Who Governs the Globe?

Academics and policymakers frequently discuss global governance but they treat governance as a structure or process, rarely considering who actually does the governing. This volume focuses on the agents of global governance: "global governors." The global policy arena is filled with a wide variety of actors such as international organizations, corporations, professional associations, and advocacy groups, all seeking to "govern" activity surrounding their issues of concern. *Who Governs the Globe?* lays out a theoretical framework for understanding and investigating governors in world politics. It then applies this framework to various governors and policy arenas, including arms control, human rights, economic development, and global education. Edited by three of the world's leading international relations scholars, this is an important contribution that will be useful for courses, as well as for researchers in international studies and international organizations.

DEBORAH D. AVANT is Professor of Political Science and Director of International Studies at the University of California, Irvine.

MARTHA FINNEMORE is Professor of Political Science and International Affairs at the George Washington University.

SUSAN K. SELL is Professor of Political Science and International Affairs and Director of the Institute for Global and International Studies at the George Washington University.

Cambridge Studies in International Relations: 114

Who Governs the Globe?

Cambridge Studies in International Relations is a joint initiative of Cambridge University Press and the British International Studies Association (BISA). The series will include a wide range of material, from undergraduate textbooks and surveys to research-based monographs and collaborative volumes. The aim of the series is to publish the best new scholarship in International Studies from Europe, North America and the rest of the world.

Cambridge Studies in International Relations

Series list continued after index

Who Governs the Globe?

Edited by

DEBORAH D. AVANT, MARTHA FINNEMORE,
AND SUSAN K. SELL

CAMBRIDGE
UNIVERSITY PRESS

CAMBRIDGE UNIVERSITY PRESS
Cambridge, New York, Melbourne, Madrid, Cape Town, Singapore,
São Paulo, Delhi, Dubai, Tokyo, Mexico City

Cambridge University Press
The Edinburgh Building, Cambridge CB2 8RU, UK

Published in the United States of America by Cambridge University Press, New York

www.cambridge.org
Information on this title: www.cambridge.org/9780521122016

© Cambridge University Press 2010

First published 2010
Reprinted 2011

Printed in the United Kingdom at the University Press, Cambridge

A catalogue record for this publication is available from the British Library

Library of Congress Cataloguing in Publication data
Who governs the globe? / edited by Deborah D. Avant, Martha Finnemore,
Susan K. Sell.
    p.   cm. – (Cambridge studies in international relations ; 114)
ISBN 978-0-521-19891-2 (hardback)
1. International organization.   2. International agencies.   I. Avant, Deborah D.
(Deborah Denise), 1958–   II. Finnemore, Martha.   III. Sell, Susan K.   IV. Title.
V. Series.
JZ1318.W486   2010
341.2 – dc22   2010007112

ISBN 978-0-521-19891-2 Hardback
ISBN 978-0-521-12201-6 Paperback

Contents

Part II Authority dynamics and governance outcomes

Figures

Tables

Contributors

Deborah D. Avant   University of California, Irvine

Clifford Bob   Duquesne University

Tim Büthe   Duke University

R. Charli Carpenter   University of Massachusetts, Amherst

Alexander Cooley   Barnard College

Allison Danner   United States Department of Justice

Martha Finnemore   George Washington University

Tamar Gutner   American University

Virginia Haufler   University of Maryland, College Park

Kathleen R. McNamara   Georgetown University

Karen Mundy   University of Toronto

Abraham L. Newman   Georgetown University

Matthew Potoski   Iowa State University

Aseem Prakash   University of Washington

Susan K. Sell   George Washington University

Erik Voeten   Georgetown University

Preface

This project was born of shared frustration. All three of us were engaged in different research about global governance but we all were dissatisfied. Something fundamental was missing in the way academics talked about what we were seeing on the ground. Traditional theoretical apparatus could not accommodate the diversity and creativity of activity we encountered. Standard academic language could not even describe it. Academic talk about global governance was about regimes, constraints, bargaining, and principal–agent relationships. It erected sharp divides between economic and security issues. Most of it was about states or intergovernmental structures. The majority described stasis or equilibrium. Creativity and innovation were not integral to global governance talk. Neither were the complex webs of varied actors pushing change. Yet the global governance we saw in our own research across very different issue areas was remarkable for its dynamics, creativity, and variety of actors.

In 2004 we came together to found a new Institute for Global and International Studies (IGIS) at the George Washington University's Elliott School of International Affairs. At IGIS, suddenly we had adjacent offices and geography bred inspiration. In a series of conversations we began to articulate what we thought was missing in both our theory and language of global governance. We also discussed the work of other scholars who were wrestling with related issues. We contacted a number of these scholars and persuaded them to participate in an organic process of discussions and research presentations that would evolve into the current volume.

We did not start with a hard and fast framework but with a series of questions and a commitment to focus on the agents who govern. Our framework and the individual chapters grew together out of the discussions at our workshops. We are extremely grateful for the smart ideas, hard work, and deep engagement of the authors who contributed to this book. Our contributors are also noteworthy for their wit and good humor. It has made the process of shaping and editing this book not only intellectually rewarding but a lot of fun.

We have had much support along the way. We are particularly grateful to Elliott School's Institute for Global and International Studies (under first Debbi's leadership then Susan's) for organizing and hosting workshops. IGIS assistants Laura Barker, Jessica Krueger, and Sarah Schaffer handled all the logistics with much dedication and professionalism. The Deans of the Elliott School, first Harry Harding and then Michael Brown, gave us both their confidence and their financial commitment. The International Studies Association provided us with a generous Venture Workshop grant that supported the project in its later stages.

A number of our colleagues and graduate students at George Washington University offered insightful comments on drafts and participated in our workshops. Special thanks go to Maryam Zarnegar Deloffre, Henry Farrell, Lee Ann Fujii, Jim Goldgeier, Craig Kaufmann, Eliot Posner, Chad Rector, and Amir Stepak. At one workshop Chad Rector grew so tired of saying "Marty, Debbi, and Susan" that he dubbed us "Medusa." Medusa was very fortunate to have committed and insightful discussants for our workshops and associated panels. Thanks to Dan Drezner, Matt Hoffman, Benedict Kingsbury, Loren Landau, Duncan Matthews, Lou Pauly, J. P. Singh, Hendrik Spruyt, and Paul Wapner for very useful indepth feedback. Risa Brooks, Nitsan Chorev, and Michael Williams were not at our workshops but nonetheless provided helpful written comments on the project. As Debbi headed off to University of California, Irvine, midway through the project we also gained useful insights from students there: Benjamin Bohr (who also deserves thanks for his help with the references), Karl Kruse, Winfred Wan, and Ashley Williams. Finally, to John Haslam and anonymous reviewers thanks for both support and enthusiasm along with excellent comments that helped us improve the manuscript.

1 | Who governs the globe?

DEBORAH D. AVANT, MARTHA FINNEMORE,
AND SUSAN K. SELL

Academics and policymakers speak frequently about global governance but do so in the passive voice. They treat governance as structure or process. Global governance is "the sum of organizations, policy instruments, financing mechanisms, rules, procedures, and norms" or "the collective effort to identify, understand, and address worldwide problems that are beyond the capacity of individual States" (Najam *et al.* 2006; Club of Rome n.d.). Global governance is something that happens; no one, apparently, actually does it. Analysts rarely talk about global *governors* and have not made the agents in this process central to their analysis.

To the extent that international relations (IR) scholars do think about who global "governors" might be, they think about states. States, after all, are widely recognized political authorities. Their job is to govern. And they do govern, or try to, in many areas of global activity. They sign interstate treaties, create international law, and promulgate wide-ranging rules to initiate, regulate, and "govern" activity in desired ways.

States are by no means alone in this endeavor, however. The global policy arena is filled with a wide variety of actors – international organizations, corporations, professional associations, advocacy groups, and the like – seeking to "govern" activity in issue areas they care about. These actors are not merely occupying global structures. They are active agents who want new structures and rules (or different rules) to solve problems, change outcomes, and transform international life. Governors are thus engaged in processes that are both quintessentially political and dynamic, even transformational. These processes are political in that power and mobilization are keys to success. They are dynamic in that nothing is ever governed once and for all time. Any understanding of governors and governance must account for constant possibility of change.

International relations theories that focus only on states are poorly equipped to understand this kaleidoscope of activity by such a wide range of agents. Functionalist theories of global governance pick up more activity but downplay the contentious politics of global governance. Neither type of theory provides much guidance about dynamics and change. Without theories about these diverse actors and dynamic processes, we do not have conceptual equipment with which to understand significant aspects of global politics.

Consequently, in this project we focus on the agents of global governance whom we call "global governors." For purposes of this inquiry, *global governors are authorities who exercise power across borders for purposes of affecting policy.*[1] *Governors thus create issues, set agendas, establish and implement rules or programs, and evaluate and/or adjudicate outcomes.* Rather than assuming that states govern, we investigate. Who actually performs the tasks involved in governing? Our investigation explicitly centers on the process by which these actors gain and use authority. Where do global governors come from? Why are they in charge? How do they accomplish their goals? What effects do their actions produce?

Answering these questions leads us to focus on two types of relationships: relationships between governors and the governed, and relationships among governors, themselves. Understanding why the governed recognize or defer to governors offers insight into why governors are influential and how they behave. Expertise might propel professional associations to the fore, inducing other actors to accept their policy proposals. Advocacy organizations often appeal to moral principles to gain authority and followers. Corporations sometimes gain authority because others perceive them as capable of achieving results. Understanding relationships among governors is similarly important. Governance is not a solo act, and governors can rarely accomplish ends alone. They divide labor, delegate, compete, and cooperate with one another in many ways to produce the outcomes we observe. Almost all governing in contemporary global politics seems to be the result of governor *inter*actions of various kinds. If their ability to achieve outcomes depends on their relations with other governors, understanding the conditions under which governors compete or cooperate can help

---

[1] There are a great many definitions of global governance. In addition to those already cited, see Keohane (2003).

explain outcome effectiveness. Focusing on these two relationships, we develop a framework for explaining both individual global governance outcomes and the dynamics of authority in global governance over time.

Our focus on governors of diverse kinds and their interactions puts us in league with a growing number of scholars who question the state-centrism of our field. Recent analyses have focused on the characteristics of *types* of nonstate actors or private authority to understand the varied effects these might cause.[2] Our hunch, however, is that it is not the type of actor but the *character of relationships*, both among governors and between governor and governed, that is key to understanding global politics. The framework we develop seeks to understand these relationships so as to explain governors, outcomes, and change.

We begin this chapter by discussing structural changes that have ushered a more diverse cast of global governors on to the world stage. Globalization, privatization, and technological change have empowered new types of actors and the end of the Cold War opened new opportunities for them to act. The next two sections elaborate our framework for understanding why actors become recognized as governors and how they go about their work. We outline five types of authority that might engender deference to governors of various kinds, allowing them to govern. We also unpack governance tasks to facilitate understanding of relationships among governors as they work to affect outcomes.

The remainder of this chapter focuses on the dynamics of global governance and its impact on both the authority of governors and governance outcomes. Exogenous shocks can certainly change governors and governing arrangements, but our interest here is in sources of change endogenous to governors and governing. We identify and discuss several such sources of change: tensions or synergies among sources of authority within a governor, cooperation or conflict among governors, and governing performance. Finally, we describe the organization of the book. Early chapters apply the aforementioned framework to understand dynamics in authority of governors

---

[2] With this focus, we build on the diverse work on transnational activists, corporations, private authority, and international organizations that shares our interest in agents other than states. A sampling includes Keck and Sikkink (1998); Cutler *et al.* (1999); Hall and Biersteker (2002); Barnett and Finnemore (2004). See also Büthe (2004).

themselves – how governors emerge and how their authority changes over time. Later chapters focus on effects of these governors on changing governance outcomes.

Bringing agents into global governance: structural changes and the poverty of statism and functionalism

Thinking of the structure of global politics as a complex web of relationships among different authorities, accomplishing different tasks and dependent on one another for outcomes, is a stark departure from the imagined world of billiard ball-like states or stratified levels of analysis that has dominated international relations theorizing. The assumption that the global political system is constituted by unitary, instrumental states and structured by the distribution of power among them has made an analyst's life easy. It strips away the many pesky and distracting sideshows on the world scene. It makes the very messy world "legible" and comprehensible to both scholars and policymakers, facilitating grand theory for the former and statecraft for the latter (Scott 1998, 1–18). The risk, of course, for analysts, policymakers, and citizens is that simplification gets things wrong and is a poor guide to comprehension and action.

Our contention is that these simplifying assumptions – unitary, asocial, instrumental states, constrained only by the distribution of state power – strip away much of what is essential for understanding contemporary politics. Perhaps it told us more in the 1980s when these theories were developed, but structural changes over the past quarter century have empowered new actors in new ways, undermining the utility of these assumptions. Four such changes have been particularly important: globalization; the privatization/deregulation revolution; new technologies; and the end of the Cold War.

Structural changes

Globalization, or the shift in the spatial reach of social action and organization toward the interregional, intercontinental, or global scale, has undermined the correspondence between social action and the territory enclosed by state borders (Held and McGrew 2000, 3). Globalization is commonly associated with the global economy but its reach extends beyond economic issues. Environmental issues, particularly problems such as global warming, join together the fates of people across the globe (Mathews 1989). Ideas about human rights have become platforms for social connections between people across the globe and have served as an impetus for military intervention (Finnemore 2003). Even security has become identified with humanity, as analysts, activists, and states develop and implement conceptions of "human security" (Paris 2001).

The Thatcher- and Reagan-led *privatization* and *deregulation* revolution has compounded this change in the relations between states and social power. Starting in the 1980s, states, led by the most powerful, began systematically to cut economic actors free from state control in hopes of improving economic performance. States transferred public enterprises and state functions to private actors, and increasingly encouraged private actors to finance policies such as education, municipal services, and even security, which had once been the exclusive responsibility of states (Feigenbaum *et al.* 1998; Avant 2005). This faith in the rationality of markets also led states to loosen regulation of economic activity and increasingly other social activity as well. While we can debate the wisdom of such policy and its impact on the economic growth of a variety of individual states, there is little doubt that it has increased the role of nonstate actors across the board: in economic, social, and security realms.[3] Although global economic growth has exploded in the past twenty-five years, states' ability to control or regulate it has diminished, while nonstate actors' efforts to shape or tame it have increased.

New technologies facilitated globalization by easing communications, population flows, and the interchange of ideas. Information technologies such as the internet and cell phones, global media, and the ease of air travel have often had mixed effects, particularly on state capacity relative to that of other global actors. The same technology that enabled corporations in the United States to outsource computer support to India (challenging the ability of the US government to affect its labor market) also allowed communication among Al Qaeda operatives. Cell phones are both essential tools of global business and vehicles for popular dissent in places like the Philippines and Burma. New technologies have also enhanced the capacities of states. They allow the creation of ever more sophisticated communications,

---

[3] But see Weiss (1998) and Drezner (2007).

weapons systems, and infrastructure support, yet each innovation also brings with it new vulnerabilities that can be exploited by those with technological expertise.

Finally, the *end of the Cold War* further fueled global change. The halt of major conflict between the United States and the Soviet Union loosened the restraints on international activity that had been imposed by the superpower deadlock. In a wide variety of social, political, economic, and security realms, activists and organizations began to push for change. The way the Cold War ended, with the triumph of the United States and the liberal model, bolstered the credence of the privatization and deregulation ideas prominent in the United States and emboldened many (generally US-supported) international organizations to drop Cold War-style "impartiality" and push for liberal, capitalist change.[4] The resulting expansion of global markets and democracy has been dramatic. At the same time this wave of change empowered a variety of actors to press for increased human rights protection, to work to restrict the spread of conflict, and to promote attention to issues of global concern. It also inspired others to take action to counter some of these activities. As Clifford Bob discusses in this volume, international efforts to restrict the flow of small arms caused transnational gun rights groups to mobilize to resist these restrictions. More deadly has been the rise of networks such as Al Qaeda to resist what they claim to be the imposition of Western cultural and economic practices on the Islamic world.

The poverty of statism and functionalism

State-centric frameworks do not capture these changes and functionalist assumptions, while useful as a starting point, provide only limited help in understanding variation in the actual governance that goes on in the world today. Only a small fraction of global governance activity involves state representatives negotiating only with one another. Decisionmakers and participants in governance are much more diverse, partly because of the trends in globalization, deregulation, privatization, and technological change, which have empowered

---

[4] Thus, some think of global governance as a liberal political project. For discussion, see Ba and Hoffmann (2005), p. 4.

nonstate actors. The process is also far more contested and political than the functionalists suggest and functionalist assumptions alone cannot explain the variation we see in global governance. Global needs do sometimes give rise to governance arrangements but on many global issues, governance mechanisms have not emerged. Even where governance exists, functionalism tells us little about which of many possible arrangements will prevail and whose "needs" it will meet. Much of the literature on global governance equates it, implicitly or explicitly, with the provision of global public goods. Practitioners complain, however, that governance outcomes are frequently disconnected from both the public *and* the good. Complaints about global inaction on climate change and lack of access to HIV/AIDS medicines are two prominent examples. The lack of regulation that led to the 2009 global financial meltdown is another.

Global governance does not unfold naturally or smoothly toward a unique equilibrium. Governance, where it occurs, is the result of a political process and is shaped by power, access, mobilization, leadership, and other political variables. These political variables are important for determining what is noticed as a global problem as well as which solution is chosen to address it. Rules and institutions are sometimes locally stable and resistant to change even when they prove to be dysfunctional from a larger environmental perspective. Governors and their environments, both international and local, also may co-evolve as their interaction changes actors' values, identities, and preferences (March and Olsen 1998; Gutner, Mundy, and Cooley, this volume). So, while governors frequently make appeals to global needs in their bid for power, knowing global needs is rarely enough to explain how and why a particular governance outcome was chosen.

Perhaps the most pervasive assumptions surrounding global governance are normative. Many analysts assume that global governance is "a good thing." When we speak of it, we link it to activities with a decidedly positive aura: cooperation, problem-solving, providing public goods. These are all things we like; indeed, they are all things that are hard to oppose. Linking global governance to these activities disposes us to think of *any* governance as good in and of itself. Often this bias is built into the very definition of the term. Consider, for example, one of the most widely circulated and accepted definitions that the UN Commission on Global Governance has provided. The Commission (1995, 2) defines global governance as "the sum of the many ways individuals and institutions, public and private, manage their common affairs. It is a continuing process through which conflicting or diverse interests may be accommodated and cooperative action may be taken." Governance here is equated with "cooperative action" but any political observer knows that governance is not always cooperative. Power, in its various forms, may make "cooperative action" hard to distinguish from exploitation or domination (Barnett and Duvall 2005). Furthermore, diverse interests are not always accommodated. In some cases they lead to competition, even conflict, within governing arrangements.

Investigating the diverse actors who govern helps foreground some of these normative issues by alerting us to the varied normative agendas governors might bring to their work. Our focus on the relationship between governors and governed highlights issues of accountability, which frequently dog global governance arrangements. In the case study chapters, and particularly the conclusion, we consider the troubling, if sometimes unintended, consequences of governance as well as its benefits.

Jettisoning statist and functionalist assumptions does not require throwing out all of IR theory. Once we conceptualize the variety of actors in world affairs, many traditional IR theories – as well as theories from comparative politics – prove quite useful for understanding the dynamics of authority and governing outcomes. Insights from the literatures on alignment, coalition building, cooperation, strategic interaction, ideas and norms underpin many of our chapters.

Rethinking agency in governors

New tools are needed to understand and investigate governors and their effects on social life, and we develop these in the next section. Our conceptual framework is based on governors' *authority relationships* with those whom they govern, their relationships with one another, and the tensions and synergies in these relationships that might produce stability or change. Governance does not require coercion. What is striking about the breadth and depth of current governance arrangements in the world is that many, probably most, of these are not obviously or explicitly backed by force. Governors may have coercive powers and may use them at times, but more often the governed actually accept the governors' authority in some fashion. Understanding the nature of this authority and how it works must be at the center of any understanding of governors.

Governors can also exercise leadership and creativity, two terms that are oddly absent in most discussions of global governance. Put in social science jargon, governance is not simply the result of structural constraints; it is also the result of generative agents. It can be *transformational and innovative* rather than simply prohibitive (McNamara, this volume). Governance involves the creation of new issues, new interests, new communities, and new modes of action by creative agents. Governors can gain acceptance from those they seek to lead by offering attractive new ideas, formulating new strategies, and persuading people of the importance of new social goals. While states may have advantages in coercion, they have no monopoly on these other aspects of governance. Leadership and creativity have many sources.

Understanding governance as more than just rule-enforcement or the provision of order encourages consideration of more kinds of governors and of how they do their work (Rosenau and Czempiel 1992, 4–5). The exercise of authority, in both generative and constraining ways, is a common feature of governors. Different governors draw on different types of authority, which affects their behavior vis-à-vis their constituents and one another. Thus our analysis starts with the concept of authority.

"Why are you in charge?": the nature of authority in relations between governors and governed

If organizations like the United Nations (UN), the International Electrotechnical Commission (IEC), and Exxon are all (potentially) global governors, why are they in charge? Why does anyone pay attention to them? Understanding why actors are authorities and are able to govern allows us to better understand their behaviors, relationships, and impacts.

We define authority as the ability to induce deference in others.[5] Authority is thus a social relationship, not a commodity; it does not exist in a vacuum. Authority is created by the recognition, even if only

---

[5] For a sampling of the rich literature on authority, see Flathman (1980); Raz (1990); Beetham (1991). Our definition and the treatment that follows draws on Barnett and Finnemore (2004), esp. ch. 2.

tacit or informal, of others. Recognizing an authority does not mean one always agrees with or likes the authority. It does mean, though, that one defers to the authority. Such deference confers power. Having a set of constituents that have signified their acceptance of an authority allows that authority to exert greater influence than would be the case if she did not have their deference.

Deference to an authority might take a variety of forms. Authority might cause actors to subordinate their own conscious preferences to the directives of the authority and thus, in Robert Dahl's (1957 and 1968) sense, get one actor to do what she would not otherwise do, but it might also have subtler effects. Authority might create new preferences in actors who were previously indifferent or at odds. It might change preferences in others who become persuaded to share the authority's views based on its moral standing or expertise. It might mobilize new or different constituencies for political action.

Deference occurs for a variety of reasons. Some actors are authoritative because of the office they hold. The President of the United States is authoritative because he or she holds that office; when that person leaves office, deference will be accorded to the next individual who holds it. Some actors may be authoritative because of inherent qualities others see in that person. Nelson Mandela, for example, has a certain amount of authority on the international stage because of his moral character and reputation. Those did not disappear when he left the presidency of his country. Actors may also be authoritative because of what or whom they represent. They may represent a respected institution, an underrepresented other, or a lofty ideal. Many nongovernmental organizations (NGOs), for example, induce deference (or try to) by claiming to represent noble ideas or deserving others.[6]

The basis on which the governed defer has another side, however; it also constrains the governor. Governors cannot do just anything they want; their actions must be seen by the governed (and others)

---

[6] Richard Flathman (1980, 16–19) distinguishes those who are "an authority" from those who are "in authority." The former have inherent qualities that induce deference. In the realm of global governance, these might be expertise or moral/reputational qualities. Nobel Prize winners, academic experts, heroes all are authorities of this first type. The latter are actors who are "in authority" by virtue of the positions they hold. UN secretary-generals, CEOs of multinational corporations, leaders of NGOs are examples of this type.

to accord with whatever authorizes them to act. An NGO that gains authority by claiming to represent noble ideas can only continue to use that authority as long as others see it as following through on this commitment. An office holder may command deference when fulfilling the duties of that office but not in a private or nonofficial capacity.

In order to understand the political consequences of the exercise of authority for global politics, we examine the various sources of authority that agents draw upon.[7] Broadly, we see five bases of authority for global governors – institutional, delegated, expert, principled, and capacity-based authority.[8]

Institutional (or institution-based) authority derives from holding office in some established organizational structure. Managing directors of the International Monetary Fund (IMF) or the heads of multinational corporations gain authority from their positions in these institutions. Their authority is defined and limited, however, by the rules and purposes of the institution that authorizes them. If the head of the IMF suddenly started pronouncing policy on nuclear proliferation, for example, he (or theoretically she) would not generate deference. Indeed, such action would probably be viewed as illegitimate and cast doubt on the person's competence. Similarly, when powerful states push the IMF to bend rules and make loans to geopolitically sensitive but otherwise not creditworthy states, people will question the authority and legitimacy of the IMF.

Delegated (or delegation-based) authority is authority on loan from some other set of authoritative actors.[9] Often, in the realm of global governance, those who delegate are states or sub-state agencies. State delegation to international organizations (IOs), firms, and NGOs has been widely studied. The nature of delegation arrangements can vary greatly, as can the ways in which global governors interpret, improvise,

---

[7] For alternative treatments of "political" authority, see Lake (2006 and 2007); Pauly and Grande (2007). For a classic and narrow view of political authority, see Schmitt (1996).

[8] This typology draws on Barnett and Finnemore (2004).

[9] Delegated authority may overlap with institutional authority. In principle, a principal could delegate to a specialized subordinate to solve the problem as the agent sees fit rather than according to the principal's wishes. Some classic principal–agent arguments make just this claim: see Pratt and Zeckhauser (1987). More common among IR theorists, however, is the assumption that agents abide by the wishes of their principals (generally states): see Hawkins *et al.* (2006).

or shirk in these delegation arrangements. Often, too, one sees "nests" or "chains" of delegation which may attenuate (or sever completely) the relationship between preferences (or intentions) of the delegators and governance outcomes on the ground. For example, Abraham Newman finds complex relationships emerging as states simultaneously delegate authority to agents "below" and "above" the nation-state in their efforts to govern. The disaggregated state can result in administrative daisy chains, blowback, and tattletale scenarios, all of which raise deep questions about bureaucratic control, autonomy, and accountability (Newman, this volume).[10] They also muddy the relationship between state preferences and outcomes. This is not to say that the delegation is meaningless, however – far from it. Governors exercising or invoking this type of authority often justify their actions with references to the wishes of their delegators – the "principals" – and are often seen as illegitimate if they circumvent those who delegated authority in the first place.

Expert (or expertise-based) authority is authority based on specialized knowledge. Unlike delegated or institutional authority, it inheres in the actor. A Nobel Prize-winning physicist or economist remains so, no matter what her or his job. Frequently, though, expertise is coupled with other types of authority. Institutions or organizations often want experts on staff or delegate complex technical tasks to experts. As with other forms of authority, expert authority is limited in its use by the content of its expertise. Education professionals are unlikely to induce much deference if they start making rules or expressing opinions about technical requirements for the electronics industry and vice versa (Mundy and Büthe, this volume). Note, too, that there is a sense in which the application of much professional expertise has a moral or principled dimension. Most professionals believe that practice of their profession and application of their knowledge is a social good and furthers goals of the larger community.[11] For example, an economist working for the IMF may well be convinced of the merits of structural adjustment policies as a means of restoring financial stability and promoting growth. Yet, her expert notions of the "social good" may

---

[10] Prakash and Potoski (this volume) also identify networks of governance chains.

[11] Steven Brint (1994) uses the phrase "social trustee professionalism" to describe this moral aspect of professions that view themselves as repositories, even guardians, of socially important knowledge necessary for human progress.

not be broadly shared. These same structural adjustment policies may lead to food riots and mass protests in borrower countries, compromising the effectiveness of expertise-based authority and its effects on outcomes.

Principled (or principle-based) authority is legitimated by service to some widely accepted set of principles, morals, or values. It can inhere in both actors and offices. Desmond Tutu probably enjoys principled authority of both kinds: he has moral authority as a bishop in the Anglican Church, but also because of his principled beliefs, personal history, and character. Principled claims might be used to galvanize partisan supporters, as with NGOs that are trying to create new issues or set agendas (Bob, this volume). Appeals to moral values like peace, security, prosperity, human dignity, and freedom are very common authorizing tools for a wide variety of actors seeking to govern globally. Some such appeals are more credible than others, and some actors are more credible in making them. Corporations may do a great deal of good in the world, but because they are by their nature profit-driven, people assume utilitarian motives, making it harder for them to attain principled authority.[12] NGOs, by contrast, almost always make moral claims and are able to do so in part because no one thinks they are in it for the money. NGOs often benefit from an aura of moral authority because of this perceived altruism, even if they happen to be incompetent and do little to further the causes they profess. Finally, different principles have resonance among different constituencies. Though much of the literature focuses on Western NGOs as the purveyors of principled authority, Osama Bin Laden also makes principled authority claims that resonate with his followers.

Capacity-based authority involves deference based on perceived competence. This has close kinship with institutional, delegated, and, potentially, expert authority, but is its own distinct form. Many scholars, including Joseph Raz (1990, 5–6), have described authority that derives from and is justified by the task the authority is supposed to perform. If the community agrees that a task must be accomplished, then satisfying the community's preferences imparts authority to the actor and creates deference to her. Solving the problem or completing the task may not depend upon the holding of a particular office

---

[12] Sell and Prakash (2004).

in an institution or possession of any rarified knowledge. Instead, the capacity for effective action is what creates legitimate authority for the governor. People defer to the governor because they believe she will produce desired results. Empirically, it is hard to think of a "pure" case of capacity-based authority.[13] Most global governors who are effective at solving problems get their opportunities to do so from some other source of authority. For example, the perceived capability of corporations working in conflict zones to monitor funds and implement policies was central to efforts to assign authority to them for reducing conflict (see Haufler, this volume). Note too that, conversely, lack of efficacy or competence can undermine authority drawn from other sources. The IMF and World Bank have had their authority questioned based on accusations of poor performance. Perceived failures in peacekeeping have strained the UN's authority to undertake such missions.

What do global governors do?

The term "global governance" describes the different policymaking activities that produce coordinated action in the absence of world government (Rosenau and Czempiel 1992). A core idea implicit in the global governance literature is that governance is more than making or enforcing rules. There are steps both before and after the explicit making and enforcing of rules that are crucial to political outcomes. Public policy scholars have long understood and analyzed these processes. Drawing on this insight, we tease out the tasks or activities implicit in the governance process.

Setting agendas and creating issues. Much IR literature implicitly or explicitly adopts a functionalist stance toward issue creation: it assumes that issues needing governance are obvious and their appearance needs little explanation. As several of our empirical chapters show, this is hardly the case. Actors often struggle to persuade others that a problem or issue exists (Carpenter, this volume; Rochefort and Cobb 1994). In many cases the "problem" is not a problem for everyone. Charli Carpenter's chapter on "children born of war" demonstrates the way that gatekeepers can keep issues *off* the international agenda. Some actors, often powerful ones, may like the status quo and

---

[13] Paul "Red" Adair's authority claims lay in successfully extinguishing fires on oil rigs. See www.redadair.com/.

either deny or refuse to acknowledge the existence of a problem at all. Governance of a problem cannot begin until someone defines a problem as an issue and succeeds in placing it on a consequential agenda.

Making rules. This might happen through strategic interaction at high-level conferences, as traditional statist analyses describe, but rules have many sources. Some are unintended consequences of decisions taken for different reasons. Tim Büthe's work on European Commission (EC)/European Union (EU) merger review demonstrates that by writing rules for anti-trust enforcement, member states inadvertently set a process in motion that extended merger review authority to the EC, thus transferring authority to a supranational body (Büthe and Swank 2006). Other rules may become codified and widely accepted simply on the basis of past practice, not through formal decisions. The US prerogative to name the head of the World Bank and Europe's right to name the head of the IMF, for example, were informal agreements that became institutionalized over time. Similarly, the regional blocs at the UN are artifacts of past practice. In many situations, competing authorities fight over the rules.

Implementation and enforcement. Once promulgated, implementing rules is almost always a contested process. Many rules that high-level government actors make are vague, even platitudinous, requiring other actors to exercise a great deal of discretion and autonomy to translate them into action on the ground. Even when states or other governors try to write specific and detailed rules, the fit can be uneasy across diverse cases. The Millennium Development Goals (MDGs) exemplify this, leaving ample opportunity for implementation to have an enormous impact on governing outcomes (Gutner and Mundy, this volume). Alexander Cooley's chapter on the surprisingly dysfunctional implementation of reconstruction by contractors in Iraq also illustrates this possibility. Virginia Haufler's description of the Chad–Cameroon pipeline deal (Haufler, this volume) highlights a proposed revenue-sharing plan that the Chadian government signed into law. Once the pipeline was built, however, the government tried to evade external oversight and claim a larger share of the profits. No specific case ever fits the rules perfectly; there will always be exceptions, modifications, and improvisations by implementing agents. Even if all actors agree on what the rules require, acting on those requirements demands resources, information, and coordination, all of which are notoriously complicated and even contentious in many transnational settings. Enforcement may be equally fraught with controversy.

Evaluating, monitoring, and adjudicating outcomes. Disputes over implementation and compliance often require evaluation, monitoring, and/or adjudication. The implementing governor may carry out these tasks (for example, the World Bank has an "Independent Evaluation Office"), but often other actors carry out these watchdog functions. In some cases it is clear who gets to decide what constitutes compliance, and those actors may become powerful governors in their own right, as is the case with international judges (Danner and Voeten, this volume). Other times, monitors and evaluators may be self-appointed as are the many NGOs that keep tabs on compliance with the UN's Global Compact. Occasionally, both insiders and outsiders take on these roles, as they do for the IMF, World Bank, and UN progress on the Millennium Development Goals. Who monitors and evaluates is sometimes unclear, however, breeding controversy. The growing use of contractors in war zones, for instance, has created actors without clear legal status (Avant 2005). Who judges and by what law remains unresolved. Sometimes, too, no one monitors, evaluates, or adjudicates outcomes. The absence of governors to fill these roles has led to common complaints about lack of oversight, transparency, accountability, and even legitimacy.

Feedback effects and overlap in governance

These stylized categories were drawn from a conception of the governance process as a set of stages. In practice, though, governance rarely takes the form of a linear staged process. Activities may overlap and feed back on each other in many ways. Adjudication may set new agendas for actors. Implementation may create issues that raise new challenges for rules. Frequently agenda setting is about not only putting an issue on the agenda but identifying *who* should govern in an issue area and why. The feedback and overlap between governance tasks plays an important role as we develop our framework below.

One might have imagined that different types of actors would perform different governance activities.[14] Our contributors demonstrate,

---

[14] Early theorizing by Keck and Sikkink (1998), for example, suggested that advocacy networks set agendas but states make rules. Also see Drezner (2007a).

however, that who does what varies at different times, on different issues, and with different degrees of formality and stability. In some cases, one governor may carry out many of these activities. The EU has developed authority and capacity for almost all governing tasks. In other cases, one governor relies explicitly on others to perform different parts of governance in an explicitly institutionalized way. The IEC relies on states or sub-state bureaucracies to enforce the standards it sets. In other instances, the tasks a governor undertakes are highly variable. An agenda setter in one instance may be an implementer or evaluator at another time. Rules may be made by one actor but implemented by many or vice versa. For instance, the World Wildlife Fund acts as an advocacy network, working to put issues on the agenda and incite state rulemaking on some issues; on other issues it – along with its umbrella consortium, the International Union for Conservation of Nature (IUCN) – makes rules that it will then lobby states to sign on to; and on still others it implements policy under contract to states, international organizations, individual members, or all three. Breaking the governance process into analytic segments and exploring the governing agents at each juncture affords a more accurate picture of how the various nonstate or private authorities matter for global governance (Cutler *et al.* 1999; Hall and Biersteker 2002; Büthe 2004).

No governor governs alone. Rather than simply portending possible competitors to states, the growing authority of a wide variety of different agents can also add potential partners to states and to each other (Raustiala 1997). Along with the relationship between governors and governed, then, the relationships *among* governors lie at the heart of current global politics.

The dynamics of global governance

Nothing is ever governed once and for all time. Even maintaining equilibrium requires effort and is thus rarely felt as such by participants in the political process. Global governance – and politics more generally – is a dynamic process. Each new governing arrangement alters the structures, rules, and opportunities that came before. Governors and would-be governors adjust well, or poorly, or not at all, to the attendant changes. Some governors seize opportunities, others become irrelevant, and still others never get a chance to govern. A legitimate governor at Time 1 may be completely illegitimate at Time 2. A workable governing arrangement at Time 1 may become utterly unacceptable at Time 2. A governing arrangement may grow weaker over time, or alternatively it may grow stronger, with more far-reaching effects. Understanding these dynamics is the key to explaining global politics.

Change in governing arrangements may be driven by exogenous factors – the end of the Cold War or new technology, for example – but emergence and evolution of governance arrangements may also be driven by features endogenous to governors' relationships with the governed and each other. We identify three endogenous mechanisms of change.

(1) Multiple authority sources *within* a single governor. These might create synergistic opportunities for enhancing authority but also tensions that may create demands for contradictory courses of action and/or authority challenges.
(2) Relations between governors. These may be cooperative and additive, leading to far-reaching effects, or tense, dysfunctional, and even conflictual relationships, leading to failed action and potentially weakened authority.
(3) Performance. While producing expected results or exceeding expectations can solidify the authority of governors, unintended, suboptimal, or undesired outcomes may erode authority and induce pressure for change.

The following sections discuss each of these possibilities in greater detail.

Multiple authority sources within a single governor

Most global governors are authorized by some mix of authority types. This is hardly surprising. We should expect creative governors to try to bolster their authority wherever possible and thus look to add new authority and new constituents to whatever they already have. Governors may expand their authority by demonstrating competence in new areas, exceeding the sources, mandates, and constituents that originally authorized them. In Lebanon, Hezbollah built its authority as a principled militant organization by pledging to protect Lebanese Shiite Muslims. It gained support among a larger constituency and a stronger base, however, by providing a range of social services. Institutional authorities often hire or delegate to experts to augment their authority. The IMF hires economists from top universities. Principled authorities often try to gain footholds in institutions to expand their power and influence. NGO activists may welcome appointment to posts in the UN or powerful national bureaucracies. Often governors creatively seek to draw on varied sources of authority to induce greater deference across a broader set of constituents.

Despite hopes for synergy, however, multiple sources of authority within a single governor do not always sit well together. Institutional rules may require behavior at odds with expert knowledge. Experts often complain about bureaucratic red tape and dysfunctional procedures when they work inside organizations like the UN that govern globally. Similarly, delegation demands from states may be at odds with the moral principles that authorize a governor. One example would be the UN's inability to intervene in Rwanda. Moral imperatives and the UN's own human rights principles required action but institutional procedures necessitated support from member states, many of which showed little enthusiasm for action on the ground (Dallaire 2003; Barnett 2002). The UN is similarly cross-pressured in Darfur when member states (its principals) decline to authorize military action, but its principled authority depends on looking like a credible opponent of genocide. Tensions in authority can create "reluctant governors" – actors that accept governing responsibilities only because those are instrumental for fulfilling their primary missions. It was largely due to the corporate social responsibility movement and associated legitimacy and market concerns that corporations joined governance efforts for the Kimberley Process and the Chad pipeline project (Haufler, this volume). Finally, delegation of demands for functional performance may be a serious threat to some governors who have trouble delivering on promises. Continued poverty in many parts of the world despite extensive and expensive World Bank efforts has produced a long string of criticism of the Bank's performance from member states and others.

According to analysts of organizational hypocrisy, this should not be surprising. Most organizations, particularly large public organizations, are actually created to embody and carry out diverse missions for broad constituencies that do not always sit easily together. The UN was created to promote both peace and human rights. When force is required to protect rights, different parts of the organization and different constituents of the organization may pull it in different, even contradictory, directions. Further, when the action demanded by one set of institutional rules, principles, or constituencies contradicts another, an organization may use talk or symbolic action to appear concerned with these multiple, conflicting requirements. Indeed, in many aspects of public life, talk *is* action and symbols create effects. Using different tools to respond to a contradictory set of pressures can be a strategy for organizational survival. If an organization has authority in part due to its representation of different constituencies, contradictory behavior should not be surprising. Indeed, organizations need hypocrisy to survive (Brunsson 1989; Krasner 1999; Lipson 2007; Weaver 2008).

By focusing on tensions among authority sources, our analysis captures this tendency. Our governors are diverse. Some are more prone to these tensions than others.[15] The organizational hypocrisy literature has focused on the ways these tensions manifest themselves in behavior. What the organized hypocrisy theorists have thought less about is whether, or the conditions under which, this behavior (what Brunsson terms "hypocrisy") feeds back on to the organization and its authority. We suspect that it does. Over time, we suspect that continued hypocrisy reduces the authority of governors.

When multiple bases of authority are in tension, we see varied outcomes. The governor may become paralyzed and choose hollow or symbolic action. The UN, for example, has taken action in Darfur that gives the appearance of "doing something" while not contradicting limitations set by the member states delegating authority. Similarly, Tamar Gutner's chapter demonstrates a variety of ways in which delegated authority over poverty reduction at the IMF sits in tension with its expertise in international financial stability. The result has been contradictory policy that is unlikely to meet poverty reduction goals. Sometimes, rather than trying to balance or fudge, governors simply choose to serve one mission over another. This may result in more coherent policy, but risks loss of authority among constituents not served. Having to choose between coherent policies and serving

---

[15] Brunsson (1989) argues that organizations operating in environments of conflicting values (what he calls "political," as opposed to "action" organizations) are much more likely to face such tensions.

constituencies should reduce the governor's authority over time. If the UN consistently ignores the humanitarian principles that legitimate it and comes to be seen as a tool of powerful member states, or the IMF fails in its efforts to support the MDGs, these governors' authority to make rules and galvanize others to action will decline.

Conversely, when sources of authority are mutually reinforcing we expect to see governors' power expand. In the early 1990s, for instance, as the United Nations' principled mandate to induce global cooperation was reinforced by fewer conflicts among the sources of its delegated authority (member states), we saw an expansion of the UN's activity in ways that met or exceeded expectations – particularly during the first Gulf War.

Governors are not simply passive recipients of deference or slaves to authorizing forces, though. They can, and often do, seize tensions as opportunities to redefine problems, create ordering mechanisms for resolving contradictory mandates, or think differently about their authority. This management of authority to *create* mutually reinforcing sources of authority is more common. Kate McNamara's analysis of the EU provides a powerful example of effective management. EU bureaucrats have taken delegated, expert, and principled authority to enhance a Union-wide identity. The authority of the EU has grown in part because its symbols are banal and nonthreatening to European states. These banal symbols, however, also fit well with many dimensions of the postmodern world and thus resonate with the lived experiences of EU members. EU authority is the result of synergies among language, visual symbols, and action that embrace the fragmentation of postmodern life.

All other things being equal, when sources of authority are in tension we should expect a governor to experience dilemmas. Some governors will take action – like trying to create new interpretations of their missions that reconcile conflicting demands for action, resolve tensions in authority sources, and allow for consistent action. These actions may succeed. Successful governing, like all successful leadership, requires constant effort to present diverse actions as consonant with authorizing goals or shared principles. If sources of authority are mutually reinforcing, or a governor is successful in redefining them as such, we should expect a governor's authority to solidify or expand. Conversely, if they fail, or if governors do not take action, we should expect the governor to be less effective and, ultimately, to lose power.

Relations among governors: synergies, tensions, and outcomes

Given the variety of governors active in a given issue area, a governor's ability to affect outcomes almost inevitably depends on her interactions with others. Our case study chapters reveal something of the diversity of possible relationship types – delegation and contracting relationships, networks, cooperative (even symbiotic) relationships, and conflictual relationships. In some instances, working with other governors can enhance the effectiveness of policy outcomes and the authority of the governors. For instance, Raustiala (1997) shows how NGO action on international environmental issues aided and enhanced the power of states in creating a regulatory regime. Slaughter (2004) has made this argument about intergovernmental networks more generally. But multiple governors engaged in an issue can also work against one another. The most obvious instances are situations of open competition or conflict. One governor might mobilize a coalition against another to defeat prospects for action. A violent instance of this is, of course, Al Qaeda's mobilization of like-minded groups around the world to affect the United States (or "Western") presence in the Middle East. Clifford Bob describes a nonviolent manifestation of this dynamic in the mobilization of guns rights groups against a coalition to regulate small arms. The result was what Bob terms a "zombie policy."

In keeping with our focus on authority, one of the key reasons we would expect governors to work at cross-purposes is the diversity of their authority sources. One governor (or a group within a governor) may push one policy as best and right on the basis of one authority claim, while another governor (or group within a governor) may advocate a very different policy rooted in a different authority base. At the World Bank and the International Monetary Fund, for example, creditor and donor states advocated for structural adjustment policies for years on the basis of both economic expertise and their institutional position as major shareholders and "principals" of those organizations. Debtor states and NGOs often fought these policies by calling on moral claims (obligations to the world's poor), buttressed by a countervailing set of economic arguments that structural adjustment policies would fail to achieve the results claimed by proponents. The result has been that the Bank implements policies in the name of poverty reduction that are often opposed by the poor. In another example of "organized hypocrisy," the Fund and Bank have formally recognized these arguments and articulated a principle of "country ownership" of these programs, but have retained de facto control in many cases. The result was what Gutner terms "taxicab delegation": the IMF and World Bank formally delegate decisionmaking power to borrowers, putting them in the driver's seat, but the Fund and Bank tell them where to go (Gutner, this volume; Weaver 2008).

Even when governors ostensibly agree upon outcomes, subtler tensions may cause them to work at cross-purposes. Karen Mundy's discussion of "education for all" demonstrates how a widely agreed-upon norm was nonetheless poorly implemented for many years owing, in part, to the fact that the various governors (UNESCO, UNICEF, and the World Bank, alongside various states and advocacy networks) had constituencies with different ideological leanings, making agreement on policy – let alone implementation – difficult.

Particular forms of governance relationships may exacerbate or ameliorate conflict among governors. For instance, Alex Cooley argues that contracting often erodes inter-governor trust. By turning a relationship based on dispositional factors into one based on a "situational" one (that is, one governed by the terms of a formal contract rather than long-term personal relationships), some contracts undercut previous sources of informal understanding that worked to mediate tensions between the authority imperatives of contractors and those of donors.

In nested institutional relationships, governors may have generally cooperative relationships but nonetheless fall prey to tensions on some subset of issues. In his analysis of the International Electrotechnical Commission and electronic standards, for instance, Tim Büthe demonstrates that there are generally synergistic relations between the IEC, states, and consumers, and that these create standards with vast reach. In individual instances, though, tensions between governors, based on competing constituencies' demands, may lead states (and/or consumers) to fail to implement or enforce standards, thereby reducing their reach. The US failure to adopt the metric system is a prominent example.

One important relationship, often overlooked and undertheorized in global governance work, is leadership. One or more governors may become leaders in a governing effort, setting agendas for other governors and coordinating their work. As Danner and Voeten suggest, the judges appointed to international criminal tribunals seized a leadership role, creating procedural rules, substantive law, and even professional standards for those who would follow in their wake. NGOs may also take on leadership roles as their social entrepreneurial efforts become institutionalized in new governing arrangements (Haufler, this volume). Of course, leaders may also restrict the power of other governors or would-be governors, as UNICEF does in Carpenter's analysis.

Regardless of why governors cooperate or compete, whether they do or do not should affect the reach of their efforts and the degree to which governance seems effective. Cooperation should enhance the reach of governance efforts, while tensions should restrict them and competition may undermine them altogether.

Outcomes and performance as triggers for change

Governing outcomes, in turn, influence the future authority of participating governors. While it is certainly the case that bad outcomes can sometimes continue for long periods, over time poor performance and unintended outcomes can create pressure for change in either policy or governing authority, or both. Undesired outcomes might undermine the authority of a governor or open space for a replacement. Undesired or unintended outcomes might create opportunities for governors to forge new relationships to try to fix these problems. Such outcomes might also result in new mandates for the governor(s), new definitions of the problem, and/or new definitions of goals or success. Virginia Haufler's description of the decision by the UN, donor states, and advocacy networks to include corporations working in conflict zones as part of a governing arrangement provides a dramatic example of this. In this case, the failure of local states to address the rise in conflict and the lack of desire on the part of the UN and more powerful states to intervene led these groups to turn to corporations (actors previously thought to exacerbate conflict) in order to mitigate or prevent conflict.

Conversely, of course, better-than-expected performance might result in expanded authority for a governor. By the mid-1990s, the World Bank's performance record was the subject of widespread criticism from NGOs and others. The IMF, by contrast, was looking relatively competent. Therefore, member states pushed the Fund to become involved in more and more development tasks that were previously the sole responsibility of the Bank, often over the objections of Fund staff. Expanded authority is often a mixed blessing, however, as Tamar Gutner's chapter makes clear. It can create a version of the

"Peter Principle" for global governors: as the reward for competence (or perceived competence) governors may receive more and different tasks for which they are *not* equipped and, ultimately, are not competent to perform.

Managing constant change

These dynamics make a global governor's job complicated. Governors who want to maintain their authority must negotiate between taking action that is consistent with the demands of multiple authority sources (and constituents) and producing successful outcomes, which almost inevitably depends on some coordination with other governors. Tensions and synergies – within authority sources and among governors – create both opportunities and constraints for governors.

As governors interact, both among themselves and with the governed, they may learn from other governors' example, as well as from new ideas. Learning is a powerful source of change in global governance in several of the chapters here. Advocacy groups, states, and international organizations learn from success and failure and refine strategies for promoting their goals (Carpenter and Bob, this volume). Sometimes learning results from a mixture of failed strategies and new ideas (Haufler, this volume). In other instances, relations between governors can actually inhibit learning (Cooley, this volume).

Governors spend a great deal of energy strategizing about how best to maintain or increase their authority and work with or against others to produce the outcomes they and their constituents seek. They try to reconcile conflicting demands for action. They present themselves strategically to different audiences, tailoring policies and justifications to satisfy institutional, delegation, expert, moral, or competence requirements. They work with – and against – other governors to achieve goals, enhance their authority, or both. Sometimes they succeed; sometimes they fail.

Overview of the book

This volume provides a framework for and examples of the analysis of global governors as actors in their own right. It begins the process of theorizing their behavior, interaction, and political impact. The contributors demonstrate the diversity of the phenomenon. They examine a variety of different governors working on a wide range of issues, from economic development to education, to small arms control and technology regulation. We sought unity and coherence in the questions each author asked but left them free to suggest different answers. The analyses that follow, then, are informed by a variety of theoretical perspectives. They all, however, identify the governors in their issue area, examine the basis of each governor's authority, and specify how governors interact on the issue at hand. They have all also attended to endogenous changes in the governor, its authority, and its behavior.

The volume is divided into two parts. The first focuses primarily on how synergies or tensions affect changes in authority – including the construction of governors. The second focuses more on how synergies or tensions affect governance outcomes – potentially feeding back into increased or decreased authority.

Governance dynamics and change in authority

The first five chapters examine governance dynamics as they affect changes in governors' authority. We begin with three chapters that focus specifically on the emergence of new governors. The chapters vary in the mechanisms through which governors are created, the tensions or synergies in their authority, and the degree to which they have consolidated their authority. The last two chart two different mechanisms through which governors' management of tensions in their authority sources enhance the overall deference they command.

Erik Voeten and Allison Danner examine how states created new institutions – international criminal tribunals (ICTs) – and how the ICTs then consolidated authority as new governors for adjudicating war crimes. Begun with authority delegated by states, judges initially appointed to the ICTs used their expertise not only to create procedural rules for the courts and substantive law but also to establish professional standards enhancing the chance that judges with particular backgrounds would serve on the ICTs. Synergies between delegated and expertise authority led to successful consolidation of authority for the ICTs. Several variables contributed to this synergy, including the absence of strong interest in the decisions of the ICTs among powerful states, the fit between judges' competencies and the task they were asked to undertake, and path dependency.

Aseem Prakash and Matthew Potoski also examine the creation of a new institution – ISO 14001 – but through the lens of collective action rather than delegation. They use club theory to explain both the creation of this governor and limits to its authority. Expertise-based (and agreed-upon) environmental standards laid the foundation for this club. Tensions between profitability and environmental standards posed a potential problem, but the fact that environmental standards were nonrival but excludable opened the possibility for launching a voluntary club and reaping benefits from being seen as responsible companies. Persuading would-be participant companies that abiding by these standards would in fact be profitable and that nonabiders would not free-ride on collective gains was crucial to their development. Prakash and Potoski describe the way in which the ISO used its expertise to triangulate between different constituencies (companies, NGOs, and consumers) in creating the 14001 standards. Those constituencies also determined limits to ISO 14001's activities and effectiveness. It made rules and set up monitoring systems but did not opt for enforcement. Though some tensions were resolved to allow the club to form at all, others were not, causing it to be, in their terminology, a "weak sword club."

Reframing issues can also generate potential new authorities. Virginia Haufler demonstrates how advocacy groups, the UN, and states, anxious to find new tools to dampen conflict, enlisted corporations as governors in conflict prevention. Though many had initially blamed multinational corporate actors in extractive industries for fomenting conflict, the absence of capable authorities in many areas led people interested in conflict prevention to think of new ways in which they could enlist corporations to be part of the solution. Some corporations have found themselves reluctant participants in these governance schemes. Though desires to manage their reputations and preserve their markets have spurred some action, the tensions between the firm's core mission (extraction of natural resources for profit) and the new expectation (being responsible for mitigating conflict) are not always neatly resolved. Furthermore, the governance arrangements involving not just corporations but also advocacy groups, international organizations, and states – all with quite different bases of authority and constituencies – may portend both less effective outcomes and fewer chances for increased authority.

Over time, governors may consolidate and strengthen, or even reinvent their governing role. Two cases from the European Union (EU) suggest this dynamic and different ways in which it might occur. Abraham Newman's chapter addresses how state-delegated authority – both to the EU and to sub-state authorities – generated opportunities for sub-state and supra-state organizations to combine their delegated authorities with expertise or principled commitment to become governors. In these "dual delegation" arrangements, governors enhance their authority through cooperation with one another. Rather than the rigid relationships one might expect from the principal–agent logic dominant in international relations theorizing, neither sub-state nor supra-state organizations faithfully carry out state interests. Nor do sub-state and supra-state organizations always cooperate as socialization theory might expect. Instead, each organization acts according to its authority and with varying effectiveness, depending on its ability to create coalitions with other governors.

Kate McNamara's chapter makes a broader claim about the EU's attempt to create a new form of institutional authority for itself. Using delegated, expert, and principled authority, the EU has manipulated symbols to promote a banal and nonthreatening form of Union-wide identity. The power of this symbolic politics implicates the relationship between the EU, as a postmodern governor, and EU bureaucrats, who seek to manage their constituents' expectations in such a way that they become willing to cede even greater authority. In her analysis, it is not only the way banal authority is nonthreatening to other governors, particularly European states, but also its fit with the postmodern era that creates the synergies she sees. Authority based on banal symbols manages one set of tensions but creates another, launching a new round of contestation over the consolidation of institutional authority.

Governance dynamics and outcomes

The next six chapters focus on the ways in which conflict, tensions, and synergies affect governance outcomes. The first four look specifically at conflicts and tensions within or among governors and the various outcomes these produce: from keeping issues off the agenda to creating suboptimal policy even with agreed-upon goals, to an example of conflict and zombie policy. The final two examine conditions under which cooperation among governors can produce expected and more optimal outcomes.

Charli Carpenter examines tensions within advocacy networks concerned about children and war. While some activists were eager to put on the international agenda the needs of children born as a result of wartime rapes, gatekeepers interested in maximizing successful campaigns were less enthusiastic. She shows how powerful gatekeepers within the network kept the issue of children born of war off the agenda. Her analysis reminds us to look for the dogs that don't bark and demonstrates how power can work even among like-minded advocates to resolve tensions in a way that denies attention to important issues.

Examining the growth of contracting between governors, Alex Cooley argues that a variety of governors frequently choose contracts that are incomplete, short-term, and renewable. These contracts, however, lead to competition that undermines both the effectiveness of outcomes and governors' continued authority. He illustrates how the dynamic is similar whether the principals are states (like the United States) or IOs (like the UN), and whether the agents are corporations (like Halliburton) or NGOs (like CARE). The tensions among governors lead to opportunism, erode trust, and generate suboptimal outcomes.

Tamar Gutner examines the poverty reduction efforts under the Millennium Development Goals (MDGs). Asking the IMF to participate in developing and implementing policy to meet the MDGs is an example of what Gutner calls "mission seep," where the same goals are delegated to a broad array of international actors. It has pushed the IMF away from its core strengths and bears all the signs of delegation pathology, in which principals delegate tasks that are unclear, unrealistic, or highly complex. Her analysis demonstrates how this leads to tensions among sources of authority – the institutional and expertise-based authority the IMF has developed versus the authority it has been delegated in a new realm. The IMF has every incentive to jump on the MDG bandwagon because that is what states have asked and that is where the money is. But in so doing, the IMF is working toward the same goals as many other organizations without coordination and with little consensus on the relationship between the MDGs and the IMF's Poverty Reduction and Growth Facility. This authority delegation has also generated tensions among governors. The IMF, while being responsive to its principals (and thus a good agent), acts in a manner that leads away from the principals' ultimate goals (poverty reduction). Though states and IOs have a common set of goals, complete with targets and timetables, no one is accountable for the outcome. Ironically, having global governors like the IMF makes it easier for states to approve global outcomes but do little to meet them.

Clifford Bob examines conflict: the mobilization of one set of governors against another to affect policy. Tensions between governors in this case create competing frames through which to think about the control of small arms – as a tool for reducing conflict or as a threat to the rights of legitimate gun owners. As Bob demonstrates, the mobilization of guns rights groups and sympathetic states led to a campaign that weakened international efforts to control the flow of small arms, creating what he calls "zombie policy."

Tim Büthe focuses on why the International Electrotechnical Commission emerged as a transnational governor in the early twentieth century and why it evolved to govern the entire spectrum of electrotechnology globally, as well as how its interactions with other governors affect its efficacy as a standard-setter. He shows how synergies between authority (based on expertise) and self-interest drew together individuals who were at once inventors and investors to launch an organization that could enhance electrotechnical harmonization in ways that led to greater profitability. He also examines who the key actors are at each stage of the governance process and describes how the Commission relies on synergies with states and scientific organizations at the domestic level to enforce IEC standards and thus lead to effective outcomes.

Karen Mundy's analysis of global governance in education begins with a paradox: despite agreement on a principle, education for all (EFA), international action on this issue remained uncoordinated and ineffective for the better half of a century. Her chapter shows how enhanced authority on the part of many different governors (in terms of either capacity, expertise, principle, delegation, or material resources) produced tensions in the way of interorganizational competition, which undermined effective action. It also suggests that shifts in relational dynamics among global governors in the period since the Millennium Development Declaration have promoted synergies among EFA's governors which invite greater accountability and effectiveness.

Together, these chapters demonstrate the rich variety of global governors at work in the world today and the utility of the proposed framework for beginning to understand them. By investigating systematically the authority of these actors – why do the governed defer? – we gain a better understanding of where these governors come from, how and why they can influence policy, and how they may fail or be challenged. Attending to the relations among governors draws attention to a complex web of (inter)dependencies, not just between governors and governed, but also among the governors, themselves.

PART I

Authority dynamics and new governors

2 | Who is running the international criminal justice system?

ALLISON DANNER AND ERIK VOETEN

On May 25, 1993, United Nations Security Council resolution 827 established the International Criminal Tribunal for the former Yugoslavia (ICTY) "for the sole purpose of prosecuting persons responsible for serious violations of international humanitarian law committed in the territory of the former Yugoslavia." The limited geographic and temporal focus of the ICTY belies its importance in the development of international criminal law. As the first international tribunal since the Nuremberg Tribunals to interpret the crimes of genocide, crimes against humanity, and war crimes, the ICTY and the subsequently established Rwandan Tribunal (ICTR) have developed an enormous new body of international law, spanning substantive criminal principles, procedural rules, and sentencing practices (Danner 2006). These courts have concluded, for example, that genocide can be committed through the crime of rape, that civilians – and not just military leaders – can be convicted under the theory of "command responsibility," and that war crimes can be committed during civil wars.[1] All of these conclusions represent a significant expansion of the legal texts that formed the basis of their decisions. Moreover, most of these principles have become entrenched in the permanent International Criminal Court (ICC), thus ensuring their influence well beyond their original limited purpose.

The judges at the ICTY and the ICTR have thus played a central role in a task that is traditionally reserved for states: the creation of international law. As such, the questions that motivate this book are

We appreciate comments and suggestions from Karen Alter, Maximo Langer, the editors of the volume, and the participants in the Global Governors workshops. The views expressed in this article do not necessarily represent the views of the Department of Justice or the United States.

[1] The ICTR statute is more explicit than the ICTY statute on the civil war issues as it includes crimes committed in violation of Common Article 3 of the Geneva Conventions.

acutely relevant Who are these judges? Where does their authority come from? How do they accomplish their goals? Whose interests are they serving? What are the theoretical mechanisms of accountability and when, if ever, have they been activated?

These questions have not yet been adequately addressed in the literature. Although there is a lively academic debate about the role of international courts (Helfer and Slaughter 2005; Keohane *et al.* 2000; Posner and Yoo 2005; Reus-Smit 2005), it has tended to treat international criminal tribunals as an afterthought, perhaps because they do not neatly fit the categories of supranational adjudication or interstate dispute resolution bodies. Moreover, individual judges (or prosecutors) rarely feature in these debates.[2] Instead, international courts are treated as black boxes that form either a solution to a particular functional problem that states face (in rational institutionalist approaches) or pieces of evidence for the existence of a "justice cascade" (Lutz and Sikkink 2001) (in sociological or ideational approaches). As with the other aspects of global governance studied in this volume, the agents in the process have not been made central to the analysis (see Avant, Finnemore, and Sell, this volume).

Despite this lack of attention, however, we suggest that both the rationalist and constructivist schools of thought offer useful insights into the origins of the authority of judges and the functioning of accountability mechanisms. From the sources of authority outlined in chapter 1, rationalists stress delegation by states and suggest that judges can and should be held accountable by these same states. Sociological approaches stress expertise and principles as the ultimate sources of judicial authority on international criminal law and point to a disaggregate set of actors that comprise international society as the ultimate guardians of accountability. We derive a set of observable implications from these theoretical starting points and offer a first empirical investigation of the agency of international criminal judges. Our analysis focuses first on the selection process, in which governments play a direct role. We investigate the professional, national, and personal backgrounds of judges and candidates for judgeships on the ICTY and ICTR until 2004 in order to better understand who is deemed appropriate by governments for running the international criminal justice system. We also study the extent to which

---

[2] Most of the literature in political science has focused on the creation of ICTs as opposed to their agency (Rudolph 2003) or their effectiveness (Bass 2000).

governments use reelection as a tool to hold judges accountable. We then turn to an analysis of how the personal, national, and professional identities of judges influence their decisionmaking in the court.

Theoretically, our findings are a mixed bag. As would be expected by rationalists, powerful states are vastly overrepresented on the tribunals and have succeeded in influencing the course of judicial decision-making in various ways. Moreover, there is evidence that governments do use oversight. For example, ICT judges lose their jobs in elections more frequently than is commonly asserted. At the same time, however, we also find evidence for some of the propositions derived from constructivist approaches. Perhaps most notably, while ICT judges were initially a diverse lot of diplomats, academics, and national judges, it appears that governments have arrived at a common understanding of what the background for an international criminal judge should be: a national-level appellate judge with extensive international human rights experience. We suggest that the move toward judges with trial experience was motivated by concerns about the inefficiency of ICTs. Indeed, instances in which judges were not reelected appear motivated by poor performance rather than the content of decisions. That states appeared almost exclusively motivated by efficiency in holding judges accountable left judges relatively free to develop legal norms and perhaps cater to an NGO constituency that did care deeply about legal norm development.

We also find interesting effects in the social interaction of judges. For instance, the likelihood that a judge will write a dissenting opinion is affected by the proportion of judges on a panel who are from common law countries – *not* whether that individual judge is from a common or civil law country. We suggest, then, that rationalists can provide convincing accounts of the creation of ICTs and some of the main constraints under which ICT judges operate. Yet, the actual operation of the tribunals does appear to have changed the perceptions of states and the expectations of nonstate actors in ways that are not easily accounted for by rationalist institutionalists, as suggested by this volume's opening chapter.

Judges and the development of international criminal law

When the United Nations Security Council created the ICTY, it had only the distant precedents of Nuremberg and Tokyo to guide it. The

Security Council was clearly ambivalent about creating a court using its Chapter VII powers – a step the Council had never previously undertaken. As a legal matter, it was not clear that the Council even had the authority to establish a tribunal under Chapter VII.[3] The discussion in the Security Council of the resolution creating the court provides evidence of the members' understanding of the ICTY. It is noteworthy that the meeting did not focus on the question of the new court's accountability to the Council. In fact, several state representatives emphasized that the tribunal must act, and be seen to act, as independent of the Security Council.[4]

Many delegates asserted that the tribunals could not create new law. The representative of Venezuela underlined that the tribunal, "as a subsidiary organ of the Council, would not be empowered with – nor would the Council be assuming – the ability to set down norms of international law or to legislate with respect to those rights. It simply applies existing international humanitarian law."[5] In his report to the Council presenting the draft statute for the court, the secretary-general declared that the "principle *nullum crimen sine lege* requires that the international tribunal should apply rules of international humanitarian law which are beyond any doubt part of customary law."[6]

Although the ICTY statute left many of the details of crimes vague, representatives on the Council made few comments on issues of substantive law. Only Canada, which was not a member of the Security Council but did submit a proposal to the secretary-general for the statute of the tribunal, argued for more specifics. Canada urged that the Security Council set out the exact offenses under the law of war that would fall within the jurisdiction of the ICTY in its statute, as well as the mental states that the prosecutor would have to prove.[7]

---

[3] For example, the Mexican delegate still remarks in every UNGA debate before an ICTY election that the Mexican delegation participates in the election despite its conviction that the founding of the ICTY was illegal.

[4] United Nations Security Council, Provisional Verbatim Record of the Three Thousand Two Hundred and Seventeenth Meeting, S/PV3217 (May 25, 1993), reprinted in 2 Morris & Scharf, YUGOSLAVIA at 179, at 194 (statement of Japan), 203 (statement of Spain) [hereinafter ICTY Debate].

[5] ICTY Debate, *supra* note xx, at 182. The United Kingdom, Brazil, and Spain made similar statements, ibid., at 190, 202, 204.

[6] Secretary-General Report at ¶ 34.

[7] Letter dated April 13, 1993 from the Permanent Representative of Canada to the United Nations Addressed to the Secretary-General, ¶ 8 S/25594, April 14, 1993, *in* 2 Morris & Scharf, YUGOSLAVIA, *supra* note xx, at 459, 460.

No other state took this approach, and it is not reflected in the final Statute. With the exception of Canada's proposal, none of the public records relating to the ICTY statute reveal any qualms with investing such discretion in an international court.

Despite the reservations expressed about judicial lawmaking, the skeletal nature of the statute made it quite obvious that the ICTY judges would have to engage in this activity. Just as treaties that contain vague standards effectively delegate lawmaking to the institution charged with interpreting them (Trachtman 1999), the brevity of the ICTY's statute implicitly delegated lawmaking power to the judges. In the case of the ICTY, the Security Council never alluded to this allocation of power, even though the state representatives must have been aware of it. In addition, the statute does contain one overt allocation of lawmaking authority, directing the judges to establish their own rules of procedure of evidence.[8]

When the Security Council created the ICTR the following year, it adopted a statute that closely resembled that of the ICTY. Although it changed some details of the ICTR's substantive law to reflect differences in the conflict in Rwanda, the crimes prosecuted at the ICTR were written in terms as vague as those of the ICTY. The statute entrusts the ICTR judges to base their rules on those promulgated by the judges at the ICTY, but it allows them to make changes "as they deem necessary" (ICTR Statute, Art. 14).

It is thus unsurprising that ICTY and ICTR judges have engaged in lawmaking in a broad range of areas. In response to the Security Council's explicit directive, they have crafted procedural rules and policies on a staggering number of issues, from attorney's fees to whether detainees should have internet access while in jail. The judges are continually refining their own rules: at the time of the writing of this article the ICTY rules had been amended thirty-seven times. In terms of substantive law, they have decided the scope of their own jurisdiction and determined that the Security Council acted lawfully when establishing these courts. The courts have developed definitions of rape, torture, genocide, crimes against humanity, plunder, and a host of other key concepts in international criminal law.

---

[8] Article 15 of the ICTY statute provides, "the judges of the International Tribunal shall adopt rules of procedure and evidence for the conduct of the pre-trial phase of the proceedings, trials and appeals, the admission of evidence, the protection of victims and witnesses and other appropriate matters."

What is most telling, perhaps, is that when states sought to establish a permanent international criminal court in 1998, they chose to take a different approach. The states creating the International Criminal Court were not willing to invest the court's judges with as much discretion as that enjoyed by the judges on the ICTY and ICTR. The treaty setting out the law of the ICC is much more detailed than those of its predecessor courts. The ICC treaty contains 126 separate provisions, while the ICTY statute has only 34. In addition, states themselves wrote the rules of procedure and evidence and elements of crimes instead of leaving these up to the judges. These were conscious decisions to rein in the discretion of the ICC judges (Schabas 2001).

Theoretical perspectives

Anne-Marie Slaughter (2004) has characterized the central issue in contemporary global governance as the "governance trilemma," which arises from a demand for global rules in the absence of a strong centralized government but requires that government actors be held accountable through a variety of political mechanisms. This trilemma, then, hinges on articulating the appropriate relationship among (1) the sources of the relevant global rules; (2) the creators of the institutions that develop them; and (3) the subjects that are governed by them. In the case of the ICTY and ICTR, even describing the relevant actors is a challenging task.

The rules adjudicated by the tribunals derive from preexisting treaties (namely the Genocide and Geneva Conventions) written by states, and from customary international law, developed principally by the post-World War II tribunals. The Security Council, presumably acting on behalf of the entire United Nations, created the ICTY and ICTR, which use this treaty-based and customary law that was not itself created by the Council. None of this preexisting law was detailed enough to support criminal trials using contemporary standards of due process, leaving the judges with the inevitable task of lawmaking. As for the subject of the rules, while the courts only have jurisdiction over a geographically and temporally limited set of defendants, the tribunals' jurisprudence has been widely described as "restating" customary international law, rendering it binding for individuals in every state. Much of this law was then incorporated by states when drafting the treaty creating the International Criminal Court.

Given this tangled set of relationships, it is a conceptual challenge to develop a set of positive and normative expectations about how to understand the courts and, by implication, their judges. On whose behalf are they acting? What is the source of their authority? What weight should be given to their decisions? How should we expect states to behave with regard to the selection of the judges that engage in this lawmaking?

The theoretical literature on international courts can be divided into two broad camps that have fundamentally different notions about the sources of the authority of judges as well the mechanisms of accountability. Rational institutionalists conceptualize the authority of international judges as resulting from explicit acts of delegation by states. Constructivists and other sociologically inclined scholars in political science and law argue that the authority of international judges resides in the extent to which they legitimately exercise rational-legal authority. Whereas rationalists see problems of accountability as emerging from a failure of judges to abide by the terms of the delegation contract, constructivists suggest that judges are primarily accountable to upholding a set of shared norms and ideas that motivated the creation of ICTs. As such, there are multiple theoretical sources of authority, as identified in chapter 1.

In the remainder of this section, we seek to derive some observable implications from these perspectives for the judicial selection process and judicial behavior.

Rationalist approaches

Rational institutionalists argue that states delegate authority to international courts because they believe that international judges might be able to achieve a set of objectives more effectively and/or efficiently than absent such delegation. The most common approach is principal–agent (P–A) theory, which stresses the conditional nature of these grants of authority (Hawkins *et al.* 2006; Cooley, this volume). States delegate authority to international judges because these judges have advantages in terms of expertise and experience in running criminal trials. In order to achieve these advantages, agents (judges) should be granted some discretion. P–A theorists thus define authority as "the right to pick a decision in an allowed set of decisions" (Simon 1947), which is narrower than the broader definition of authority in chapter 1. P–A approaches paint a picture of international judges who enjoy "constrained independence" (Helfer 2006). They operate in a "strategic space" (Steinberg 2004), whose boundaries are defined by the terms of the delegation and the effectiveness of the tools of control at the disposal of governments.

The fundamental question at the heart of any P–A analysis is how principals can achieve the benefits from delegation while minimizing the (policy) losses associated with surrendering authority. As such, the selection and reselection of judges become central. However, the P–A approach is too general to yield specific expectations about what types of judges governments are likely to select or how these judges would behave once selected (Voeten 2007). To create such expectations, we need to make further assumptions about what governments and judges want from an ICT. We discuss two such assumptions.

Credible commitments

Delegation to judicial institutions that are truly independent and whose judgments cannot easily be overruled may help governments make credible commitments (Alter 2008; Majone 2001). In the case of ICTs, independent tribunals that are not subject to state intervention plausibly help states make a credible commitment to the court's explicit goals (deterring future violations through the punishment of perpetrators, breaking the cycle of violence by substituting individual accountability for collective accountability, and providing an accurate record of the atrocities) rather than the politicized exercise of victor's justice. If establishing a credible commitment to impartial justice were the primary aim of governments, then the grant of discretion to judges has a fiduciary character, with little use for oversight or *ex post* accountability to states. In fact, any perception that judges or prosecutors could be removed for failing to implement the wishes of their principals undermines the purpose for which the tribunal was created in the first place.

Governments could make their commitments to refrain from imposing victor's justice more credible by appointing judges from countries that have independent legal systems and were not directly involved in the conflict under consideration. Moreover, those with experience as judges in independent domestic legal systems or as academics, who are used to acting with relative autonomy, would be more natural candidates for international judgeships than diplomats or other government officials, who by training are more likely to be concerned with the legal position of their home governments. Judges are accountable in this framework, not to the parochial interests of their principals, but rather to the broader set of ideas that motivated the founding of ICTs – that war criminals should be brought to justice through fair trials.

In this view, we would expect governments to intervene infrequently in ongoing cases. In addition, governments would not oppose access to the court by independent[9] nongovernmental organizations (NGOs), which serve to monitor the proceedings, contribute amicus briefs, and issue reports on the performance of judges. The reelection process should be used to dismiss only judges who have undisputedly failed to perform based on the assessments of such reports rather than any particular dissatisfaction states may have with judicial performance. In this framework, then, judges and prosecutors are "trustees" (Alter 2006) who enjoy considerable agency before they meet the scorn of powerful states. Yet, judges should also realize that the commitment of states to the ICTY and ICTR is only temporary, thus creating incentives to expand the tribunal's authority immediately rather than going through the gradual building of legitimacy that characterizes behavior of other international courts (Danner 2006).

Realpolitik

Realist scholars in law and political science have a much narrower vision of the extent to which international courts, and hence international judges, are and should be independent and exercise agency (Posner and Yoo 2005; Goldsmith and Posner 2005; Snyder and Vinjamuri 2003). ICTs present an apparent problem to realist theorists as they regulate what should be the ultimate prerogative of states: their conduct in war. Yet, to a considerable extent, the creation of ICTs is a story that can be told by realists without flinching (Rudolph 2003). The ICTY was created amidst the failure of UNPROFOR and certainly was a much cheaper alternative to expanding that mandate. Richard Holbrook has acknowledged that, within the US government, the tribunal was widely seen as a public relations device (Williams and Scharpf 2002). Similarly, the ICTR was a relatively inexpensive

---

[9] "Independent" here means independent from the governments that created and fund the court. It does not necessarily imply impartiality with respect to what occurs at the court.

gesture in the aftermath of the international community's failure to prevent genocide. This is even more so given that few if any of the governments that created the ICTs and voted for their judges expected one of its citizens to be subject to the tribunal's proceedings. More generally, targets of ICT proceedings tend to belong to unpopular and less powerful regimes.

Realists would point out that the functioning of ICTs depends greatly on the continued cooperation of powerful governments. First, tribunals are largely dependent on governments to apprehend the accused (Danner 2003). Second, the funding of the ICTY and ICTR was frequently inadequate and insecure, to the extent that the United States privately stepped in to supply the prosecutor's office with (its own) prosecutors (Danner 2006). Realists, then, would not be surprised by the ICTY prosecutor's decision not to investigate NATO for potential war crimes in Kosovo (Danner 2003).

With regard to judicial selection, realists are worried that judges will be overly expansive in their rulings. Studies of judicial behavior on the European Court of Human Rights (ECHR) have shown that international judges who were primarily diplomats or government bureaucrats in their previous careers tend to be more sympathetic toward the state than those who were national judges, academics, or private practitioners. They also would expect that governments would use prestigious and lucrative appointments to reward loyal functionaries, something that was of great concern to the founders of the ICTY.[10] Finally, realists would expect an overrepresentation of judges from powerful countries that had a direct stake in the conflict. Many of these expectations contrast directly with the credible commitment rationale.

With regard to judicial behavior, judges may have considerable agency on those issues that are of little concern to the great powers, but are heavily constrained when an issue generates the wrath of a powerful state. We would expect to see amicus briefs or other intervention by states in the "big cases" and a close adherence by judges to the views of their own states (Posner and de Figueiredo 2005). Judges that exceed these limits should be punished during reelection. Thus, the selection and reelection of judges should primarily be about issues of loyalty.

[10] Interview with John Crook, January 9, 2006, and interview with Michael Matheson, December 13, 2006.

Constructivist approaches

Constructivists and other sociologically inclined scholars in political science and law argue that rationalist approaches have an overly narrow conception of authority (Barnett and Finnemore 2004; Goodman and Jinks 2004; Avant, Finnemore, and Sell, this volume) and, by implication, of the agency that international judges can exercise. First, the creation of ICTs does not necessarily meet functional demands by states but rather reflects an "international justice cascade," in which nonstate actors demand some form of justice for egregious war crimes (Lutz and Sikkink 2001). Thus, the ultimate stakeholders for ICT judges are not states but NGOs and the victims and citizens they seek to represent. Although early constructivist research stressed the benign principled nature of NGOs, recently more attention has been paid to the possible pathologies resulting from their partisan nature and financial insecurities (see especially the chapter by Clifford Bob in this volume). These pathologies become especially important because constructivists reserve a large role for NGOs in publicizing judges' deviations from appropriate behavior (as do rationalists who follow the credible commitments logic).

Second, international judges can, through their decisions, help change the way governments perceive their own interests. For example, Michael Barnett and Martha Finnemore (2004) have argued that international organizations can exercise power by creating new categories and definitions, which then become accepted by states, generally because states respect the rational-legal authority of international institutions. As mentioned in the previous section, ICT judges have developed definitions of rape, torture, and genocide that could potentially have consequences well beyond their original intent, so long as they are implemented in ways deemed legitimate by the international community. Judges may also develop procedural models. For example, some legal scholars argue that ICTY judges shifted from an adversarial model to a managerial model to prosecute international crimes (Langer 2005).

With regard to judicial selection, sociological theorists would expect the development of a common conception of the appropriate qualifications for an international criminal judge. As such, we may see initial diversity in qualifications but over time should see more homogeneity in the kinds of candidates that governments nominate and elect. This process of acculturation need not necessarily reflect a move toward judges who dispose of trials more efficiently or effectively but could reflect pathologies that creep into organizational culture. In addition, constructivists would expect that governments that particularly identify with the global production of public goods, such as peace and justice, would be among those most enthusiastic about having a national serve as an ICT judge.

Other sociological theories point to professionalization as an important potential source of judicial behavior. Slaughter (2004) has argued that transnational networks of judges have been extraordinarily influential in shaping judicial decisionmaking around the globe by facilitating learning through the exchange of information. Although her focus is primarily on the emergence of a global community of human rights law, similar concepts may apply to the area of international criminal law. In network terms, international criminal law constitutes a small and dynamic world. Prosecutors, counsels, and judges move freely between the various tribunals. Academics move from analyzing the tribunals to serving on them. Thus, it would seem useful to study the development of transnational networks of international criminal lawyers and the norms embedded in such networks. Indeed, some scholars have already begun the process of considering the relevant networks in international criminal justice (Turner 2007).

International criminal justice networks are likely to become increasingly important as the number and type of international criminal institutions increase. International prosecutors from the ICTY, ICTR, ICC, and the Special Court for Sierra Leone have gathered together to share best practices and discuss prosecutorial strategies. The prosecutors at the ICC have also provided legal resources to the Iraqi Special Tribunal.

If this kind of networking is a key feature of international criminal justice, we would expect judges to serve routinely on multiple courts in the international system. We would expect them to work actively in the dissemination of the norms they have developed by writing books, giving speeches, and the like (Terris *et al.* 2007).

Three somewhat skeptical perspectives deserve attention here. First, it may be that networks do not so much facilitate cross-fertilization, as Slaughter argues, but rather help spread dominant norms and practices. Of particular concern is the perceived dominance of Anglo-Saxons, a frequent complaint from continental Europeans. Furthermore, it is entirely possible that international criminal judges retain a stronger sense of national or previous professional identity, especially because, on average, ICT judges are in their mid-fifties when initially appointed to the bench. As a result, we would expect, for instance, that conflicts between judges from common and civil law systems might arise. Second, networks are not only useful for spreading information but also serve other professional purposes, most notably career objectives. It would be useful to assess the extent to which members of the international criminal law community are in a position to distribute desirable jobs, committee assignments, and so on. If career prospects become dependent more on the evaluation of peers than on the prerogatives of states, then we would expect this to affect judicial behavior. Third, networks are not invulnerable to the influence of governments or INGOs. These organizations can convene or participate in conferences, or otherwise seek to influence the flow of information inside networks.

Judicial backgrounds and the selection process

The judicial selection process at the ICTY and ICTR

The nineteen "permanent" judges at the ICTY and the sixteen permanent judges at the ICTR are elected through a majority vote by the members of the United Nations General Assembly from a list of candidates provided by the Security Council.[11] The Security Council, in turn, develops its list of candidates from a list compiled by the secretary-general based upon state nominations. Each state may nominate up to two candidates, but these candidates cannot both be of the same nationality or of the same nationality as any sitting judge at either the ICTY or the ICTR.[12] On at least one occasion, the secretary-general has had to extend the nominating period for lack of sufficient candidates.

The courts' statutes instruct the Security Council to construct its list "taking due account of the adequate representation of the principal

---

[11] The designation "permanent" distinguishes these judges from a pool of "temporary" judges, known as *ad litem* judges. These *ad litem* judges were first added by the Security Council in 2000 in order to increase the capacity of the ICTY to conduct multiple trials at one time. See SC Res. 1329 (2000).

[12] ICTY Statute, Art. 13*bis*; ICTR Statute, Art. 12*bis*.

legal systems of the world."[13] (There is no mention of gender diversity in either the statute of the ICTY or that of the ICTR.) In terms of qualifications, the tribunals' statutes state that the judges "shall be persons of high moral character, impartiality and integrity who possess the qualifications required in their respective countries for appointment to the highest judicial offices."[14]

Once elected, the judges serve four-year terms, although they may stand for reelection. After their election, they are assigned to a trial or appeals chamber. The trial chambers are made up of three permanent judges and up to six *ad litem* judges, of which three serve on any given trial. The three-judge panels manage the pre-trial phase of the courts' cases and conduct the trials of the defendants, serving both law-finding and fact-finding functions. At the end of the trial, they issue a judgment that sets out detailed analysis of the relevant law and facts and states whether the defendant is found guilty or not guilty. The judgment also contains an explanation of any criminal sentences assigned to convicted defendants.

If either the defendant or prosecutor appeals, the trial chamber's decision is reviewed by the seven-member appeals chamber, which will eventually issue a lengthy decision of its own on the case, often revising the trial chamber's conclusions. Although the ICTY and ICTR technically have different appeals chambers, the same judges serve on both the ICTY and ICTR appeals chambers. They do not sit on a trial chamber while serving on the appeals chamber, although some judges have sat on both.

Nationality

As is true for most UN postings, informal conventions play an important role in the geographic distribution of judgeships. With regard to the ICTY, the major NATO member states (the United States, the United Kingdom, France, and Italy) were de facto guaranteed judgeships if they desired them (which they did). Judges advanced by the five permanent members of the Security Council were usually elected, the only exception being the Russian candidate for the first ICTY

---

[13] ICTY Statute, Art. 13*bis*; ICTR Statute, Art. 12*bis*.
[14] ICTY Statute, Art. 12; ICTR Statute, Art. 13.

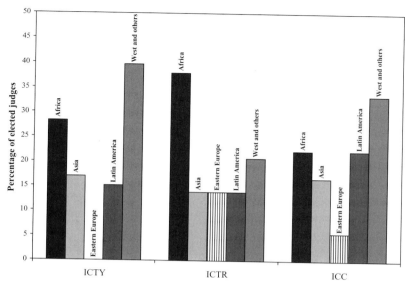

Figure 2.1 Regional distribution of ICT judgeships

election in 1993.[15] Russia's partiality to Serbia evidently disqualified Russian judges from partaking in the tribunal. By contrast, Russia has been the only P-5 country with representation on the less prestigious ICTR.

Figure 2.1 shows the regional distribution of judgeships for the ICTY, ICTR, and – for purposes of comparison – the ICC.[16] It is immediately evident that the ICTY is dominated by judges from the West and the ICTR by African judges. Thus, judges from countries that presumably have an interest in the functioning of the tribunals are overrepresented on both courts. On the other hand, Eastern European judges were excluded from the ICTY (and slightly overrepresented on the ICTR, perhaps as a form of compensation). Judges from Latin American countries, who had little at stake in either conflict, were underrepresented on both courts.

These findings are perhaps surprising from the credible commitments perspective. After all, if governments wanted to use the national origin

[15] Valentin Kisilev. He obtained only seventy-one of the ninety-four votes necessary for election on the first ballot.
[16] Regional classifications follow the official UN groupings.

of judges to signal impartiality, judges from democratic Latin American countries would seem like ideal candidates. Instead, it appears that the distribution of nationalities reflects interests in the outcome of the tribunal, or at least in the stability of the region upon which the court focuses.

Another issue that inevitably surfaces when staffing international courts is the representation of the world's main legal systems. There has long been a charge that individuals from common law countries have dominated the ICTs. The ICTY was largely modeled after a common law criminal court. The prosecutorial office was primarily staffed with Americans and, later, Australians.[17] This is also evident in the composition of the bench: whereas 30 percent of the world's countries have a legal system of common law origins, 47 percent of elected ICTY judges were from common law countries.[18] Perhaps more surprising is that this also holds for the ICTR, where 45 percent of elected judges came from common law countries.[19]

The relevance of this is hard to gauge. Various scholars have asserted that judges have significantly different roles in civil and common law legal systems (Glaeser and Shleifer 2002). Judges have generally played a subordinate role in legal systems designed after the French civil law system. In common law countries, on the other hand, judges are frequently asked to engage in broader interpretations of legal principles. This would make judges from common law countries, the argument goes, more likely to be activist in their role orientation than judges from French civil law countries. This difference should be especially apparent on the appeals chamber. The role of judges in criminal trials also differs considerably. In civil law systems, judges generally have an active inquisitorial role. In common law systems, there is a much stricter separation between the trial judge, the investigator, and the prosecutor. The resulting heterogeneity in socialization among ICT judges may well affect judicial performance and result in tensions on mixed judicial panels, a point that we will briefly return to later in the chapter.

---

[17] The United States offered to fill staff positions in response to initial problems due to UN budget shortfalls.

[18] Data on legal origins is from La Porta *et al.* (1999).

[19] There was a perception that the ICTR was going to be dominated by civil law judges, owing to the civil law origins of Rwanda and the likelihood of finding good judges with fluency in French (interview with Michael Matheson, December 13, 2006).

Table 2.1 *Poisson regressions on the number of ICT candidates and judges for countries, 1993–2004*

	No. candidates		No. judges	
	coefficient	SE	coefficient	SE
(Constant)	−0.26	0.28	−1.02**	0.42
Civil liberties	−0.06	0.05	−0.16**	0.07
CINC capabilities	1.04***	0.44	1.68***	0.47
Peacekeeping participation	0.89***	0.20	1.15***	0.31
Common law origin	0.53***	0.16	0.78***	0.22
Latin	0.09	0.22	0.45	0.29
Asian	−0.59**	0.24	−0.36	0.33
R^2_{adj}	0.15	0.21		
N	154	154		

Notes: **p < .05, ***p < .01. All tests are two-tailed.

In all, there are eighty-six countries that have sought at least once to have a judge elected to an ICT and forty-nine countries that have succeeded in having a judge elected. Table 2.1 reports results from an analysis of some correlates of the number of candidates a country nominated who were successfully elected to either ICT. The model is estimated using a Poisson regression, to take account of the nature of the count data. The results are meant to be illustrative.[20]

If a realist model dominates international justice, we would expect that more powerful countries would be more likely to advance candidates and certainly more likely to succeed. We measure relative material capabilities using the Composite Index of National Capability (CINC) score from the Correlates of War project.[21] Capabilities have an effect on both the number of candidates and the number of judges

[20] We analyze the data cumulatively to avoid difficulties resulting from the rule that a country cannot have a judge serving on both the ICTY and the ICTR. The main results also hold in a negative binomial regression and a simple OLS regression.

[21] This indicator was originally developed in Singer *et al.* (1972). It is more fully discussed in Singer (1987). This measure is based on six components of material power: total population, urban population, iron and steel production, energy consumption, military personnel, and military expenditure. The CINC score is computed by summing all observations on each of the six components for a given year, converting each state's absolute component to a share of the international system, and then averaging across the six components.

a country had successfully elected but, as expected, the effect is much larger on the latter.

In a credible commitments framework, we would expect countries with a tradition of judicial independence to be more successful in judicial elections. We find that countries with high levels of domestic civil liberties[22] were often successful in having candidates elected, although they did not advance more candidates, controlling for other factors. This suggests that candidates from countries with high levels of civil liberties enjoyed an advantage in elections but that liberal countries were not necessarily more enthusiastic about having their nationals serve on the ICTs. We test the first hypothesis more explicitly on candidate-level data later in this chapter.

Third, the sociological perspective implies that a desire to fill prestigious international posts may be correlated with more general tendencies of a country to participate in the international community. Some governments have a greater inclination to be a part of international society and contribute to its collective enterprises, especially with regard to the production of peace and justice. Having a national serve on an ICT may be more valuable to those governments than to governments that do not identify themselves as much with global international society. Moreover, ICT judgeships may be a reward for cooperative behavior in the UN.

We suggest participation in UN peacekeeping missions as a good indicator for voluntary contributions to international public goods (see also Lebovic and Voeten 2006). This indicator is useful as participants in peacekeeping missions are diverse in terms of their relative power and levels of domestic liberalism. The results in Table 2.1 provide evidence in favor of our intuition: countries that contributed frequently to peacekeeping missions much more frequently advanced candidates for ICT judgeships than did countries that rarely participated.[23] Moreover, they also ended up with more ICT judgeships than did other countries, controlling for other factors.

Fourth, the results in Table 2.1 reveal a strong bias in favor of judges from common law countries but we found no evidence that Latin

---

[22] As measured here by the Freedom House civil liberties index, which runs from 1 (high level of civil liberties) to 7 (low level of civil liberties); see www.freedomhouse.org.

[23] The precise measure is the proportion of years between 1993 and 2004 that a country contributed troops to a UN peacekeeping operation.

American countries less frequently advanced candidates or less frequently succeeded. It is true, of course, that Latin American countries are generally not common law countries (except for some Caribbean nations), so the two variables are not completely independent.

There is some evidence that Asian countries less frequently advanced candidates for judgeships, although this is not reflected in the number of judgeships held by Asian nationals.

In all, then, it appears that more powerful, more liberal countries and countries that are generally inclined to participate in UN efforts to achieve peace and justice are also better represented by judges on the ICTs. Thus, these results find some support for aspects of the realist, international society, and credible commitment models.

Professional backgrounds of elected judges

We coded the previous experience of ICT judges and candidates for judgeships primarily based on the curriculum vitae that their governments submitted to the UN as part of the election process.[24] This reliance on official sources has advantages and disadvantages. On the pro-side, this is the information that country representatives rely on when they vote on ICT candidates. On the con-side, judges and their national governments have considerable control over what qualifications they may or may not report. This proved somewhat of a problem in the European Court of Human Rights, where some candidates understated their political experience, sometimes in rather blatant ways (Flauss 1998). Unlike ECHR elections, however, ICT elections are competitive in the sense that not every country is guaranteed a judgeship.[25] Thus, country representatives have incentives to reveal glaring omissions or misrepresentations on the CVs of rival candidates. Yet, this potential check is limited to only the most obvious misrepresentations, given that country representatives generally have little information about the candidates beyond the official vitae.[26]

---

[24] For the ICTR, these can be found in UN Documents: A/49/894, A/53/444, A/53/444/Add.1, A/53/1003, A/55/873, A/57/493, A/57/802, S/2003/689, S/2004/291.

[25] ECHR elections are competitive in the sense that each government has to submit a list of three candidates from which the Parliamentary Assembly of the Council of Europe elects one.

[26] Interview with Michael Matheson, December 13, 2006.

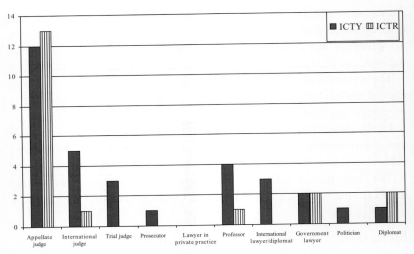

Figure 2.2a Position at time of election, ICTY and ICTR judges

For each judge, we coded official job descriptions as well as other relevant reported experience, including education, military experience, and international (including UN) experience. Figure 2.2 plots the main job descriptions of ICTR and ICTY judges. Figure 2.2a categorizes judges by the main position that they held at the time of the election.[27] Figure 2.2b denotes the job description that best characterizes the judge's career before entering the court.[28] Obviously, assigning judges to these categories required some judgment, as most judges had experience in multiple professions. We take note of this issue in our descriptive analyses.

The primary job descriptions of ICT judges fit into four broad categories: judges, domestic legal practitioners, full-time professors at universities (academics), and government officials (politicians, diplomats, and bureaucrats). Judges were by far the most common: 67 percent of all ICT judges were judges at the time of their election. This percentage is notably lower when we code the category that best describes the overall career of ICT judges (37 percent). A number of (especially ICTR) judges worked as government lawyers or in some

[27] In cases where the candidate had retired before the election, we coded the main position at the time of retirement.

[28] Judges of the appeals chamber are assigned to the court in which they were elected.

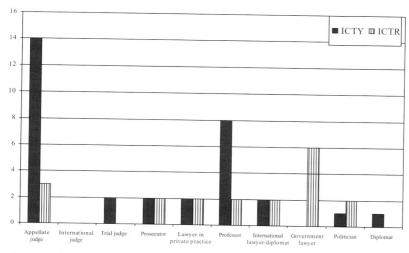

Figure 2.2b Primary career position, ICTY and ICTR judges

other capacity before becoming an appellate or international judge, which then launched their careers as international criminal judges.[29]

Among the candidates who were judges at the time of election, most (74 percent) were judges at an appellate court. Some also had experience as trial judges, although only 9 percent were primarily trial judges. A total of fifteen ICT judges reported experience as a national trial judge on their CVs.[30] Yet, the primary experience of ICT judges is not in running trials but in reviewing the decisions of lower courts. Since most of the judges at the ICTY and ICTR in fact act as trial judges, this heavy representation of appellate judges may have contributed to the difficulties in trial management that have been the focus of much criticism leveled at these courts.[31]

Only five ICT judges were full-time professors at a university at the time of their election; twice that many could be characterized as career

---

[29] This description applies, amongst others, to Jean-Claude Antonetti (France), Lennart Aspegren (Sweden), William Hussein Sekule (Tanzania), Erik Møse (Norway), Winston Churchill Maqutu (Lesotho), and Asoka de Zoysa Gunawardana (Sri Lanka).

[30] Eight at the ICTY, seven at the ICTR.

[31] It should be noted that many of the judges have had some trial experience prior to their election. For example, nine permanent ICTY judges and eight ICTR judges report that they have prosecutorial experience. Twenty-two ICTY judges and seven ICTR judges mention extensive experience in private law practice. Therefore, many judges have had experience at the trial level, although not as trial judges.

academics whose primary job at the time of election was no longer in academia. For example, Belgian judge Christine Van den Wyngaert had been a professor of criminal law at the University of Antwerp for almost twenty years, when she became an *ad litem* judge for the ICTY in 2001. She was elected as a permanent judge to that court in 2004. About half of all ICT judges (twenty-six) report that at some point in their careers they had a full-time position at a university. Many of the remaining judges held positions as visiting professors or lecturers. Thus, even though few ICT judges were full-time professors at the time of their election, many have had extensive experience in academic life.

In all, 22 percent of ICT judges could best be described as government officials at the time of their election (this rises to 28 percent when we code the category that best describes a judge's career). We split the category of government officials into several subcategories: *diplomats* are those who represented their country abroad (for example, as ambassadors) or in international organizations; *international-lawyer diplomats* are lawyers who spent significant time in the domestic bureaucracy on international issues; *government lawyers* are those who worked in a domestic bureaucracy not devoted to international issues (generally, the justice department); and *politicians*, usually former ministers of justice. The vast majority of ICT judges with a government background are lawyers who made a career in their national ministry of justice or foreign affairs.

Professional background of candidates for judgeships

We can gain an even better sense of what might be motivating states when they choose judges by looking at the backgrounds of all the candidates presented to the General Assembly for judicial elections. Figure 2.3 reports the number of successful *and* unsuccessful candidates for ICTY (3a) and ICTR (3b) judgeships. For purposes of exposition, job descriptions are collapsed into the four main categories: judges, domestic legal practitioners, academics, and government officials. The figures are based on the jobs ICT candidates held at the time of election. We also created a separate category for judges who were up for reelection.[32]

---

[32] This category does not include current *ad litem* judges but it does include judges who were appointed by the secretary-general during a regular term.

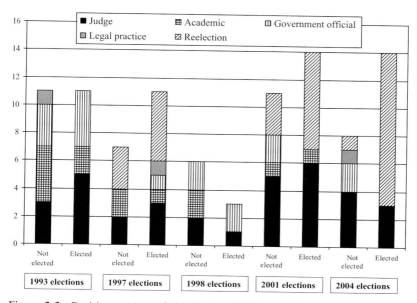

Figure 2.3a Position at time of election for ICTY candidates

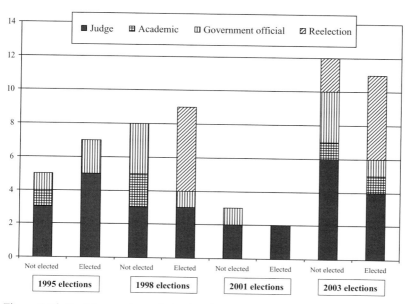

Figure 2.3b Position at time of election for ICTR candidates

A few interesting trends are immediately visible from the figures. First, the model of the academic as international criminal judge has decreased in popularity. After the first round of ICTY elections, only three academics were newly elected on to the court. All three were from P-5 members (who were relatively assured of election): US law professor Theodor Meron (ICTY, 2001), Russian professor Sergei Egorov (ICTR, 2003), and Chinese professor Tieya Wang (ICTY, 1997). This suggests that academics have become an unpopular choice as ICT judges. A first glance at the data confirms this: professors were elected 28 percent of the time, diplomats 39 percent, and judges 58 percent. The next section tests this hypothesis more rigorously in a multivariate setting but the selective behavior of governments is consistent with the hypothesis: whereas six of twenty-two candidates in the 1993 ICTY election were full-time professors, none of the new candidates in 2004 were primarily academics.

In addition, the percentage of government officials elected to the ICTY and ICTR has gone down over time. After 1998, only one candidate whose position at the time of election was best characterized as a government official was successfully elected to either ICT (eight such candidates stood for election over the same period).

This trend suggests that, when these courts were established, states were more concerned with nominating individuals who would be responsive to their governments, although we interpret the election of academics as responding to a need for expertise in international law. We view this early history as providing some support for a principal–agent model. The increasing success of judges in the ICTY and ICTR elections suggests that, as governments become more comfortable with these courts, they are willing to elect professional judges to these posts. This fact could support the credible commitments model or simply confirm that, as the principals become less concerned with agency slippage, they are willing to provide more discretion to their agents.

These results are also consistent with a vision of the courts less tied to the theoretical models we have advanced. Selecting more academics and government officials at the beginning of these courts' existence and then gradually turning to individuals with more judicial experience makes sense if you consider the evolution of these courts. When they were established, their legitimacy was uncertain and their law indeterminate. There was less a need to run trials than to develop the law, rules, and support for the courts that could make them function properly. As a consequence, many of the candidates for the initial ICTY elections were those who were well connected at home, despite concerted efforts by the United States at persuading governments to advance experienced trial judges.[33] As the courts faced increasing caseloads, however, the need to have judges who can run trials became more acute. Indeed, one of the primary criticisms that have been leveled at the ICTY and ICTR in the past five years has been the length of their trials (and, consequentially, their cost). In this environment, it is unsurprising that states are increasingly turning to experienced judges.

The International Criminal Court may be experiencing a similar pattern. In contrast to the ICTY and ICTR, in the ICC's first election four of the eighteen elected judges had primarily academic backgrounds, and two of these were serving as academics at the time of their election.[34] Four of the eighteen judges served significant roles as government lawyers, principally in the ministries of foreign affairs and justice.[35]

Reelection

Reelection serves as one of the most important potential mechanisms for accountability for judges at the ICTs. The efficacy of this mechanism, however, depends upon whether or not judges are routinely reelected and, if they are not, for what reasons their reelection campaigns fail. In all, there were forty-two occasions on which an ICT judge stood for reelection. While the success rate for sitting candidates (78 percent) was notably higher than that of novel candidates (45 percent), there were still nine instances in which sitting judges desired reelection but failed to secure sufficient votes. This may well underestimate the true extent to which judges fail to secure reelection, as

---

[33] Interview with John Crook, January 9, 2006 and interview with Michael Matheson, December 13, 2006.

[34] The two academics were Sang-hyun Song (Korea) and Akua Kuenyehia (Ghana), and the longtime academics were Renee Blattman (Bolivia) and Anita Usacka (Latvia). The career backgrounds of the elected ICC judges are summarized at www.humanrightsfirst.org/international_justice/icc/election/chart_el_judges.pdf.

[35] These were Tuilona Slade (Samoa), Philippe Kirsch (Canada), Erikki Kourula (Finland), and Hans-Peter Kaul (Germany).

candidates unlikely to be successful could be discouraged from standing for reelection.

Seven of the failures to secure reelection occurred on the higher-profile court, the ICTY. Especially interesting is the 1997 election when Judges Saad Saood Jan (Pakistan), Adolphus Karibi-White (Nigeria), and Elizabeth Odio Benito (Costa Rica) failed in their bids for reelection. The three judges served on the trial chamber in the Celebici trial (the first trial that charged Muslims with war crimes)[36] in which, according to one NGO report, "the uninterested judges – led by the presiding Judge Adolphus Karibi-White from Nigeria, sometimes assisted by Judge Jan – are falling asleep more and more often, only to be woken after the third or fourth cry from defence or prosecution lawyer: 'Objection, Your Honour!'"[37] The allegation that Judge Karibi-White slept through large parts of the trial also featured in the appeal by the defendants, who argued that the tapes of the trial "clearly and unambiguously paint a disturbing picture of a Judge prone to fall asleep during all phases of the trial, at almost any time when he was not speaking, examining a document, or otherwise being actively engaged."[38] The appeals chamber, however, held that "his sleeping was only of secondary concern."[39] The appeal also alleged that Judge Odio Benito was not qualified to be a judge and that she should have disqualified herself owing to a conflict of interest (conclusions that the appeals chamber did not accept).

More generally, the running of the Celebici trial was subject to severe criticism as a result of its length (twenty months), the leaking of confidential information to the press,[40] and the judges' tolerance of disruptive tactics by defense lawyers who, according to then ICTY President Gabrielle Kirk McDonald, "behaved as if they were in the O. J. [Simpson] trial, and not before the International Criminal

---

[36] Prosecutor vs Delalic, ICTY Case No. IT-96–21-T (The Celebici Case).

[37] "Tribunal Update 36: Last Week in The Hague" (July 7–12, 1997), Institute for War and Peace Reporting, www.iwpr.net/.

[38] "Selective Prosecution." Trial Judgement in Prosecutor vs Zejnil Delalic, Zdravko Mucic also known as "Pavo", Hazim Delic, Esad Landzo also known as "Zenga", Case No. IT-96–21-T, Trial Chamber, ICTY, 16 Nov 1998. www.un.org/icty/celebici/appeal/judgement/cel-aj010220e-10.htm.

[39] Ibid.

[40] "Tribunal Update 36: Last Week in The Hague" (May 19–24, 1997), Institute for War and Peace Reporting, www.iwpr.net/.

Tribunal."[41] Although this evidence is merely circumstantial, the fact that the only three judges not reelected were precisely the three judges publicly criticized for incompetence is at least suggestive.[42]

There were also three judges who failed to secure reelection in 2001: Judges Rodrigues (Portugal), Vohrah (Malaysia), and Nieto Navia (Colombia). They served together on the trial chamber of the Aleksovski trial. The chamber rendered a non-unanimous judgment. The majority argued that the alleged offences did not take place during an international armed conflict, whereas Judge Rodrigues in a dissenting opinion found that the prosecutor had demonstrated the international nature of the conflict and the guilt of the accused. However, so far we have not found similar allegations of judicial incompetence in the public record. The same is true for the other cases in which sitting judges lost their tenure: the Egyptian Judge Elmahdi (2004) and the ICTR Judges Dolenc (Slovenia) and Maqutu (Lesotho).

Nevertheless, we find this evidence of failure to win reelection to suggest that states do pay attention to the quality of the judges they elect, and that judges do run the risk of failing to be reelected because of incompetence.

Statistical analysis of elections

In the previous sections, we speculated at various points that certain characteristics of candidates and of their countries of origin could correlate with their relative success in elections for vacancies on international criminal tribunals. In this section, we test these hypotheses explicitly using a multivariate framework. Our dependent variable is the number of votes a candidate obtains in the first ballot of elections relative to the threshold for being elected. So, if the absolute majority threshold is ninety-four, then our dependent variable takes the value 1 if the candidate received ninety-four votes on the first ballot, the minimum number needed to secure election. The first ballot is the

---

[41] "Celebici Trial: Judges Strike Back. Tribunal Update 77: Last Week in The Hague" (May 18–23, 1998), iwpr.net/?p=tri&s=f&o=180577&apc_state= henitri1998.

[42] Judge Karibi-White received only sixty-two of the ninety-four necessary votes for reelection. Judge Jan had seventy-one votes, and Judge Odio Benito eighty-three. Note that the ICTY election was during the trial, although the judges were allowed to finish it.

best measure to assess preferences for candidates as later rounds are more strategic, with representatives generally shifting votes away from candidates with a poor showing on the first ballot.[43]

With regard to the characteristics of judges, our main substantive hypothesis was that candidates who were academics fared less well in elections than did others. To test this hypothesis, we inserted a dummy variable that takes the value 1 if the candidate was a full-time professor at the time of election. We also included dummy variables indicating whether the candidate was a government official and whether the candidate was standing for reelection. Thus, the reference category becomes candidates who were judges and domestic legal practitioners at the time of election.

We also included three variables for characteristics of countries. First, candidates from countries with better domestic human rights records may do better in ICT elections. This may be because UN representatives may believe that a judge representing a country with a good human rights reputation would be more open to (and experienced in) finding governments guilty of human rights violations, and better accustomed to judicial independence. As introduced earlier, we use Freedom House civil liberties scores as a measure.

Second, we expect that judges from powerful countries will be more successful in elections. There are various rationales for this: the ICTs need the support of strong countries; weaker countries may feel compelled to vote for candidates from stronger nations; stronger states have greater capabilities to lobby others; and stronger states may be able to bring forth stronger candidates. We measure relative material capabilities using the Composite Index of National Capability score from the Correlates of War project.[44]

Third, we suspect that judges from countries that are known to be contributors to global public goods obtain more votes. As such, ICT judgeships may be rewards for generally cooperative behavior in the UN. We measure such behavior as the proportion of years in which a country contributed troops to UN peacekeeping missions in the four years prior to the election.

---

[43] In fact, the candidacies of those at the bottom of the first ballot are frequently withdrawn after one round of voting.
[44] See the discussion around Table 2.1.

Table 2.2 *Regression of candidate and country characteristics on the proportion of votes (of the majority threshold) that a candidate receives in elections to ICTs, 1993–2004*

	ICTY		ICTR		combined	
	coefficient	SE	coefficient	SE	coefficient	SE
(Constant)	0.87	0.10	0.68	0.00	0.84***	0.08
Country characteristics						
Civil liberties	−0.05**	0.02	0.00	0.03	−0.04**	0.01
CINC capabilities	0.60***	.15	0.47	0.34	0.59***	0.13
Peacekeeping participation	0.17*	0.09	0.23**	0.09	0.17***	0.06
Candidate characteristics						
Reelection	0.26***	0.00	0.27***	0.09	0.26***	0.06
Academic	−0.18*	0.09	−0.18	0.14	−0.18**	0.07
Government official	−0.10	0.09	−0.18	0.09	−0.13**	0.06
ICTR	—	—	—	—	−0.01	0.05
N	94		54		141	
R^2_{adj}	.48		.39		.44	

Notes: *p < .1, **p < .05, ***p < .01. All tests are two-tailed.

Table 2.2 reports the results from the linear regression analysis on the ICTY, ICTR, and the combined elections. The table reports coefficients as well as standard errors and the outcomes of two-tailed significance tests. (We also estimated models including common law origin. This variable was never significant and did not change the other results.) The results are generally favorable to our hypotheses, although with some interesting twists.

First, being an academic at the time of election disadvantaged candidates considerably: compared with the reference group (candidates who were judges and domestic legal practitioners at the time of election), academics were expected to gain one-fifth less of the share of the vote needed to get elected. The size of the coefficients on academic are nearly identical across the courts, but the coefficient is only significant at p = .07 for the ICTR case owing to the smaller sample size. In all, though, this is reasonably strong evidence that candidates who were academics at the time of election had a reduced chance of success.[45] As a whole, government officials were also less successful in ICT elections. These results confirm our descriptive analyses.

Second, both civil liberties and power had strong significant effects in the expected direction for ICTY elections but not for ICTR elections. An ICTY candidate from a country with the best Freedom House score was expected to obtain 35 percent more of the necessary majority vote than a candidate from a country with the worst Freedom House score. For the ICTR, the effect is essentially zero. Both effects were robust to the introduction of regional controls.[46] Capabilities were positive in all three regressions, but only significant for the ICTY and combined models. (This result also holds when including a dummy variable for P-5 members.)

The only country characteristic that had a strong effect on the electoral fortunes of ICTR candidates was their country's participation in peacekeeping missions. A candidate from a country that participates every year in peacekeeping missions is expected to obtain 23 percent of the necessary majority vote more than a candidate whose country never participates. Thus, the idea that ICT judgeships are partially rewards for good social standing receives support.

It is evident that elections for international criminal judges are not random events. Four variables, the current position of a judge, her country's human rights record, capabilities, and peacekeeping participation, together explained 48 percent of the variation in the vote proportion for ICTY candidates. Thus, the simple model has considerable explanatory value for the electoral fortunes of ICTY judges, although less so for the ICTR, which clearly received less attention from the powerful states.

Decisionmaking of elected judges

Introduction

We now turn to the difficult matter of studying whether and how it matters who serves on the ICTs. In the discussion so far, we have

---

[45] If we instead construct the measure based on the overall careers of candidates, the measure for academic becomes insignificant.

[46] These are dummy variables for Africa, Latin America, Asia, and Eastern Europe.

rendered some impressions on this issue, suggesting that some judges may well be more capable of running an impartial and efficient trial than others. Moreover, we have suggested that judges may have varying perspectives on matters of substantive or procedural international criminal law. That this can be consequential is illustrated by the following quote from a dissenting opinion by Judges Schomburg and Güney, who argued that "It should not happen that due to shifting majorities the Appeals Chamber changes its jurisprudence from case to case."[47]

The difficulty is to measure judicial behavior systematically. The most common approach is to examine separate and dissenting opinions. Such studies are widespread in the study of domestic courts and have been undertaken for some of the international courts that allow public dissents,[48] in particular the International Court of Justice (Posner and de Figueiredo 2005) and the European Court of Human Rights (Voeten 2007 and 2008). Most of the studies on judicial behavior in the international context focus on the extent to which judges are biased. Bias, in these studies, typically refers to a revealed preference among judges toward their own government or governments that share alliances and/or cultural traits with their national government.

This conception of bias is particularly relevant in the contexts of supranational adjudication and interstate dispute resolution where judicial decisions can be categorized as being either for or against a government. In the context of ICTs, bias is less easily defined, although not irrelevant. For example, judges from NATO countries might be predisposed toward convictions and long sentences since NATO was a primary party on the "other side" from most of the defendants. The only study of this phenomenon, however, found no evidence for this thesis, although the study was limited to the trial chambers on which there was very little dissent (King *et al.* 2005).

Our interest goes beyond bias. Primarily, we wish to test whether personal attributes of judges, especially their previous job experience

[47] Prosecutor vs Dario Kordic and Mario Cerkez, ICTY Case No. IT-95–14/2, Judgment of December 17, 2004, www.un.org/icty/kordic/appeal/judgement/index.htm. The dissent was on the accumulation of convictions for sentencing purposes, an issue on which the ICTs have not been consistent.

[48] The most prominent international courts that do not allow public separate opinions are the European Court of Justice and the World Trade Organization's Dispute Settlement Body.

and their domestic legal systems, influence the way they run trials and make decisions. Studies of the effects of personal attributes on judicial behavior are common in the domestic context but rare for international courts.[49] They are important, however, for understanding how ICTs exercise their agency. This section limits its attention to the extent to which judges vary in their propensities to write separate opinions.

Propensity to write separate opinions

We gathered data on all judgments issued by the ICTY's trial and appeals chambers until March 2006.[50] This yielded a total of 104 decisions, 34 by the appeals chamber (a five-judge panel) and 70 by the trial chambers (three-judge panels). On 31 (30 percent) of these judgments, there was at least one dissenting opinion, separate opinion, or separate declaration by a judge. In all, 53 of the 376 individual choices by judges included a dissent, separate opinion, or declaration.[51] Separate opinions were much more common on the appeals chamber, where 60 percent of all decisions included at least one separate opinion (as compared with only 16 percent on the trial chambers).

Judge Mohamed Shahabuddeen, who is from Guyana and has served at the ICTY since 1997, was by far the most frequent issuer of separate opinions: he wrote a separate or dissenting opinion on thirteen of the twenty-three decisions in which he partook and was thus responsible for 25 percent of all separate opinions issued by ICT judges. In many of these opinions, Judge Shahabuddeen did not depart from the substantive conclusions of the majority but rather set out (often at great length) a different rationale for reaching those conclusions. The American and other Western delegations were initially hopeful that Judge Shahabuddeen, a former judge on the International Court of Justice, would become the next president of the court. Apparently, however, his behavior on the court did not endear him to his initial supporters.[52] The next most frequent writers of separate opinions were Judge Patrick

---

[49] For an exception, see Bruinsma (2006).

[50] Based on publicly available information at www.un.org/icty/cases-e/index-e.htm.

[51] For the moment, we do not distinguish between these. We will undertake a more fine-grained analysis once we have a full and appropriately checked dataset.

[52] Interview with Michael Matheson, December 13, 2006.

Table 2.3 *Probit regression on issuing a separate opinion on trials at ICTY (entries are marginal effects and robust standard errors clustered on judges)*

	Model A		Model B		Model C	
	Marginal effect	SE	Marginal effect	SE	coefficient	SE
Appeals chamber	.20***	.02	.17***	.03	.17***	.04
Common law	.07**	.04	.06	.04	–	–
Shahabuddeen	–	–	.14***	.06	.19***	.05
Proportion of common law judges on panel	–	–	–	–	.13*	.08
Academic	.04*	.05	.03	.05	.03	.05
Judge	.16***	.04	.13***	.04	.12***	.04
N	321		321		321	
Pseudo R²	.175		.185		.190	

Notes: *p < .1, **p < .05, ***p < .01. All tests are two-tailed.
Constant in equation but omitted from table as marginal effect has no meaningful interpretation. Predicted probability at x-bar was .103 and .106 for the respective equations.

Lipton Robinson (five of twenty trials), a judge from Jamaica who has served on the ICTY since 1998, and Judge Wolfgang Schomburg (four of fourteen), a judge from Germany who has served on the ICTY since 2001.

Table 2.3 reports the marginal effects and robust standard errors clustered on judges from a probit regression. The dependent variable takes the value 1 if a judge wrote a separate opinion, dissent, or separate declaration in a judgment or decision. The analysis controls for whether a decision was issued by the appeals or trial chamber.

We test two explicit hypotheses. First, we would expect that judges from common law countries would be more likely than their counterparts to write public separate opinions. A central difference between common law and civil law legal systems is that public dissents are generally allowed in the former and not in the latter. Hence, socialization theory would suggest that judges from common law countries are more likely publicly to display separate opinions, whereas judges from

civil law countries are more inclined to keep silent when in disagreement. The results from model A confirm this expectation: judges from
common law systems were significantly more likely to write a separate opinion than were judges from other legal systems. The effect,
however, did not reach conventional levels of statistical significance
once we accounted for the unusual behavior of Judge Shahabuddeen
through the inclusion of a dummy variable. Moreover, the size of the
effect was modest: being from a common law legal system increased
the probability of a separate opinion by only 7 percent. These results,
then, indicate that the influence of domestic legal systems on individual
judicial behavior is minor.

The effect could, however, reside in the interaction between common and civil law judges. Common law judges, who are generally
more comfortable writing separately, might influence their civil law
colleagues once they are working together in an international setting.
Indeed, it would be only natural for judges on international courts to
learn from each other, despite differences in their professional background and legal cultures.

Interestingly, we find some support for such effects. Of the twenty-
three judgments in which no common law judge partook, twenty-two
were unanimous.[53] Moreover, there is a moderately positive statisti-
cally significant correlation between the proportion of common law
judges on a panel and the proportion of minority opinions.[54] Model C
in Table 2.3 lends more rigorous support to this hypothesis: the larger
the proportion of common law judges on a panel, the greater the probability (by 13 percent) that *any* judge writes a separate opinion. It is
notable that model C fits the data better than does model B. This suggests that the proportion of common law judges on a panel is a better
predictor for whether a judge will write a separate opinion than the
actual domestic legal system of origin of that judge. We believe that
this does provide some evidence of influences that emerge once a judge
joins the international bench.

A second thesis is that professional socialization may affect the tendency to write separate opinions. Most notably, we would expect those

---

[53] This could, of course, be due to a selection effect where unbalanced panels (in
terms of representation of domestic legal systems) occur on minor cases where
dissents are unlikely.
[54] Pearson R = .19, p = .059.

ICT judges whose previous experience was primarily as a judge or as an academic to be more inclined to write separate opinions than those who primarily earned their living as government officials.[55] Academics tend to have strong opinions on matters that concern their subject area and are generally inclined to share those opinions with others. Judges are also more used to expressing public dissent, certainly compared with government officials who are generally socialized to keep their disagreements behind closed doors.

The results strongly confirm the finding for those whose primary experience was as a judge: judges were 16 percent more likely to write separate opinions than were government officials (13 percent after controlling for Judge Shahabuddeen). The effect is less strong for academics (3–4 percent) and only significant in one specification (model A).

We also tested whether there were similar composition effects as for domestic legal systems but we did not find that judges were more likely to write separate opinions when they served on panels with disproportionally large numbers of academics or judges.[56] Thus, the effect of professional socialization does appear to influence judges at the individual level.

Conclusion

This chapter has offered a first investigation into the agency of international criminal judges. With the advent of the ICC, this has become an increasingly important category of global governors but we know very little about who these judges are, how they were selected, and how they behave once selected. Our analysis has shed some light on these questions, although much remains to be done, especially with regard to the last question.

Our first contribution was to identify theoretical accounts of the selection process and of judicial accountability. We then tested the implications of these accounts with data from the ICTY and ICTR. It is clear that none of the individual theoretical perspectives provides an entirely satisfactory account of agency in the international criminal justice system. This is not surprising, given the relative lack of attention

---

[55] See Bruinsma (2006).
[56] Results not shown in Table 2.3 but are available from the authors.

for global governors in the theoretical literature, as identified in chapter 1 of this volume. The challenge, then, is to find ways to combine insights from these perspectives into a cohesive theory.

We are not fully there yet, but we would like to point to some ways in which synthesis is possible. First, it is clear that the approaches are not always fundamentally in contradiction with each other. The realist and P–A accounts rely on highly similar mechanisms, with realists being somewhat less convinced by the need for independent international judges and somewhat more impressed by the tools governments use to rein in ICTs. Both the credible commitment and the constructivist logic stress legitimacy as an important source of authority and point to the role of NGOs as watchdogs. Moreover, the credibility of a commitment to an independent ICT may be a matter of degree (or one of multiple goals that states have) rather than an absolute tying of hands. This reaffirms the point from chapter 1 that different sources of authority overlap.

Second, the P–A and realist accounts point to areas where governments should constrain judges but they also provide convincing rationales for why states often do not have strong interests at stake in issues that concern ICTs. Most notably, none of the ICTs' powerful supporters expected to be directly subjected to their rulings. It is not entirely unreasonable, then (and the empirical record suggests as much), that the development of international criminal law was of little concern to most governments. If anything, governments cared about the efficiency of the courts and the perception that the rulings were fair. Perhaps sociological approaches provide the most promising account of how the ICTs used this opportunity to exercise authority, maybe in ways not anticipated by the ICTs' founders, yet still within a broad set of constraints made clear by powerful states (for example, no prosecution of members of NATO).

A picture emerges of an issue area where governments were generally quite happy to let others (judges) develop rules as long as these remained within a rather wide zone of discretion. Governments mostly exercised fire-alarm oversight by, for example, replacing judges who fell asleep during trials. They also developed a common understanding of a profile of an international criminal judge, a vision that culminated in a new process for the election of ICC judges that specifically highlights experience in criminal trials. This does not mean that governments generally agreed with the rules that judges developed. Quite to the contrary, many of the new rules and interpretations of international criminal law would have been unlikely candidates for passage in the traditional lawmaking settings, such as multilateral treaty negotiations. As such, these new ways of creating rules deserve our attention even if they do not run against the immediate interests of the powerful. Moreover, these new rules, especially new interpretations of the definition of genocide, may well affect states in unanticipated ways in the long run.

3 The International Organization for Standardization as a global governor: a club theory perspective

ASEEM PRAKASH AND MATTHEW POTOSKI

This chapter examines the emergence of the International Organization for Standardization (ISO) as global governor in the area of international product and management systems standardization. We outline a novel theoretical approach rooted in the theory of clubs (Buchanan 1965; Cornes and Sandler 1996; Prakash and Potoski 2006b) that analytically connects actors (governors) with institutions (governance systems). Unlike much of the regime literature, which tends to focus on governance systems established to mitigate international governance failures, this volume focuses on actors who establish, monitor, and enforce these rules. After all, given the lack of a global sovereign, it is not clear which actors govern at the international level, how, and with what consequences. As the introductory chapter notes, scholars often discuss global governance issues in passive voice, treating governance as a structure or a process. These discussions are not sufficiently agentic in that it is not clear how and why specific actors are involved in the unfolding of governance processes and the establishment, monitoring, and enforcement of governance systems.

Both governments and nongovernmental actors supply governance systems. While we illustrate our club theory approach in the context of a nongovernmental governor – the International Organization for Standardization and a specific governance system it has created, ISO 14001 – our perspective is sufficiently general to be employed to study intergovernmental as well as hybrid governors – an important issue given that we seldom find policy monopolies in policy domains.

The introductory chapter defines global governors as "authorities who exercise power across borders for purposes of affecting policy. Governors thus create issues, set agendas, establish and implement rules or programs, and evaluate and/or adjudicate outcomes." In this chapter, we explore (1) how the design of governance systems is endogenous to the attributes of the governor and (2) how this affects the ability of the governance system to address the twin challenges of recruitment (attracting participants) and shirking (ensuring that the participants adhere to the system's requirements). We illustrate how governance systems can fail and how they can be successful. Our club theory approach should therefore help in comparing nongovernmental governors across policy domains, as well as comparing governance systems sponsored by different governors within a given domain, along analytic dimensions such as institutional emergence, functioning, and effectiveness.

For analytical clarity, we term the actors that establish governance systems as the primary governors and actors performing monitoring, enforcement, and sanctioning as secondary governors, in recognition of the fact that the entire gamut of governance activities need not be performed by the same actors. In some cases, the primary governor may "outsource" monitoring, enforcement, and sanctioning to others.[1] In other cases, outside actors may themselves step in to monitor and enforce the rules without necessarily seeking permission from the primary governor. While some of this division of governance between the primary and secondary governors might follow Williamson's (1985) "make or buy" logic, noneconomic logics might be at work as well. The key point is that the array of governance services are typically not provided by a single, hierarchically organized governor. Instead, we should think in terms of varying configurations of the governance chains (akin to a supply chain or a value chain), the key governors in such networks, and what factors might drive such variations.

Our chapter contributes to this volume's aim of addressing the broader debates on the relative salience of agency and structure in influencing individual and collective behaviors. We take the agency–structure debate beyond its usual dichotomies by emphasizing the role of structurally embedded agents in supplying new (and different) global governance structures. Agents work in an institutional environment where some extant structures have important bearings on their preferences and normative proclivities. Agents often themselves create institutions to constrain their own and others' behaviors. The question then is what drives the supply and configuration of these institutions? As our chapter illustrates, the supply of new governance structures is

---

[1] This issue can be examined via the perspective of agency theory, as we have done elsewhere.

influenced not only by the collective action challenges confronting agents and stakeholders' demands for responses to governance deficits, but also by the institutional space afforded to agents by existing structures.

As a global governor, the International Organization for Standardization supplies product[2] and process standards to commercial actors.[3] Later we will show how these standards can be viewed as clubs in a theoretical sense. Of course, the International Organization for Standardization is not the only governor in the international standardization sector; others include the IEC (International Electrotechnical Commission; see Tim Büthe's chapter in this volume) and the ITU (International Telecommunication Union).[4]

This volume's editors have identified five bases of authority for global governors: institutional, delegated, expert, principled, and capacity-based authority. The International Organization for Standardization derives its authority from the expertise it has offered to the standardization sector for more than six decades. An interesting aspect of the ISO story is the tension between two objectives it seeks to achieve. It seeks legitimacy via technical expertise which should lead it

---

[2] Also see the special issue of the *Journal of European Public Policy* on the politics and economics of international institutional standards, Volume 8, Issue 3, 2001.

[3] For illustrative purposes only, here is an example of an ISO technical standard. ISO 5151 specifies the standards for testing and rating performance of nonducted air conditioners and heat pumps. This forty-three-page standard was created by Technical Committee #86. This standard "Specifies the standard conditions on which the ratings of single-package and split-system non-ducted air conditioners employing air- and water-cooled condensers are based, and the test methods to be applied for determination of the various ratings. Is limited to systems utilizing a single refrigeration circuit and having one evaporator and one condenser. Also specifies the test conditions and the corresponding test procedures for determining various performance characteristics of these non-ducted air conditioners and heat pumps" (see www.iso.org/iso/en/CatalogueDetailPage.CatalogueDetail?CSNUMBER=11156&ICS1=27&ICS2=80&ICS3=&scopelist, accessed January 19, 2007).

[4] All three governors are based in Geneva. To coordinate their activities, they have formed the World Standards Cooperation, a kind of a supra-governor. Unlike the IEC and the ITU, the International Organization for Standardization's focus is not limited to any particular sector: it is the key cross-sectoral governor in the field of international standardization. See www.iso.org/iso/en/aboutiso/introduction/index.html (accessed January 19, 2007).

to create stringent standards. At the same time, it also seeks legitimacy though high participation levels by offering affordable standards which firms can profitably adopt. Since its inception in 1946, the International Organization for Standardization has developed more than 16,000 international standards (or clubs), most of which are technical product standards. Its website notes:

When the large majority of products or services in a particular business or industry sector conform to International Standards, a state of industry-wide standardization can be said to exist. This is achieved through consensus agreements between national delegations representing all the economic stakeholders concerned – suppliers, users, government regulators and other interest groups, such as consumers. They agree on specifications and criteria to be applied consistently in the classification of materials, in the manufacture and supply of products, in testing and analysis, in terminology and in the provision of services. In this way, International Standards provide a reference framework, or a common technological language, between suppliers and their customers – which facilitates trade and the transfer of technology. (ISO 2007a)

Starting in the 1980s, the International Organization for Standardization expanded its governance offerings to include process and management system standards in the fields of quality control (ISO 9000), the environment (ISO 14001), and food safety (ISO 22000). Recently, it has begun developing corporate social responsibility standards (ISO 26000).[5]

Our discussion of the International Organization for Standardization focuses on one particular club, ISO 14001, the most widely adopted voluntary environmental standard in the world. As of 2005, 110,000 facilities from 138 countries have received ISO 14001 certification to become what we call club members. While ISO 9000 was the International Organization for Standardization's first process standard, it has not generated much controversy because its key stakeholders – firms, nongovernmental organizations (NGOs), and governments – tend to have converging preferences on quality issues.

---

[5] It has also signed a Memorandum of Understanding with the United Nations to ensure that this standard coheres with the United Nations Global Compact, another global governor in the area of corporate social responsibility. See www.iso.org/iso/en/commcentre/pressreleases/2007/Ref1062.html (accessed July 30, 2007).

Quality control is predominantly a technical rather than a political issue with distinctive regulatory, distributive, or redistributive dimensions (Lowi 1964). Indeed, there are strident debates about whether governments should retain a governance monopoly in the environmental area because nongovernmental governors may not have incentives to create effective and democratic governance systems. By and large, activist groups are more concerned with and agitated about clubs (such as ISO 14001) designed to mitigate the Pigouvian externality problems (Pigou 1960) and less with clubs designed to mitigate coordination problems (as in ISO 9000) (Abbott and Snidal 2001).[6] Given these important political dynamics, ISO 14001 is an interesting illustrative example through which to explore the politics and economics of global governorship and governance.

Following this volume's themes, by "governance" we mean the organization of collective action through a set of rule structures, also termed "institutions" or "regimes." Creating institutions is often expensive.[7] Actors tend to establish institutions where collective endeavors are expected to be enduring rather than one-off affairs. By permitting, prohibiting, or prescribing actors' behaviors (Ostrom 1990), institutions stabilize expectations about other actors involved in the collective endeavor. Because institutions can and do fail, their effectiveness – their ability to shape actors' behaviors in desired ways – should be viewed as a variable to be examined rather than one whose value can be assumed.

While institutions are expected to alter actors' incentives, they also inculcate or "teach" norms (Finnemore 1996) about appropriate and inappropriate actions, which can then alter actors' future incentives. Different institutions are likely to employ varying strategies, which

[6] This is not to say that coordination problems are bereft of distributional conflicts; they are not. The controversy over the technical standards of high definition TV is a case in point (Hart 2004).

[7] While some institutions might spontaneously emerge (Sugden 1989), a substantial proportion of policy-relevant institutions are conscious artifacts of human agency. Indeed, while establishing new institutions, actors take into account and are constrained by existing ones (Thelen 1999). Our theoretical narrative takes into account historical institutional legacies by emphasizing the varying institutional contexts in which actors and the institutions they create or join function. A key point our research has made is that nongovernmental clubs operate in the shadow of public regulation (much of which is a carryover from the past) and their efficacy is influenced by their fit with public institutions.

are embedded in the sometimes competing and sometimes reinforcing logics of instrumentality and appropriateness (March and Olsen 1989). While the International Organization for Standardization tends to employ instrumental rationales to encourage firms to adopt ISO 14001, the logic of appropriateness is often embedded in its communication strategies. Instead of apportioning the variance between these logics, an almost impossible task, we examine the institutional design behind this governor's quest to create and communicate the usefulness of this unique governance "product" and therefore encourage firms voluntarily to join ISO 14001.[8]

Nongovernmental programs, sometimes also described as private authority regimes, are recognized as important policy tools across countries, industries, and issue areas (Cutler *et al.* 1999; Haufler 2001; Mattli and Büthe 2003; Cashore *et al.* 2004; Prakash and Potoski 2006b). These programs seek to create institutional incentives for participating actors (typically targeting firms, but also NGOs[9] or even governments) to adopt specific codes of conduct and practices beyond what is legally required of them. The governors of voluntary regulatory programs claim that such programs encourage program participants to create positive social externalities, although in practice this expectation is not always met. If the claims are justified, the creation of such externalities is a direct consequence of program participants' beyond-compliance practices. Some social externalities might have the attributes of public goods, such as a cleaner environment, while others may have more private goods characteristics, such as higher wages. Different types of externalities create incentives for different stakeholders to organize in favor of or against a voluntary program, and thereby influence the propensities of actors to join the program.

The challenge for a governor sponsoring a voluntary program is to motivate firms to pay the costs of producing a broader social good. Why would a firm – or any instrumental actor – voluntarily do so?

[8] The epistemic community perspective is also inadequate for this task because it downplays the instrumental motives of participating actors. While actors participating in the ISO's governance and rulemaking processes certainly have technical expertise, standard development is fundamentally a political process where instrumental concerns of actors often play an important role. This is particularly evident in the development of standards to govern environmental issues.

[9] See Gugerty and Prakash (2010) in the context of NGO clubs.

Voluntary programs offer monetary and nonmonetary payoffs for producing social externalities that firms would not capture as cheaply without participating in the program. An apparel company, for example, might join a fair labor practices program to enhance its brand image and escape criticism from social activists (Bartley 2009). For the stakeholders, these programs reduce information asymmetries regarding the firm's unobservable practices, such as whether the firm is employing child labor. By participating in a credible voluntary program, firms can signal their intentions and practices along dimensions that are difficult for external stakeholders to observe, and therefore lower stakeholders' transaction costs for identifying "progressive" firms. Stakeholders can reward participants or punish nonparticipants as they deem fit, depending on their own preferences and abilities.

An important analytic challenge is to understand how program governors create and communicate the meaning and value of participation in their voluntary program – its "brand" image – because it is this brand identity that entices firms to join the program and thereby produce positive externalities.

Global governors and governance: a club theory perspective

Social dilemmas pertain to situations in which actions by self-interested individuals do not improve the welfare of the larger group, and in the pursuit of self-interest these individuals end up harming their own interests as well. A well-known example is the Prisoners' Dilemma game where two prisoners kept in different cells "confess" in the hope of securing lenient sentences for themselves although it would have been better for both prisoners to "not confess." At a more fundamental level, collective action dilemmas can be traced to the attributes of goods and services and the institutional context in which actors seek to produce, exchange, and consume them.

Two attributes are especially important: excludability and rivalry. Excludability means that it is technologically, institutionally, and economically feasible for one actor to exclude others from appropriating the benefits of a good. The actor wants to exclude others because it has contributed resources for the production, maintenance, or protection of the good while others have not. An absence of excludability creates incentives for other actors to "free ride," that is, to enjoy the good's benefits without contributing to its production, maintenance, or protection (Olson 1965). After all, on average, why would actors incur costs if they cannot be prevented from appropriating a good's benefits?

Rivalry (or subtractability) means that if one actor consumes a particular unit of a good, it is no longer available for another actor to consume. Rivalry in consumption can create incentives for actors to overconsume resources (the logic being, if I do not consume it, then somebody else will and therefore deny me the benefits from future consumption). Overconsumption by several actors can lead to resource degradation, as is the case in the "tragedy of the commons" (Hardin 1968). If rivalrous resources are excludable, their scarcity would lead to higher prices, thereby lowering consumption. Problems arise when rivalrous goods are nonexcludable because their scarcity does not translate into higher prices that curb consumption.

Based on these characteristics, products can be classified into four stylized categories: private goods (rival, excludable), public goods (nonrival, nonexcludable), common-pool resources or CPRs (rival, nonexcludable), and impure public goods (nonrival, excludable). Private goods can generally be produced and exchanged through markets without significant collective action problems. In other words, when individuals produce, buy, and sell private goods, they not only make themselves better off but also improve the lots of those with whom they are exchanging resources. Such rosy win-win scenarios are less likely to occur in the cases of public goods, club goods, and common-pool resources. For public goods and common-pool resources, nonexcludability is an obvious source of collective action problems. Not surprisingly, then, the production of positive externalities creates collective action problems: individuals are not willing to pay the private costs of producing externalities that others cannot be excluded from enjoying (but see Coase 1960). The net benefit of these externalities, the value their producer and everyone else enjoys, may be much greater than their costs, but since the producer experiences only a fraction of the benefit and all the costs, she is not likely to produce them. Such market failures are often the rationale underlying government market interventions via command and control regulations: because firms are likely to overproduce negative externalities and underproduce positive ones, governments enact regulations that compel actors in socially desirable directions.

Voluntary governance clubs can also mitigate collective action dilemmas and therefore induce participating firms to incur private costs to produce positive externalities. In the economic sense of the term, clubs are institutions that supply impure public goods (Tiebout 1956; Wiseman 1957). James Buchanan (1965) identified clubs as institutions for producing and allocating goods that are neither fully private (rivalrous and excludable), nor fully public (nonrivalrous, nonexcludable). Club theory has been applied to examine policy issues pertaining to zoning, busing, road congestion, city size, and military alliances (Cornes and Sandler 1996).

Where voluntary programs differ from traditional clubs is that their purpose is to produce social externalities and they use branding benefits that have the characteristics of club goods to induce social behavior. Clubs create externalities by requiring members to incur private costs, as codified in the club's membership standards and its mechanisms for ensuring compliance with those standards. Unlike the traditional Buchanan club, the main costs in voluntary programs are not direct payments to club sponsors. Rather, they are the monetary and nonmonetary costs of adopting and adhering to the club's requirements.

Clubs generate three kinds of benefits: social externalities, private benefits, and branding benefits. *Social externalities* constitute the policy payoff of voluntary programs. Clubs' positive externalities can have the attributes of private goods (e.g., a club requiring participating firms to pay higher wages), public goods (e.g., a club requiring participating firms to lower air pollution), or even club goods (e.g., a club requiring participating forestry firms not to cut trees that are revered by an aboriginal group).

Private benefits accrue to a single member only and are denied to other club members and nonmembers. For example, a voluntary program designed to protect the environment might require policies that help firms identify waste and therefore reduce costs and improve profits. Such private benefits, however, have limited utility for evaluating voluntary programs because an instrumental actor (such as a profit-oriented firm) is likely to take these actions unilaterally, without joining the club, in order to enjoy the private benefits such actions produce. If the private gain from unilaterally taking such action were sufficient, then voluntary clubs would not be necessary to produce the social externalities we desire.

Club benefits, the central analytical feature of voluntary programs, accrue to club members only and are key incentives for joining the club. They are something valuable that club sponsors can offer to participants and exclude nonparticipants from appropriating. Club benefits can take the form of goodwill, improved reputation, or other compensation that members receive from external stakeholders in response to their club membership. Club members often receive a branding that enables them to advertise that they are different from nonmembers by virtue of their club participation. Because stakeholders have different preferences regarding the externalities they want firms to produce and have varying abilities to reward or punish firms, the stakeholder context in which firms are located crucially bears upon the branding benefits firms perceive in joining the club.

The issue of optimal club size has been widely discussed in economics literature. Although our voluntary program notion of a club differs from a traditional Buchanan club, club size is equally germane in our case.[10] Indeed, the size of a club's membership roster influences the value of its branding benefits in important ways. While voluntary clubs might be susceptible to overcrowding, by and large voluntary clubs have been challenged to attract sufficiently large rosters. Additional members create positive network effects (Bessen and Saloner 1988);[11] that is, the branding benefits participants derive increase when a new firm joins the club because additional members help advertise a club more broadly since each member's activities generate positive reputational spillovers for others.[12]

Some firms take unilateral actions to boost their reputation with stakeholders. If such unilateral action is effective, why should firms join voluntary clubs? Club membership offers several advantages over

---

[10] For a formal model of the implications of voluntary program size, see Kotchen and Van 't Veld (2009).

[11] It should be noted, however, that there is a tipping point beyond which excessive club size can pretty much eliminate the special club benefits. If everyone is a member, no one is. For example, if nearly all beef producers turned organic, the reputational benefits to all would be greatly reduced while even nonorganic beef producers would be able to reap the benefits because consumers would be more likely simply to assume they are organic. In addition, more members increase diversity in ways that may blur the club's distinctiveness and cohesion.

[12] This issue should be examined in future research given the heterogeneity among firms. Arguably, an additional firm with identical characteristics may not help in putting the message across to new stakeholders. Perhaps the club sponsors should seek to attract a diverse array of firms each with links in different stakeholder networks. Our future work will investigate how organizational reputations are created and advertised.

unilateral action for enhancing firms' reputations among stakeholders. From the stakeholders' perspective, unilateral commitments by firms to socially desirable action are less credible. When individual firms make and enforce their own rules, they can more easily change them. If they consciously separate membership from control, as institutionalized systems clubs can enjoy a degree of credibility that firms alone may find difficult to acquire. Because clubs can also capture economies of scale and network externalities, progressive actions taken as part of a club can do more to boost a firm's standing with stakeholders than the same actions taken unilaterally.

We have suggested that by separating membership from control, clubs may seek to signal to stakeholders that the club is not a sham but instead imposes serious beyond-compliance requirements on its participants. But stakeholders also need to be assured that over time the governors (club sponsors) will not dilute their club's standards, a plausible scenario if the club is sponsored by an industry association or an actor that tends to favor business interests. To satisfy the skeptics, club governors need credibly to commit to not lowering standards opportunistically. The attributes of the club governors can affect the nature of credible commitment challenges.

Consider two types of governors: pro-business and anti-business. When a club is sponsored by a pro-business governor, it needs to signal to its stakeholders that it will not opportunistically loosen the rules. When a club is sponsored by an anti-business governor, the credible commitment challenge is in relation to its potential members: governors need to make a credible commitment that they will not opportunistically tighten the rules. Think of a scenario in which firms consider joining an NGO-sponsored club. Potential members recognize that exiting a voluntary club might be costly; club membership might require them to acquire competencies or establish systems (in short, invest in assets) specific to the club but that are difficult to apply to alternative uses (Williamson 1985). Thus, such asset specificity might make them vulnerable to opportunistic exploitation by the governor.[13]

---

[13] Arguably, in the long run, such governors would not be able to attract new members. Hence, they might not have incentives to behave opportunistically. As our fieldwork in this area for more than a decade suggests, these assurances are not likely to persuade managers in "staff" functions who are often planning how to survive the next round of corporate downsizing.

The second issue is the potential retribution costs. For firms, membership in a voluntary club provides an intangible asset in the form of branding benefits. By joining a voluntary club, firms make a public commitment to pursue socially progressive practices. If they exit, they are likely to be spotted and perhaps sanctioned by stakeholders.[14] In fact, club governors have incentives to advertise the exit and shame the exiting firm. Anticipating the structural predicament potential participants face, club governors might be tempted opportunistically to raise the stringency of their club's requirements over time. Potential members who recognize the incentive incompatibility problem may therefore want a credible commitment from club governors that they will not exploit their advantage. Thus, in many ways, club design and club governance are endogenous to the attributes and reputations of club governors.

Mere words to assuage potential members' concerns may not suffice to solve credible commitment problems: potential members may want safeguards in the rulemaking processes (such as a super-majority requirement for changing standards) and perhaps representation of countervailing interests in the rulemaking bodies. Thus, whether the club is sponsored by governors sympathetic to business interests or hostile to them, club design must respond to credible commitment issues.[15]

Mitigating collective action dilemmas

Like any other governance mechanism, clubs are vulnerable to institutional failures if they do not solve their collective action dilemmas. For voluntary clubs, two collective action dilemmas are analytically most salient. First, what we term the "Olsonian dilemma" centers on

[14] All other things being equal. Of course, power dynamics are important. Extremely powerful members may be less likely to be sanctioned. For example, the USA has rarely been sanctioned for operating against Security Council and Geneva Convention "club rules."

[15] While we do not have space to illustrate this issue with an example, we wish to note that the dynamics in the forestry industry seem to support our predictions. The NGO-sponsored club, Forest Stewardship Council, and the industry-sponsored club, Sustainable Forestry Initiative, have implemented changes in the rulemaking processes in response to credible commitment problems (Cashore *et al.* 2004).

a club's capacity to attract participants to its roster and to capture the economies of scale and network effects for building the club's reputation. Second, what we term the "shirking dilemma" pertains to a club's ability to compel participants to adhere to its program standards once they have joined the club. Participants might have incentives to free-ride on the club's reputation: they could join the program and enjoy the benefits of its reputation, but shirk their responsibility to adhere to its standards. Widespread shirking reduces production of positive social externalities and therefore undermines the club's credibility and viability. If the club strictly monitors noncompliance with rules and sanctions, shirking can be mitigated. A club with a reputation for effective policing is likely to have a stronger standing among its stakeholders.

Club standards

Club standards specify what firms need to do to join the club and remain members in good standing. Club standards can come in different forms. They might specify performance expectations (sometimes called "outcome standards"). Other standards are more process-oriented, such as requirements that members adopt a management system, or that members regularly consult with community groups. Finally, some club standards limit membership eligibility through descriptive preconditions, such as whether firms operate in a specific industry or have already established high standards of social performance.

Lenient club standards require marginal effort from potential participants in moving beyond the requirements of public law and regulations. They are low-cost clubs for firms to join. Of course, even lenient club standards must mandate at least some nontrivial membership costs, or else the club would be merely an empty gesture. While many firms might easily join a lenient voluntary club, we expect its reputation to be weak because word would spread that it makes only marginal demands on its participants and therefore requires them to produce little additional social externalities. We also expect such clubs to face adverse selection problems because firms with superior social performance would not want to subsidize or identify with laggards. In the long run, this would further lower a club's credibility and make it unattractive even for laggards. It should be noted, however, that while clubs designed to mislead stakeholders (and preempt regulations) exist, attentive scholars and policymakers do not take claims made by club governors for granted. Given the active scrutiny by activist groups of such clubs, they are likely to be exposed. Our theory predicts that, over the long haul, such "Astroturf" clubs[16] would have marginal membership and, importantly, marginal impact on public policy.

Stringent club standards require members to produce social externalities well in excess of what government laws require. Such actions are likely to be costly, although the nature of these costs varies across firms, even across those operating in the same institutional settings. The advantage of stringent standards is that the club brand would be more credible and serve as a low-cost tool for signaling club members' commitment to the club's social objective. Armed with this information, stakeholders could reward or punish firms accordingly.

Designing voluntary clubs requires balancing competing imperatives. On the one hand, to enhance the club's credibility with external stakeholders, sponsors may prefer stringent standards. On the other hand, such standards may lead to low membership – and few network effects and scale economies in building the club brand – as few firms are able to meet demanding membership requirements. Thus, pitching the club standards at a level appropriate for potential participants and yet acceptable to key stakeholders is a key institutional design issue club governors must confront, a task that has been accomplished reasonably well by the International Organization for Standardization in the context of ISO 14001.

Monitoring and enforcement rules

Shirking is a second major source of institutional failure in voluntary programs. Shirkers formally adopt the club's standards but do not adhere to them. They nonetheless continue to claim to be socially progressive by virtue of their club membership. While clubs can exclude nonmembers from enjoying the benefits of club membership, shirkers slip by unless they are identified and expelled. If the word spreads about large-scale shirking – and it is difficult to keep such information under wraps – the club's reputation is likely to slip and its brand

---

[16] We owe this term to Henry Farrell.

reputation be weakened. Thus, club sponsors have incentives to curb shirking, unless, of course, the club is an "Astroturf" club designed to fool stakeholders rather than impose real requirements on its members.

Willful shirking occurs because (1) the goals of the participants and the club governors diverge, and (2) participants are able to exploit information asymmetries (regarding their adherence to club standards) in relations with club governors and stakeholders.[17] Eventually, information asymmetries prevent stakeholders from differentiating program shirkers from nonshirkers. As we discuss below, because measures to curb shirking impose costs on potential participants, club governors have to balance competing imperatives.[18]

We identify three components to effective and credible monitoring and enforcement systems that mitigate information asymmetries and sanction shirkers: third-party monitoring, public disclosure of audit information, and sanctioning by club governors. While club governors might themselves serve as monitors in voluntary clubs designed to produce social externalities, third-party monitoring is the gold standard if not the norm (Gereffi *et al.* 2001). Third-party monitoring means that club governors require participating firms to have their club-related requirements or policies audited by accredited, external auditors to verify that they are adhering to membership requirements. Firms are less likely to shirk under third-party auditing because they recognize that accredited, external actors have the ability and incentive to identify and report shirking. In some cases, the governors may require public disclosure of audit information to empower external actors (secondary governors) to scrutinize participating firms' club obligations and then expose the shirkers. Sanctioning by external stakeholders might follow, thereby mitigating club participants' incentives to shirk in the first

---

[17] Arguably, shirking might be inadvertent. While there might be goal convergence between participants and club sponsors, the participants may not correctly understand club requirements or possess means to adhere to them. While this is theoretically possible, we have not found examples in the context of management standards where club requirements are seldom in the form of complex, technical terms that some participants might not comprehend. Club requirements are often quite simple and straightforward. Hence, we expect that much of the shirking is likely to be willful.

[18] Shirking might be curbed by sociological pressures (normative, mimetic, and coercive) from other participating firms or stakeholders which in the first place persuade program members to join the club. Instead of relying on sociological pressures alone, a club can mitigate shirking through its institutional design.

place. Finally, the governor may itself act upon the audit information and sanction the members who have been found to be shirking on their obligations. This might be a credible threat because the governors have a vested interest in ensuring the club's credibility. However, at the same time, governors may not want to acquire a reputation for being harsh and adversarial. Anti-business governors, in particular, need to be careful about the level and type of sanctioning. Arguably, in such clubs the governors may have a greater impact on public policy if they retain firms with imperfect compliance as opposed to expelling them and thereby losing the leverage they exercised over them as members. Thus the design and practice of the monitoring and sanctioning rules is likely to be endogenous to the attributes of the club governors, as is compliance with consensual norms.

We call clubs' monitoring and enforcement programs "swords." "Strong sword" programs have all three components: audits, disclosure, and sanctioning mechanisms. While they are most likely to curb shirking because they mitigate information asymmetries between participants and governors/stakeholders and allow sponsors to sanction shirkers, for participants they are high-cost clubs. "Medium sword" programs require third-party audits and public disclosure. Although their institutional design does not provide for sanctioning of the shirkers by the governor, they are likely to curb shirking because, with public disclosure of audit information, the club's stakeholders can punish shirkers. "Weak sword" programs require only third-party audits. For the participants, these are low-cost clubs that seek to mitigate information asymmetries between the governor and club members by audits alone. Because external stakeholders do not have access to information regarding adherence to club obligations by individual participants, they cannot reward or sanction firms. As we discuss below, ISO 14001 is an example of a weak sword club. Its governor, the International Organization for Standardization, is not known to sanction shirkers aggressively, and the absence of public disclosure of audit information weakens stakeholders' ability to sanction shirking.

To summarize, we expect voluntary programs to produce the most social externalities (measured in terms of improvement in social performance of participating members beyond legal requirement) in clubs with stringent standards and strong swords. However, these are also high-cost clubs that might discourage firms from joining. We expect the production of social externalities to be small in clubs with lenient standards and weak swords. While these are low-cost clubs, they are likely to create only marginal branding benefits for their participants. Given that political and economic implications of voluntary clubs vary across participants, governors, and stakeholders, different club types are likely to serve as the most appropriate fits for varying policy contexts. In some instances, policymakers might favor a lenient club with wide membership as opposed to a stringent club with a very limited membership. We expect heterogeneity of clubs in various policy environments instead of the domination of one specific type.

ISO as a global governor and ISO 14001 as a governance club

The International Organization for Standardization is a nongovernmental governor established in response to functional demands for harmonizing technical standards and processes. It is now an international leader in the field of standardization. Similar to the case described by Danner and Voeten in this book, where the judges appointed to international criminal tribunals seized a leadership role by creating procedural rules, substantive law, and even professional standards for those who would follow in their wake, the International Organization for Standardization has established the procedural and substantive rules for the international standardization movement.

The ISO is made up of representatives from 158 national standards bodies. These national bodies, in turn, are agents of the various stakeholders within their countries; they are not official representatives of their countries' governments. Some of these representatives might be governmental bodies (such as the Standardization Administration of China), while others have nongovernmental status (such as the American National Standards Institute). The International Organization for Standardization was not established via an intergovernmental treaty. It is a nongovernmental governor in which governmental bodies in their individual capacities can serve as principals.

While the International Organization for Standardization has launched about 16,000 clubs, we explore its environmental management club, ISO 14001. This club prescribes broad principles for firms' environmental management systems and does not mandate environmental standards for firms' products or technologies. Further, it does not stipulate environmental outcomes firms must achieve. The rationale for focusing on management standards is that if appropriate systems are in place, desired outcomes will follow. Firms that wish to join ISO 14001 must draft and approve an environmental policy, establish systems, document compliance, regularly review their progress, and designate a top manager to oversee implementation of their environmental programs. In practice, ISO 14001 typically commits member firms not only to comply with or exceed domestic laws, but also to adopt the best available environmental technologies, assess the environmental impact of their operations, and establish programs to train their personnel in environmental management systems.[19] For most firms, the management systems are extensive. They require substantial investments in personnel, training, and, most critically, establishing paper documentation for their environmental operations (Sayre 1996).

Unlike some other voluntary environmental programs, ISO 14001 requires participants to receive an initial certification audit, conducted by certified external auditors who themselves are audited and approved by their domestic national standards body. Firms must then receive annual recertification audits to verify that their management systems continue to meet ISO 14001's standards (ISO 2004b). These audit and certification measures are designed to prevent participants from shirking their program responsibilities as ISO 14001 members (Kolk 2000).

While not conclusive, recent research suggests that ISO 14001 certification improves firms' environmental and regulatory performance. In a study of 236 Mexican firms in the food, chemical, nonmetallic minerals, and metal industries (which together generate 75–95 percent of Mexico's industrial pollution), Dasgupta *et al.* (2000) find that ISO 14001 adopters show superior compliance with government environmental regulations. This is important because developing country governments often find it difficult to enforce their own regulations. Instead of undermining public regulation, ISO 14001 may improve firms' compliance with it, even when firms are located in alleged pollution havens. Echoing Dasgupta *et al.*, Potoski and Prakash (2005b) found in an analysis of more than 3,000 US facilities that ISO 14001 certification improves regulatory compliance among US facilities regulated under the Clean Air Act. There is also evidence that firms

[19] See www.iso.org/iso/en/iso9000–14000/index.html (accessed January 27, 2006).

joining ISO 14001 pollute less. In an analysis of 316 US electronics facilities, Russo (2001) found that ISO 14001 membership is associated with decreased toxic emissions. Potoski and Prakash (2005a) report that ISO 14001 adopters reduce pollution as reported in the EPA's Toxics Release Inventory. In sum, while ISO 14001 alone will not solve all industrial pollution problems, there is some evidence that ISO 14001 adoption leads to lower facility-level pollution and improved facility-level compliance with public law.

A very brief history of the International Organization for Standardization

In 1906, the International Electrotechnical Commission (IEC) was founded to develop technological standards for the burgeoning electronics industry (for details on the IEC, please see Tim Büthe's chapter in this volume). In 1926, the International Federation of the National Standardizing Associations (IFNSA) was established to develop standards in the field of mechanical engineering. IFNSA was fairly active in Europe through the 1930s, although it became dormant with the onset of the Second World War. Nevertheless, business interest in establishing common international standards did not fade away. The United Nations Standards Coordination Committee (UNSCC) was established in 1946 to aid allied postwar efforts and subsequent reconstruction. That same year, delegates from twenty-five countries met to discuss merging the IFNSA and UNSCC, leading to the creation of the International Organization for Standardization in 1946 (ISO 2004a).

Effective and widely accepted international clubs facilitate international trade by reducing the transaction costs inherent in negotiating contracts. The identification and agreement on the International Organization for Standardization as a governor to develop global clubs helped mitigate coordination dilemmas inherent in multiple standards. The challenge was to bestow this governor with sufficient technical expertise and legitimacy so that the clubs would be viewed as authoritative across countries. The ISO has benefited from businesses' desire to reduce transaction costs stemming from cross-national variations in government regulations. As the argument goes, businesses are increasingly global and should be allowed to manage their global operations with minimum friction or bureaucratic interference. Clubs created by the International Organization for Standardization provide one route for accomplishing this end. They enable multinational corporations to reduce the transaction costs of dealing with varying clubs across their subsidiaries and with their trading partners. However, we recognize that such global clubs might also be motivated by the desire of businesses to thwart the emergence of new national-level regulations and standards – an important issue that has undermined the ISO's legitimacy among some stakeholders (Prakash and Potoski 2006b).

The ISO's legitimacy also stems from its technical expertise and its participatory process for developing new standards. While the clubs it creates serve business interests, nongovernmental organizations can be included in the national delegations and therefore can (and do) participate in the rulemaking processes that take place via technical committees. It is fair to say that given the transparent and bureaucratic nature of its rulemaking processes, the International Organization for Standardization has been able credibly to ensure that its clubs will not opportunistically and surreptitiously dilute their requirements in the future. It has not, however, committed to creating a level playing field between business and nongovernmental actors in the rulemaking processes, especially in the context of more politically sensitive clubs such as ISO 14001. As a consequence, key environmental organizations remain skeptical of ISO 14001 and some of them even oppose it.

This has political consequences for and erodes the credibility of this club in some contexts. For example, the active opposition from environmental groups has led the United States Environmental Protection Agency (EPA) to disallow attorney–client privilege for the environmental audits which are essential for securing the ISO 14001 certification. Not surprisingly, American firms are relatively wary of joining ISO 14001 lest the environmental audits uncover environmental violations, thereby creating evidence for the EPA to use against them (Kollman and Prakash 2001). Indeed, the United States is one of the few countries within the Organization for Economic Cooperation and Development (OECD) that have lagged in adopting ISO 14001.

Rulemaking

The International Organization for Standardization creates and modifies clubs (which, once established, are open to any firm or country) based on specific procedures and voting rules, all directed toward making its working participatory. It assigns voting rights according to three types of membership: 103 member bodies, 46 correspondent members, and 9 subscriber members.[20] Only member bodies can be considered principals because they have full voting rights and are entitled to participate in any technical committee responsible for developing standards. Others can be termed "quasi-principals" because, while they are kept informed about the work in the technical committees, they do not have voting rights (ISO 2004b).[21]

Every year, the International Organization for Standardization convenes a meeting of its General Assembly to vote on various proposed standards, with each full member receiving one vote. Proposals are submitted to the General Assembly by the ISO Council, which serves as the executive committee for the organization. Representation on the ISO Council rotates every three years among full members. The Council itself does not develop the proposed clubs. Instead, it forms ad hoc technical committees to develop specific standardization clubs and then disbands them once the clubs' rules are in place. Technical committee members represent specific countries. Typically, those on the committee are technical experts-on-loan from industry, technical bodies, and governmental agencies. Although NGOs and trade associations do not have an independent standing in the International Organization for Standardization, they can serve on technical committees as a part of a national delegation. To retain voting rights in technical committees, the ISO requires that members regularly attend meetings. Absence from two consecutive meetings can trigger punitive action. To approve a new standard, the International Organization for Standardization requires a two-thirds majority approval in the technical committee and a three-fourths majority in the General Assembly. It reviews and, if necessary, revises each club at least every five years (ISO 2004b).

Along with rulemaking, governors need to monitor compliance and sanction noncompliance. How does the International Organization for Standardization approach rule monitoring and enforcement? To explore this question, we briefly contrast the World Trade Organization (WTO), as an intergovernmental governor, with the International

[20] See www.iso.org/iso/en/aboutiso/isomembers/index.html (accessed August 12, 2008).
[21] See www.iso.org/iso/en/aboutiso/isomembers/index.html (accessed August 12, 2008).

Organization for Standardization (a nongovernmental governor), both charged with promoting world trade.[22] Institutionally, the WTO has club-like features – its benefits are excludable and nonrival. It seeks to govern the policies of governments, not firms, supplies rules that restrain governments from erecting tariff and nontariff barriers, and provides grievances settlement services. The WTO has outsourced the monitoring function to member countries (secondary governors), which have incentives to monitor their competitors' behaviors. To minimize monitoring costs, the WTO's institutional logic favors a "fire alarm" approach over a "police patrol" approach (McCubbins and Schwartz 1984). If country A believes that country B has imposed import restrictions in violation of WTO rules, it can file a complaint with the WTO. The WTO offers adjudication services and decides on the merits of the complaint. Interestingly, the WTO does not provide sanctioning services. It decides the level of retaliation that the plaintiff is allowed and it is up to the plaintiff to enact specific policies in this regard.

Unlike the World Trade Organization, the International Organization for Standardization promotes trade by erecting international voluntary clubs for reducing trading costs among countries. The ISO 14001 club extends the International Organization for Standardization's transaction-cost-reducing logic in a new way. It seeks to reduce transaction costs stemming from information asymmetries between firms and their stakeholders regarding firms' unobservable environmental practices. Firms that join ISO 14001 must adopt an environmental management system for their internal operations, as codified in the ISO 14001 standards. By requiring firms to adopt beyond-compliance environmental management practices, ISO 14001 certification signals to stakeholders that firms have adopted environmentally responsible policies that lead participating firms to create positive environmental externalities. Thus, stakeholders are able to differentiate

---

[22] Activist groups routinely criticize the WTO for not providing them a "voice" during the trade negotiations. They contrast this with the United Nations, which solicits the views of nongovernmental actors. The World Trade Organization, however, has made an exception for the International Organization for Standardization by granting it an observer status, arguably because of the close convergence in the objectives of the two governors. This can be viewed as additional proof of the pro-business bias of the International Organization for Standardization.

environmental leaders from laggards at low costs and, depending on their preferences, can reward or punish participating firms. To compensate for the nontrivial costs of adopting environmental management systems, ISO 14001 provides branding benefits so that firms can advertise to stakeholders that they are ISO 14001 certified. The perceived payoff of this brand signal is contingent on ISO 14001's institutional design, as well as firms' characteristics and the stakeholder and the institutional context in which they operate.

In the case of ISO 14001, the International Organization for Standardization does not provide monitoring services or enforcement services. These services are provided by third-party auditors (secondary governors) who are accredited by national-level accreditation bodies. While the ISO has the authority to sanction participating firms that shirk on their program obligations by revoking their ISO 14001 certifications, it is seldom exercised. Because it does not require participating firms to disclose audit information, it is a weak sword club that has a relatively high likelihood of prompting shirking. On both these counts, the ISO 14001 has been criticized by activist groups. Given that ISO 14001 has attracted a large number of firms and that its requirements have been criticized as insufficient, we expect that the club governors will come under a great deal of pressure to ratchet up the club's requirements. While changing such rules is not easy, it is not impossible. It will be very interesting to see how the governor responds to such demands in the future. On one hand, it needs to shed its pro-business image to garner wider acceptability and legitimacy. However, by becoming a strong sword club, it might create disincentives for firms to join it. This is a nontrivial concern because ISO 14001 faces competition from several industry-level environmental clubs.

Competition

There is seldom a single governor or a single club in a policy domain. Do clubs have first-mover advantages in terms of attracting members? These advantages might be substantial given that the propensity among firms to join any club depends, in large measure, on the "network effects" they can capture (Farrell and Shapiro 1985). This is because the benefits for a firm of joining the club critically depend on how many other firms have joined it as well. In the context of technical clubs, the ISO does not face much competition, especially given the market division agreed upon with the IEC and the ITU (Büthe, this volume). In this role, by providing a focal point for standard development for firms, this governor mitigates coordination dilemmas facing them.[23] The widespread acceptance of technical standards is aided by the fact that new ISO rules need to be approved by a super-majority of national delegations (which often include representatives from leading national firms). Once firms commanding a substantial global market share in an industry subscribe to ISO standards – which they do because industrialized countries are the active members in the rulemaking processes – the emergence of a rival club becomes less feasible. Thus, a participatory and consensus-based standard-making process helps the International Organization for Standardization secure its place as the preeminent global standardization governor.

Unlike technical standard clubs, there is competition among governors, each offering its own club, within the context of management standards clubs such as ISO 9000 and ISO 14001. The International Organization for Standardization's foray into management standards clubs has created interesting competition dynamics. While its first management standard, the ISO 9000 quality control program, has been widely adopted, its adoption levels vary across countries even after controlling for the usual suspects such as the size of the economy. An important reason for this variance is the presence of competing quality standard clubs such as the Six Sigma, as well as industry-specific standards established by industry associations.

ISO 14001 faces an even more intense competition. Even if we were to think of a restricted domain for ISO 14001 – voluntary environmental clubs – we can identify several governors that supply competing clubs: (1) industry-level governors, such as the American Chemistry Association's Responsible Care and the American Forestry and Paper Association's Sustainable Forestry Initiative; (2) regional governors, such as the European Union's Eco-Management and Audit Scheme (EMAS) club; and (3) governmental governors, such as the EPA, which have created more than sixty clubs, such as the Performance Track Initiative.

Many of the competing clubs target specific industries and arguably provide more compelling branding benefits for the firms simply because the stakeholders can identify the club with the industry type. Further,

---

[23] See Spruyt (2001) in the context of demand for and supply of standards.

ISO 14001 faces competition from regional clubs, which again can provide more compelling branding benefits, and government-sponsored clubs which, in many cases, can provide tangible benefits in the short run. In short, the competition for membership in the voluntary environmental governance policy market is substantial.

Firms can surely join multiple clubs at the same time but this increases their costs. An important challenge for the International Organization for Standardization is to make ISO 14001 standards appeal across industries and countries. While ISO 14001's standards are indeed generic and apply across industries and regulatory contexts, this flexibility has come at the cost of specificity and some environmentalists have criticized its lack of transparency. Some of the competing clubs have stronger credibility because they have more stringent and specific club standards or monitoring rules. The crucial challenge for the governor is to identify how potential participants make tradeoffs between increased credibility (and the subsequent branding benefits) flowing from stringent rules and the higher costs of joining such clubs. In the case of ISO 14001, the International Organization for Standardization seems to have opted for a weak sword club with moderate club standards. It will be instructive to observe how this governor responds to the activist pressure to upgrade the quality of "swords" and club standards.

Who governs?

Many view the International Organization for Standardization as a pro-business governor. Our theory predicts that club governors would seek to allay this suspicion in the design of their various clubs. To respond to the credible commitment problem, the ISO works with specific voting rules. Standards need to be approved by two-thirds of the members that have participated in the standards development process and by three-fourths of all voting members.[24] Thus, the standards cannot be changed easily. In any case, the process of standard development is reasonably transparent, and outside observers, even when not represented on technical committees, have a fair amount of information about the deliberations.

---

[24] See www.iso.org/iso/en/stdsdevelopment/whowhenhow/how.html (accessed August 12, 2008).

Nevertheless, the ISO's rulemaking processes have been criticized as unjust and inequitable. While the procedures may serve the interests of the principals, the clubs can create negative externalities for nonprincipals. Why is the process unjust? First, the ISO club development process does not grant NGOs independent standing, which often leaves them on the outside of the standards development process. This is unlike much public regulation in democracies, particularly in the United States, where NGOs deliver input through established institutional mechanisms. Second, the costs of participating in the standards development meetings and the difficulty in supplying technical experts tend to exclude participation by national standards bodies from developing countries, leaving some principals structurally disenfranchised (Clapp 1998). Consequently, although developing countries account for about 75 percent of the national standards bodies in the ISO, they contribute less than 5 percent to the technical rulemaking work. The United Nations Conference on Trade and Development (another global governor) has thus recommended that the ISO provide financial support to developing countries to facilitate their participation in standards development. Despite these criticisms, the International Organization for Standardization continues to maintain its central position, arguably because it enjoys credibility for its technical expertise and relatively open and fair rule standards development processes.

In addition to the rulemaking issues, one can also examine the "who governs?" issue by exploring the factors that drive the diffusion of ISO 14001. Arguably, at both the rulemaking and diffusion levels, developed countries seem to be most privileged. Our empirical work suggests that important drivers of ISO 14001 adoption lie in the structure of the international political economy. Recall that we made the argument that in addition to club design and the attributes of the club governors, the attractiveness of the club depends on the institutional and stakeholder context in which potential participants are located. A given club may have varying levels of credibility (and therefore branding benefits) in different contexts, probably because different stakeholders have varying perceptions of the branding signal. Our research suggests that exports and inward foreign investment are important drivers of ISO 14001 adoption. Specifically, we find that international trade serves as a vehicle for transmitting importing countries' ISO 14001 preferences to exporting countries (Prakash and Potoski 2006b). Given that developed countries with high levels of ISO

14001 adoption (with the exception of the United States) absorb the bulk of developing country exports, international trade has encouraged ISO 14001 adoption in developing countries through a supply chain requirement. For many developing country firms, ISO 14001 certification has become an important requirement for exporting to developed countries. In another paper, we find that inward foreign investment stocks are associated with higher levels of ISO 14001 adoption in host countries when foreign investment originates from countries that themselves have high levels of ISO 14001 adoptions (Prakash and Potoski 2007). In other words, countries' ISO 14001 adoption levels are associated not with how much foreign direct investment host countries receive but with the identity of the actors from whom they receive it. In this way, the value of the ISO 14001 brand becomes contingent on the value attached to it by foreign investors. Thus, a careful study of ISO 14001's cross-national diffusion reveals how the structural power enjoyed by some principals (the rich, developed countries) in the rule-making processes has enhanced their ability to exploit their structural power in international trade and investment to encourage the diffusion of ISO 14001 standards. As it stands now, ISO 14001 is becoming a de facto requirement for tapping into trade and investment networks that the ISO's key principals seem to dominate. The normative implication is whether such weak sword clubs, although with third-party monitoring, are the most appropriate for tackling the environmental challenges faced by the developing world where the enforcement of public law anyway tends to be lax. Would such weak sword clubs trap the developing world in low-equilibrium situations from which neither public nor private law can extricate them?

Conclusion

The proliferation of nongovernmental governors supplying voluntary clubs raises important questions about their efficacy as policy tools. These clubs vary in their ability to shape actors' behavior, and their policy usefulness has been called into question. While these instruments are not a policy panacea, prematurely rejecting nongovernmental clubs might miss an important opportunity to strengthen global governance. Yet uncritically accepting them might exacerbate the structural inequities in the world.

This chapter outlines some initial steps for a theoretical framework for evaluating voluntary clubs on two crucial dimensions – club standards and enforcement rules – to guide inquiry concerning the promise and pitfalls of different types of voluntary clubs. Through the theoretical lenses of club theory, we seek to explain how club attributes can induce members to produce positive social externalities and contribute to overall welfare. We examined how these attributes can mitigate the Olsonian dilemma of inducing members to join the club and the shirking dilemma of having members adhere to club standards once they have joined.

Our perspective suggests important directions for further study. Although this chapter has focused on how club standards and enforcement rules affect clubs' collective action dilemmas, other club dimensions are likely to influence club efficacy. As our discussion of the International Organization for Standardization has shown, the reputation of the governor and the processes for establishing club rules are likely to influence the club's credibility among members' stakeholders. Clubs sponsored by governors with reputations for technical expertise are likely to be perceived as more legitimate and effective. The ISO 14001 club benefits from the International Organization for Standardization's reputation as a global standards authority, not just for technical standards but increasingly for management standards, as reflected in its successful ISO 9000 program. Likewise, transparent and inclusive rulemaking procedures can improve a voluntary program's credibility. The ISO's rulemaking process for ISO 14001 included participants from many sectors and regions, though NGOs and developing countries could have been better represented.

This club theory perspective on governance has profound potential for advancing scholarly inquiry. We believe that club theory offers powerful insights for studying the production, provision, and distribution of collective goods through mandatory (for example, governments), as well as voluntary, clubs. Often times, scholars insist that voluntary programs are fundamentally different from public regulation and need a different theory of governance. We submit that public regulation can be viewed as a mandatory club for those within the government's jurisdiction. Monitoring and enforcement issues suggest that individuals often have considerable de facto (rather than de jure) autonomy in responding to governmental law. At a broader level, whether actors in a mandatory club have credible exit options might be debatable; mandatory clubs require strictly defined boundary conditions to keep insiders in and to let in only selected outsiders. But boundaries can be porous – firms and labor can vote with their feet (Tiebout 1956; Hirschman 1970). In fact, much like voluntary clubs, the boundary conditions of mandatory clubs (as reflected in free trade agreements and immigration laws) are not fixed; regulations for the inflow and outflow of capital and labor are often subject to heated public debates. Intergovernmental clubs also reflect similar debates about boundary conditions, membership rules, and broader collective goods issues. Thus, mandatory clubs share with their voluntary cousins similar challenges with regard to institutional design and the production and distribution of collective goods. Indeed, several scholars have employed the club perspective to study intergovernmental clubs such as the European Union (Ahrens *et al.* 2005), the North Atlantic Treaty Organization (Sandler and Hartley 1999), the World Trade Organization (Keohane and Nye 2001), and regional trading blocs (Fratianni and Pattison 2002). Thus, the club approach can help identify the key characteristics of governance systems, link them to the attributes of the governors, and move toward a general theory of governance. Our chapter contributes to this endeavor.

Some other cases presented in this book can be usefully examined by employing insights from club theory. Indeed, as the introductory chapter correctly points out, a comparative analysis of cases presented in this volume can shed light on how the relationship among governors influences the institutional design of the governance system. In this regard, Büthe's chapter and this chapter present interesting overlaps and contrasts. In both cases, self-interested actors seek to establish rule systems that can be modeled as clubs. In the ISO 14001 case, the governors came up with a weak sword club to ensure that high numbers of firms found it affordable and joined the club. The opposition by the American delegation to a strong sword club contributed to the final outcome. Thus, ISO sought to reconcile the tension between its twin sources of legitimacy – expertise as well as wide levels of acceptability – by opting for a middle path of a weak sword club but with third-party monitoring. In Büthe's case, there tend to be more synergistic relations between the International Electrotechnical Commission (IEC) club, states, and consumers. Consequently, the governors created a club with a vast reach, and arguably with stronger self-enforcing swords.

In sum, this chapter suggests that nongovernmental governors have the potential to serve as important global governance instruments. They are neither a panacea nor a curse, but they can certainly complement the efforts of existing global, intergovernmental governors. They merit careful examination to understand their operations so that policy decisions can harness their potential and avoid their pitfalls.

4 | Corporations in zones of conflict: issues, actors, and institutions

VIRGINIA HAUFLER

Since the end of the Cold War, many observers have commented that civil war and local violence have increased dramatically, with Kaplan pointing to "The Coming Anarchy" as a feature of the twenty-first century (Kaplan 1994).[1] These "new wars" of the post-Cold War era have been described as being about identity issues and not the geopolitical and strategic issues underlying earlier conflicts (Kaldor 1999; Newman 2004). But in the past ten years, scholars, policymakers, and activists have also increasingly highlighted the material economic factors that are critical features of many contemporary conflicts. They have pointed to the importance of natural resources, especially oil and diamonds, in fueling long-running civil wars in Africa. A corollary of this attention to economic factors is that the spotlight of international attention regularly focuses on the role of private investors in facilitating and even causing conflict, corruption, and criminality in weakly governed states. Given the high profile and influence of major corporations operating in the developing world, some activists and policymakers argue that the private sector is critical to conflict *prevention* efforts. They seek to integrate business into a variety of voluntary governance regimes intended to control or reduce the links between economic transactions and civil war. Why has this shift in understanding and action occurred? Since when is the private sector given responsibility for peace and security issues that are normally reserved for public authorities? Why has governance by the private sector been adopted as the "obvious" solution to these conflicts?

This chapter explores the dynamics of issue definition and agenda setting, seeking to explain how and why efforts to address conflict

---

[1] This perception is contradicted by the reality that the numbers of conflicts and of people killed in war have declined over the past ten years; see Gurr and Marshall (2006); Human Security Center (2006).

today include a role for the private sector, and how that issue has been taken up to varying degrees by governments, activists, and international organizations. The issue was defined and the agenda set as a result of two processes: the development of a broader corporate social responsibility agenda, which has become a focal point for activism, with activists engaging in a learning and emulation process across issue areas; and the movement by public authorities to strategically delegate authority and contract out conflict prevention to nonstate actors, in order to reduce the costs of intervention and respond to domestic and transnational pressures. The campaign by activists defined civil conflict as an issue area in which corporations had exacerbated the violence and prevented the establishment of peace, whether they intended to or not. They then took this a step further to assign a role to those same companies in preventing conflict and fostering peace. Companies could do this by adopting a prescribed set of conflict-sensitive business practices and participating in multi-stakeholder governance initiatives designed to reduce conflict. This "business-and-conflict" agenda led to a broad effort to institutionalize corporate participation in conflict-prevention activities, although, as will be discussed below, the results have been fragmentary and incomplete.

This has resulted in a disaggregation of global governance, in which different state and nonstate actors perform separate governance functions regarding conflict prevention. Two consequences flow from these innovations in the governance of conflict: first, companies have found themselves reluctantly participating in conflict-prevention regimes in order to manage their political and reputational costs and preserve their markets and "license to operate." These companies operate mainly in extractive sectors and are unable to pack up and move to a new location in response to a breakdown in order. Second, the nongovernmental organizations (NGOs) that initially sought to blame the companies now find themselves partnering with them in governance – even though they generally consider these firms "bad" governors – in the expectation that their behavior can be changed for the better. Ultimately, these efforts support the evolution of increased authority for corporations over conflict issues. This outcome is not entirely in the interest of either NGOs or firms, and yet both actors have contributed to the expansion and institutionalization of the business-and-conflict agenda. The resulting tensions reflect a delicate balance in which either side may find it all too easy to defect and give up this particular governance role.

The role of the private sector in governance is highly contested, with heated debates in particular over the relative benefits of public *regulation* of corporate behavior versus corporate *responsibility* for providing public goods (Haufler 2001; Vogel 2006). The idea that regulation or self-regulation of corporate behavior may contribute to settling conflicts is a new one, though the fact that companies might contribute to conflict is not new at all.[2] This particular solution to contemporary conflict in the developing world was created and defined by specific NGOs in the 1990s, but interest in it was sustained by the institutional support of other actors. A variety of related issues – conflict, corruption, and criminality – came together in a business-and-conflict agenda promoted by the United Nations (UN) Global Compact and a small number of leading donor governments. But there has been continuing contestation over the relative power and responsibility of private agents in addressing these difficult issues. This contestation reflects competing bases for authority of both public and private actors. Corporations may have the resources and expertise to act effectively in this arena, but they do not have the legitimacy for others to look with equanimity on their increased role in political affairs, even in the pursuit of peace. At the same time, there is clearly some tension between this agenda and the sovereignty and policymaking autonomy of the target states, which reflects a divide over whether actors based in the developed world are imposing their solutions on the states and societies of the developing world.

This chapter begins with a short discussion of agency, governance, and the private sector. This is followed by a section on different approaches to issue definition and agenda setting, and how they may apply to the identification of economic actors as critical players in conflict prevention. The next section examines the business-and-conflict agenda and the manner in which this agenda was defined and expanded in different ways over a relatively short period of time. The conclusion discusses the implications of this process for institutionalization and broader governance issues.

---

[2] For an excellent historical overview of the many ways in which foreign firms have become entangled in local politics, including war, see Litvin (2003).

Agency and authority in global governance

Traditionally, the study of global governance has been equated with the creation and operation of intergovernmental organizations and international regimes. In recent years, the term increasingly has been used to denote the fact that governance at the global level includes a wide variety of actors, both public and private, national and international. As Avant *et al.* describe it in this volume's introduction, *"global governors are authorities who exercise power across borders for purposes of affecting policy. Governors thus create issues, set agendas, establish and implement rules or programs, and evaluate and/or adjudicate outcomes."* Often, this governance involves contributions from different types of actors performing different tasks or functions, sometimes in partnership and sometimes separately and in contention, disaggregating the governance process. We have many different labels for this: public–private partnerships, global public policy networks, nonstate market-driven governance, etc. (Reinicke *et al.* 2003; United Nations Foundation n.d.; Cashore *et al.* 2004).

In the case of business and conflict, transnational NGOs set the international agenda by effectively raising the issue of natural resource revenues as a source of conflict financing, blaming international firms, and seeking to "govern" them. Both state and nonstate actors responded in part by negotiating new rules and practices for a particular firm, sector, or project. Companies generally led the implementation phase in programs to limit the negative effect of resource development, in cooperation with local government leaders and at times with contributions from intergovernmental organizations and donor governments. NGOs typically took on the role of assessment and monitoring of projects, officially or unofficially. Enforcement and adjudication processes, when they existed, might be in the hands of home or host governments, international organizations, or even the private sector itself.

The focus of this chapter will be on how a particular set of issues was defined by one set of actors (initially NGOs and subsequently international organizations and donor governments) in order to establish governance tasks for another set of actors (individual companies, industry associations, and business groups). Those other actors only reluctantly acceded to the pressure to establish rules, norms, and institutions governing their behavior and in many cases have struggled against this expansion of their responsibilities. The relationships among these various actors have produced a diversity of new forms of governance, but as noted in the introductory chapter to this volume, their interactions are often in tension.

Corporations are often theorized in a simple way: they are the ultimate rational actors, driven by profits alone.[3] Their interests are defined by their position within a capitalist economy, and their actions are determined by their class interests and/or their need to sustain and expand the capitalist system.[4] While this certainly is not entirely wrong, it misses the complexity of motivations driving corporate actors today, their varied organizational features, the ways in which they act collectively, and the manner in which they define and redefine their interests. In a world in which the "spotlight" of international attention is difficult to avoid, businesses increasingly find that maintaining their reputation has market value (Spar 1998). When they operate in multiple jurisdictions, they may be subject to too many contradictory rules and learn to value a common framework to address particularly contentious issues. They respond variously to the need to preserve their reputation, prevent government regulation, and adopt evolving norms about corporate behavior (Haufler 2001). Scholarship on business behavior points to many motivating factors beyond profit alone, including market share, risk management, reputation, principal–agent problems, organizational learning, and values-based concerns (Fort and Schipani 2004; Dunning 1993; Casson 1994; Sell and Prakash 2004). Large multinational firms are in constant interaction with a wide range of organizations and individuals, engaging in a kind of modern corporate diplomacy on a global scale (Stopford, Strange, and Henley 1991; Haufler 2004; Hocking 2004; May 2006).

The private sector acts as an agent of global governance in a number of different ways. Individually, multinational corporations (MNCs) are large hierarchical organizations that govern their employees, suppliers,

---

[3] Milton Friedman (1970) famously argued that profits are the only goal the firm *should* have, though that position has been extensively critiqued; see Wilcke (2004).

[4] This chapter takes a deliberately agent-centered focus, and does not address the structural power or place of business within the capitalist system. Critical perspectives tend to be divided on whether corporate interests favor war or peace, with literature and evidence on both sides.

and distributors on a transnational basis. The twenty-first-century company is highly networked, with many tasks outsourced to firms around the world. This involves complex chains of delegation, partnership, and outsourcing that extend the reach of the firm organizationally, creating bonds and relationships even among keen competitors (Gereffi and Korzeniewicz 1994). Dunning (1993) refers to this as the rise of "alliance capitalism," in which the boundaries of the firm are no longer coincident with ownership. This makes it difficult to identify the legal and official reach of the firm – and thus the limits of its responsibilities. Some firms claim that they have no control over or responsibility for the outcomes that are decried by activists. For example, Nike, which owns no factories itself, initially responded to criticism from labor activists by denying that it was responsible for the labor standards of its subcontractors.

Collectively, firms participate in a variety of initiatives that establish rules, principles, and norms guiding their behavior internationally. These may be based on existing industry associations, such as the standards organizations discussed by Büthe in this volume. Firms also organize as issue-based interest groups that cross sectoral boundaries, such as the World Business Council for Sustainable Development. These groups can be fairly fluid, as consensus about interests held in common waxes and wanes. New groups may form in response to particular campaigns and crises, or old ones may be reformed to address new issues. These new groupings are "clubs" that provide both public and private goods to their members, as discussed by Prakash and Potoski in their work, in this volume and elsewhere (Prakash and Potoski 2006b).

The basis for private sector authority varies across issues and initiatives, but it is typically drawn from their expertise, resources, and perceived efficacy. Company managers have more knowledge than potential regulators or outside observers about markets and technologies. They have resources in the form of personnel, organizational capacity, and money that other actors lack. And they are often viewed as being very effective at implementing programs and achieving goals. This is particularly true for companies operating in conflict zones, where by definition the government lacks significant capacity. There are limits to how far and in what areas the firm's governance role is viewed as legitimate. Analysts often distinguish between the immediate area of corporate operations where they have clear responsibilities (for

example, a mining company having direct responsibility for its mining operation), and the larger arenas in which companies have influence (the community, the nation, the globe) but their role is contested
(Nelson 2000; Banfield *et al.* 2003).

In these larger arenas, private sector authority often derives from
delegation by other actors, including donor governments and international agencies. Corporations may be instruments of foreign policy
for particular states. In the case of conflict issues, powerful states may
want to see conflicts in the developing world settled and espouse a commitment to the norm of humanitarian intervention, but shy away from
direct intervention themselves owing to the costs and difficulties of
achieving success (Finnemore 2003). International organizations such
as the United Nations may have a clear role in peacekeeping but face
severe political and financial limits on their capacity to act. Domestic
and intergovernmental development agencies have increasingly linked
development and conflict agendas, but are unsure of their own capacity to address the problems they have identified (Duffield 2001). Peace
may be viewed by all these actors as a public good, but like many public goods, it tends to be undersupplied. Handing this off to the private
sector appears to be a second-best solution, but one that is pragmatic
about the political limits of public action.

In this chapter, I focus primarily on the issue definition and agenda-
setting phases of governance activities. It is impossible in most cases to
separate these phases from rulemaking and implementation processes,
but the earlier steps are especially interesting in the case of business
and conflict. Why the sudden turn to the private sector to resolve
conflict in the developing world? The business-and-conflict agenda is
one in which NGOs (advocacy organizations, think-tanks, and foundations), governments, the UN, and the World Bank all attempt to
establish new responsibilities for another group of actors: the business
community. The business community, in turn, generally opposes these
attempts to put limits on some kinds of behavior while expanding corporate responsibilities. They are concerned that any new commitments
will establish precedents that they did not intend concerning their role
as agents of conflict prevention. As will be discussed in more detail
below, the business-and-conflict agenda has included the creation of
new rules and norms regarding corporate transparency, supply chain
management, revenue management, security management, and conflict impact assessment. Each of these has been institutionalized in a

different manner, but all include corporate actors at the center of implementation. And all include a redefinition of the identity and interests
of these central actors.

Setting the agenda for international business

The process of issue definition and agenda setting can be broken down,
somewhat artificially but usefully, into a number of different steps.
First, we can identify objective conditions that have distributive or
moral consequences for particular sets of people. If objective conditions
are not seen as costly by anyone, then there is no issue to be identified or
resolved. Observers may note that conditions have differential effects
and may even point out potential sources of grievance, but it is when
an individual or group puts a name to those conditions, identifies the
nature of a problem, and calls for action that it truly becomes an
issue. In this second stage, by identifying costs and values involved
in maintaining or changing the status quo, the participants typically
make connections between cause and effect that no one had identified
previously. In this stage, injuries are enumerated and blame is laid
(Keck and Sikkink 1998). But similar objective conditions may not
always lead to identification of the same issues, injuries, and causes, as
Carpenter has noted. An identifiable issue does not always become a
part of the international agenda (Carpenter 2005a). The third step is
one in which collective action is or is not mobilized to put that issue on
the agenda of those who can do something about it. As Mancur Olson
(1965) perceptively argued, the existence of a problem that needs to be
resolved does not necessarily mean that a group will form to address it.
Collective action faces many barriers. At the international level, such
barriers are formidable indeed.

Most of the literature on agenda setting assumes a domestic context
where the goal sought is to change government policy.[5] Baumgartner
and Jones (1993) describe a model of "punctuated equilibrium" in
which both issue definition and the control of institutions within
a country interact and can produce sudden shifts in domestic policy instead of incremental evolution and change. Kingdon's "policy

---

[5] There is a vast literature in the communications field on issue definition,
focusing on the media. Although the media constitutes a very important part of
the story in agenda setting, it is not the focus of this chapter.

windows" model also looks at how opportunities for change may emerge from the way in which problems, policies, and politics converge (Soroka 1999). Much of the foreign policy literature, especially on US foreign policy, posits a cycle in which external events and presidential attention are key factors in getting an issue on the domestic agenda (Wood and Peake 1998). In all these cases, the models for agenda setting assume an existing policy framework and set of institutions which interact with other factors to determine the point at which change is possible.

This is very different from the international arena, which is much less structured than the domestic one. The stages of a policy cycle (for example, issue definition, agenda access, and policy choice) are less clearly defined, the appropriate point of access is unclear, and the institutional framework is fragmented. When problems are constructed at the international level, affected groups must choose among different actors and different institutional forums to determine where to expend their effort. The sites at which agendas are made and policies are changed are dispersed across different levels, institutions, and actors, and may change over time. At the domestic level, electoral politics are a critical element of issue definition, as political parties compete to dominate policy debates. Internationally, the UN General Assembly plays a somewhat similar role, but one that is much weaker and less significant to the overall global agenda than what we see in domestic electoral politics. Globally, there are multiple bureaucracies, both public and private, which are competing sources of expertise, information, and policy change. This makes agenda setting in the international arena a complex and slippery topic.

The business-and-conflict agenda is particularly interesting, in part because the main target for policy change is not a public actor or institution – it is the private sector. The private sector generally takes the position that the business of business is to make money, not policy.[6] And yet, it is obvious that the private sector is deeply involved in influencing a range of public policies, both at home and abroad. The analysis of corporate policy change on issues of global governance is not well developed as yet, though it is emerging as an area ripe for better developed scholarship (Büthe 2004).

---

[6] Milton Friedman wrote that the main social responsibility of business is to make money for shareholders, within the limits of law and social norms (Friedman 1970).

In the beginning, it was not clear to activists what were the appropriate points of access to the private sector and the mechanisms by which it could be drawn into new arenas of governance. Multiple strategies were tried, and the outcomes took a variety of forms. Many advocacy organizations underwent a learning process as the broad "corporate accountability agenda" matured over time. Over the course of the past decade, activists have targeted the private sector directly in transnational campaigns that sought to influence consumer and investor sentiments, but they have also targeted international agencies and donor governments to find a way to influence corporate policy. They have utilized rational appeals to the corporate bottom line, describing conflict as bad for business, while also framing the issues in moral terms, pointing to the suffering and hardship of the victims of violence. They have adopted an array of activist tactics, from street protests to litigation. Seeking to promote this new agenda, advocacy organizations learned from previous campaigns on other issues. As stated in the introductory chapter, learning is a powerful source of change, and the actors involved in this issue have learned over time about their sources and techniques of influence.

Issue definition and agenda setting on the international stage are closely linked to the actions of particular agents of change who mobilize to promote a specific set of ideas. As Risse (1994) said, "ideas do not float freely," they are attached to particular groups or institutions. In the business-and-conflict case, activists identified a pressing need to deal with violence and victimization in conflict-ridden countries, and proposed a new solution utilizing the private sector. This matched the emerging norms surrounding corporate social responsibility and preexisting strategies activists had already been using to influence corporate behavior in other issue areas. It also matched the strategic goals and constraints of key actors – donor governments and international organizations – which sought to address the problems of failed states but had limited resources and political will to act aggressively.

International NGOs defined – or in some sense *re*-defined – the issues involved in civil conflict, pointing to market actors as a cause of suffering, and sought to establish a new solution involving private sector action (Rochefort and Cobb 1994; Keck and Sikkink 1998). This kind of reframing of an issue may be taken up by a wider community when the new idea or norm is congruent with old ones; when actors learn from new evidence and behaviors that challenge traditional perspectives; or when experts and particular social groups redefine what is appropriate (Simmons *et al.* 2006; Cortell and Davis 2000).[7] Key players are more likely to see congruence, learn about new ideas, and emulate experts if these all match their strategic needs at a particular point in time. Once a new idea or norm is adopted by key players, they must identify the processes and opportunity structures in which to use political reframing strategies, information communication, and values identification to mobilize a larger and influential audience (Tarrow 2002; McAdam *et al.* 2001; Keck and Sikkink 1998). As increasing numbers of actors come to the same understanding about the definition of the issue, its character, and possible solutions, a network of experts and policymakers may be created. When the consensus extends to a larger audience, such wider acceptance may result in what Keck and Sikkink (1998) describe as a "norms cascade" (see also Haas 1990).

The reframing of an issue to include new actors or solutions is not automatically diffused within a wider community. While NGOs may identify an issue and attempt to place it on the international agenda, they are not always successful; they may not even take up an issue in the first place, as Carpenter discusses in her contribution to this volume (see also Carpenter 2007b). Contestation among different groups may be based on different perceptions of cause and effect, and competing actors may identify different factors and actors as being at fault (Tarrow 2005; Carpenter 2005a; Bob 2005). Internationally, this contestation may occur within particular institutional arenas, such as the UN, or in a space that is detached from an institutional framework, which is primarily the case in the business-and-conflict agenda. What makes NGO–business interaction particularly complex is that transnational campaigns target audiences in one (developed) country in support of an issue that directly affects an audience in another (typically underdeveloped) country.

---

[7] In a recent special issue of *International Organization*, Simmons *et al.* (2006) lay out four possible mechanisms of policy diffusion: coercion, competition, learning, and emulation. This chapter does not address coercion and competition since the focus is on issue definition and agenda setting and not behavioral change. Coercion and competition would logically be more important in analysis of the impact or outcomes of this agenda, that is, in looking at whether the private sector actually changes its behavior.

The first response of most of the business community to new demands, as in this case, is to stonewall. They oppose all attempts to impose new obligations. They typically argue that they cannot change their behavior because they will lose out to competitors, suffer higher costs, or be subject to unreasonable expectations. Stonewalling strategies are particularly common as a response to transnational advocacy campaigns. As anti-corporate campaigns become more intense or sophisticated they can impose more direct costs on companies – loss of markets as consumers refuse to buy the goods of "bad" firms, loss of financial resources as investors turn elsewhere, litigation costs as advocates bring their issues into the justice system, and increased electoral support for potentially costly regulation of corporate behavior. As these costs escalate, stonewalling becomes harder to sustain. When stonewalling becomes too difficult to maintain, however, many firms pursue a national strategy favoring local regulation, since they typically have more influence in the domestic political arena than in the international one and will be able to preserve their domestic competitiveness with favorable regulations. In an increasingly globalized world market, however, leading MNCs may pursue a strategy of harmonization, that is, support for international regulation and opposition to national regulation. This reduces the costs of operating under multiple regulatory regimes and is often viewed as a means to "level the playing field." One final option is to adopt voluntary self-regulatory strategies as a way to avoid local and international regulation yet ameliorate societal demands (Haufler 2003). Different companies and industry sectors adopted a mix of these strategies in response to the new business-and-conflict prevention agenda, generally favoring voluntary self-regulation over other strategies.

We can trace the emergence of the business-and-conflict agenda to a number of factors. First, the social entrepreneurship of key individuals and NGOs was critical to the initial definition of the problem. In this case, they saw the problem as ongoing conflict and then redefined it as a problem of how business was conducted in conflict-affected countries. Blame was assigned, and big business became the symbol of the ills of these countries. The solution – a change in business behavior – became an integral element of defining the problem. Second, the definition of the problem was reinforced by the existence of the broader corporate accountability movement, which was increasingly successful in promoting corporate social responsibility in other issue areas such as the environment and human rights. This movement made the "business case" for corporate action, emphasizing the long-term bene-fits of responsible action, in addition to making values-based appeals. This was further reinforced by the parallel emergence of academic research and policy analysis that examined the political economy of conflict, "teaching" relevant actors about the links between private sec-tor behavior and conflict. Third, the agenda was set when the cause was taken up by international organizations and major donor states, which saw this as a low-cost solution to a problem they were under pressure to resolve. They wanted to see the end to conflict in the developing world for strategic and humanitarian reasons. At the same time, they were justly wary of direct intervention. For these actors, the business-and-conflict agenda and its call to involve companies in conflict prevention provided the illusion of concerted action while responsibility for action had, in fact, been delegated to the private sector. As more key actors participated in the campaign, the set of issues and solutions became increasingly clear. Repeated negotiations over rules and the design of implementation mechanisms occurred among a changing constellation of actors. The result was a variety of systems, involving different sets of actors, each addressing a narrow subset of the business-and-conflict agenda.

The political economy of conflict

Empirical and policy-oriented research has identified a number of fun-damental mechanisms by which foreign trade and investment can con-tribute to the political economy of conflict by creating conditions that facilitate the eruption of violence or its continuation (Berdal and Malone 2000; Collier 2003a and 2003b; Ballentine and Sherman 2003; Humphreys 2005). Some mechanisms are general in nature, while others are specific to the development and exploitation of nat-ural resource wealth, thus leading to the special targeting of the extractive sector. The main mechanisms are: (1) the attractions and depredations of resource wealth itself; (2) the politics of inequitable distribution of economic activity, often exacerbated by ethnic divi-sions; and (3) problems stemming from security or protection ser-vices provided to firms, which arise at the project, community, and state levels. In recent years, the economic causes of war have become a fruitful area of research and have generated an extensive debate over "greed versus grievance" as factors explaining the outbreak of violence.[8]

There are two different types of problems that derive from natural resource wealth: the use of revenue gained from trading in high-value commodities to finance war and criminal activity; and the inequitable and too-often corrupt management and distribution of revenues from major long-term resource development, such as gas and oil projects. A number of scholars have examined empirical evidence regarding various mechanisms by which natural resource wealth may be linked to violence, and it is not clear whether it is natural resource wealth that undermines good governance, or weak governance that allows natural resource development to have such dire consequences (Collier 2003a and 2003b; Humphreys 2005).

High-value natural resources can be categorized according to whether they are "lootable" or "non-lootable," which have different patterns in their relationship to the outbreak of violence (Ross 2004; Ballentine and Nitzschke 2005). Lootable resources are easily obtained and carried from place to place, with high value for their weight. The best-known example is that of diamonds. Although deep-mined diamonds may be difficult to obtain and trade illegally, many areas of West Africa have alluvial diamonds, which do not require deep mining. Much of the diamond business in alluvial fields is by artisanal miners, who sell their diamonds to middlemen. These then become part of a chain of diamond sales, polishing, and marketing that stretches across the globe and spans legal and illegal markets. At the initial stages, the diamonds can be captured by rebels or secessionist movements and used to finance the purchase of weapons and provide money for troops.[9] The income from diamond sales may also be captured by the governing elite, who may use it to fight rebels and prop up their own power regardless of popular support. In the diamond sector, there is a legitimate industry that could be further developed, and an

---

[8] This characterization in terms of greed or grievances simplifies complex arguments. Some of the early work included that of David Keen (1998), Mats Berdal and David Malone (2000), and Paul Collier and Anke Hoeffler (2000). These factors are also linked to analyses of the "new wars" described by Mark Duffield (2001) and Mary Kaldor (1999), and critiqued by Edward Newman (2004).

[9] For excellent overviews of the role of resource flows in conflict, particularly regarding diamonds, see Smillie *et al.* (2000); Humphreys (2005).

illegitimate one that needs to be regulated or controlled to cut its link to violence.[10]

Fixed-resource development ("non-lootable"), such as gas and oil projects or deep mining, typically requires contracting between governments and investors. Such contracts stipulate, among many other things, the percentage of revenue from the project that must be paid to the government as taxes and fees. These revenue payments can be a windfall to the government, allowing it to loosen fiscal controls, expand its budget, and distribute benefits through patronage to friends and relatives. If it is not managed well, resource development distorts the economy and encourages poor macroeconomic policy choices by governments.[11] Politically, it makes the government less dependent on taxation and thus less accountable to citizens. The payments can become a source of competition among elites, corruption among bureaucrats, and discrimination among citizens. This "resource curse," as some have called it, has been associated with the outbreak of conflict (Karl 1997; Ross 1999; deSoysa 2000). The massive revenues from these projects may support authoritarian rulers by providing them with the financial means to increase the repressive capacity of the state. The end result is that revenues from legitimate business that is meant for positive development goals instead produce conflict and underdevelopment. An already weakened state is particularly susceptible to the dangers of mismanaged resource development.

In many cases, these problems are exacerbated by the lack of security. When it comes to private sector trade and investment, fixed investments face a much bigger security risk than others. Most mobile industry and services simply leave conflict-ridden areas, but large projects may remain in place (although they may cease operations at the height of violence).[12] Foreign companies are often obligated by their contracts

---

10 The policy debates over what to do about so-called "conflict diamonds" acknowledge the difficulty of distinguishing between legitimate and illegitimate diamonds and diamond trading. The fear is that any action against conflict diamonds might undermine legitimate markets and states with well-managed diamond sectors, such as Botswana.

11 This is often referred to as the "Dutch disease," named after the Dutch experience. With the discovery of North Sea gas, investment dramatically shifted out of all other areas of the economy, leading to severe macroeconomic imbalances.

12 Most businesses flee violence, but some do not. If the violence is in a distant or inaccessible part of the country or the firm is not itself a target of attack, then

with governments to secure protection through the use of government military or police forces. In a number of high-profile cases, particularly in Nigeria and Sudan, these very forces proved to be a threat to civilians. Government forces have used company facilities – private airports, helicopters, and trucks – in order to carry out repressive operations against local communities.[13] In other cases, as in Colombia, foreign companies have tried to avoid the danger of being implicated in government human rights violations and repression by hiring private security companies.[14] In another set of high-profile incidents, such private forces also proved to be a source of danger to the civilian population and were accused of corruption.[15] In all these cases, the inequity of providing security to companies and their employees instead of local communities can become a significant source of grievance.

The business-and-conflict agenda: issue definition and agenda setting

The idea that foreign investment can contribute to instability and violence is nothing new. We can look at the history of the British East India Company for a well-known example from the past. In his recent historical survey, Litvin (2003) points out the commonalities across time and space in how companies that are reluctant to get entangled in local politics inevitably get caught up in local disputes, and in too many cases their actions make the situation worse. During the 1960s and 1970s, there was an outcry in the United States and elsewhere against corporate intervention in local politics in places like Guatemala and Chile. Extractive industry development, especially oil and mining,

---

business can continue. For example, the oil industry continued operating throughout the Angolan civil war because it was not a target of attack and most of the fighting was outside the oil-producing areas; see Berman (2000) for managers' views on conflict.

[13] There are conflicting reports about the degree of direct complicity by companies in these repressive operations. The definition of complicity in cases such as these is a subject of evolving practice; see Ramasastry (2002).

[14] For a thorough analysis of the global private security sector, see Avant (2005).

[15] There are disputes about the exact relationship between company managers and public and private security forces. Some within the companies defend themselves as unwitting accomplices in atrocities, while others accuse them of acting in full knowledge of the dangers of using any sort of security force in such an uncertain environment (Avant 2005).

was implicated in authoritarian repression, corruption, and instability (Karl 1997). After the end of the Cold War, there was widespread concern about what appeared to be an increase in civil conflict. Civil wars in Africa seemed to be enveloping greater numbers of people, spilling across borders, and defying all attempts to resolve the issues at stake. The Cold War competition for allies in the developing world had come to an end, and many rebel movements and governments had to seek new sources of financial support. This led to an expanded use of natural resources to provide the money for soldiers and guns.

The emergence of the business-and-conflict agenda in the 1990s started with the recognition that trade and investment contributed to intractable civil conflict. At this stage, the analysis could have stopped. Instead, however, some social entrepreneurs identified a culprit in these economic transactions: international firms. In the early 1990s, international NGOs such as Global Witness, Partnership Africa Canada, and others produced investigative reports on the role of commodities such as oil, diamonds, and timber (in addition to banks) in supporting continued conflict. The turn from identifying the problem to targeting the private sector as the solution was congruent with the emerging corporate social responsibility movement. The initial impetus toward a corporate social responsibility agenda can be traced back to the 1960s, but it gained speed with the anti-apartheid movement and its targeting of investors (Broad and Cavanagh 1998; Bendell 2004). While the anti-apartheid movement demonstrated the potential effectiveness of targeting multinational corporations, it was not until the 1990s that a real "movement" could be said to have emerged. Many groups active on issues of the environment, development, health, labor standards, and human rights began to develop guidelines, principles, and codes for multinational corporations to adopt. By the end of the 1990s, there were a variety of separate and disconnected campaigns against corporate misbehavior, as more and more advocacy organizations learned about the potential for social change through reforms to corporate behavior. It is against this background that the debate over corporate complicity in human rights abuses and continued conflict in developing countries emerged on the international agenda. Voices in the international community called for the withdrawal of corporations from investment in countries with illegitimate governments or unstable political environments, such as Burma and Sudan.

At the same time, the research community began to pay attention to economic factors in civil war. It produced scholarship on the so-called "resource curse" or the "paradox of plenty" (Karl 1997; deSoysa 2000; Auty 1994; Ross 1999 and 2004; Collier 2003a; Collier and Hoeffler 2000; Berdal and Malone 2000). Paul Collier (2003a) established a research program at the World Bank that was very influential in both academic and policy circles and helped establish conflict as an appropriate issue for the World Bank to address. He and his colleagues conducted empirical research indicating that the more a country is dependent on a single or small number of highly valuable commodities for a majority of its export revenues, the more likely it is to suffer from corruption and underdevelopment.[16] The International Peace Academy established a program on Economic Agendas in Civil Conflict and conducted a series of workshops and conferences on the topic that brought together scholars, policymakers, and activists, and produced a series of high-quality research publications (Ballentine and Sherman 2003; Ballentine and Nitzschke 2005). Over the next few years, many different academic and policy institutions would organize workshops and conferences on this topic.

The notion of bringing businesses into conflict-prevention efforts emerged primarily from activism over oil in Angola, diamonds in Sierra Leone, and the use of security forces in Nigeria and Colombia (Global Witness 1998 and 1999; Freeman 2000; Smillie *et al.* 2000). Norm entrepreneurs such as Global Witness highlighted in the global media the role of specific companies that profited from turmoil in Africa, especially from oil and diamonds. Global Witness and Partnership Africa Canada were particularly effective in helping launch the "blood diamonds" campaign. They sought to target consumers and persuade them not to buy diamonds because of their links to bloodshed and terror in West Africa.

Around this time, three NGOs produced a groundbreaking report that attempted to persuade the business community that active and direct involvement in ensuring peace was in their own self-interest. The

---

[16] Collier's work generated controversy, both from those who put more weight on issues of identity, such as ethnic and religious causes of conflict, and from those who challenged the empirical analysis and conclusions drawn from it. For instance, see Woodrow Wilson International Center for Scholars and International Peace Academy (2001); Fearon (2005).

Council for Economic Priorities, International Alert, and the Prince of Wales Business Leaders Forum (now the International Business Leaders Forum) cooperated to publish *The Business of Peace*, which set the agenda for the emerging interest in corporate conflict prevention. This report made the economic and moral case for why businesses should view conflict-prevention activities as financially sensible. International Alert established a program on business and conflict, engaged in and facilitated dialogue between oil companies and communities in places such as Azerbaijan, and produced a number of reports linking business action to conflict prevention (Banfield *et al.* 2003). Amnesty International, Human Rights Watch, Oxfam International, and other well-established human rights and development NGOs also began to set up programs linking business action to the prevention of human rights abuses, corruption, repression, and violence.

Interest in this topic was reinforced by the United Nations Global Compact, under which the business community committed to nine (now ten) principles drawn from UN conventions on the environment, labor, human rights, and anti-corruption. The UNGC was established by then Secretary-General Kofi Annan as a global tool to promote particular norms for the business community. Its very first policy dialogue addressed issues of business in zones of conflict. This topic was pushed to the top of the UNGC agenda by business leaders, particularly those in the diamond industry who were feeling the pressure of an effective activist campaign against "blood diamonds." The industry players were seeking a forum in which to explore their options and demonstrate a commitment to change. Although some leading diamond industry players were eager to participate in the UNGC dialogue, it was difficult to persuade other leading international companies – particularly American ones – of the value of this exercise. The eventual participants in this first policy dialogue included representatives from the private sector, other international organizations including the UNDP and World Bank, and NGOs. The NGOs initially defined the general problem, and it was at this forum that participants established a number of recommendations that have continued to be at the core of the business-and-conflict agenda to this day. These include the need for corporate transparency, particularly regarding financial payments to host governments; revenue management, in which businesses participate in ensuring that the revenues from natural resource development are utilized for public purposes; management of security in a way that protects human rights; and the development of "conflict-sensitive business practices," including the use of conflict impact assessments (United Nations Global Compact 2002).[17]

Some of the initial effort went into trying to persuade companies to undertake "conflict impact assessments." While foreign investors typically undertake an analysis of political risk to their own operations, there were calls for them to be proactive in assessing the impact of their operations on local political and social conditions. It has been surprisingly difficult to persuade companies to collect the data for such an assessment, let alone use it in strategic planning. Advocates believe that when company management understands the variety of channels through which its operations can impact a locality negatively, then preventive policies at the individual company level can be implemented. The UNGC and International Alert developed "toolkits" for systematic assessment to try to facilitate more widespread adoption of this practice.

The emergence of the broader business-and-conflict agenda encompassed a number of simultaneous strands. The first to gain traction addressed the need to control trade in commodities, with the "blood diamonds" issue gaining the most attention. Under pressure from a very effective campaign launched around 1998 that blamed the diamond sector for funding conflict in Sierra Leone, an initially reluctant diamond industry formed a new group – the World Diamond Council (WDC) – dedicated to ending the trade in conflict diamonds. Industry leaders, notably DeBeers, initially stonewalled and did not take the campaign seriously. Some industry leaders, however, realized the political environment had changed in ways that made the influence of transnational advocacy campaigns more apparent. They had the examples of other corporations that had been targeted on other issues: Nike on labor standards, the fur industry on animal cruelty, etc. The value of diamonds hinges so heavily on image and perception that some feared an extended campaign linking bloodshed to the gems would influence consumer buying habits.[18] In 2000, the WDC proposed to develop a certification system that would identify diamonds that did not come from conflict regions and were "legitimate." They proposed a

---

[17] Information was obtained by personal participation in UNGC meetings.
[18] The conflict diamond campaign threatened markets but did not actually have a huge impact on diamond sales.

chain-of-custody system that would track rough diamonds from the ground to the retail store to ensure that conflict diamonds did not enter legitimate market channels. In order to ensure this system would be viewed as legitimate and to increase its effectiveness, the WDC advocated the establishment of an intergovernmental system of export-import controls.

Given the importance of the diamond sector to its economy, South Africa launched negotiations with other diamond producers in May 2000 to develop a system of trade controls. The UN General Assembly passed a resolution later that year endorsing the establishment of a certification system for rough diamonds. After two years, producer governments, the diamond industry, and key NGOs reached consensus on what is known as the Kimberley Process Certification System (KPCS). KPCS members commit to export and import controls on diamonds and agree to oversight by other members, as well as two NGOs: Global Witness and Partnership Africa Canada. The KPCS integrates into its process the certification and chain-of-custody system developed by the diamond industry. Since its implementation, members have moved to strengthen oversight and have been willing to exclude participants who do not meet KPCS standards. The process has been undermined by diamond smuggling, corrupt officials, and violence in Zimbabwe. Nevertheless, it is credited with helping to cut off the flow of funds to rebels in Sierra Leone, thus facilitating the negotiation of a peace agreement there. While the KPCS has achieved a relatively high degree of institutionalization and acceptance, activists have been unable to gain support for similar certification systems for other conflict commodities, such as coltan and timber.

The issue of corruption was quickly linked to the business-and-conflict agenda, since corrupt leaders and their often supportive business allies helped undermine legitimate government. In the 1990s, activists and development specialists began to view corruption as a barrier to development and a precursor to social breakdown. Transparency International, an NGO dedicated to changing law and regulation regarding corruption issues, launched a highly successful campaign to "name and shame" countries by publishing its annual Corruption Perception Index of the most corrupt political environments. It promotes the negotiation of "integrity pacts" between business and government. In 1997, member states of the Organization for Economic Cooperation and Development (OECD) finally passed a Convention on Combating Bribery of Foreign Public Officials in International Business Transactions. The World Bank, as part of its program of good governance initiatives, began to incorporate anti-corruption elements into its development programs and has supported the idea that both government and the private sector need to provide more information to the public about commercial transactions.[19]

Increasingly, the payments made by oil and mining companies to host governments became a central target. Global Witness, whose key goal was "breaking the links between natural resources, conflict and corruption," was a key actor in arguing for transparency and responsible revenue management. It produced investigative reports detailing the links between oil revenues and conflict in places such as Angola and lobbied governments and international organizations to take action. A Canadian company, Talisman, came under intense public pressure regarding its participation in an oil development project in Sudan. The Sudanese government was fighting a civil war in the south, and oil development was both a source of conflict and a source of military finance. Talisman's CEO initially condemned the criticisms and refused to withdraw. Eventually, as the company's share prices declined in response to the barrage of bad publicity, it sold its share in the project to a Chinese-owned company. While the diamond case hinged on the potential action of consumers, in this case action by investors and the threat that the government of Canada would step in with regulations led Talisman to change its policy. In response to this incident, as well as similar ones involving the mining sector, the Canadian government became an active player in the business-and-conflict agenda, sponsoring research and debate at home and internationally.

The British government, under Tony Blair, made corporate social responsibility a key element of its foreign policy. It established a Corporate Citizenship Unit in the Foreign Office, and the Department for International Development provided support to organizations such as International Alert for research in this area. The British took the lead

---

[19] The anti-corruption drive by the World Bank divided policymakers concerned that the most disadvantaged people would be victims twice over: once by the corruption of their leaders, and again if the World Bank cut off its aid. Anti-corruption efforts were further undermined when World Bank President Wolfensohn, a champion of the program, came under fire for corruption himself.

in promoting transparency in revenue payments through the Extractive Industries Transparency Initiative (EITI), announced in 2002 at the World Conference on Sustainable Development. This policy effort targeted host governments to persuade them to be more transparent about natural resource revenues and where the money goes. Although initially a UK initiative, over time it has built up support and now has twenty countries that have committed to or are implementing its principles, though with varying levels of success and enthusiasm. EITI has established a Secretariat and has sought to become more institutionalized. Unlike the Kimberley Process, however, EITI relies more on voluntary action by governments and does not directly target industry. As a counterpart, the Publish What You Pay Campaign, launched with the support of George Soros, combines the efforts of more than a hundred NGOs that seek to pressure companies directly to make public their payments to host governments.

The entire area of revenue management, going well beyond transparency, became a subject of concern. Scholars, policy analysts, and development practitioners studied the models of "good" oil revenue management in places such as Norway and Alaska. These model systems typically required transparency about the amount of oil development and revenue; established a fund for future generations; and made commitments regarding the distribution of revenues to support social welfare and equitable development. The goal was to avoid the resource curse and the macroeconomic distortions known as "Dutch disease."[20] The question was whether such models could be transported to states that were desperately poor, generally undemocratic, corrupt, and not genuinely committed to any of the elements of such a model. The need for a new way of doing business took on more import as the international petroleum industry began to explore for oil in some of the most unprepossessing corners of the world: Sudan, Chad, and Equatorial Guinea.[21]

---

[20] The "resource curse" refers to the ways in which natural resource wealth undermines broader development and fosters corruption and conflict.

[21] In a report by the Overseas Development Institute and the UN Development Programme (UNDP) in 2006, they list twelve countries in Africa alone that can expect to receive windfall revenues from commodity price increases; see Overseas Development Institute and United Nations Development Programme (2006).

The first attempt at implementing such a model in a poor country occurred during this time period, as part of the project to develop a gas pipeline from Chad to Cameroon. Oil had been discovered in Chad in the early 1970s, and a consortium of foreign oil company investors led by Esso (now ExxonMobil) conducted exploration and planning. Decades of civil unrest and the challenges of working within a multi-ethnic state were viewed as barriers to development at first. However, the oil majors were all looking for new sources of oil and began seriously to consider development in Chad in the 1990s. In order to manage political, social, and environmental risks, Exxon began consultations with communities beginning in 1993 and initiated work with the World Bank. The consortium leaders realized that revenues from this project could destabilize the corrupt and weak regime in Chad, and perhaps in Cameroon as well, and that the violence would not be good for business. At the same time, international activists were warning of the inevitability of political breakdown and the destruction of the natural environment, mobilizing a "green" consortium to oppose it. But by 1997, the World Bank had committed to participate in the project.

This would be a huge project, estimated initially at $3 billion. The major consortium partners were Esso/ExxonMobil, Shell, and Elf, which would finance about 70 percent of the project. Another large percentage would come from the International Finance Corporation, along with export credit agencies in the United States and France and commercial banks. The World Bank would contribute only about 3 percent of the pipeline costs, but it established conditions for the disbursement of the loan (*Petroleum Economist* 1998). The oil companies looked upon World Bank participation as critical to managing the risks they faced. The Bank insisted on environmental assessments prior to investment, and the companies were willing to apply the same standards in Chad that they would apply in a developed country (*Financial Times* 1997). Although initial opposition to the project centered on environmental and resettlement concerns, as the situation in Chad and surrounding countries deteriorated over the course of the 1990s, increasing concern was voiced about human rights abuses, corruption, and the potential for war. The World Bank was under pressure from activists, who had been campaigning against World Bank programs and were particularly vocal in opposing Bank financing for major oil development projects such as this one. The Bank staff supporting this project viewed a revenue management plan for the Chad–Cameroon pipeline project as an innovative way to promote responsible development and address critics' concerns.

The most onerous conditions were contained in a revenue management plan. Once the companies paid the taxes, fees, and royalties they owed the government, they were willing to go along with World Bank conditions on the use of those payments by the Chadian government. There were still many voices opposing this plan, including some World Bank staff, who held it up in 1998 over continuing environmental concerns. Nevertheless, the Chadian government passed a law institutionalizing the revenue management plan in 1998. Under this plan, 10 percent would be saved for future generations, 80 percent would go into a separate account (not controlled by the government) for health, education, welfare, and development projects, and 5 percent would go for special development in the oil-producing region. The development account was established in London, managed by an NGO, and overseen by an "International Advisory Group" of eminent persons, from both Chad and elsewhere. This group would monitor the use of pipeline profits and ensure transparency regarding oil production and revenue streams.

Implementation was nearly derailed, however, when the Bank hesitated to provide a final commitment, and then the oil companies themselves hesitated about whether to go forward. Shell and Elf did in fact withdraw from the consortium in 1999, citing economic concerns. The project teetered on the edge, generating heated opposition from NGOs and "green" politicians in Europe, targeting the World Bank as much as the companies. Other central African states, however, expressed solidarity with Chad and urged the Bank to go forward with its plan. Throughout 2000, the World Bank wavered regarding final approval, even as Chevron and Petronas replaced Shell and Elf in the oil development consortium. The Board of the World Bank finally voted to approve the project in 2000. The pipeline was built, and revenues began flowing. However, the Chadian government consistently tried to undermine external oversight and claim a larger percentage of the revenues. When it tried to change the law that underlies the revenue management plan, the World Bank ended its programs in Chad; after months of negotiations, the relationship was resumed and the revenue management plan remained in place. It is not clear whether this can be a model for other projects. Oil exploration and development in other equally unstable environments is going forward, but despite concerns about the resource curse, nothing like the Chad revenue management plan has been attempted elsewhere.[22]

One final issue became a key element of the business-and-conflict agenda: corporate security arrangements. Most foreign investment in extractive industries involves negotiations and contracts with the host government, which often require them to rely upon the government for protection. In some cases, observers accused host governments' military and police forces of violating the human rights of ordinary civilians and using corporate resources (helicopters, for instance) to violently attack local communities (in places such as Nigeria and Colombia). A few companies sought to avoid such entanglements by hiring private security companies but found themselves partnering with organizations that were accused of fraud, human rights abuses, drug running, and human trafficking. They – and often their home governments – came under critical pressure for the way in which corporate security conflicted with the protection and human rights of local communities.

In response, the US and UK governments facilitated a dialogue among extractive industries and NGOs on security and human rights issues. The goal was to develop international voluntary norms for hiring security forces, both public and private. In 2000, they announced the adoption of the US–UK Voluntary Principles on Human Rights and Security by a small core group of countries and companies. The Voluntary Principles have not been widely adopted, but they are slowly being incorporated into some contracts and laws. The initial group has slowly expanded and has tried to become more institutionalized by establishing a steering committee and holding regular meetings. A recent effort to tighten oversight mechanisms led to intense negotiations, with a number of companies unwilling to make deeper commitments than they originally had. But the system is still in place and taking on more significance, particularly given rising popular concern over the actions of private security forces.

---

[22] The oil development law for Iraq, as currently discussed, will have some features of a revenue management plan. Which regions within the country will control the oil fields and how the revenues will be distributed regionally are at the core of Iraqi political decisions over oil development.

Conclusion: setting the agenda for business

The turn toward a corporate role in conflict prevention came from twin governance failures: the failure of governments to resolve violent and bloody conflict in the developing world, and the failure to regulate the negative impact of trade and investment on conflict. But in assigning companies this new role, the harshest critics of corporations may have given the private sector new authority in the arena of conflict and security. The debate over corporations and conflict is one which evolved within a remarkably short period – from approximately 1998 to 2002, when most of the initiatives described above had been instigated. The issue was defined by an assortment of NGOs addressing peace and conflict prevention, human rights, and humanitarian concerns. The agenda was set – and then expanded – by them with the support of the United Nations (especially the UN Global Compact), a handful of donor governments and key exporting states, and a few leading corporations. Rules were negotiated by a variety of actors at the local, national, regional, and international levels and within both the public (state and intergovernmental) and private sectors. Implementation has been primarily a task for a reluctant private sector in partnership with states, IOs, and NGOs. In most cases, monitoring has been sustained by NGOs and intergovernmental organizations. Although it was not described in detail here, the enforcement and adjudication of the rules have been contested by the private sector and its critics.

This very brief overview tells a story about how an old issue became defined in new ways. Setting agendas and creating issues is a central piece of governance, as noted by Avant *et al.* in the introductory chapter. In this case, these processes assigned corporations a more prominent role and authority over the governance of conflict. We can trace this back to NGOs that essentially began to transfer the ideas of corporate social responsibility from the environmental, labor, and human rights fields into the debate over the role of corporations in conflict zones, extending learning from one issue area to the next.[23] The appropriate sites of contestation and access for addressing the

---

[23] The characterization of this as an extension of corporate social responsibility (CSR) is contested by some analysts, who argue that corporate *security* responsibility of companies is very different from traditional social responsibility. See, for instance, Banfield *et al.* (2003); Wolf and Engert (2005).

corporate role in conflict were not at first very clear, and activists engaged in an evolving strategy to establish this on the international agenda. They brought in a widening array of other actors to propel this agenda forward, and found receptive ears in the halls of the UN and in a handful of donor governments. As was noted in the introduction to this volume, the relationships among the actors are key to understanding evolving forms of governance.

What is striking is the range of governors involved, the diversity of "triggers" for the new governance initiatives, and the different governance mechanisms and rules they produced. "Name and shame" activism was involved in all cases but had particular impact in the cases of Talisman, blood diamonds, and the security principles. The revenue management mechanisms in Chad–Cameroon and EITI essentially built upon these and earlier activism. Rules and standards were established in both the Voluntary Principles case and EITI, but only diamonds developed an extensive certification system and legal framework. The Chad–Cameroon case is the only one where an international organization took the lead; in EITI and the Voluntary Principles, and to some extent Talisman, particular governments pushed the issue forward: the United Kingdom, the United States, and Canada. The private sector was instrumental in the diamond case, but much more passive in all the other instances.

The ultimate aim of those supporting this agenda is to create more peaceful societies with an equitable distribution of natural resource wealth and improved governance. This is the goal of the NGOs, donor governments, and international organizations. The companies involved in conflict-prevention initiatives see it as contributing to an improved ability to manage their political risks and reputation, gaining "cover" for their operations in failed states. The hope of those advocating this agenda is that it will be a win-win situation for states, societies, and companies. But who loses? Corrupt local leaders clearly lose, as do rebels attempting to finance the takeover of government. Another set of losers is those who oppose natural resource development projects: local communities that might be devastated by depletion and degradation of their environment; those displaced by major project development; and those who do not believe that any of these initiatives will reduce corruption, inequity, and instability. Finally, the losers include those who oppose the transfer of some authority over conflict and security issues to the private sector. For them, sovereignty and legitimacy lie with either the government or the people of the country involved.

The public sector has not completely abdicated its role in international governance on conflict and security issues. All of these new mechanisms include a significant role for public authorities, either governments or international organizations, and they often include the direct participation of civil society representatives. In other words, these are all about a business role in governance of conflict and security issues, but the business role is narrowly defined. In fact, most participants agree that the private sector cannot legitimately act alone in these areas and requires some sort of partnership with other more legitimate actors – states, international organizations, and NGOs. The authority of nonstate actors in this arena remains tentative and has not been fully institutionalized or accepted. More importantly, their willingness to be a part of governance arrangements will remain a source of weakness that may lead to their breakdown in the future.

5 International organization control under conditions of dual delegation: a transgovernmental politics approach

ABRAHAM L. NEWMAN

Domestic officials increasingly play a decisive role in international affairs. States, for example, appoint oversight committees (for example, comitology, congressional supervision, or regulators groups) to monitor the behavior of international organizations (IOs) (Pollack 1997 and 2003). While such committees are frequently studied as mechanisms that track delegated authority, this chapter examines how and why the introduction of such actors may open up the possibility for new governors to emerge, altering the very terms of global governance.

Existing research tends to take two dominant views of these committees. From the principal–agent perspective, they serve as a "police patrol" that represents state interests. They report to national executives on excessive international organization activism, reining in such behavior. Research from the constructivist strain has argued, by contrast, that international cooperation socializes participants, undermining ties to national interests (Joerges and Neyer 1997; Wessels 1998). Over time, then, oversight committees come to reflect the preferences of international bureaucracies. Empirically, there is evidence to support both claims. In some cases, oversight committees have dutifully fulfilled their delegated role. But in others, they have become loyal defenders of their international organizations. Neither argument has developed a theoretical framework that satisfactorily explains variation in oversight outcomes.

Building on the insights from transgovernmental theory (Keohane and Nye 1974; Slaughter 2004), I argue that this variation can be understood by making two additional assumptions: states are not unitary actors but are composed of multiple sub-state units and these sub-state units have their own preferences distinct from national executives. International oversight, then, takes place in an environment

131

of dual delegation, whereby states have simultaneously delegated to international organizations and to sub-state actors. Using transgovernmental politics as an alternative starting point, I construct a deductive model that generates clear hypotheses as to when oversight bodies should act to rein in IO activism and when they should encourage it. Employing delegated, expert, and principled authority, oversight bodies can carve out a place in potential coalitions with states, IOs, or other sub-state or nonstate actors. Rather than being an appendage of states or IOs, these transgovernmental actors can reinvent their governing role, becoming an important global governor. This chapter, then, highlights the agency of global governors. Significantly, governors may actively forge authority-based coalitions that can increase their independence and influence.

In addition to explaining variation in international oversight effectiveness, the chapter builds on a long-dormant line of transgovernmental theory emphasizing the coalitional interaction of international organizations and sub-state actors. In their seminal work, Keohane and Nye (1974) speculated about such interactions, specifically the ability of transgovernmental actors to form alliances that could shape international organization politics. Recent work, however, has stressed the capacity of transgovernmental actors to work through policy coordination to conduct global governance. Acting through informal networks, sub-state actors have the ability to harmonize standards, share information, and cooperate on enforcement, creating a fast and flexible solution to cumbersome global governance problems (Slaughter 2000; Raustiala 2002). This chapter complements this work by focusing on transgovernmental coalitions – the political interdependencies, tensions, and synergies between transgovernmental networks and international organizations (Newman 2008b; Eberlein and Newman 2008; Alter 1998; Thurner *et al.* 2005).

More generally, it digs into complex issues of delegation that emerge in global governance and underscores the unexpected and unintended alliances that can form as multiple global governors interact. In contrast to principal–agent arguments, which follow a clear instrumental logic of implementation oversight, the transgovernmental perspective blurs the arbitrary distinctions between agenda setting, rulemaking, and implementation. At the same time, it underscores the importance of preexisting domestic institutional bargains for global governance, challenging a purely functionalist explanation for the dynamics of dual delegation. These dynamics are then highly dependent on the varying levels of authority enjoyed by the web of international organizations and transgovernmental actors as they engage with the demands of national executives.

The chapter is organized around four sections. First, I present the control dilemma that states face as they delegate to international organizations. This section presents in more detail the oversight mechanisms that states deploy to rein in international organization activism. The second section builds the deductive model that explains variation in oversight committee outcomes. After presenting the logic behind the model, I offer a set of empirical expectations. The third section scrutinizes the argument in the case of data privacy in the European Union. Starting in 1997, the member states of the European Union agreed to create a cooperative body comprising national data privacy regulators to monitor supranational policymaking. The case offers a least likely case for a monitoring failure under the existing principal–agent perspective as data privacy is grounded in long-fought national civil liberties traditions. Additionally, because the group regularly publishes its revealed policy preferences, an empirical record exists to scrutinize the chapter's claim. The fourth and final section of the chapter examines the more general implications of the argument for questions of IO cooperation and transgovernmental politics.

International organization autonomy and state control

Since the end of World War II, states have turned to international organizations as a cornerstone of global governance. National governments have agreed to create centralized and independent bureaucracies working to resolve conflict and promote cooperation at the international level. Such delegation has accelerated in the past twenty years across a broad range of issue areas including financial regulation, security cooperation, and health and safety preparedness. Research on international cooperation has identified a number of justifications for such delegation including globalization, deregulation, new technology, and the end of the bipolar world order (Avant, Finnemore, and Sell, this volume). Despite the diversity of justifications, no one doubts the explosion of these global governance institutions.

The delegation of authority to international organizations by states poses an important control challenge (Nielson and Tierney 2003).

As international organizations evolve, the threat of bureaucratic drift emerges. That is to say, these organizations develop independent preferences from the governments that created them, and they assert these preferences in international debates. The ability of these institutions to achieve their goals is then a function of a number of factors, including the extent of delegated power, their rational-legal foundations, moral authority, and expertise (Barnett and Finnemore 2004). Confronted by international organizations endowed with a range of power resources, states may lose control of the agenda-setting process or the monitoring and oversight of international agreements.

Given the possibility that international organizations may deviate from their original mandate, scholars in the rational institutional tradition have focused on the design mechanisms available to states to minimize bureaucratic drift (Hawkins *et al.* 2006). Borrowing from principal–agent theory, research has demonstrated that when states (i.e., the principal) delegate authority to international organizations (i.e., the agent) they have an incentive to construct monitoring mechanisms to alert them if their agents go astray (Pollack 2002; Dogan 1997; Franchino 2000). The major dilemma facing most principals is that, while they want their agents to follow their original mandates, the cost of monitoring is quite high. Principals often lack the expertise necessary to identify bureaucratic drift, and direct oversight presents high costs in terms of time and resources.

According to instrumental theories, principals devise institutional mechanisms that reduce the cost of monitoring and rein in bureaucratic drift. One of the most common forms of this arm's-length oversight is "police patrols" (McCubbins and Schwartz 1987; Shipan 2004). Principals may appoint committees to oversee agent activities and then report back to a broader set of principals. These "police patrols" develop expertise in their particular monitoring area and reduce the burden of oversight. Nations often construct committees of national representatives to oversee the activities of international organizations, creating police patrols for this international setting.

While this literature has made an important contribution to our understanding of state control within the context of delegation to international organizations, considerable empirical evidence casts doubt on the argument. Within the context of European Union governance, where the most detailed studies on the topic have been conducted, empirical findings demonstrate that police patrol committees have often failed to identify bureaucratic drift (Joerges and Neyer 1997). In fact, committees of national representatives have frequently sided with the European Commission, which is the ultimate example of an international agent. Some researchers suggest that this monitoring failure results from a socialization process, whereby the members of such oversight committees adapt their preferences through their interactions with international organizations (Wessels 1998; Egeberg 1999; Jachtenfuchs 2001). This explanation, however, is still unsatisfying as it cannot account for variation in oversight. The theory would expect that, given a similar level of interaction, representatives would uniformly move toward the preferences of the international agents over time. Additionally, empirical work has cast considerable doubt on the ability of the socialization hypothesis to explain this behavior (Hooghe 2005).

Dual delegation and transgovernmental politics

This chapter builds a model that addresses the outstanding empirical concerns by complicating the control relationship. In short, the model recognizes the fact that the monitoring mechanisms employed by states to check international bureaucratic discretion rely on the work of additional agents. While international relations literature has increasingly examined the role that multiple principals play in altering the dynamics of global governance (Nielson and Tierney 2003), it too has often assumed that oversight institutions share the preferences of state executives.

The model therefore makes two additional assumptions derived from the transgovernmental politics literature, which produce a set of testable expectations. First, states are not unitary actors. They comprise multiple sub-state actors including ministry bureaucrats, independent regulatory agencies, judges, and parliamentarians. While early international relations theories assumed away such complexity, changes in technology, organizational behavior, and levels of interdependence challenge the credibility of such a position. Large literatures on global governance and transgovernmental actors highlight the need to integrate sub-state actors into theories of international affairs (Milner 1998; Slaughter 2004; Risse-Kappan 1995). Additionally, as states have moved from Keynesian demand management to arm's-length regulatory oversight, the number of sub-state officials has proliferated.

The institutional complement of the domestic regulatory state is a host of agencies, administrative bodies, and ombudsmen (Gilardi 2005).

Second, I assume that these sub-state actors develop independent preferences from their national principals. Extensive work from the fields of American and comparative politics has demonstrated that executive agencies (i.e., agents) forge preferences distinct from national parliaments (i.e., the principals) (Carpenter 2001; Goodman 1991; Wood 1988). No reason exists to assume such preference development would be less likely to occur in a policy space dominated by international concerns. In fact, there are a number of reasons why this preference differential should be accentuated in the foreign policy realm. As many of these agencies were created primarily with domestic concerns in mind, national executives often have fewer monitoring tools to examine the behavior of transgovernmental actors. The US federal government, for example, could not have predicted the extensive international activities of the Securities and Exchange Commission when it was founded in response to the Great Depression. Additionally, appointments to sub-state agencies often reflect left–right domestic cleavages, while transgovernmental activities typically reflect other political dimensions. At the same time, sub-state actors are independent and autonomous from international organizations and thus their preferences will not automatically converge. In short, sub-state actors become potential coalition partners for international organizations but hold no strict loyalty to them (Trondal and Veggeland 2003; Alter 1998).

The model then raises two logical questions: what do sub-state units want and when can they assert themselves? Drawing on work from organizational theory that has been applied in both national and international contexts, I argue that these actors derive their preferences from their bureaucratic culture (Carpenter 2001; Barnett and Finnemore 2004). The organization's mission, standard operating procedures, and professional staffing help shape the set of policy goals (both intentional and unintentional) that it pursues. The environment in which bureaucrats work affects what they want. Such bureaucratic culture is the product of ongoing institutional reproduction, which is typically quite resistant to change. It is important to note that these preferences do not necessarily reflect the goals of national executives at the time, as bureaucratic interests develop through long-term historical interactions (Skowronek 1982; Pierson 2004).

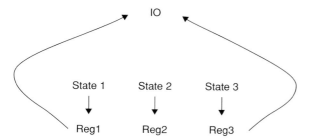

Figure 5.1 Dual delegation in global governance

Just because such actors have developed their own preferences does not mean that they will be able to assert them in international control debates. Sub-state actors have a number of potential power resources at their disposal, including expertise, authority delegated at the national level, and network ties to other regulators and constituents (Newman 2008a). In contrast to national executives, these sub-state units often have a far greater technical grasp of the activities being conducted by international organizations. They also have a variety of delegated authorities over national markets, ranging from public shaming to control over market access. Finally, they gain legitimacy through their interconnections with parallel sub-units from other countries and regulated groups. A statement by the securities and exchange commissioners of the world has far more legitimacy than one by the Commission of Spain. Combined, these power resources transform transgovenmental actors into additional players in the control equation. As with the case of preferences development, the availability of such resources is frequently historically determined by the state-building process and is adjustable to momentary circumstances (Pierson 2004). The expertise-based or delegated authority of an institution is largely determined by its institutional design and previous day-to-day operations. Variation in these authority resources, then, conditions its ability to play an independent role.

State oversight of international organizations occurs within the context of dual delegation. States simultaneously cede authority to institutions above and below the nation-state, each of which has unique preferences and resources to achieve its goals. The monitoring of international agents is conducted not by the principal but by committees comprising subnational agents (see Figure 5.1).

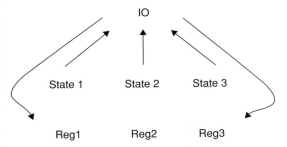

Figure 5.2 Daisy-chain delegation in global governance

Further complicating actor allegiances, sub-state actors (e.g., Reg1, Reg2, Reg3 in the figures) who monitor international organizations often implement policy for international organizations. In this daisy-chain of delegation, states not only delegate up to international organizations and down to sub-state officials but international organizations then delegate again to sub-state officials. This form of daisy-chain delegation is depicted in Figure 5.2.

Integrating these assumptions into existing models of international organization control, I shift the focus of the debate from institutional monitoring mechanisms to the preferences and capacities of the monitoring agent. The relative preference alignment between the international organization (IO), the national executive (NE), and the monitoring agent (MA) will influence the degree of autonomy enjoyed by the international organization. To simplify the model, I assume only one monitoring agent with the resources to assert its interests and a unidimensional preference array.[1]

I then construct a set of three preference arrays. I intentionally chose three extreme possibilities to accentuate the implications of the model's assumptions. The first case exists when the monitoring agent's preferences are identical to those of the national executive. This is also identical to the status quo assumption made by those who employ rational institutional theory to understand control in the international setting. Here, the monitoring agent will serve as a police patrol,

---

[1] Both of these conditions will be problematized in future work. The goal of this chapter, however, is to amend current theory first before moving too stridently into untested theoretical ground.

Figure 5.3 Preference array for police patrol

Figure 5.4 Preference array for IO ally

Figure 5.5 Preference array for tattle tale

warning national executives of excessive bureaucratic drift by international organizations.

In a second case, the monitoring agent's preferences fall nearer to those of the international organization than to those of the national executive. Monitoring agents will have a weak incentive to report on international organizations and may even report the activity of national executives to international organizations. In short, the information stream may be reversed by monitoring agencies, creating a blowback for national principals. In such cases, the sub-state actor serves to facilitate international organization autonomy. In an important difference from socialization models, the monitoring agent may share a policy preference with an IO for different underlying reasons.

Finally, in a third set of cases, the preferences of national executives and international organizations may align while monitoring agencies may have divergent preferences. In these cases, the monitoring agency serves as a "tattle tale," alerting third parties, the news media, and other political organizations to the activities of the national executive and the international organization. As a result, international organizations and national executives become constrained by the behavior of sub-state actors.

The transgovernmental approach offers expectations that explain variation in monitoring outcomes. In addition to the two primary outcomes identified in existing literature (police patrol and international organization ally), the model predicts a third outcome, tattle tale. The amended model then provides an explanation for considerable descriptive work that has identified links between sub-state actors and third parties such as nongovernmental organizations, multinational corporations, and other international organizations.

In the following section, I use two analytic narratives to demonstrate the importance of integrating the dual delegation assumptions into explanations of international organization control. In each, I take the police patrol hypothesis as the null and then test it against the expectations generated in the transgovernmental politics model. The narratives scrutinize the competing hypotheses within two politically charged policy decisions involving the regulation of data privacy by the European Union. I chose the European Union as the site for the exploration as it has been used in a number of leading studies examining the issue in question. I therefore hold constant, with previous studies, many institutional and environmental factors that affect questions of international organizational control. The chapter focuses on the area of data privacy as it offers the empirical evidence necessary to test the derived expectations. Many committees in the European Union are quite opaque. While national voting patterns are often discernible, few records indicate the actual participants and their institutional affiliation. In the case of data privacy, the Article 29 Working Party is composed of national regulatory agencies with considerable independence from their national executives. Additionally, the regulation of data privacy creates shifting and cross-cutting cleavages in the multilevel governance setting. There is no clear "national" vs "supranational" position or clear left–right partisanship. The narratives allow for considerable variation in the preferences of the actors involved, permitting an evaluation of the dual delegation hypotheses. The narrative begins by presenting a brief introduction to the field of data privacy regulation in the European Union, which is then followed by an examination of specific committee oversight over telecommunications data retention and airline passenger data records.

Shifting institutional alliances in the field of data privacy

Background and institutional map

Before analyzing the politics of control, it is important to introduce the policy domain of data privacy. The regulation of the collection and use of personal information started in the 1970s, when national governments first implemented computer technology. To prevent the abuse of new databanks, legislatures in many European countries passed rules that required public and private organizations to follow a basic set of fair information practice principles concerning personal data (Bennett 1992; Hondius 1975). These data privacy laws created new regulatory institutions – data privacy authorities – that monitor the implementation and enforcement of such legislation. Data privacy authorities are independent agencies that enjoy considerable autonomy from their national executives. While the exact institutional designs differ, they often have separate budgets, extended leadership tenure, and discretion over personnel. Data privacy authorities conduct a diverse set of functions: they receive and investigate citizen complaints, advise the government and parliament on emerging data privacy issues, and regulate the cross-border exchange of personal data (Flaherty 1989).

In 1995, the European Union adopted a data privacy directive, which elevated the issue of data privacy to the supranational level. Divergent rules across the member states had created serious frictions. Prior to the adoption of the directive, a third of the member states had no privacy regulations in place. Data privacy authorities from high-regulatory countries began to block the transmission to other member states, threatening the emerging internal market (Newman 2008a). The directive harmonized rules across the member states and created an extraterritorial provision, which bans the transfer of personal data from Europe to countries that fail to maintain "adequate" privacy regulations (Farrell 2003).

Institutionally, the 1995 directive created two oversight committees that monitor the implementation and enforcement of the directive. The Article 31 Committee comprises national member-state government representatives and oversees the Commission's implementation of the directive. Reflecting daisy-chain delegation, most of the directive is implemented at the national level by domestic data protection supervisors and therefore the Article 31 Committee has a rather limited mandate. It is most active in international negotiations between the Commission and other countries.

The second committee, and the focus of this investigation, is the Article 29 Working Party. The Working Party comprises representatives from national data privacy authorities. It has a secretariat that is funded by the European Commission and is located in Brussels. The Working Party has a broad mandate to advise the Commission on emerging data privacy concerns facing the EU, make recommendations regarding the implementation and enforcement of the directive, and evaluate the adequacy of levels of protection in countries outside the EU (Newman 2008b). The Working Party regularly releases opinions and recommendations that make its preferences on European data privacy policy quite transparent.

From a principal–agent perspective, the Article 29 Working Party contains those national representatives with the proper expertise to advise the Commission and monitor its behavior. This perspective assumes that the Article 29 Working Party would serve as a police patrol, reporting back on Commission behavior to national executives. Research suggests that the creation of the Working Party was a result of member-state concerns that the Commission would garner too much power under the new regulations (Bignami 2005).

Forcing the unitary state assumption, which is often used in international relations literature, on to the principal–agent model, which is derived in the American and comparative subfields, however, obscures several critical features of the relationship. First, the Working Party may develop preferences distinct from national governments. National data privacy agencies are often staffed by politically active lawyers who want to check the expansion of power and surveillance in society. Their mission is to balance the interests of organizations that hope to exploit data with the privacy concerns of citizens. Generally, they see themselves as filling an important advocacy void for citizens who would not otherwise be able to defend their privacy interests. Since data privacy agencies often defy their national governments domestically, it is logical that the same independent streak might emerge at the international level.

Second, data privacy authorities enjoy substantial authority. They are independent agencies that have been delegated the authority to monitor the collection and use of personal information. Many agencies have the power to sanction inappropriate cross-border transfers of data. Since their inception in the 1970s, these agencies have built considerable expertise in the domain. Staffed by activist lawyers, they are among the few technical resources for governments and businesses seeking to understand the policy domain. As a transgovernmental network, the Article 29 Working Party has come to enjoy considerable institutional authority. Increasingly, international business, media, and government officials refer to the Working Party as the European data privacy regulator.[2]

Third, the Working Party is an example of daisy-chain delegation, complicating traditional notions of delegation. The members of the Working Party have been delegated the authority to oversee national regulation by their national executives. At the same time, the directive delegates to the Working Party the authority to monitor and harmonize supranational implementation. The following narratives demonstrate the implications of adopting the dual delegation assumption for the politics of global governance.

The data retention debate: monitoring communication

The surveillance of telecommunications is a highly sensitive issue touching upon cross-cutting concerns of national security, economic competitiveness, and civil liberties. Starting at the turn of the twenty-first century, this issue was elevated to the supranational level as member states began calling for data retention legislation at the European level. Data retention legislation requires communications firms to store all customer data for a given period of time. The intent of these regulations is to guarantee access to such archived data for police and security organizations. It differs from a data preservation regime, wherein police authorities can request data records for an individual once that individual has been identified as a criminal suspect. With the explosion of digital networks, national security organizations pressed for

---

[2] For example, a recent article in the *International Herald Tribune* discussing an Article 29 Working Party investigation, titled "EU Panel to Question US Spying on Banks" (September 26, 2006, p. 4). Similarly, an article in the *Washington Post* discussing a recent opinion of the Working Party reads "IP Addresses are Personal Data, EU Regulator Says" (January 22, 2008, p. D1).

data retention legislation as a mechanism to bolster their criminal investigations (Schwartz 2003).

The debate over data retention offers an important window into a discussion of global governance, highlighting the multiple players involved, their diverging preferences, and the interaction of complicated delegation chains. National executives, most vocally represented by their national security apparatus and their ministries of the interior, feared that existing data privacy legislation would hamper their ability to guarantee security in a world marked by digital networks and transnational terrorism. Supranational cooperation was important for two reasons. First, many of the strongest advocates of data retention from the security community feared that other member states would not pass legislation. This risked incomplete data trails for criminals who increasingly operate across national boundaries. Second, even some of the most vocal national executive supporters of data retention faced strong opposition at home to their proposals. In the United Kingdom, prior to the European initiative, the government was forced to compromise and enact a voluntary system. A coalition of member-state governments thus looked to supranational cooperation as a mechanism to harmonize retention standards across the member states and to overcome domestic opposition. Belgium offered an initial proposal for four years of data retention in 2002 that was circulated among the member states. It was not until 2004 that an official draft was submitted to the Council of Ministers, which called for mandatory retention of up to three years.[3]

The European Commission greeted such proposals with caution.[4] As its central mission had long focused on the integration of internal markets, the Commission did not want to enact rules that might weaken the competitive position of companies within the European Union. The communications industry was strongly opposed to retention rules, as they imposed new storage requirements. Preexisting data privacy rules limited the ability of telecommunications firms to

---

[3] See Council of the European Union, *Draft Framework Decision on the retention of data processed and stored in connection with the provision of public communications networks for the purpose of prevention, investigation, detection and prosecution of crime and criminal offences including terrorism* (Brussels: European Union, 2004).

[4] See Tatum Anderson, "Major European Institutions Divided on Data Retention," *Telecom Markets*, February 22, 2005: online.

use such data for their own purposes; thus retention implied a set of new responsibilities without new business opportunities.[5] Trade associations estimated that the cost of such legislation would reach hundreds of millions of euros.[6] Additionally, the Commission was ultimately responsible for overseeing the privacy directive, which guaranteed a high level of protection. The Commission, then, entered the debate concerned with how such legislation might affect competitiveness and civil liberties within the Union. The first draft legislation written by the Commission reflected these concerns and proposed a year of mandatory retention, including a number of data privacy provisions.

Far from monitoring and reporting on the behavior of the Commission to national executives, the Article 29 Working Party lobbied the Commission extensively to restrain the proposal of the member states. As early as 2002, as national executives began discreetly to circulate retention proposals, the Working Party condemned such an effort. The Working Party released a set of opinions arguing that retention should be for no longer than six months and that such data should still fall under protections guaranteed under data privacy legislation.[7] The Working Party called on the Commission to respect data privacy rights within the Union. Drawing on its legal expertise in data privacy issues, the Working Party argued that the Council's initiative violated the European Charter of Human Rights and required

[5] See International Chamber of Commerce, *Common Industry Statement on Storage of Traffic Data for Law Enforcement Purposes* (Brussels, 2003).

[6] The German Telecommunications Association (BITKOM) conducted a study that forecast this cost of retention. See *Frankfurter Allgemeine Zeitung*, "Telekom-Branche gegen Datensammler," September 23, 2004, p. 13.

[7] The Commissioners released a statement at the International Conference of Data Protection Commissioners that concluded, "Where traffic data are to be retained in specific cases, there must therefore be a demonstrable need, the period of retention must be as short as possible and the practice must be clearly regulated by law, in a way that provides sufficient safeguards against unlawful access and any other abuse. Systematic retention of all kinds of traffic data for a period of one year of more would be clearly disproportionate and therefore unacceptable in any case." See Article 29 Data Protection Working Party, *Opinion 5/2002 on the Statement of the European Data Protection Commissioners at the International Conference in Cardiff on mandatory systematic retention of telecommunications traffic data* (Brussels: European Union, 2002), p. 3.

a disproportionate level of data retention. Not only did this governor actively lobby at the supranational level, but the national regulatory agencies also expressed their opposition in national parliaments. The German data privacy commissioners, for example, called
on the national legislature to resist the German government's support
for the EU proposal.[8] After the terrorist attacks in the United Kingdom and Spain, the Working Party moderated its position slightly
but still argued that retention should not exceed one year, once again
citing the basic privacy principles enshrined in the directive.[9] The arguments developed by the Working Party were taken up by many players in the policy debate, including the European Parliament and the
Commission.

As the legislation entered its final phase of negotiation, the national
executives found no support from the Working Party. In fact, the
Working Party position, which had been developed over the course of
several years, more closely resembled that of the Commission. Despite
the convergence in policy goals, this was no simple case of socialization
in so far as the justifications of the two bodies differed dramatically.
The Working Party argued for the protection of civil liberties while
the Commission argued for ensuring economic competitiveness. Thus
instead of an international socialization process, the two parties came
to the negotiations with distinct reasons derived from their unique
bureaucratic cultures. The final bill struck a delicate compromise,
which required all member states to enact retention legislation. The
period of retention could range between six months and two years.
While potentially longer than the one-year maximum advocated by
the Working Party and the Commission, the final rule reflects important concessions from the security establishment, represented by the
national executives.

---

[8] In June, the data protection commissioners of Germany called on the
federal government to reject the EU data retention proposal; see
Datenschutzbeauftragte Deutschlands, Presseinformation (June 25, 2004). The
Federal Data Protection Commissioner's warning to Minister Schily was
reported in *Die Stern*, "Schily weist Datenschuetzer-Kritik zurueck," April 20,
2005: online.

[9] See Article 29 Data Protection Working Party, *Opinion 9/2004 on a draft
Framework Decision on the storage of data processed and retained for the
purpose of providing electronic public communications networks with a view
to the prevention, investigation, detection, and prosecution of criminal acts,
including terrorism* (Brussels: European Union, 2004).

International conflict over airline passenger data

Moving from a regional to an international governance debate, the area of air transportation safety offers a second important case demonstrating the complexity of global governance in a world of dual delegation. After the terrorist attacks in the United States, the US government enacted a set of terrorism protection measures, many of which had international ramifications. One of the fiercest transatlantic debates centered on US demands that foreign air carriers provide detailed airline passenger records to US Customs. The Aviation and Transportation Security Act of 2001 authorizes US Customs and the Immigration and Naturalization Service to levy fines of thousands of dollars for every plane that lands without transferring passenger data. The European privacy directive, however, prevented the transfer of personal data to countries lacking adequate data privacy standards. And given the limited nature of privacy rules in the United States, the European Union did not grant it adequacy status. European airlines then faced a double bind – transferring data to US authorities risked sanction by European data privacy authorities, and failing to transfer data risked sanction by US authorities.

Given the importance of air transport to transatlantic tourism, member states and the European Commission hoped to resolve the conflict quickly. The Commission, supported by the Council, began talks with the US Homeland Security Department that would permit the transfer of data and secure air transport. These talks produced a Joint Statement in February 2003, whereby the Commission agreed as a stopgap measure to delay enforcement of European privacy laws and permit data transfers while a more robust agreement could be negotiated. The Joint Statement detailed that the United States would limit the exchange of sensitive data and the scope of agencies with access to it.[10]

Prior to the conclusion of the agreement, however, the Article 29 Working Party actively lobbied to guarantee data privacy protection in the area of air transport. The Working Party offered a recommendation in October 2002, claiming that such transfers of traveler information were in direct violation of the 1995 privacy directive and breached Community law. The Working Party was particularly concerned with

[10] See European Commission (2003).

direct access of US agencies to the databases of European firms, the sharing of sensitive data such as meal choices that might indicate religious affiliation, the extended retention period, the vague standard for collecting and transferring the information to other agencies, and the lack of a formal monitoring mechanism.[11] In March 2003, just after the release of the Joint Statement, the chair of the Working Party, Stefano Rodotà, warned the European Parliament that continued transfers threatened to result in regulatory or judicial intervention. Given the requirements of the European privacy directive, he asserted, data privacy authorities might be forced to sanction carriers that transferred data under the Joint Statement. This, in turn, could further escalate the conflict.[12] The Working Party used its monitoring capacity and expertise to serve as a fire alarm but not for the national executives. Rather, the Working Party used its information advantage to alert the European Parliament to its concerns surrounding the legality of the negotiations.

The Parliament concurred and argued that the demands placed by the United States were unacceptable, especially the request for direct access to carrier databases. European Parliamentarian Sarah Ludford (UK-Liberal), citing the argumentation of the Article 29 Working Party Chair Rodota, summarized the dispute: "This is a stunning rebuff to the Commission. He [Chairman Rodotà] said in essence that National Data Protection Commissioners and courts were not free to suspend application of relevant laws just on the say-so of the Commission. That must be right. It is a reminder to the Commission that if it will not be the guardian of Community law, then others have to be" (quoted in Statewatch 2003).

The ability of the Working Party to complicate the global governance of the issue further rested on the daisy-chain of delegation. Not only had the EU created the Working Party to oversee implementation of the directive but its members also acted individually as national regulators. After the release of the Working Party Opinion, national regulators began to enforce their national legislation. The Italian data privacy

---

[11] See Article 29 Data Protection Working Party (2002).
[12] See the letter from Chairman of the Article 29 Working Party Stefano Rodotà to Jorge Salvador Hernández Mollar, Chairman of the Committee on Citizens' Freedoms and Rights of the European Parliament. Brussels, March 3, 2003. Available at www.statewatch.org/news/2003/mar/art29ch.pdf.

commissioner, for example, limited data transfers from Alitalia to the United States to information contained in a passport. Similarly, the Belgian authority ruled in late 2003 that US–EU transfers violated data privacy laws.

The Working Party's position, then, forced the Commission to renegotiate the agreement with the United States.[13] The constraint placed by the Working Party on the Commission can be seen in a letter sent from Frits Bolkestein, the EU's Internal Market and Services Commissioner, to Tom Ridge, head of the US Homeland Security Department: "Data protection authorities here take the view that PNR [Passenger Name Record] data is flowing to the US in breach of our Data Privacy Directive. It is thus urgent to establish a framework which is more legally secure . . . The centerpiece would be a decision by the Commission finding that the protection provided for PNR data in the US meets our 'adequacy' requirements."[14]

After extensive negotiations with the United States, the Commission agreed in December 2003 to a new agreement. This would not include access to carrier databases, and the information transferred would be filtered. The compromise solution included: reduction of the number of categories of data collected from thirty-nine to thirty-four; deletion of sensitive data; limits on information collection to terrorism and transnational crime; a retention period of three and a half years; a sunset clause that forces renegotiation after three and a half years; and annual joint audits of the program.

Despite these concessions, however, the Working Party and the European Parliament did not believe that the agreement went far enough. The European Parliament eventually took the Commission before the European Court of Justice, arguing that the Commission did not have the jurisdiction to negotiate the agreement and that the

---

[13] The Working Party detailed its concerns in June 2003. They focused on the "pull" system, which allowed direct US access into European databases, the lack of an enforcement or audit system, the possibility that data would be shared with other agencies, the collection of sensitive data, the retention period, and lack of correction rights for passengers (Article 29 Data Protection Working Party 2003 Opinion 4/2003 on the Level of Protection Ensured in the US for the Transfer of Passengers' Data Brussels.

[14] Letter from European Commissioner Frits Bolkestein to US Secretary of Homeland Security Tom Ridge, June 12, 2003. Available at www.statewatch.org/news/2003/sep/Bolkestein-12JUN2003.html.

agreement violated basic privacy principles along the lines of the argumentation offered by the Working Party. The Court ruled in favor of the European Parliament but only on the issue of jurisdiction. As a result, the Council of Ministers was forced to renegotiate the agreement.

Demonstrating that national executives and the Commission shared a fundamentally similar position, the final agreement negotiated between the Council and the Department of Homeland Security removed many of the privacy protections inserted by Working Party lobbying. Returning to a compromise similar to the Joint Statement, the final agreement reflected the national executives' interests in guaranteeing security and tourism. Ironically, the European Court of Justice effectively removed the European Parliament and the Working Party from the negotiations. As authority shifted to the Council, neither the European Parliament nor the Working Party had delegated authority to oversee the process.

The narrative, then, demonstrates the complex role that transgovernmental actors play in global governance. Far from serving as an oversight mechanism of an international organization, the Working Party "police patrol" warned a third party – the European Parliament – of actions taken by the Commission and the member states. The case underscores the importance of delegated authority as a power resource for global governors. As the Lisbon Treaty of the European Union will reduce the distinction between the various policy pillars, the Working Party and the Parliament could be in a much stronger position in domestic and justice affairs in the future.

Conclusion

A central question concerning global governance deals with how states maintain control over the behavior of international organizations. In order to address this question, scholars of international relations have borrowed extensively from principal–agent theory developed in the context of American and comparative politics. Principals generate mechanisms to monitor and police the activity of agents. In instances when agents drift from their original mandate, principals may then employ a set of punishments to rein in autonomous actors.

In the national context, authors have examined a diverse number of formal relationships among political actors, including legislative committees, executive agencies, and civic organizations. At the international level, these models have also progressed in their complexity and richness, incorporating the possibility of multiple principals (for example, several nations delegating to an international organization) and private actors monitoring international organization activity. The persistent assumption within the international relations literature of the unitary state, however, has missed an important development in delegation relationships within global governance.

At the same time that states have looked to a widening number of international organizations to manage complex international issues, the same states have delegated domestic decisionmaking to a host of sub-state officials. Regulatory agencies, ombudsmen, and administrative courts now oversee day-to-day operations in many economic and social areas. This dual delegation alters the control dynamic, injecting transgovernmental actors into the mix. These transgovernmental actors are often appointed by national executives to monitor the behavior of international organizations, and they are simultaneously appointed by international organizations to implement and oversee the policies of the international organization.

Far from being only a control mechanism, these transgovernmental actors may alternatively serve as an important ally to international organizations or other global governors. As the simple model illustrates, sub-state actors' role varies depending on their preferences relative to the other major players involved. Often the product of long-term state-building processes, these preferences and resources reflect the context of domestic institutional design and evolution and not necessarily the optimal configuration for monitoring and reporting on international organizations. The two cases discussed above offer an initial illustration of the argument. In the area of data retention, the Article 29 Working Party allied with the European Commission to rein in national executive demands for sweeping surveillance powers. In the area of airline passenger data, the Article 29 Working Party alerted the European Parliament to the activity of the European Commission and the national executives. In neither case did transgovernmental actors serve the simple police patrol role predicted by the standard principal–agent model but rather they acted as allies of various other international actors. Data privacy authorities injected civil liberties concerns into the security-dominated debate. While research has questioned the democratic legitimacy of transgovernmental activity (Slaughter 2001), this chapter suggests that such "bureaucratic" actors may inject under-represented views into international policymaking, serving to destabilize a politics based on concentrated interests (Sabel and Zeitlin 2007).

Importantly, the cases suggest that varying levels of authority across sectors and time significantly shape the dynamics of global governance. The airline passenger data case illustrates this point. The decision of the European Court of Justice to shift the debate from the first pillar of the EU concerned with the internal market to the third pillar concerned with police cooperation undermined the delegated authority of the Working Party. It weakened the Working Party's ability to affect the later round of negotiations. Transgovernmental actors are not universally positioned to alter global governance dynamics but are dependent on shifting sources of authority.

Transgovernmental actors come to global governance with their own preferences and authority resources, which they enact in their relationship with both national executives and international organizations. In considering these preferences and power resources, this chapter has attempted to reignite a debate about transgovernmental coalitions and how they may transform global governance. In so doing, it challenges purely functional accounts of oversight and implementation and seeks to highlight the highly contentious political nature of dual delegation.

6 Constructing authority in the European Union

KATHLEEN R. McNAMARA

Where do governors come from, what makes them authoritative, and how do they accomplish their goals? This question is perhaps nowhere more intriguing than in the case of the European Union (EU). Despite its dramas of constitutional disarray and financial discord, the EU stands as possibly the most successful innovation in political authority of the past century. The EU is a powerful governor: its rules and decisions are highly consequential for its twenty-seven member states, and it has an international presence across a variety of policy spheres and in ongoing formal international forums such as the World Trade Organization (WTO) and the G-8. At the same time, the EU's legitimacy continues to be contested by academics, politicians, and citizens alike, in no small part because of its unique nature – not a nation-state, but not an international organization as generally understood. What are the sources of the EU's authority, and how has it managed to be legitimate despite its novelty and in the face of severe constraints and competition from other political actors? How robust is this authority and its legitimating foundations?

To answer these questions, I focus on the social processes involved in constructing a political entity as legitimate. Legitimate authority, for my purposes, is a descriptive term, not normative. Authority is "the ability to induce deference in others," as the editors of this volume state, and an actor can be viewed as legitimate if it achieves a significant level of acceptance without coercion. For newly emergent governors, or those that seek to take on new powers, one necessary and prior component of this legitimacy is the governor's status as a "social fact" or as a taken-for-granted political entity. As the editors note, "governance requires more than big sticks," and "generative agents" can create and transform politics in profoundly consequential ways. Throughout history, a critical source of this sort of political power has been an actor's ability to create, through discourse and action, the sense of its own authority as natural and unremarkable. Bourdieu

(1991, 170) has called this the ability to "construct the given," that is, to make natural and unremarkable certain categories and actions that reinforce and legitimize political agency.

(In this chapter, I focus on the role of symbols, and their interaction with practice, in creating the cultural infrastructure for such naturalization of authority.) These symbols do not simply represent the EU as an actor, but also empower it, creating Europe as a political entity. The blue and yellow stars on the EU flag, the unconscious use of the phrase "European foreign policy" by a journalist, the publication of statistics denoting economic growth or inflation in the "European economy" all invent the EU, in an act of imagination (To take hold, however, these symbolic representations need to be underpinned by the lived experiences, or practices, of its citizens) A European passport has symbolic weight, but its meaning becomes internalized through the practice of breezing through the "EU Nationals" line at Charles de Gaulle airport. (Despite the ubiquity of these symbols and practices, the EU departs from the modern nation-state in its almost exclusive emphasis on seemingly "banal" forms of authority) such as a European currency, rather than the more passionate nationalist symbols that played into the development of the nation-state (Billig 1995; Cram 2001). While this technocratic approach has been the bedrock of successful integration in the EU, it is questionable whether the sanitized symbols of EU community, such as EU license plates, are a potent enough glue to hold together the potential "imagined nation" of Europe.)

Ultimately, the symbols and practices of any newly emergent political entity will not gain traction unless they are congruent with their broader cultural setting. As technology shifts our conceptions of time and place toward the postmodern, the EU's overlapping and fragmented governance structures seem to resonate culturally even as they depart from the familiar hierarchical territorial sovereignty of the modern nation-state. Will this allow European citizens comfortably to take on overlapping political identities as well? Or will fragmented and potentially clashing political identities challenge the robustness of the EU's new form of governance?

The chapter proceeds as follows. I begin by outlining the EU's potent governance capacities and note the myriad ways in which its actions profoundly shape the lives of people inside and outside Europe. I then turn to the puzzle of the EU as an authoritative political entity, examining how other authors have probed the question of the EU as an emerging governor. I sketch out one specific framework for thinking about the social construction of authority. I focus on the role of symbolic power in constructing legitimate political authority and parse out the specific ways in which symbolic representation of and practices within the EU have naturalized the concept of "Europe" in myriad ways previously aligned with the nation-state. I focus on one particularly salient area of EU policymaking – citizenship policies – and discuss the EU's activities in terms of how they construct, however imperfectly, an imagined EU political community. The conclusion cautions, however, that there are several important challenges to the EU's status, in particular the tensions in the combination of modern and postmodern governance in the EU today and the potential limits of the "banal" symbols that currently construct the EU.

The EU as a global governor

The EU today exercises significant power over the citizens of its member states and plays a key role on the world stage. Notwithstanding periodic episodes of cross-national bickering amongst its members, the EU has decisively altered national governance in Europe. There is arguably no area of national policymaking among the twenty-seven members of the EU that is not in some way shaped by EU decisions. Historically, the EU has played a key role in market regulation, agriculture, trade policy, and monetary policy. Most prominently, the Single European Act of 1989 began a revolutionary market integration program that brought down barriers to trade and dealt with conflicting standards in everything from electrical outlets to financial reporting. The push to move policy capacity to the EU level in this area has resulted in the EU setting "over 80 per cent of rules governing the exchange of goods, services and capital in the member states' markets" (Hix 1999, 3). Early on, EU states agreed to develop a single position in trade policy negotiations and formulated trade policy through the Brussels bureaucracy for decades (Meunier 2005). The EU also exercised a heavy hand in shaping member-state monetary policy, first indirectly through its longstanding exchange rate regime and, more recently, directly controlling the twelve participating members' money supply through the European central bank and its euro (McNamara 1998).

Less well known, perhaps, is that the EU has now moved beyond strictly economic policy areas and has a reach spanning across all areas of social and other nonmarket policies. In the area of social policy, which has historically been jealously guarded by national actors, the EU has begun actively to shape welfare and social safety nets across its members (Johnson 2007). Citizenship and interior affairs have likewise been penetrated by EU programs (Maas 2007). In the area of the environment, the EU has formulated and passed some of the most extensive policies designed to stem global warming (Bailey 2003; Gower 2001). Public health, education, and cultural programs have also become part of the EU's policy arsenal, perhaps most visibly in the ERASMUS student exchange program that promotes movement of students throughout the EU. Regional policy, primarily in the form of economic development, has also evolved into a major part of the EU's purview, as these initiatives and targeted programs have significantly affected the development path of longstanding member states like Ireland and Portugal, as well as the newer enlargement countries. In all, this comprehensive intertwining of EU involvement in the member states' economies and societies has resulted in a "Europeanization" of political life within member states (Risse *et al.* 2001).

Outside the EU's borders, its posture as a unified actor in certain areas of international politics has also fundamentally altered the dynamics of the international system (Cooper 2003; Ginsberg and Smith 2007; McNamara and Meunier 2002). Contrary to the conventional wisdom that the EU lacks foreign policy power, many observers note that the EU's influence in the world lies precisely in its distinctive nonmilitary and noncoercive character – in particular the spreading of its norms and values (Manners 2002; Meunier and Nicolaïdis 2006). The EU has already had tremendous influence on many of its neighboring states, most often through the lure of membership, and as such has exercised considerable power on the international scene (Jacoby 2004; Vachudova 2005). It also exercises power through example, promoting regional integration arrangements that mirror its image, and through normative suasion (Farrell 2007).

In addition, the capacities of the EU as a more traditional foreign policy actor have vastly increased in recent years, even though it is a development that has failed to capture the headlines (Ginsberg 2001 and 2007; Smith 2003). The EU has deployed military and police forces and crisis management personnel to sixteen conflicts and has taken over from NATO the responsibility for providing security in

Bosnia-Herzegovina. It also has a distinct security strategy that provides a guiding framework for its widening foreign policy activity.

The EU institutions that are responsible for this deepening of the EU's policy capacity are the European Commission, the European Parliament, the Council, and the European Court of Justice.[1] The Commission is made up of a "college" of national political appointees who serve as Commissioners, as well as a standing bureaucracy divided into functional policy bureaus or Directorate Generals. The Commission can initiate policy proposals and implements policy decisions. The European Parliament, made up of European Members of Parliament elected in EU-wide contests every five years, has strengthened its role over the past decade, with the power to amend, veto, and advise, and the authority to oversee EU institutions and censure the Commission. The Council is the more intergovernmental arm of the EU, being made up of representatives of the national governments serving either in Councils or as specific national ministers (of finance, for example). Finally, the European Court of Justice, sitting in Luxembourg, acts in concert with the national courts to uphold EU law and has proved an important actor in the integration process through its interpretations of the EU's laws, or *acquis communautaire*.

These extensive and penetrating governance regimes emanating from the EU level have created what many refer to as a "European constitutional order," where states and their citizens appear to be bound together institutionally in ways far surpassing traditional international organizations. Yet the EU has obviously not simply replaced the nation-state in terms of political identity or policy functions. In the following section, we examine more closely the nature of the EU as a global governor.

The puzzle of EU authority

My brief overview above has sketched out some of the key dimensions on which the EU is a global governor. Many scholars have further detailed the capacities of the EU policy regime, as well as the limits and implications of this shift to Brussels. Yet still elusive is the broader question of how to think about the nature of authority in the EU. How has the EU accrued what this volume's editors conceptualize

---

[1] For an extensive overview of the structure and function of the EU institutions, see Hix (1999 and 2005); Wallace *et al.* (2004); Peterson and Shackleton (2006).

as "institutional authority" over the citizens it governs (Avant, Finnemore, and Sell, this volume)?

Scholars have made important inroads into this question by starting with the more fundamental issue of what, exactly, the EU *is*. If we are going to understand the nature of its legitimacy, in this view, we need first to think about how to conceptualize the EU, in terms of both the continuities that it represents and its truly transformative characteristics. Some have focused on the unique qualities of the EU's structure, offering alternative and innovative templates such as "multilevel governance" to try to capture the dynamics of EU politics (Hooghe and Marks 2001; Bache and Flinders 2004). Others have more explicitly drawn comparisons with historical forms of governance, using the past to draw out the differences and similarities with past political orders (Bartolini 2005).

These works and others have brought the study of the EU far from the place it was in 1993, when John Ruggie took IR theorists to task for having "impoverished" mindsets that are unable even to find the vocabulary to describe the EU. Yet the challenge that Ruggie issued and the hints he provided for thinking about the puzzle of EU authority remain salient and provide a very fruitful springboard for thinking about how authority is socially constructed within specific cultural contexts.

In his seminal essay Ruggie (1993) argues that the end of the Cold War opened up a period of unusual fluidity in international politics, akin to the remaking of the modern system of territorial states, and asserting that the EU may be the most powerful example of emerging political forms. Yet, he notes, our conceptual toolkit is woefully limited in its ability to depict the transformations in the form and content of rule evinced in changing forms of governance, such as the EU. As a starting point for understanding the rise of profoundly new global governors, Ruggie's strategy is to go back in time, examining the transformation that occurred with the last "big bang" in political authority: the rise of the territorial state. In contrast to the medieval system of rule, the period around the seventeenth century ushered in today's dominant form of the state as "territorially disjoint, mutually exclusive, functionally similar, [and] sovereign" (Ruggie 1993, 151). In the process, political authority became consolidated from the personal and parcelized authority of the medieval era into the public and externalized central authority of the territorial state. Ruggie also notes that the monopoly over the legitimate use of force by the central authorities was a key constituting part of this public sphere. Sovereign states embodied a distinct expression of individual, exclusive territoriality, a historic and profoundly consequential innovation in political rule.

The sources of this epochal transformation are threefold, in Ruggie's view. First, material changes in the lived experience of human populations contributed to the reorganization of rule, particularly in terms of changing climate and demographics, shifting relations of production, and transformations in the relations of force (Ruggie 1993, 152–3). Second, social arrangements – in the sense of the strategic interactions, institutions, and behaviors of actors – were shaped by responses to these material changes. The Champagne Fairs that allowed for long-distance trade are an example of the intricate economic and social institutions that developed.

Ruggie's final source of transformation in international systems of rule is the one that will concern us most as we consider the emergence of the EU. Ruggie argued that these more functional stories fail to determine the form of the state that emerged; to understand that, we need to understand the "social epistemes" or "mental equipment" that people drew upon in "imagining and symbolizing forms of political community" (Ruggie 1993, 157). Broadly speaking, in this view, the Westphalian state is intimately connected to the universe of discourses and practices that can loosely be defined as "modernity" (148–52). As will be discussed, the conceptions and experiences of space and time under modernity have been viewed by many as critical to the ability of nation-states to be imbued with legitimacy, as part of the creation of an imagined political community so eloquently written about by Benedict Anderson (1983). Ruggie suggests, but does not expand on, the idea that conceptions and experiences of today's European citizens reflect a more postmodern form of time and space relations, one which is fragmented and overlapping in ways that "implode" modern space–time relations.

A second critical contribution establishing the puzzle of the EU as an emergent governor is James Caporaso's (1996) overview of governance metaphors for understanding the EU. He proposes three general categories for understanding what Robert Cox (1983) calls "forms of state," that is, the many types of "conceptually possible expressions of political authority organized at the national and transnational levels," what in this project we refer to as "global governors" (Caporaso 1996,

31). For Caporaso, the categories Westphalian, Regulatory, and Post-modern are metaphors that capture particular societal constellations of interest and their institutional settings over time and place. The Westphalian state category is the familiar model where "monopolies of legitimate violence, rational bureaucracies and centralized policy-making authority correspond to territorially exclusive political orders" (1996, 34). The functions of the regulatory state are more aligned with transnational global governors such as those described by this volume's authors. These regulatory regimes serve to facilitate transna-tional economic exchange and deal with market failures by increasing information or creating incentives for cooperation and the provision of public goods. Caporaso notes that this sort of governance solution rests on theories of new institutional economics and microeconomic rationality. Finally, he proposes a third category of state as organized political expression: the postmodern state. Here, governance is "frac-tured, decentered, and often lacking in clear spatial (geographical) as well as functional (issue area) lines of authority" (Caporaso 1996: 34).

In addition to finding elements of the other two governance models, Caporaso suggests certain characteristics of the EU that seem to fit the postmodern metaphor. First, he argues that the EU has a "weak core," in the sense that the most central functions of domestic governance – namely foreign policy, social policy, citizenship, and internal and exter-nal security – are not developed at the EU level. While this argument could be contested by developments in the decade since his essay was published, it is certainly the case that concrete policy capacity in these areas continues to lag the national setting. More on target, perhaps, is his assertion that the multilevel governance theory of Marks (1993) neatly mirrors the notion of a fragmented, multiperspective postmod-ern consciousness. EU governance relations (among states, EU agen-cies, and subnational actors) are interconnected, rather than nested, and take on the "marble cake" qualities of interpenetrating interac-tions, rather than being neatly layered (Elazar 1987; Risse 2003).[2]

---

[2] Caporaso (1996, 47) also points to the globalization of production and the lessening power of labor vis-à-vis capital as a potential part of the move toward postmodernity, as the state "creates transnational spaces for capital where the opposed forces of organized labour are not prevalent." In this view, capital is postmodern in its spatial expression, but labor remains stuck in twentieth-century modernity.

Ruggie's and Caporaso's accounts set up the puzzle of the EU as a global governor quite effectively and begin pointing toward post-modernity as one path to understanding the social foundations (and tensions) of its legitimacy. However, they offer only a very preliminary discussion of how legitimate governance in such a postmodern form might be constructed in a global governor like the EU. My next section turns to the question of the social basis for authority and tries to work out the ways in which the EU evidences both historical continuities and important discontinuities with past forms of governance.

A social theory of political authority

How is authority generated by governors like the EU, or as the editors (Avant, Finnemore, and Sell, this volume) ask, "why are they in charge?" Governance implies self-regulation, rather than direct control, and therefore involves subjective identification and compliance. Political authority rests on the consent of the governed, the product of which is legitimacy and the ability of those in power to rule without continual coercion. While political philosophers have debated the nature of legitimacy for centuries, here we will follow the pragmatic example of historical sociologists, who have pinpointed the role that culture and social construction play in the exercise of legitimate authority. The concept of symbolic power is central to this exercise. Symbolic power, in Bourdieu's (1991, 170) phrase, can be thought of as the power to construct or "constitute the given" and as such is critical in securing the consent of those governed. As the scholar Mara Loveman (2005, 1655) has written, symbolic power "is the ability to make appear as natural, inevitable, and thus apolitical, that which is the product of historical struggle and human invention. Through practices of classification, codification, and regulation, for example, modern states not only naturalize certain distinctions and not others, but they also help constitute particular kinds of people, places, and things."

This process is dependent on the recognition of a political authority as legitimate but, notably, it is most effective when it is least obvious, that is, when the practices and rules of governance are so taken for granted that they are not noticed as creating the very basis for the political action that is occurring. Note that this is entirely different from the cataloging of policy capacities that many would use to measure the

EU's power. Here, the taken-for-granted quality of governance results, most likely, in the *lack* of recognition that any obvious assertion of power has taken place.

An essential part of this process is the creation and acceptance of the status of the governor itself as a "social fact." Social facts are so obvious that most people think of them as *objective* facts, forgetting that they are dependent on shared, intersubjective understandings for their existence (Searle 1995). Social facts are distinctive in that they are viewed as stable, neutral, and having an existence separate from the speaker who is articulating them as fact, even as they owe their existence to that speaker's words. Searle (1995, 27) notes that while there are brute facts in the world (such as the distance of the sun from the earth), there are also institutional facts (such as the fact that Condoleezza Rice was the US Secretary of State). These institutional facts require particular human institutions for them to be meaningful (such as the system of US government). Marriage and football are examples of social, institutional facts: without a shared understanding of what those things are, they would not exist.

The language we use to describe these social facts is itself a social institution, a system of symbols with rules that by the act of naming defines and brings into being within our consciousness the objective world. Brute facts, such as the sun, exist without language, but it is only through language that we can state their existence. Similarly, the terrain of the continent that makes up the EU exists as a brute fact, but the European Union is an institutional fact, invented through our intersubjective understandings.

Moreover, as Searle (1995) points out, social facts rest on sets of institutional rules that may be constitutive and/or regulatory in nature. His classic example is chess: its rules regulate the playing of the game, while also creating it as an activity. Chess does not exist prior to the constitutive rules that call it into being. Likewise, the activities of every political entity, such as the EU, are regulated by a series of institutional rules that, in turn, are themselves created and shaped through those institutional activities. The rules that govern the use of the euro are regulative, for example, but also constitutive because the single currency itself is brought to life through those rules.

Quite importantly for our discussion of the EU, these phenomena can be recognized as social facts despite contestation over how they should be defined or what they represent. For example, marriage is understood in a broad sense as a category within and across different cultures, despite contentions over whether it is defined only as a union between a man and a woman. Football exists despite the different American and Canadian rules regarding the size of the football field, among other things. Likewise, despite contentious political battles over what the EU is, it has taken on the status of a social fact: no one denies that it exists, even if people's subjective understandings of what it is, or what it means, differ dramatically.

The EU must become a social fact if it is to be legitimate. It must be seen by a majority if not all people as a distinct actor, with a large-scale, collective social identity. Moreover, legitimacy is fatally compromised if there is no sense of belonging on the part of the governed. Their political identity must in some way be located in the imagined community being constructed around and through them. A sense of "Europeanness," "European public," "European interest," and "European identity" – even if contested and embryonic – comes into play when a governor is constructed as legitimate. As Walzer (1967, 194) has famously said, "The state is invisible; it must be personified before it can be seen, symbolized before it can be loved, imagined before it can be conceived."

But the EU is challenged by its very novelty: it is a social fact without the vocabulary to identify it as such. It has a much more uncertain ideational existence than a nation-state, even as it is experienced in a multitude of ways. It also does not have the galvanizing motivation and constitutive experience of fighting and dying for the homeland that pushed forward the love of the state in other historical experiences. Neither does it extract revenues and redistribute them in the ways used by the modern state to create bounded political entities. Indeed, there is a skeptical literature that has arisen amongst scholars of Europe that stresses the low rates of Europeans' self-identification with the EU in interviews and polls (Diez Medrano 2003; Checkel and Katzenstein 2009; Fligstein 2008; Favell 2003). It is clear from this work that people do not have the nationalist fervor or pride in being citizens of the EU that they have as Swedes or Greeks.

But perhaps our yardstick of comparison is incorrect. Instead of looking for the nationalist fervor as we traditionally think of it, we might also find consequential evidence of what has been called "banal nationalism" (Billig 1995). Billig has noted not only that nationalism arises in crisis and conflict, but that nations are reproduced on a daily

basis through banal and mundane ways, and it is those habits of mind
and practice that underpin national identity. He argues that even those
activities and representations that seem the most clichéd (flags and
anthems, for example) matter, for they reproduce national identity
in ways that prime populations for supporting their states in more
emotional or difficult times, such as war. He argues that established
nations continually "flag" or remind their populations of nationhood
in myriad seemingly innocuous ways. Billig writes that "this reminding
is so familiar, so continual, that it is not consciously registered as
reminding. The metonymic image of banal nationalism is not a flag
which is being consciously waved with fervent passion; it is the flag
hanging unnoticed on the public building" (1995, 8).

This concept of banal nationalism well captures the under-the-radar,
taken-for-granted rhetoric and practices that create Europe as a legitimate actor and an authority structure that reverberates back on individual identity in ways not captured in the polls.[3] For example, the
acceptance of a public entity, the Eurostat Agency, commissioning
Eurobarometer polls, asking people whether they feel European, may
be creating a chain of representations and practices that reinforces the
concept of the EU as a legitimate actor and "European" as a legitimate
category of identity. The work of seemingly mundane bureaucrats and
telephone polling agents does not excite the mind the way a national
day of independence with fireworks and fervent anthem singing might,
but it may have important effects in creating the foundation for EU governance by legitimating a range of statistical and information-gathering
activities. Ironically, from this perspective, Eurobarometer is constructing European identity even as it is reporting its nonexistence. So, it is
not the degree of felt or activated "Europeanness" (although that is
important in other contexts) that matters for this argument but rather
the normalization of the EU as a legitimate governor and site of political authority. Banal nationalism may be just one step in the route
toward Walzer's beloved state, but it might be an important one in
the symbolic activity that he argued is the key to the political art of
unification.

So how might a political actor accrue this important governance resource? Through the creation of pervasive, often banal

---

[3] Laura Cram has explored this idea, as well; see Cram (2001) and her recent
work on inventing a European public (2006).

representations that symbolize, construct, and constitute, and through a larger structure of practice that connects those representations to lived experience.)

Creating Europe

The EU uses "political technologies," as Foucault (1988) has called them, to construct categories and frame reality. Cris Shore (2000), in an innovative study of the role of cultural construction in EU bureaucracies, has called these various forms of representation and activities "agents of European consciousness." But these created realities may not gain purchase on the mental and emotional frames of EU citizens unless they resonate successfully. Such resonance can occur when these symbolic representations are reinforced or supplemented by experience through practice. Speaking about the EU is a way of putting the representation through language into practice. Standing in a line for "EU Nationals" at the airport is a practice that engages with the symbolic boundary created by the Schengen agreement and the laws on EU citizenship and mobility. Transacting in euros is simultaneously an experience and a practice, one that engages both the functional and the symbolic.

We see this occurring across a variety of areas, including the construction of boundaries and categorizations, as represented in language and visual images. Names of political entities across the EU reinforce the notion of a bounded European polity, from the European Central Bank (and Euroland, as the area where the euro is used is commonly called) to the European Court of Justice and the European Food Safety Authority (Europe's version of the Food and Drugs Administration, located in Parma, Italy). While this seems completely unremarkable, remember that these organizations not only have functional administrative roles, but can also serve to represent Europe symbolically as they become part of daily discourse. Likewise, visual symbols of the EU, such as the "CE" marking on toys, which denotes their compliance with EU toy safety guidelines, or the placement of EU flags and other symbols on road construction signs where the EU is contributing funds, reinforce the notion of a bounded political actor at work.

The euro itself is a potent political symbol. The very name reinforces the presence of Europe in domestic and international market exchanges. Money itself is, of course, a social construction, predicated on a widely shared belief in its value: the success of the changeover from national currencies to the Euro in twelve European states indicates a high level of acceptance of the EU as a governing authority, one that is strengthened through the practice of using euros. Likewise, the carefully chosen images on the euro seek to represent Europe through maps and architectural imagery (building bridges and so on). Unsurprisingly, policymakers within the EU thought carefully about the social implications and symbolic foundations when planning the public relations around the launch of the new currency (Shore 2000).

The entire field of EU studies itself, which initially arose in the 1950s and 1960s but did not become a large and established organizational field until recently, acts to legitimate the EU as a political actor, worthy of its own group of scholars and experts. The EU has spent a great deal of money in the past two decades to assist in the development of this field. Dozens of universities in Europe now have Jean Monnet Chairs, named after one of Europe's "founding fathers" and funded by the EU, for scholars of European integration. I myself was the recipient some years ago of a Fulbright to the European Union (funded by the EU), which is atypical among Fulbright awards in centering on an entity other than nation-states.

All of these activities work to create the conceptual foundations for imagined communities of Europe and citizens' place in it (or outside it). These symbolic representations exhibit internal tensions, such as the "unity in diversity" slogan of the EU, some of which we will explore in the conclusion. But even as these symbols seek to constitute the EU as a legitimate actor and site of political authority, without a larger structure of practices that can validate and sustain them the EU would not be able to maintain its governing authority. Below, I explore one area of EU policymaking that blends both symbolism and practice in the invention of Europe: citizenship and mobility programs.

EU citizenship practices as constituting the given

Rather than relying on extractive or coercive practices, the EU has overwhelmingly relied on the inherently social power of more subtle forms of administrative and ideological cooptation (such as categorization and classification) to produce cultural legitimacy for its innovative form of governance, just as state- and nation-building actors had done before. The accrual of symbolic power, the capturing of an administrative realm, and its normalization as part of the EU's governance capacity have functioned to further the constitution of a new political community. I briefly highlight some of these processes in the area of European citizenship.

Nowhere is the question of the status of the EU's political authority more central than with citizenship, where the EU has created a new legal – and conceptual – category of the EU citizen. These developments have occurred slowly, and often under the radar of observers.[4] The formal category of "European Union citizen" was introduced with the Maastricht Treaty in 1993, but de facto citizenship, in the sense of rights evolving over time, had been growing since the initial efforts to increase labor mobility with market integration decades earlier. Free movement throughout the EU has been a crucial component of the economic, social, and political project of European integration, starting with the Coal and Steel Community, and it is a critical component of both citizenship and the creation of an imagined community. As Maas (2007) notes, "One of the modern state's most notable functions is to facilitate the free movement of people within its boundaries, and the essence of full-fledged state citizenship, as distinct from earlier local citizenships, is its uniform applicability throughout the state's domain." The EU has likewise pursued the promotion of mobility within the framework of an overarching European set of rights. This has created new lived experiences – the practice of crossing borders without frontiers, inspections by EU customs agents, and having a common external border with the world – that can serve to underpin the various symbolic constructions of Europe. Below I tease out the connections between the legal developments and policy practices, and the implications they may have for the construction of European political authority. This case is particularly rich because it engages different types of dynamics in the creation of a social fact: representation in language and symbol and experience or practice that reinforces a new social reality. In citizenship and mobility policy, the EU is involved in the constitution of itself as an actor through both ideas and practice.

Abolishing borders, creating community

In the post-Westphalian order, borders tend to be thought of first as those politically drawn boundaries established by war and/or

---

[4] Willem Maas (2007) provides a succinct overview of the history of citizenship; Antje Wiener (1998) offers more extended discussion of many of these issues.

negotiation and subject to formal law. But mental boundaries matter as well. Our mental maps of the geography of a political community are influenced by personal experience (for example, daily routines segment the space around us into particular neighborhoods), by sharp demarcations of physical geography (traditionally mountains or rivers), but also by ethnic, racial, or socioeconomic divides (the inhabitants of Morningside Heights by Columbia University in New York City are sharply divided in their mental imagery of boundaries from the inhabitants of 110th Street). The redrawing of boundaries, legal or mental, can be thought of as extending the power of the actor who is located at the center, while simultaneously reinforcing its legitimacy if its boundaries are accepted.[5]

The single market, envisioned fifty years ago in the Treaty of Rome, with its promotion of "the four freedoms" – that is, the free movement of goods, services, money, and people – has provided an anchor for the redrawing of the lines of community through the eradication of national borders (and the construction of a common external border), the granting of free movement rights, and later, the legal and political infrastructure to support such movement. After its initial introduction in the narrowly defined confines of the European Coal and Steel Community, the 1957 Treaty of Rome conferred on workers "the right to accept offers of employment, to move freely among the member states for this purpose, to reside in any member state if employed there, and to stay in any member state if formerly employed there" (Maas 2007). The European Commission was given the authority to implement these provisions and largely did so within the decade.

Progress toward more mobility continued over the decades of the 1970s, '80s, and '90s, but did so in a seemingly erratic way – ideas introduced but not acted on for many years were not atypical during this period. A major step toward the creation of a borderless Europe occurred in 1985, in the Luxembourg town of Schengen, where Germany, France, Belgium, Luxembourg, and the Netherlands signed an agreement to eliminate border controls. Schengen was created outside the normal treaty protocol of the EU, but the next major development – the Single European Act – was within the treaty system, coming into force in 1992 and encompassing all EU members. The Single

---

[5] On the relationship between maps and the centralization of power, see Anderson (1983) and Scott (1998).

European Act radically pushed the concept of a borderless EU, with free movement for all, squarely into the accepted public discourse, with the Commission serving as a critical actor in reframing and legitimizing this move forward in European integration (Fligstein and Mara-Drita 1996). The Maastricht Treaty later reinforced the political status of EU citizens through four sets of rights: free movement rights, political rights, the right to common diplomatic protection, and the right to petition Parliament and appeal to the Ombudsman.

In response to concerns that backers of EU citizenship would introduce language making EU citizenship superior to national citizenship, the Amsterdam Treaty contained the following text: "Citizenship of the Union shall complement and not replace national citizenship" (Art. 8A, para. 2). The Nice Treaty

subsequently extended qualified majority voting to free movement which meant that decisions about the right to move and reside freely within EU territory would no longer require the unanimous support of all member states. The member states did exempt passports, identity cards, residence permits, social security, and social protection from qualified majority voting. Provisions in those areas would continue to require unanimity, but decisions about free movement provisions could now be made more easily. (Wiener 1997)

Most recently, the Constitutional Convention has been the focus of the debate about the nature of European citizenship. The Convention was viewed by some as an opportunity to consolidate further the idea of a European citizen, and sometimes dramatically so, as the discussion centered on the concept of "dual citizenship." But the push to make explicit and obvious the fact of already significant rights and reclassification at the European level backfired. The citizenship dimension ended up being part of the broader political debate about the direction of the EU and the necessity of the constitution, and may have contributed to its rejection in referendums in France and the Netherlands.[6]

The overall effect of this historical path has been to create a rule-based regime that, despite being highly contentious, has profoundly

---

[6] Many of the elements of the failed constitution were repackaged into the Lisbon Treaty, which came into force December 1, 2009. The most politically sensitive symbolic aspects were tempered, although others, such as a European President and High Representative for foreign policy, remained.

changed the pertinent category of reference for human mobility from the national border to Europe as a whole. Moreover, flowing from these decisions have been a whole host of changes in the territorial basis for specific political, social, and economic rights and entitlements that now provide those within the EU with a single political space in which to work, play, study, and retire.

More explicit political effects flowed from the adoption of the 1976 Council decision to implement direct universal suffrage and the European elections in 1979. This decision created a direct link between the public and the European Parliament, bypassing the national governments which had previously been an intercedent in the electoral process. Changing EU laws regarding the basis for EU citizenship subsequently enabled reforms granting the right to vote in municipal and European elections according to one's state of residence, rather than national origin. In addition, a variety of social rights such as healthcare, the right to establishment, old age pension, and the recognition of diplomas, developed along with the EU social charter (Wiener 1997, 9). Again, these changed laws have had both de facto and de jure effects on the mental images and assumptions that people have about what constitutes Europe and what their relationship to it is.

One of the policy areas where mobility is the most advanced and administratively elaborate is in the Europeanization of education. The EU has an extensive series of programs to encourage the movement of students (and professors) across borders. The ERASMUS program, set up in 1987, provides for reciprocal study programs (in which students do not have to pay the fees of the university where they are visiting), stipends, and credentials for exchange-students across Europe. By its twentieth anniversary, more than 1.5 million students had taken advantage of ERASMUS to study abroad. The EU plans to double that number to 3 million by 2012. In the early 1980s, a network of information centers was set up to advise students on cross-border education and transfer of qualifications. The administrative mechanics are in place to allow for cross-border recognition of education credits in the "European Credit Transfer System," a program introduced by the European Commission that requires the study abroad credits to be recognized across the EU. There are standard formats available from the EU to capture credits, training, and qualifications and "translate" them into a standard format – a "European CV" – in what the EU calls the effort to promote the "recognition and transparency of qualifications."[7] The appendix to this chapter has a copy of the text of the EU's information booklet, "Europe on the Move," which informs young people of the many programs available to them and proselytizes about the benefits of such trans-European social and economic action.

Finally, one of the policy activities the EU has used to construct European citizenship is the evolution of passports toward a common European format and away from discrete national designs. The very idea of passports is such a taken-for-granted state right that we might not find the activities remarkable. But passports are a relatively recent invention, dating to World War I, when states sought to monitor and control the passage of potential foreign nationals.

In *The Invention of the Passport*, John Torpey (2000) describes why this document that we take for granted was an important milestone for the development of authority in the state. Similarly to James Scott's (1998) observations about the ways in which states have made their populations "legible" and in so doing built state capacity, we can think of how the EU passport enhances a political authority bounded not by national territory but by a new, imagined EU. Treaty language established a standardized EU passport, issued from 1988.[8] At that point, the words "European Community" were placed on the front of all member-state passports, and other elements were required, such as the translations of certain parts of the text inside the passport into official languages of the European Community. In 1997, the words "European Community" were replaced with "European Union." At the end of 2004, the EU Council decided to require member states to adhere to new "biometric" passport regulations with machine-readable facial images and room for fingerprints, stored on microchips.[9] In this realm,

---

[7] See http://ec.europa.eu/education/policies/rec_qual/rec_qual_en.html for information on all these programs.

[8] Wiener (1997, 7) reports on the communiqué for the treaty, which stated: "the fact remains that the introduction of such a passport would have a psychological effect, one which would emphasize the feeling of nationals of the nine Member States of belonging to the Community" (26) and, second, "[o]ne should take into account not simply the psychological effect of a uniform passport as justifying its existence but that such a passport might be equally justified by the desire of the nine Member States to affirm vis-à-vis non-member countries the existence of the Community as an entity, and eventually to obtain from each of them identical treatment for citizens of the Community."

[9] As part of the Schengen body of laws, or *acquis*, the United Kingdom, Ireland, and Denmark may "opt out" from these regulations.

after 9/11 and the Madrid and London bombings, the EU has extended its administrative reach, rather than surrendering internal policing and homeland security concerns to member states.

The advent of a European passport is the clearest physical expression of the drive toward mobility and citizenship status within the boundaries of the EU. This physical presence is also made apparent when one arrives in an airport or train station from outside the EU: the signs point to two categories of person: "European Union Nationals" and everyone else. This makes tangible the mental redrawing of EU citizenship in a way that is quite striking and yet very quickly became a taken-for-granted part of the natural landscape of things. As in our earlier discussion of symbolic power, it is these invisible and unquestioning modes of interaction and experience that serve to reinforce political authority most potently.

In sum, this brief survey has pointed out the ways in which the highly developed EU legal system has created a new category of European citizen, who is granted rights under the EU body of laws that are definitive and supersede national law in the ever-expanding areas covered by EU treaties. With this category of citizenship come important implications for the imagined European community. On a symbolic level, the creation of the European citizen as an everyday term in language helps constitute Europe and is part of the process of banal nationalism described above. In the area of practice, it has entailed the official sanctification of mobility with few legal and administrative barriers. Students and professionals can study and work abroad with their credentials and training mutually recognized across borders. In so doing, they need not worry about surrendering their financial benefits or political rights, as the EU legal regime now protects both. While personal and other reasons may keep many people in Europe from exercising these rights, their existence has been transformative nonetheless, both for those taking advantage of this mobility and for those receiving the other EU nationals into their locales.[10]

Citizenship policies are clearly only the tip of the iceberg when it comes to the construction of a European political space and identity; a multitude of effects flow from the various policy programs of the EU. The single market itself by definition constructs a social space. The EU's

---

[10] For one popular cultural exploration of this phenomenon, see the movie *L'Auberge Espagnole* (2002).

activities have been crucial in creating the administrative infrastructure for the single market to branch out into a multitude of areas that have the potential gradually to reorient the mental frameworks people use when they think of themselves in Europe. Such seemingly banal phrases as "the European economy" work to construct an image of a bounded political and social space in ways perhaps as important as the concrete policy programs they embody.

Yet for this extension of the administrative reach and the redrawing of political community to be successful, the nature and form of political authority has to match the underlying cultural frames that ultimately work to underpin governance. Is there a discontinuity in the basic form and content of that exercise of bureaucratic power by the EU, seen in our discussion of the construction of the European citizen? If the current nation-state owes some of its legitimacy to the rise of instrumental rationality and related mental changes reflected in the visual arts and elsewhere, as Ruggie argues, what are the changes in the basic social foundations that make the EU's unique form of nonexclusive territorial power possible? My concluding section, below, takes up the argument that the postmodern cultural turn has been a critical legitimizing force enabling the EU's success at the same time as it creates unique stresses and strains for this global governor.

Conclusion: the cultural foundations of EU authority in a postmodern era

The discussion above has focused on the ways in which the EU is constructed as a social fact. In its symbolic representation in myriad areas, it has extended its administrative reach and accrued power while creating an imagined community of Europeans. I examined the area of citizenship policy and mobility to demonstrate the interaction between this symbolic construction and the practices needed for governance to be accepted. However, in conclusion it is necessary to return to the question of how robust this banal nationalism in the EU truly is.

Clearly, being constructed as a social fact is not enough for successful governance; what is the content of that fact, how is it contested, and how is it viewed – as inclusive or exclusive, democratic or not? One of the main criticisms of the EU is that it has long been an elite project, both driven by political elites without mass participation in decisionmaking and, to the extent European identity exists at all, confined to a cosmopolitan elite that travels freely between the national capitals, speaking several languages while working for multinational investment banks – what Adrian Favell (2003) has termed "Eurostars." How far does the accrual of EU symbols go when it comes to whether EU citizens feel they have rights and obligations as EU citizens? How big is the difference between what the EU says and what people feel and do?

There are also a series of rival narratives that have gained traction across some parts of the European public, and which construct the EU as illegitimate. In a prominent example, Jean-Marie Le Pen has long challenged the basic legitimacy of the EU, as have other far-right political activists throughout the Union. For Le Pen and others, the taken-for-granted nature of the EU is, in fact, a highly contestable proposition. The ever-enlarging EU, now expanded with Romania and Bulgaria to twenty-seven members, also challenges the continued construction of the idea of Europe. While the history of nation-states shows us an amazing ability to invent traditions and reconstruct history to provide for inclusion of previously warring and disparate peoples (Weber 1976; Hobsbawm and Ranger 1983), this is certainly not a foregone conclusion but rather a serious challenge to the EU's political authority.

A more profound challenge to the EU's governance may lie deeper, in shifting social foundations and the tensions between the EU's modern and postmodern characteristics. When Benedict Anderson wrote about the rise of the last new political form, nation-states, he focused on the cultural roots of authority. For him, the imagined communities of the state were dependent on social transformations of modernity; he viewed the novel, newspaper, map, and museum as agents of modernity that made possible nation-states by linking people in the same space–time plane. Are those agents of modernity are still the solid social foundations for today's transformation of governance described in the chapters of this volume? For the case of the EU, we should ask what the EU's cultural foundations are, and whether the transformative effects of technology and changing norms of interaction might impact the EU's success as a global governor.

First, whereas in the modern age political authority has been tied closely to sovereign, territorial states, the EU departs in important ways from this model. Instead, the EU can be characterized as postmodern in form, made up of overlapping and fragmented governance structures that are not territorially exclusive and where sovereignty is located at different levels of governance depending on the issue area.)

The term "postmodern" has been used in numerous and no doubt conflicting ways such that it conveys an inherent fuzziness that should make us wary of relying too heavily on it for any precise explanations. Nonetheless, when considering the political development of the EU, it seems that *contra* Gertrude Stein, "there is a there there."[11] Harvey (1990) defines postmodernism in part in reaction to modernity and its positivistic, technocratic, and rational universalism.[12] In contrast, postmodernism "privileges heterogeneity and difference as liberative forces in the redefinition of cultural discourse. Fragmentation, indeterminacy, and intense distrust of all universal or 'totalizing' discourses" all share a rejection of "meta-narratives" (1990, 9). One way to explore the question of how these broad cultural changes may impact the legitimacy of different forms of political authority is to focus on the changing conceptions and experiences of space and time. Arguably, practice in the era of the internet and of EasyJet or Ryanair travel around Europe has qualitatively changed EU citizens' perceptions of time and space. The scale and speed of media in Europe is also profoundly different today; with the rise of Eurosport and Euronews on satellite TV, we can now see Benedict Anderson's simultaneity, which he viewed as key to any imagined community, as taking hold with a vengeance.

Likewise, the rise of fragmented perspectives, nonlinear thought, multiple narratives, and a raising up of the individual to speak with the same authority as a credentialed expert can be found in something that millions use many times a day – the internet. But what might the implications be for political authority? Wikipedia is built on the notion that collaboration between millions of individuals around the planet can produce information thorough enough to have become the first

---

[11] Stein was speaking of Oakland when she announced "There is no there there." She seemed to view Europe in a more favorable light.
[12] Harvey (1990) is a touchstone for any analysis of the condition and consequences of postmodernity. A remarkably clear template for understanding the relationship between culture and international relations is provided by Nexon and Neumann (2006).

entry in many a Google search. YouTube has likewise become a global phenomenon that operates on a completely uncurated basis, unfiltered and open to anyone with the desire to communicate. Blogging, in a similar way, removes the authoritative editor or fact-checking committee and allows direct communication and a forum for anyone with a computer and an internet connection. The uncurated museum shares this decentering and raising to prominence of nonexperts, as is the case with the Museum of the American Indian in Washington, DC, and the Musée du Quai Branly in Paris, which do not seek to offer a meta-narrative about the objects and their meanings, with a story following a particular arc, but rather to present objects without a constructed narrative. How might these practices translate into expectations and understandings of European citizens today?

On the one hand, the EU's structure aligns well with certain aspects of this contemporary cultural context. Arguably, the EU rests today on a set of postmodern experiences, images, and cognitive equipment, which enable the creation of a nonexclusive, nonterritorial political community. This particular cultural constitution of postmodern life may be one of the critical "raw materials" allowing the citizens of Europe to be part of an imagined political community whose territorial expression is overlapping and blurred, where political identities may be simultaneously Provençal, French, and European.

On the other hand, however, the accrual of symbolic power has relied heavily in the EU on more traditional modes of bureaucratic authority similar to those that nation-states have long relied on. This Weberian authority may be made more difficult in this postmodern landscape, where metanarratives are disdained and authority is decentered through technology and cultural practices. In particular, the question of fragmented and potentially clashing political identities challenges the robustness of the EU's new form of governance. Scholarly conceptions of the role of bureaucracies in political life are almost exclusively attached to the idea of a sovereign nation-state exercising administrative power. Academic literature and popular conceptions alike tend to view the development of policy capacity as taking place in the hands of centralized, exclusive authorities, existing in a hierarchical system where lines of accountability and decisionmaking are clearly circumscribed. The mental acquiescence needed to make such sites of authority legitimate, as argued by Weber and many after him, is tightly bound up with the rise of instrumental rationality and modernity itself.

(It remains to be seen whether the tension between the postmodern and the modern in both the governance of the EU and its social foundations will plague the EU and limit its activities.)

I have argued here that the EU has emerged as a full-blown global governor over the postwar era, profoundly shaping the lives of its inhabitants, as well as the lives of many across the globe through its foreign policies. The EU, as a political actor, faces a situation similar to that faced by other newly emerging forms of political organization throughout history, in that there are both challenges and opportunities in the new. Just as political rule has been transformed and morphed in the case of city-states, empires, federations, and nation-states, the EU as a new form draws on political technologies and mental categories while simultaneously changing them. The symbolic construction of legitimate authority and the notion of "imagined communities" continue to be critical to this process, even as the nature and meaning of those terms evolves and changes.

APPENDIX: TEXT OF A EUROPEAN COMMISSION DOCUMENT ACCESSED THROUGH THE CENTRAL "EUROPA.EU" WEBSITE

European Commission
Directorate-General for Press and Communication
Manuscript finalised in June 2003

It's your Europe

Living, learning and working anywhere in the EU

Europe on the move

The European Union – wide open with opportunities for all

In the early 1990s, the European Union became a truly open area in which people, goods, services and money can move around with almost total freedom. Every EU citizen, regardless of age, has the right to travel, live, work, study and retire anywhere in the EU. And there are plenty of opportunities!

This booklet tells you about those opportunities. It encourages you to think seriously about the benefits and personal fulfilment to be gained through living, learning or working in another EU country.

Information and advice – at your fingertips

As an EU citizen you have the right to live and work in any EU country. However, when planning your move abroad, you will naturally be asking a whole range of practical questions. Where to live? What about schools and child care facilities? Can I move to another country without having a job offer? Will my qualifications be recognised? How do I get residence and work permits? Is my driving licence valid in other countries? Do I have the same health care and social security rights as at home? What is my tax situation if I work in another EU country? How will my pension be paid? And so on.

In the past, hunting for all this information could be a frustrating and time-consuming business. But no longer. The European Commission and EU government departments have been working very hard to provide you with guides and up-to-date factsheets on all these topics and many more besides.

Answers to your questions

We have now made all these sources of information available on line via the "Your Europe" internet portal: europa.eu.int/youreurope

Click on it and follow the links for all the information you need. You will find very detailed guidance on all the issues that concern you – from social security and tax systems to practical details like finding a school, renting accommodation and opening a bank account, in whatever EU country you choose to go to.

Need more help? Two direct services at your disposal

1 Citizens Signpost Service

Do you want expert advice about

- Difficulties buying or renting property in another EU country?
- Trouble registering your car?
- Problems having your professional qualifications recognised?
- Problems with the tax authorities?
- Technical difficulties transferring your pension rights to a new country of residence?

Then follow the link to our Citizens Signpost Service (CSS). It provides free tailor-made information and advice on your rights and will point you to the organisation or service that can best help solve your problem. Experts will reply to your enquiry, in your own language, within three working days.

2 European Consumer Centres

You want advice about your rights as a consumer, or help in solving a consumer protection problem? Do you need expert information about

- Shopping online?
- Package holidays?
- Timeshare deals?
- Cross-border banking?
- Food safety?

Then follow the link to the European Consumer Centres. These centres have been (or are being) set up in all EU countries and the network is expanding to cover all the countries due to join the EU in the next few years. Your local centre can given you the information you need as well as specific help with cross-border disputes.

PART II

Authority dynamics and governance outcomes

7 Packing heat: pro-gun groups and the governance of small arms

CLIFFORD BOB

International relations scholars now recognize the important, if limited, influence of nongovernmental organizations (NGOs) and transnational advocacy networks (TANs) in global governance. Yet even as we have expanded our vision of "global governors" (defined in this volume as "authorities who exercise power across borders for purposes of affecting policy") and potential governors who seek such authority, we have done so with a kind of tunnel vision. Most of the literature analyzes only groups promoting human rights, the environment, women's rights, sustainable development, and global justice. Yet as the activists involved with these organizations well know, they do not act unopposed, and states are not their only foes. Rather, on a host of international issues, NGOs and TANs with conflicting values, ideologies, and policy ideas contend against one another.

Recognizing the contentious nature of transnational politics places key governance activities in a new light. The argument here is that in any issue area in which there is serious political conflict, it is not enough for analysts simply to examine those groups promoting new policies.[1] There is often a temptation to do so because, superficially, at least, these actors appear to be moving debate forward. On the other hand, if analysts take a broader view, they will typically find that such "change agents" do not act alone. Often opponents will mobilize too and dog policy proponents at every stage of the process. In these dynamic situations, "policymaking" is in some ways a misnomer. In reality, it is simultaneously an effort at making and unmaking, in which opposing sides vie for influence. The competition between would-be governors is often politically contentious and ugly. The parties seek to keep their foes out of policy arenas, they attack the others' ideas, and they seek to sully their reputations. And these battles simultaneously

---

[1] This chapter is a much-condensed version of empirical materials and theory arguments in Bob (forthcoming).

span multiple forums at varying levels of the international system. There are many groups vying for influence, and they do so both directly by promoting policies and lobbying decisionmakers, and indirectly by undermining their opponents.

To make this argument, this chapter provides an overview of one important area of global governance: international policymaking on small arms and light weapons (SALW).[2] I make no claim that the SALW case is representative of other issue areas. But in my conclusion, I give reasons to think this might be so, suggesting that this study can form the basis for developing hypotheses testable in other areas of global governance. Within the broad area of SALW policymaking, I focus primarily on the United Nations (UN) and organizations that have used it as a key forum for their activities. To be specific, much of the chapter focuses on the formation and interaction of two contending advocacy networks that have used the UN as a venue for their activities: the International Action Network on Small Arms (IANSA) which, along with numerous component NGOs, has promoted international controls on the trade in small arms; and the World Forum on the Future of Sport Shooting Activities (WFSA) which, together with national-level gun groups, in particular America's National Rifle Association (NRA), has opposed the proposed controls.

Theory

Like this volume as a whole, this chapter argues that international policy does not merely respond to global "needs." Instead, policymaking is a political process. To understand it, one needs to grasp both the strategies that policy proponents use to promote their ideas and the structural constraints they face. In that sense, this chapter resembles Carpenter's. However, where her story highlights intra-network contention, this chapter assumes that networks have reached some degree of consensus on their goals. Of course, such agreement is always temporary, shifting both as different elements within a network vie against one another and as the network interacts with the broader political environment. Nonetheless, this chapter gives relatively little attention

---

[2] While there are a variety of definitions, SALW will be defined here as pistols, rifles, assault rifles, machine guns, mortars, rocket-propelled grenades, and other weapons easily carried by an individual (small arms) or on a civilian vehicle (light weapons).

to the way in which the component groups within IANSA and WFSA agreed on their goals.[3] Instead, it focuses on the strategies the networks used and the constraints they faced in promoting their policy goals to external audiences, particularly within the UN.

Second, and more importantly, this chapter argues that governance, whether global, national, or local, is not only about making or enforcing new policy. A key aspect, as well, is policy opponents' efforts to attack, eviscerate, or kill policy processes – and more generally, the contending sides' attempts to neutralize one another. At the extreme, "nonpolicy" constitutes a form of governance every bit as powerful as policy, even if its perpetrators leave no fingerprints and its "products" are invisible (Crenson 1971). Even when opponents cannot extinguish a policymaking process, they can often stall it. And even when delay ends, opponents can overtly or subtly shape the results. In some cases, their power is such that the policies produced are little more than "zombies," so devoid of content that, while alive on paper, they are in reality dead.[4]

For scholars of global governance, the upshot is that one should seek to explain not only policy outcomes but also policy "might have beens": the ideas that might have been debated, the voices that might have been heard, and the provisions that might have been included – but for the power of opponents (Gaventa 1982). In this, the chapter runs counter to the international relations literature's emphasis on cooperative aspects of global governance. It also helps remedy pervasive selection bias that has made "global governance," at least by nonstate actors, appear more successful than it may in fact be. Governance certainly occurs, and every policy process by no means ends in failure or in a zombie policy. But the extent to which NGOs, IOs, and activists have direct effects on outcomes is less certain (Drezner 2007a). In a formal sense, of course, states have the ultimate say on international

---

[3] As in other policy arenas, certain actors within each network have more power than others and in effect act as "gatekeepers." Using this power or the deference that it sometimes induces, such actors have greater ability than others to achieve their goals. For discussion of gatekeeping and factors that contribute to an NGO's status as gatekeeper, see Bob (2005, 18–19; 2009c).

[4] In a regulatory context, this dynamic is similar to what Daniel Drezner (2007a) refers to as "sham standards." These are standards that exist on paper but that everyone ignores. In Drezner's more state-centric account, they are the result of fundamental conflict or disagreement among great powers. Thus, as in zombie policy, unresolved conflict between opposing sides is at the root of inaction.

policy. Nonstate actors, however, can play important roles at various stages. Moreover, like interest groups in domestic politics, they seek to shape state views on international policies. Indeed, one of this chapter's conclusions is that NGOs and TANs behave much like interest groups and coalitions in democratic polities (Willetts 1982).[5] In many cases, in fact, they are one and the same, jumping seamlessly between domestic and international institutions as they pursue their goals.

The making and unmaking of SALW policy

In this section, I examine the clash of opposing networks in the SALW area. I do so roughly following a "stage" model of the policy process, but an important caveat is in order: policymaking/unmaking is a recursive process. For analytic purposes, it may be possible to divide the process neatly into "stages," but the reality is that these stages overlap one another and occur in large measure simultaneously. That is, in any policy area there is a constant stream of ideas that are being formulated into one issue or another. Even as one discrete part of the issue may be rising on the policymaking agenda, other parts are still in formation, while still others may have been the subject of rulemaking or are now being implemented or assessed. This is particularly the case if one takes into account opposing networks. Even as a policy process appears to be progressing steadily through stages, opponents frequently seek to return it to an earlier stage by redefining the problem or introducing an entirely new problem that cross-cuts the old one (Schattschneider 1960). Meanwhile, opponents work hard to attack the proponents' bona fides, empirics, and logic at every step of the way. The agency of governors and these political dynamics shape both the processes and the outcomes.

Issue formation, late 1980s–1997

Small arms have been weapons of choice in conflicts around the world for centuries. For centuries too, journalists, artists, scholars, and others have shone light on the horrors of wars fought with such weapons.

---

[5] The interest group literature, at least in American politics, has noted the clash of contending groups in the policy process, e.g., Kingdon (1995, 49, 69).

But SALW as a discrete international policy area – one having an infrastructure of issues, ideas, solutions, proponents, and opponents – can be dated to the early 1990s. At that time, international analysts working on "conventional weapons" control began to expand their traditional focus beyond heavy weapons and major weapons systems. The traditional focus is evident, for instance, in the 1978 First Special Session of the General Assembly on Disarmament, calling for reductions in conventional arms and limitations on their transfer. Heavy weapons were the major concern of the outcome document. This traditional focus was also evident as late as 1991, when a UN expert panel issued a report on Ways and Means of Promoting Transparency in International Transfers of Conventional Weapons (UN doc. A/46/301, Sept. 9, 1991). Its primary recommendation – the establishment of a voluntary Register of Conventional Arms covering trade in major weapons systems – was accepted by the UN General Assembly in December 1991 (GA Res. 46/36). The report also included discussion of illicit arms transfers, but SALW as such were not its focus.

With the end of the Cold War, however, a number of factors converged to provide a context for the promotion of SALW as a separate issue. First, with an apparent reduction in the likelihood of nuclear war, conventional arms issues as a whole had greater space on the international agenda. Experts who had worked for years on nuclear weapons or heavy arms now saw opportunities to tackle SALW, an issue they increasingly viewed as more relevant and of greater gravity than either of the traditional arms control issues.[6] Second, as the Cold War receded, intra-state conflicts drew greater international attention. In these conflicts, SALW were heavily used, leading to large death tolls among combatants and civilians.[7] Third, as the UN (and various aid agencies) became more involved in international actions concerning such conflicts, its personnel also became victims of attacks by groups using rifles, pistols, and machine guns. Fourth, these international developments dovetailed with the activities of domestic

---

[6] In this, the SALW issue resembled landmines control. Indeed, leaders of the SALW control movement frequently cite the International Campaign to Ban Landmines as an important impetus and precedent. Edward Laurance, telephone interview by author, June 8, 2007.

[7] However, it is unlikely that the numbers killed by SALW at this time were larger than at other times in recent history (Human Security Center 2005). Thus, a "functional" basis for the SALW movement's growth is questionable.

gun control movements in many developed states, which framed the issues as a matter of public health and crime control. In the early 1990s, gun control movements in the UK, Canada, and Australia were galvanized by high-profile shooting incidents in which dozens were killed.

In this increasingly receptive context, a number of experts long active on heavy weapons issues began to formulate SALW as a distinct issue, one combining civil conflict, public health, and crime control aspects. There was frequent and easy interaction between pro-gun control experts and the UN. Among those most active in the nascent movement in the early 1990s were Michael Klare, Carl Kaysen, Jeffrey Boutwell, Edward Laurance, and Natalie Goldring. These individuals received crucial institutional support from the organizations to which they were attached, most of which had long been active on conventional arms or crime issues. These included the British American Security Information Council (BASIC), Saferworld, the International Peace Research Institute (Oslo), and the Federation of American Scientists (FAS). Perhaps most importantly, the Ford Foundation provided a $224,000 multi-year grant starting in 1994 to help build infrastructure for international promotion of the SALW issue. The grant sponsored a series of expert conferences on SALW that dealt with empirical issues (e.g., definitions and measurement), policy issues (alternative solutions to the problem), and strategic issues (e.g., how best to promote the issue and in what forums). The first and arguably most important of these occurred in 1994, a meeting sponsored by the American Academy of Arts and Sciences (AAAS), leading to the publication of *Lethal Commerce: The Global Trade in Small Arms and Light Weapons* (Boutwell *et al.* 1995). A second major conference took place in 1997, leading to the publication of *Light Weapons and Civil Conflict* (Boutwell and Klare 1999). Among those supporting this conference were the Ford Foundation, AAAS, the Carnegie Commission on Preventing Deadly Conflict, the Ploughshares Fund, and the John D. and Catherine T. MacArthur Foundations.

From the start, the UN was closely involved in this activism by experts. In large part, this was because some of the key figures noted above also worked with or for the UN. For instance, Edward Laurance served as a consultant to the UN Center for Disarmament Affairs beginning in 1992 and with the Panel of Experts on Small Arms later in the decade (Boutwell and Klare 1999, 261). As a result of this interchange, expert reviews of the UN Register of Conventional Arms included discussions of light weapons as early as 1994 (Goldring 1999, 108). On a more formal basis, in the spring of 1996 the UN Disarmament Commission adopted nonbinding guidelines for international arms transfers, focusing on ways of reducing the illicit trade in light weapons. And in 1997, the Economic and Social Council's (ECOSOC) Commission on Crime Prevention and Criminal Justice passed a resolution urging improved domestic firearms regulation as a means of reducing crime. Finally, in the late 1990s, the UN formed the Panel of Government Experts on Small Arms to study ways of reducing SALW transfer and use in conflicts in which UN forces were involved. In its 1997 report, which was adopted by the General Assembly, the Panel called for a variety of measures, including destruction of light weapons in the aftermath of conflicts, buy-back programs, marking weapons, and restricting sales to government purchasers only. Around this time, too, Canada and a number of European states began major involvement in the small arms control issue, supporting an emerging transnational network and developing their own programs promoting international gun control.

Notably, arms control proponents were well aware from the beginning that making small arms into an international issue would raise opposition.[8] Awareness of the likelihood of opposition (as well as of political and economic realities, namely the power of the arms industry and the likely responses of key states) shaped the way in which the issue was defined by proponents. For instance, rather than an unrealistic attempt to ban SALW production or even promote universal gun registration, proponents increasingly defined the issue around controlling illicit international trade in weapons. For many proponents, this was a major retreat from their preferred goals, a position they felt forced to adopt given the political realities of opposition from civil society organizations and key states.[9]

The pro-gun response

Pro-gun groups began their involvement with the issue in the early 1990s, just as SALW was beginning to emerge from the larger conventional arms control issue. While this international activism was to some degree "reactive" to the UN process and to the emerging SALW

[8] Natalie Goldring, personal interview by author, May 11, 2006.
[9] Lora Lumpe, telephone interview by author, May 9, 2007.

control movement, it also had its own logic. This stems primarily from the fact that major gun organizations have been active participants in the politics of developed countries for many decades. In these contexts, they have, of course, participated in national debates over gun control, safety, registration, and other issues. In their efforts, pro-gun groups worldwide have worked together with the aim of enhancing their domestic goals. For instance, at the NRA's 1992 annual board meeting, a leader of the Sport Shooting Association of Australia (SSAA) asked the NRA to help establish an international conference on firearms laws to "protect ... the rights of firearms owners wherever they are threatened" (quoted in Goldring 1999, 111). The NRA agreed to do so, leading to the founding of the International Conference on Firearms Legislation (ICFL). The ICFL held its first meeting in Australia in 1993, attracting representatives from the United States, Canada, South Africa, Australia, and New Zealand (Goldring 1999, 112).

In 1997, in the wake of the growing civil society activism and UN processes noted above, pro-gun groups from around the world formed WFSA. (Notably, this network organization predated the formation of IANSA in 1999.) Its early members included the NRA, five other US gun groups, and organizations from Belgium, France, Germany, Italy, the Netherlands, and the United Kingdom. According to contemporaneous reports, WFSA's main "challenges" included "efforts by the United Nations to promote international gun control schemes as well as proposed gun bans that could put an end to the shooting sports in several nations" (NRA-ILA 1997, quoted in Goldring 1999). Among its activities, WFSA would "establish a presence during discussions of global gun control to insure that correct and unbiased information is available to international decisionmakers."[10] As part of this effort, WFSA applied for and later received NGO Roster status with the UN's Economic and Social Council. Meanwhile, for its domestic American audience, the NRA began portraying the UN process as a dire threat to American gun ownership, the Second Amendment, and US sovereignty – themes that it continues to trumpet today.

Notably, pro-control forces were well aware of WFSA's formation, and there were discussions among activists about the wisdom of challenging pro-gun groups' applications for ECOSOC consultative

---

[10] *Gun News Digest*, "World Forum Seeks to Save Sport Shooting," Fall 1997, 20; quoted in Goldring (1999, 112).

status, on the basis that their goals were antithetical to the UN's. No such challenges actually occurred, however, in part because the UN quickly admitted the pro-gun groups, in part because of the pro-control forces' limited resources, and in part because any controversy over the issue seemed likely to backfire by suggesting that the pro-control forces were seeking to thwart debate.[11]

Agenda setting, 1997–2001

By the late 1990s, SALW had become a clearly defined, if low-profile issue both in civil society and in the UN. Even as pro-gun groups began to attack the issue, its proponents sought to promote it further. A key step in this regard was the creation of formal organizations dedicated solely to international small arms control. The most important of these were the Small Arms Survey and IANSA, both founded in 1999. Small Arms Survey acts as a source of research-based information on the issue and is based in Geneva, Switzerland, at the Graduate Institute of International Studies.[12] Its claim to authority on SALW issues rests primarily on its scientific and policy expertise. While opponents have challenged this source of authority, the Small Arms Survey has also earned backhanded praise, with the NRA calling it "one of the most unique and dangerous antigun organizations in the world" (LaPierre 2006a, 12).

IANSA is an advocacy network that now spans more than seven hundred NGOs from around the world. It includes national organizations long active exclusively on gun control issues, as well as international NGOs whose missions are far broader than gun control alone (for example, human rights NGOs such as Amnesty International and Human Rights Watch). IANSA's claim to authority is primarily moral: it aims to speak as a voice for victims of gun violence – although the NRA and WFSA dispute this assertion. Central to IANSA's activism

---

[11] Natalie Goldring, personal interview by author, May 11, 2006.

[12] Among its funders, according to its website, are the Swiss Federal Department of Foreign Affairs, the governments of Canada, Finland, France, the Netherlands, Norway, Sweden, and the United Kingdom, and the United Nations Development Programme, the United Nations Institute for Disarmament Research, the Geneva International Academic Network, and the Geneva International Centre for Humanitarian Demining. The survey has also received project-specific support from the governments of Australia, Belgium, Denmark, and New Zealand. See www.smallarmssurvey.org/files/sas/about/mission.html.

is the view that "gun proliferation is a global problem" and therefore requires a "global solution" (IANSA 2006).

Finally, the UN itself served as a platform for pro-control activism, rather than a neutral arena in which SALW issues might play themselves out. From the early 1990s, UN organs, particularly the Disarmament Commission, promoted SALW control. At a minimum, such controls might help protect UN personnel in conflict zones. More ambitiously, they might reduce bloodshed and conflict worldwide. This institutional view biased the UN process in favor of those seeking controls on SALW. Of course, since governments ultimately vote on any binding issues in the UN, this bias did not mean that the outcome of the UN process was foreordained. Indeed, pro-gun groups attended the "hostile territory" of UN forums precisely to influence national delegations on these issues. Nonetheless, the Disarmament Commission offered friendly ground for sowing the seeds of the international SALW movement.

In the late 1990s, the UN, IANSA, and like-minded states sought to raise the issue's profile on the international agenda. Their primary vehicle for doing so was a major international conference on small arms control. Not surprisingly, WFSA and the NRA opposed such a conference, albeit unsuccessfully given the UN's interest in one occurring. At the conference itself, however, the power of pro-gun forces became evident, less through direct action by civil society organizations than through that of the US government, whose delegation included several NRA board members.

Rulemaking: the UN Programme of Action

The 2001 UN Conference on the Illicit Trade in Small Arms and Light Weapons in All Its Aspects opened with hopes among the pro-control forces that it would not only raise the international profile of the SALW issue but also produce a relatively strong final document. The first set of goals was arguably achieved. The conference attracted media attention and helped build ties among IANSA member NGOs, as well as with like-minded states in many regions. In the wake of the conference, the SALW issue appeared to have gained a higher international profile than before, and IANSA has remained quite active.

But the second set of aims was not realized, primarily because of US opposition. Here the relationship between the US government and the

NRA was synergistic: NRA members participated in the official delegation and thereby had direct voice in the deliberations. Together they blocked the opposing side. This synergy was sufficient to stalemate the process and produce "zombie policy." In a dramatic opening speech to the conference, US spokesperson John Bolton laid down a series of "red lines," issues that the United States could not accept in any final document: restrictions on trade and manufacture of legal SALW; promotion of activism by NGOs and international organizations (IOs); limits on SALW sales to nonstate groups; a mandatory review conference; and a commitment to discussion of a legally binding agreement. For the UN, which sought a consensus in the conference, the US red lines played a formative role in shaping the final outcome document – even though UN leaders and many states would clearly have preferred far stronger language.

IANSA and the pro-control network not surprisingly attacked the red lines. Nonetheless, IANSA ultimately endorsed the Programme of Action on Small Arms (PoA) produced by the conference as the best that could be achieved given US opposition. Among its key provisions were *nonbinding* commitments by governments to: criminalize illicit gun production and possession; create national coordinating agencies on small arms; destroy surplus weapons; track officially held guns; issue end-user certificates for export and transfers; notify original supplier nations of re-export; disarm, demobilize, and reintegrate (DDR) excombatants; support regional small arms agreements; mark guns during production for identification and tracing; keep records of gun manufacture; engage in information exchange; improve enforcement of arms embargoes; and include civil society in SALW control efforts (UN 2001).

As IANSA noted, however, the PoA "provides no international mechanism for monitoring compliance, and the UN's role has been limited to compiling information submitted by states on a voluntary basis" (IANSA 2003). Many of the main international proponents of SALW control made similar criticisms of the PoA, with Human Rights Watch (2001) labeling it a "Program of Inaction." In fact, Human Rights Watch, formerly a key member of the IANSA network, was disheartened enough to reduce its activism on the issue. Notwithstanding increases in public awareness about SALW stemming from the 2001 conference, the PoA stands as a case of zombie policy.

Notably, for the NRA and WFSA, their apparent victory at the PoA also served to maintain their activism. Despite the PoA's weakness, the NRA and other national gun groups stridently portrayed it as the opening wedge of a UN assault on private gun ownership. And even as some countries began implementing the weak provisions of the PoA, pro-gun groups repeatedly emphasized that guns were not in fact a problem. For instance, NRA Executive Vice President Wayne LaPierre's 2006 book *The Global War on Your Guns: Inside the UN Plan to Destroy the Bill of Rights* includes lengthy chapters on the UN's threat to Americans' gun rights and the world. Regarding the latter point, the book includes detailed descriptions of recent genocides and massacres that, LaPierre argues, might have been prevented if the victims had been armed (LaPierre 2006a, 91–104).

Assessment

Under the PoA, two Biennial Meetings of States were held in 2003 and 2005. But the major international assessment effort occurred in July 2006: the Review Conference on Small Arms (RevCon) in New York. In spite of the PoA's impotence, IANSA and the UN Disarmament Commission sought to have it extended and strengthened at the RevCon. For its part, WFSA and the NRA continued their efforts to kill it, using the RevCon as a forum to do so. In these efforts, both sides deployed a wide variety of parallel tactics. They both engaged in "grassroots" politics in the lead up to the event. IANSA and the associated ControlArms campaign mounted the "Million Faces" campaign, which submitted a petition (accompanied by photos of more than a million signatories from sixteen countries) urging the UN to adopt global arms export standards. For their part, NRA members flooded the UN with letters and email messages in the weeks leading up to the conference, demanding that the UN keep its hands off their guns.[13] This NRA campaign attracted significant press attention, and in response the UN issued a special press release, "Setting the Record Straight: The UN and Small Arms" (2006b).

---

[13] At the NRA's "Stop the UN Gun Ban" website, prewritten letters to Kofi Annan, the Chairman of the RevCon, and John Bolton were available for immediate download.

There were many other parallels between the actions of the two networks. Both sides issued lengthy reports assessing the PoA – in profoundly different lights. They both sought and in some cases received representation on country delegations to the RevCon. They both sent top leaders from NGOs around the world. They both issued lengthy documents bolstering their positions and addressed the conference during its NGO sessions. They both buttonholed delegates, pumping them for information about the UN sessions and seeking to pass on information about specific issues. And they both set up rival campaign tables full of literature in the "NGO hallway" next to the meeting room.

Ultimately, the RevCon ended in failure, without any final agreement reached on the PoA's extension and strengthening. Although there were a variety of reasons for this, US opposition on several issues dear to the NRA played a major role. Thus the United States objected to language about how domestic gun laws might affect national rates of gun deaths, to discussion of possible impacts of small arms proliferation on development, and to provisions calling for a second review conference. A number of other major countries also objected to any strengthening of controls on arms transfers.

The PoA's weakness and the RevCon's failure, however, have by no means ended the conflict over SALW control. Searching for a venue in which to avoid the veto power of the United States and other major countries, IANSA, Oxfam, and Amnesty International formed the ControlArms campaign to promote an international treaty to "end the suffering caused by irresponsible arms transfers."[14] Working with a group of like-minded states, the ControlArms group lobbied for a UN General Assembly resolution to create an Arms Trade Treaty (ATT). The resolution passed overwhelmingly in December 2006, despite US rejection and abstentions by twenty-four countries, and since then the UN has begun moving forward on the treaty. If passed, such a treaty could come into force with or without ratification by the United States, China, or others. Of course, this form of governance would be far from "global" and would leave much of the SALW "problem" unsolved. But such "governance" is probably the best that those seeking controls can achieve, given the strength of the opposition among key governments and powerful sectors of global civil society represented by WFSA.

---

[14] See www.iansa.org/campaigns_events/documents/actioncard_en_artwork.pdf.

Conclusion

This chapter has focused on the role of NGOs, IOs, and TANs in global governance. To be specific, it has identified two networks of competing global governors on the gun issue: on one side, the UN bureaucracy, IANSA, and a set of states, primarily European and African; and on the other side, WFSA, the NRA, and another set of governments, most importantly the United States. Members of each network ground their authority in conflicting claims to expertise and morality – claims disputed by the opposing sides. Ultimately, of course, states make final decisions on most international policy issues (Drezner 2007a), and the US government was instrumental in making/unmaking the PoA, notwithstanding the contrary goals of other states. But the nonstate actors examined in this chapter also play significant roles in defining issues, setting agendas, assessing outcomes, and sometimes even contributing to rulemaking. As this chapter has shown, however, current understandings of nonstate actors and transnational networks as global governors require amendment.

First, it is important to recognize that NGOs by no means speak with one voice. Scholars often note this point, examining tensions within transnational advocacy networks, particularly over specific policy solutions to commonly agreed-upon global problems (Keck and Sikkink 1998, 19). The reality of unequal power and "gatekeeping" within advocacy networks underlines this point (Carpenter, this volume; Bob 2005). It suggests too that hierarchy is a central, if often hidden, feature of transnational networks themselves (not merely, as the introduction to this volume suggests, an alternative to networks). Moreover, such hierarchies are likely to be contested by network members themselves, regarding both particular strategies or broader goals and the hierarchical structure itself. For this reason, NGOs compete with one another for members and funds – not only to achieve substantive goals but also to gain clout in the networks they join. This competition is often hidden in the interest of achieving a network's commonly agreed goals, but it is nonetheless real, revealed, for example, in the schisms that frequently rend networks (Bob 2005, 95).

But this chapter emphasizes a deeper issue: on many significant policy issues, there are rival networks, often ones that do not even recognize the same problem. Beyond the gun case analyzed in this chapter, there are many others: on global warming, environmentalists confront networks of climate change skeptics; on family planning, feminists vie with religious fundamentalists; on development, free market enthusiasts oppose aid, while aid groups support it (Spiegel Online 2005). Every issue does not necessarily raise such conflict. By hypothesis, more "technical" issues – for instance, the kind of standard setting discussed by Büthe in this volume – seem less likely to generate conflict than more "political" issues linked to conflicting ideological or moral visions that have long pervaded modern societies (Sowell 2007). But in many cases, the very question of what is technical and what political remains contested.

Thus, in analyzing global governance, at least on nontechnical issues, it is not enough simply to examine proponents of change and their interactions with states. Rather, scholars must expand their analytical scope, examining how protagonists on various sides of issues anticipate and strategize with their foes very much in mind. Just like policy proponents, therefore, opponents act as "global governors." And just like policy proponents, opponents may gain "authority" on an issue, based on factors such as constituency size, scientific expertise, or moral claims. But the authority of contending networks is also reciprocally disputed. For instance, notwithstanding assertions of expertise-based authority by IANSA, the Small Arms Survey, and the UN, WFSA's own academic and scientific experts present rival analyses and harsh critiques. WFSA's Research and Statistics Committee, for instance, seeks to establish "a bedrock of unimpeachable statistics and research ... to document the economic, cultural and social benefits of sport shooting." Meanwhile, its "Project on Myths," necessary because "[m]isinformation knows no borders in the modern world," specifically targets "statistical myths and pseudo-scientific facts being used against the hunting and sport shooting community."[15]

IANSA and UN claims to moral authority, as the voice of gun violence victims or as the conscience of the world, also come under fire. For instance, Wayne LaPierre (2006a) charges the UN with illogic and hypocrisy: first, it repeatedly fails to prevent genocide in Rwanda and elsewhere; then it argues for policies that would limit potential victims' ability to obtain guns to defend themselves, particularly against repressive states. In this view, the pro-control network's claim to

---

[15] See WFSA's website at www.wfsa.net/Statistics_&_Research_Index.htm (accessed August 12, 2008).

moral authority is bankrupt. Indeed, the "UN is complicit in genocide, and international gun haters are complicit in evil" (LaPierre 2006a, 149). Reciprocally, IANSA members suggest that the gun groups are stalking horses for the global arms industry (Goldring 1999, 110). In any event, a network's (contested) authority is probably less important in determining policy outcomes than its linkages to powerful states, particularly, as in the case of the PoA process, if the state is a veto player, as the US government has been.

But even if a network's policy preferences fall victim to a veto player, conflict seldom ends there. In this, international politics closely resembles domestic democratic politics. As students of democracy have long noted, interest groups whose policy ideas are thwarted in one venue usually do not cease their activism. Rather, they maintain opposition in the press, shop for a new forum, seek to repeal current policy, exploit loopholes in it, differentiate it in a subnational political institution, undermine its implementation in an administrative agency, or challenge it in court (Meyer and Staggenborg 1996). In international arenas, such behavior is all the more likely, as the new ATT process suggests, because of the lack of authoritative decisionmakers and the wealth of possible institutions in which to advance political claims. Notably, however, in technical areas such as those discussed by Büthe in this volume, persistent conflict may be less likely as a result of "lock-in" effects once a particular standard is set; the dominance of the QWERTY keyboard is an example of this from the English-speaking world. But on less technical issues, even after a particular decision is made in one arena, the parties will typically fight on – in other institutions, new venues, or on related issues. And, as noted previously, the battle to make an issue "technical" rather than "political," a matter of administration rather than argument, is itself crucial.

Second, conflict pervades all stages of the policymaking process. Of course, for conflict to occur, those who oppose a policy must organize, mobilize, gain resources, and choose to attack. These are by no means trivial requirements. In some cases, of course, powerful oppositional networks may already exist within states and need only cooperate across borders. WFSA exemplifies this possibility, as it grew from preexisting national gun and gun rights organizations. In other cases, particularly when a policy issue is novel, it may be more difficult for a counter-network to develop. In either case, however, there is nothing automatic (or purely functional) about a rival network's rise and challenge.

Nor is there anything predetermined about where and how competing networks will contend with one another. The most direct conflicts occur in institutional arenas where rulemaking is occurring. Here the contending sides face off, usually trying in one way or another to influence decisionmakers in international organizations or states. But even in stages where issue entrepreneurs act more autonomously, especially in issue formation and agenda setting, the influence of opponents is felt. Choices about the problem's framing, promotion, and solution all occur in the shadow of opposition, whether existing or expected. Proponents may hope to keep opposition latent. Thus in the SALW case, a decision was made early on to focus on illicit trade in SALW, rather than an outright ban on such weapons. But, as in the SALW case, it is unlikely that opponents will long remain on the sidelines, particularly if they already have powerful, preexisting domestic networks. Not surprisingly, most interest groups closely protect their interests. As part of that guardianship, they ceaselessly scour the world for threats to their goals (as well as opportunities to realize them). Any activism on SALW control, however limited or camouflaged, would likely provoke interest and action from pro-gun groups.

Such responses and counter-responses also suggest that policymaking is path dependent, just as in domestic politics. Anxious to realize their goals, the NGOs and networks involved in international issues ceaselessly calibrate their actions to the prior thrusts and expected parries of their opponents. They take heed of institutional opportunities and limitations. And they accommodate themselves to the policy and statutory legacy they are bequeathed. As a result, particular policy processes are constrained by historical decisions and practices. At the international level, however, there are fewer authoritative decisionmakers and more institutional venues than in most states.[16] As a result, it is probably easier for policy proponents and opponents to jump from one venue to another – thereby opening new paths if the old ones prove too rough or unpromising. The recent opening of the ATT

---

[16] As between particular countries, those with more institutional toeholds also experience greater activism by social movements and counter-movements (Meyer and Staggenborg 1996, 1637).

process provides one example of this. As a result, dependency on a single path may be reduced, and international actors may have greater freedom of action than those operating in purely domestic arenas.

Finally, this study challenges current understandings of "global civil society" positing harmonious relations among like-minded transnational activists (Barber 2003; Florini 2000). In this view, NGOs express popular preferences better than governments do, and their participation is crucial to democratizing global governance (Falk 1995). But scholars have consistently overlooked such movements' ideological opponents, at best dismissing them as GONGOs or BONGOs (government- or business-organized NGOs). Often, too, they have sung the praises of a "moral" civil society fighting corrupt corporations and repressive states.

But this chapter suggests that certain NGOs cannot be written off as tools of corporate or state interests. Instead, the chapter shows transnational politics to be ideologically riven (cf. Risse 2000). Nor does it seem possible to create some kind of moral hierarchy between WFSA and IANSA or other NGOs and TANs by, for instance, differentiating their degrees of legitimacy, accountability, or democracy. Like most advocacy groups, they are not democratic, and their accountability to constituents comes primarily after the fact, through members' exercising their option to exit the organization. Yet, for advocacy groups, this lack of internal democracy seems unproblematic – even if for states, democracy is a worthy goal and accountability a must. Notably, most advocacy groups within democratic states are not themselves democratic, and they are held accountable primarily through domestic laws. At the international level, there seems to be no reason for groups like WFSA or IANSA to be treated any differently: internal democracy is unnecessary for advocacy groups; conversely, any claims such groups make about "representing" the global interest or civil society as a whole should be regarded primarily as political rhetoric. Regarding accountability, since NGOs and formal network organizations such as IANSA and WFSA are necessarily based in some states and inevitably operate in others, state laws will normally be sufficient – combined with additional, if informal, accountability mechanisms, such as a free media and opposing NGOs.

This chapter also raises questions about scholarship arguing that rational "deliberation" is the primary means of transnational persuasion and policy change (Risse 2000; Habermas 2001). Certainly such sober and reasoned interactions do occur in some arenas. For instance, it seems likely that part of the gatekeeping described by Carpenter involves precisely such respectful debate among ideologically compatible entities. In such contexts, differences, while important to outcomes, are primarily tactical, strategic, or rhetorical – and for that reason may be bridgeable. But when one moves beyond such circuits of agreement, the deliberative model breaks down. Fundamental disagreements – such as on the very nature of the "gun problem," let alone its "solution" – are likely to divide contending networks for long periods. And while rival networks may proclaim such broad goals as justice, human rights, sustainable development, or human security, these terms often conceal disagreement over specifics and conflict over practical applications. For instance, Mundy's chapter in this volume documents wide agreement on the idea of "education for all," but sharp contention over how best to achieve it – whether through fee-based or free education.

In sum, this chapter suggests the need to broaden our conception of global governors to include not only policy proponents, but also opponents. The SALW case is far from the only one in which such contention occurs. While nonpolicies or zombie policies are not the only result, they occur more commonly than the international relations literature has often suggested. Thus, analysts should recognize global governance as a highly contentious process, as the protagonists in numerous international policy battles already do.

8 | Governing the global agenda: "gatekeepers" and "issue adoption" in transnational advocacy networks

R. CHARLI CARPENTER

In early December 2006, human rights activists from several countries met in Cologne, Germany, to discuss strategies for addressing the social problems generated by the fathering of children by foreign soldiers during armed conflicts. It was noted that such children, born as a result of wartime rape, sexual exploitation, and consensual relations between foreign troops and local women, face a variety of adverse social circumstances in war's aftermath, including infanticide, discrimination, stigma, statelessness, and denial of the means to track their birth fathers or establish their biological identities (Grieg 2001). Activists and researchers at the meeting drew on historical case data from the post-World War II era in Scandinavia, as well as evidence from more recent conflicts in Bosnia, Uganda, and Rwanda, to make the case that "children-born-of-war" faced specific vulnerabilities and had special needs in conflict and post-conflict zones.

The meeting had been organized collaboratively by social scientists at the University of Cologne and the War and Children Identity Project in Bergen, Norway, a nongovernmental organization (NGO) that had formed on the heels of a successful domestic campaign to secure an apology and reparations from the Norwegian government for adult "war children." The event drew together researchers from Eastern Europe, the United States, and Africa to "consolidate the evidence base" on children-born-of-war. But rather than being a purely academic conference, it was also a meeting at which a small network of "political entrepreneurs" aimed to discuss and develop a strategy for policy changes to address the needs of this population.

Present also at the meeting was a representative from the United Nations, a UN Children's Fund (UNICEF) officer with some involvement in that organization's considerations of how to address the issue of babies fathered by peacekeepers and UN personnel. The official had

202

originally been invited to speak about the UN's emerging policy on sexual exploitation and whether the provisions regarding paternity in that policy might serve as a best practice for holding states and individuals accountable for protecting children left behind in conflict zones. However, as the meeting wore on, the conversation increasingly turned toward whether or not the United Nations, and UNICEF in particular, should pay specific attention to this set of human rights issues: in effect, whether it should "adopt" children-born-of-war as a category of concern in its broader child rights advocacy and programming, and how it might assist activists working on this issue. The political entrepreneurs at the meeting proposed that the support and legitimation of such a powerful authority in the child rights movement would lend credence to their concerns, assist in the process of awareness-raising throughout the child rights network, and provide valuable contacts throughout global civil society.

Over the course of the two days, the UNICEF representative consistently argued against this idea, stressing a variety of organizational, conceptual, and logistical issues. While deeply sympathetic to their concerns, his position was that the issue was too multifaceted to be encompassed under one rubric, that it was not obvious that such children's needs were unmet by existing human rights programming, and that any additional threats to their rights (such as stigma) did not fall properly under UNICEF's mandate. Toward the end of the conference, despite the case data, statistical evidence, and eloquent rights-based arguments proffered by several of the activists, the UNICEF representative stated, "I remain to be convinced of the merit of UNICEF treating these children as a specific group."[1] His remarks echoed the position of other leading child rights organizations, none of which, at that time dealt explicitly with stigma against "war children" (Carpenter 2007a).

This apparent failure of global agenda setting at Cologne is not an isolated incident in world politics. Many domestic groups covet international attention to issues of vital concern to them, often never breaking into the advocacy discourse constitutive of global civil society. There is a campaign to require governments to compensate victims of collateral damage from legal war operations; so far, efforts to create

---

[1] Author's meeting notes, Cologne, Germany, December 2006.

a "global norm" in this area have been unsuccessful.[2] There is a campaign to treat infant male circumcision as a form of genital mutilation and a human rights abuse, but this issue is given no lip service by major organizations concerned with human rights or gender violence (Delaet 2007).[3] There is a well-organized movement to outlaw conscription in national armies as a form of slavery, but global organizations working to eliminate forced labor have largely accepted that conscription is a nation's right, except in cases of conscientious objection or when the recruits include children aged less than fifteen (Jones 2007). At the same time, advocates arguing for the *right* to bear arms, on the basis that it serves as a bulwark against state repression and tyranny, have received short shrift from the international human rights movement (Bob, this volume).

These anecdotes suggest that the construction of transnational issues requires more than dedicated "norm entrepreneurs" (Finnemore 1996; Finnemore and Sikkink 1998). A permissive or inhibiting role is also played in issue emergence by actors with the ability to disseminate and promote new issues but who pick and choose among the range of possible emerging claims, launching some issues to prominence and sidelining others. Some issues are "adopted" on to the agendas of major international organizations (IOs) and NGOs, and of these, a few result in major transnational campaigns and new treaties, norms, and state policy reforms. Some are pitched by political entrepreneurs but systematically ignored by global civil society authorities. Because of this, there is at any time a dizzyingly inconsistent potpourri of causes taken up by transnational advocacy networks, interspersed with myriad problems that go unrecognized or on which progress is made much more slowly.

Even transnational social problems with which we are now familiar once went through such a process, emerging not simply as a result of the dedication and persistence of altruistic entrepreneurs, but with the acquiescence of authorities in global civil society who, facing a menu of competing claims for their attention, engaged in a process of

[2] Author's interview with Sarah Holewnski of the Campaign for Innocent Victims in Conflict, Pittsburgh, PA, March 2008.

[3] The 2006 UN Study on Violence against Children avoids mention of this issue. For an example of a norm entrepreneur on this issue, see www.nocirc.org/. For an analysis, see Delaet (2007).

vetting causes on the basis of more interest-based concerns (Bob 2005). Raphael Lemkin pitched the concept of "genocide" to a number of governments and celebrities before his idea found a home at the UN in 1948 (Schmitz 2004). Women's rights groups worked unsuccessfully to mainstream their concerns into the human rights movement until Charlotte Bunch constructed the issue of "violence against women" and brought leading human rights NGOs such as Amnesty International on board (Thompson 2002). Institutionalized violence and discrimination under India's caste system was tolerated for decades until Indian activists persuaded human rights gatekeepers to address their concerns under the rubric of "work-based discrimination" (Bob 2009c).

This chapter focuses on the role played by leading authorities in specific transnational issue domains in controlling the construction of new problems as issues in advocacy networks. Following Clifford Bob's (2005) influential study of human rights organizations, I refer to this role as "gatekeeping" and argue that it constitutes a powerful form of global governance.[4] Gatekeepers in major international organizations have the power either to lend credibility, brand value, and resources to an emergent "issue," or to block its entry into a transnational issue pool. They can also affect how the issue is framed in global civil society, dramatically influencing how it is perceived by stakeholders, its potential for linkage with other issues, and its relational attributes within the ideational landscape of global civil society.

The empirical grounding for my remarks is found first in the case literature on transnational advocacy networks and global civil society; and, second, in data I have collected over the past seven years on the activities of the child rights network. During this period, a number of civil society actors have attempted to situate the difficulties of children-born-of-war in a human rights frame, and these activities have largely been countered by leading child rights' organizations which have resisted such constructions. In the first part of the chapter, I draw on examples of UNICEF's role as a gatekeeper in this

---

[4] However, while Bob emphasizes "NGO gatekeepers," I see a gatekeeper as any global actor densely connected to a particular issue network and thereby possessing particular influence over the issue agenda within that network. These can include think-tanks, international organizations, and governmental agencies, as well as leading NGOs.

area and the organization's efforts selectively to engage such political entrepreneurs without formally incorporating the issue into its child protection agenda. In the second half, I discuss data gathered in the broader advocacy network concerning children and armed conflict. Focus groups that I conducted also aimed to gauge the extent to which such organizations viewed this issue as relevant to their own work, and why. This case of issue *non*-adoption is helpful in suggesting avenues for theory-building on the role played by such gatekeeping activities in transnational civil society.

The chapter proceeds in four sections. First, I stress the importance of conceptualizing issue emergence in global civil society as a two-step process that distinguishes issue definition by political entrepreneurs from the recognition or "adoption" of those issues by leading organizations in an issue domain. Second, I situate the governing role played by such network "gatekeepers" within the theoretical orientations suggested by the opening chapter in this volume. Third, I survey existing explanations for variation in "issue adoption" drawn from the literature on transnational advocacy networks, and argue for more systematic research on this important dynamic in world politics. Fourth, I articulate some empirical challenges to such research, and suggest a methodology for capturing and analyzing variation in this area.

Theorizing "issue adoption" by transnational gatekeepers

Transnational advocacy networks are composed of a variety of nongovernmental organizations, international organizations, governments, and myriad individuals located within these bureaucracies and other levers of symbolic power in world affairs, including academia and the media. As the literature has demonstrated, networks such as these do a great many things, including lobbying, standard setting, monitoring of compliance with standards, and shaming norm violators (Keck and Sikkink 1998). But two of the most pivotal, yet understudied, aspects of transnational network politics are the construction and acceptance of specific problems as international issues in the first place (Price 2003). These twin steps, together constituting what I call *issue emergence*, are logically prior to building campaigns, negotiating treaties, and holding states accountable to new norms.

Yet because studies of advocacy networks to date have typically worked backward from *existing* items on advocacy network agendas,

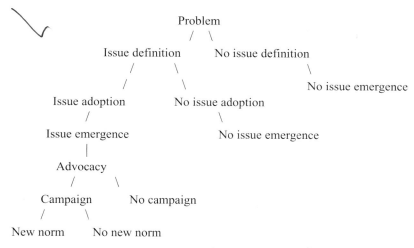

Figure 8.1 Stages in global issue advocacy

most of the theorizing has dealt with later steps in the advocacy chain, such as the process of creating and diffusing new norms (which occurs when states sign up to treaties) or the process of campaigning for the creation of new norms, which occurs once a critical mass of civil society actors converges around a specific platform such as "create an international criminal court" or "ban landmines." Thus, we know a fair amount about why campaigns form around certain issues but not others, and the conditions under which campaigns, once formed, succeed or fail (Burgerman 2001; Khagram *et al.* 2002). Less has been written about the crucial early question of why advocates and advocacy networks pay attention to certain issues and not others in the first place.

I argue that understanding the dynamics of *issue emergence* is crucial to assessing the role of transnational advocacy networks (TANs) in world politics. Not all human rights issues become codified as international norms: once an issue has emerged within a TAN issue pool, it may or may not elicit a campaign or concerted action. But if an issue never enters the agenda, no effective advocacy is possible, since all subsequent advocacy politics depend on an issue being defined as such by a norm entrepreneur and accepted as such by a critical mass of activists and gatekeepers (see Figure 8.1). In short, issue emergence is the conceptual link between the myriad bad things out there and the persuasive machinery of advocacy politics in world affairs.

Problem,
issues
&
campaigns

In mapping out these relationships, it is helpful to recall Keck and Sikkink's distinction between problems, issues, and campaigns.[5] In the human rights area, for example, *problems* are preexisting grievances that may not yet have been defined as issues. *Issues* emerge when (1) advocates name a problem as a human rights violation, and (2) major human rights NGOs begin referencing the issue in advocacy materials. *Campaigns* involve concerted efforts by multiple organizations lobbying for a specific outcome around a certain issue. Campaigns and coalitions sometimes form around, but are distinct from, specific issues (Khagram *et al.* 2002, 7).[6]

For a time, the literature on TANs was criticized for failing to analyze "dogs that didn't bark," or unsuccessful campaigns. A fair amount has now been written explaining the success or failure of campaigns (Price 1998; Thompson 2002; Khagram *et al.* 2002; Bob 2005), and this chapter adds little to our understanding of those questions. But significant variation also exists at earlier stages of the process: as Keck and Sikkink's original study recognized (1998, 7), many issues on a network agenda do not result in specific campaigns as did the child-soldier issue. For example, the human rights problems specific to "girls in armed conflict" have been recognized as an issue within the Children and Armed Conflict (CaAC) network, but have not resulted in a specific campaign. At the same time, other problems exist for war-affected children that are not recognized as issues at all, such as stigma against children born of war (Carpenter 2010).

What is of interest here is how to explain variation in the issue emergence stage: how do problems become issues, and why do some issues end up on TAN agenda space while others fall by the wayside? Although existing TAN literature tends to talk only vaguely about "norm entrepreneurship" as a permissive condition, it is useful to

---

[5] What Keck and Sikkink call "problems" are described as "underlying conditions" by scholars of agenda setting, who use the term "problem" where Keck and Sikkink use the term "issue." See Kingdon (1995) and Baumgartner and Jones (1993). Since this chapter contributes more to the TAN literature than to the domestic agenda-setting literature, I rely on the terminology popularized by Keck and Sikkink.

[6] Thus, the Campaign to Stop the Use of Child Soldiers was framed around the issue of child soldiers, aimed specifically at codifying a prohibition on child recruitment in international law (and, presently, at encouraging ratification). The child soldiers issue, however, is much broader, as is the issue pool within the "children and armed conflict" network.

distinguish at least two necessary phases of transnational issue emergence, either of which may fail to occur: *issue definition* by an entrepreneur and *issue adoption* by one or more major human rights organizations.[7] The distinction is vital for understanding issue emergence, because as the example from the Cologne meeting above demonstrates, an issue may be defined by an entrepreneur but not adopted into the mainstream TAN discourse by human rights "gatekeepers," including major NGOs and/or human rights intellectuals. Only when both issue definition and adoption have occurred can an issue be said to have been "formed" in a network's discursive space.

Issue definition involves demonstrating "that a given state of affairs is neither natural nor accidental, identify[ing] the responsible party or parties, and propos[ing] credible solutions" (Keck and Sikkink 1998, 19). Problems are defined when actors articulate the case that existing conditions are wrong and are changeable. But problem definition does not ensure that an issue will be constructed as such on the policy agenda.

By contrast, issue adoption occurs when the issue is championed by at least one major player in the broader network (Bob 2009b). Issue adoption by gatekeepers is a defining moment in the emergence of new issues on the global stage, a hurdle that must be passed for an idea to move from a nascent state to political salience within global civil society and a prerequisite for the development of a campaign that might result in new international norms.

This chapter focuses on the issue adoption stage and tries to understand how individuals in powerful, preexisting organizations, when faced with new or emerging claims by lesser known activists, make choices as to whether or not to incorporate them into their formal agendas. In the next section, I explain why this process of "gatekeeping" – choosing which issues warrant advocacy attention by the most influential organizations in an issue domain – constitutes *governance* at the global level, and why therefore individuals in gatekeeping organizations must be understood as global governors at specific points in time in relation to specific issues. I then consider explanations for variation in gatekeepers' decisionmaking practices and discuss methodological issues with respect to studying this process more systematically.

---

[7] I am grateful to Michael Goodhart for this analytical insight.

Are gatekeepers "governors"?

In determining what enters or is excluded from the transnational agenda, leading advocacy organizations govern the ideational content and reinforce or strategically alter the structure of global civil society, contributing to the regulation or nonregulation of political outcomes affecting the lives and security of individuals. This fits the definition of global governors informing this volume: "authorities who exercise power across borders for purpose of affecting policy" (Avant *et al.* 2008, 1). Defining what counts as a legitimate advocacy claim within an issue domain constitutes an exercise of three of the types of power outlined by Barnett and Duvall (2005).

First, it offers or denies *institutional* power to claimants on the material resources and ideational influence of respected advocacy organizations in global civil society. Within advocacy networks, constituent parts' authority and influence is based on moral legitimacy and persuasive power (Barnett and Finnemore 2004). As Lake and Wong (2005, 2) have demonstrated, in transnational advocacy networks, "nodes in networks are not equal": that is, some entities have much greater influence than others. Their analysis describes the contagion effect on the human rights community when leading NGOs such as Human Rights Watch or Amnesty International begin referencing new issues; correspondingly, many problems are never defined or, once defined, never spread because they are not endorsed by such powerful gatekeepers, whose "choices have powerful demonstration effects, signaling that certain causes are important" (Bob 2005, 6). By articulating a new problem as an "issue," a gatekeeping organization legitimizes that problem and defines it in a particular way, thus triggering donor attention, mobilizing material resources, and affecting the visibility of that issue within the informational content of global civil society.

Second, the gatekeeping process does not simply channel the soft power of global civil society, relative to states, toward some issues and away from others; it is also in itself an expression of *structural* relations of power *within* advocacy networks. The asymmetrical influence of powerful organizations in a network stems from factors such as relative connectivity to the rest of the network, name recognition, financial capacity, linguistic, diplomatic, and technological mastery, and access to states and global policymakers. In a global sector defined by its ability to endow symbolic meanings with legitimacy and disseminate information effectively (Barnett and Finnemore 2004; Holzscheiter 2005; Lipschutz 2005), these are coveted resources. Granting or denying access to such resources is itself an expression of power that reproduces the central place of such gatekeepers within the structural hierarchy of a transnational network. The creation of rules and procedures by which such requests are considered is itself a form of governance.[8]

Third, selecting issues for adoption constitutes a form of *productive* power (Barnett and Duvall 2005, 21). The construction of "child soldiers" or "HIV/AIDS orphans" as specific categories of concern signals a need for policies to address such populations and produces new claims on the governance activities of states, NGOs, and international organizations (Hayward 2000).[9] Conversely, to determine which voices shall not be given credibility in such forums constitutes an exercise of power that decisively shapes the global agenda. As Holzscheiter (2005, 731) writes, "The subjugation of minority voices originates in a manipulation of the issues that are talked about, in the limitation of legitimate participants in the discussion and of the ways of talking about the issues."

Such a practice of "non-decisionmaking" – to draw on Bachrach and Baratz's (1963) famous articulation of the process – constitutes an exercise of what these authors refer to as the "second face of power" (Bachrach and Baratz 1962). "When the dominant values, the accepted rules of the game, the existing power relations among groups, and the instruments of force, singly or in combination, effectively prevent certain grievances from developing into full-fledged issues which call for decisions . . . a non-decisionmaking situation exists. To pass over this is to neglect one whole face of power" (Bachrach and Baratz 1963, 641, 632).

---

[8] For example, as Bob notes (2005, Appendix 1), organizations as diverse as Human Rights Watch, the Sierra Club, and the Worker's Rights Consortium have internal documents outlining the criteria they use in sifting the various requests for assistance they receive from civil society.

[9] This does not necessarily ensure that new norms will be implemented or that governance will be effective, as Karen Mundy's analysis of "education for all" in this volume demonstrates. However, had there been no consensus among organizations associated with child rights and education, such as UNICEF and UNESCO, that education for children was a human right, implementation of such a right would have been impossible: the adoption of education as an issue for these organizations provided a permissive context in which a discussion of governance was made possible.

Limiting the scope of decisionmaking to "safe" or politically "acceptable" issues constitutes power. Thus, actors in a position to determine which issues their leading organization shall formally adopt govern the global agenda by influencing definitions of what constitutes a public good (Avant *et al.* 2008, 11). When Amnesty International and Human Rights Watch acknowledged women's rights as part of their global human rights agenda, they lent strength to women's mobilization by signaling the fundamental, rather than subsidiary, importance of gender issues; by situating women's concerns within, rather than separate from, the broader movement; and by committing their own advocacy influence to the movement.

The decisions of gatekeeping organizations nested in different issue domains also have an important effect on *how* issues are framed. It is one kind of political act to deal with the protection of civilians within the humanitarian arena; it is a different political act to begin treating this as a security problem at the level of the UN Security Council. Similarly, landmines were once treated primarily as an arms control problem; reframing them as a humanitarian concern required the mobilization of prominent civil society organizations, and this reframing had consequences for eventual governance in this area, as well as the chances of related problems (such as cluster munitions) themselves receiving attention (Price 1998). In Africa, lead organizations and donors often ask whether an issue is security- or development-related, given that these are the current master frames driving the human security issue agenda.[10] Thus, gatekeepers place conditions on the way in which a problem can be articulated in order to receive their endorsement, and issue entrepreneurs must often resist having their problem definition watered down. For example, the Campaign for Innocent Victims in Conflict (CIVIC) has been encouraged to emphasize women and children as victims, which would draw donor attention but constitute a significant narrowing of their vision. So far the organization has refused. This principled stand has affected CIVIC's ability to spread its message.

Handing over the keys: sources of gatekeeper authority

What attributes provide certain organizations the ability to exercise this influence? Why do others allow prominent organizations in an area

---

[10] I am grateful to Erin Baines for this insight.

to gatekeep? From where is the authority of gatekeepers derived? The simple answer is that gatekeeping is a relational construct dependent on particular configurations of resources, power, and interests between established players in a network and issue entrepreneurs within or outside the network.

No one organizational actor or type of actor always plays this role, as suggested by some analyses. Clifford Bob's (2005) analysis focused on NGO gatekeepers within transnational advocacy networks, but international organizations and governments can also play either role. In her book *Agenda-Setting, the UN, and NGOs* (2007), Jutta Joachim describes several sets of players that are typically sought after by NGOs aiming to promote a new issue on the international agenda. She includes governments, the media, foundations, and UN Secretariats, and in many respects she treats these players as "gatekeepers" in the sense that their choice whether or not to support a new transnational movement can exert a powerful effect on the likelihood of the movement gaining attention.

However, Joachim's view too is unnecessarily static in assuming that issue entrepreneurs come from outside these dominant groups, or that NGOs themselves cannot also serve as gatekeepers. Sometimes, governments have been issue entrepreneurs relative to UN Secretariats. Sometimes, members of the media have served not as influential allies to norm entrepreneurs, but as entrepreneurs themselves. Journalists have attempted to cover the plight of children-born-of-war, but if anything their coverage of the issue has created disincentives for leading child rights NGOs to pay serious attention to the problem (Carpenter 2007b). The "glitterati" can likewise both enhance attention to an issue (Drezner 2007b), as Princess Diana did with landmines, or attempt to create it from scratch, as Leonardo DiCaprio has attempted to do – though with less success – with respect to coltan mining in the Democratic Republic of Congo.[11]

---

[11] See "DiCaprio Touts Gorilla-Friendly Mobile Phones." Available online at www.theregister.co.uk/2001/09/10/di_caprio_touts_gorillafriendly_mobile/. Sometimes, both the issue entrepreneur and the gatekeeper occupy different subject positions within the same organization. Joel Oestreich (2007) argues that issue adoption within international organizations, such as the adoption of gender equity as an operational principle in the World Health Organization, typically involves an ongoing dynamic between "true believers," issue proponents to whom NGOs have successfully pitched a problem, and those

Thus it is not that some players (governments or IOs) are gatekeepers and others (NGOs) are entrepreneurs. The relationship between the gatekeeper and the issue entrepreneur is constituted by the *relative* political resources the gatekeeper can offer in a given context. These resources are varied; moreover, there is a recursive relationship between all of these factors.

One type of resource is formal authority or recognition as a credible voice in an issue area, or what Avant *et al.* (2008, 9) refer to as "institution-based authority." Because of its role in the enforcement of the Geneva Conventions, for example, the International Committee of the Red Cross has a unique role to play in the development of international humanitarian law (Finnemore 1996). NGOs attempting to develop a new understanding of the humanitarian effects of particular weapons, for example, are most likely to succeed if they first secure the endorsement of the ICRC Secretariat and persuade its representatives to speak out publicly on behalf of the issue. Similarly, UNICEF occupies a special position, an "official role" in the area of child rights (Oestreich 2007, 26), providing incentives for issue entrepreneurs in this area to lobby UNICEF for endorsement just as much as they lobby governments for change.

A reputation as an established expert in a niche area also helps. In any given issue area, two or three well-established NGOs are typically associated with that agenda space, and their definition of the agenda has important contagion effects. In the issue area of "women, peace, and security," the Women's International League for Peace and Freedom (WILPF) has a century of experience on the international stage. This translates into overwhelming recognition by activists of the organization's importance in the area of women and peace.[12] Persuading WILPF to adopt a particular issue on its agenda could bring attention to the issue in a way some newcomer to the network on "women, peace, and security" might not. As Anna Snyder (2003) has detailed, WILPF's relatively powerful position within the women's network gave it and other Northern organizations an advantage in framing the women's

senior personnel in the organization whose acquiescence must be secured to achieve policy change.

[12] A survey of subscribers to two "women, peace, and security" listservs in 2007 found that WILPF was the NGO most often mentioned when respondents were asked to list "organizations that come to mind when you think of 'women, peace and security.'" See Carpenter, Jose-Thota, and Rubin (2008).

agenda at the 1995 Beijing Conference, as compared with women's groups from the developing world.

An organization's early entry into an emerging niche market for advocacy can earn that organization a gatekeeping status down the line, as other organizations attempt to piggy-back on its success. Global Witness was the first organization to establish itself in the new issue area of "conflict resources," focusing originally on diamonds – an issue that became salient once large human rights NGOs like Amnesty International adopted it[13] – but more recently expanding its agenda to include timber, oil, water, and other natural resources that can be said to contribute to the political economy of armed conflict. In so doing, Global Witness has not only constructed a new advocacy arena in which a variety of issues will surface over time, but has situated itself as the lead player in this area; it has gone from being an issue entrepreneur pitching new problems to global civil society NGOs to being an authority in a newly defined issue area. As of October 2007, it topped the list for a Google search of the topic "conflict resources." NGOs interested in launching a campaign against the trade in coltan or in exposing the links between coffee companies and human rights abuses will therefore likely attempt to solicit the assistance, publicity, and networking opportunities that an alliance with Global Witness can provide.[14] This example underscores the point that gatekeeping ability inheres not in a specific organization or organization type but in their relative authority within a specific issue arena at a specific time: entrepreneurial actors can construct entirely new issue arenas and then control access to them (turning themselves into gatekeepers).

Organizations that have proven themselves within a particular issue area are more likely to attract additional foundation grants for projects in that issue area, which also explains Sally Merry's (2006, 31) observation that NGOs tend to focus "on a single issue such as reproductive

---

[13] Global Witness launched its original report on the problem in 1998 and began pitching it to the news media, industry, and governments as early as 1999; nonetheless, only after Amnesty International picked up the issue and launched its media campaign in 2000 did the issue proliferate into a large-scale transnational campaign (Grant and Taylor 2004).

[14] Indeed, Global Witness's minimal attention to coltan as an analogous problem may explain the lack of a campaign or strong governance in this area, alluded to by Haufler in this volume.

health, land mines, mental health or aging." But not all such organizations will receive this initial support. The types of resources that
make them more likely to get their foot in the door with foundations and other donors include command of professional English or
French; access to the internet; enough resources to send delegates to
international conferences or other networking opportunities; and a
professional website conforming to standard advocacy templates that
clearly defines the organization's mission.[15] Newcomers to transnational advocacy often do not have these resources, expertise, or professional visibility within global civil society. Established organizations
do have greater capacity to shape the agenda within the issue area in
which they have credibility.

Such attributes translate into access to the targets of influence, be
they states, UN agencies, or others. Some theorists consider access to
be an aspect of "a political opportunity structure," but access also
constitutes a resource because it is a quality conferred on certain issue
proponents in an advocacy sector but not on others. Consultative
status at the United Nations is one such type of access. While this has
been cast by some studies of global agenda setting as a component of
a political opportunity structure (Joachim 2007), this is not a political
opportunity that is available to all NGOs equally. A complex set of
institutional norms governs which NGOs can benefit from it: those
that have already mastered the procedural skills, the marketing and
fundraising strategies, and linguistic norms that enable them to fit the
guise of a standard nongovernmental actor.[16]

---

[15] To some extent this question of differential economic resources leading to
differential access is only a reflection, within global civil society, of the same
dynamic among governments. For example, as Tim Büthe points out in this
volume, the organizational features of the International Electrotechnical
Commission virtually assured the exclusion of governments from the
developing world, which could not afford to send delegates to landmark
conferences where global regulatory mechanisms for electrical and electronic
technology were established. This disadvantaged developing countries within
the regime and reinforced perceptions of the global South as technologically
backward.

[16] The application process for consultative status can take more than a year.
According to the UN Committee on Non-Governmental Organizations, an
applicant's "activities must be relevant to the work of ECOSOC; the NGO
must have been in existence (officially registered) for at least 2 years in order to
apply; the NGO must have a democratic decisionmaking mechanism; the
major portion of the organization's funds should be derived from

Because some NGOs lack this status, many want it, and few can achieve it, alliances with those that have it constitute resources for newcomers to the international scene.[17] Those NGOs with access to UN bodies themselves can become targets of influence for issue entrepreneurs. Their decision to adopt or ignore a particular problem within their issue pool and their decision regarding how to frame it constitute acts of power that shape the types of governance that become possible in international society and also reinforce their position in the transnational hierarchy. In short, gatekeeping practices exert regulative, as well as constitutive, effects (Wendt 2000).

These are recursive processes, such that organizations that gain early notoriety in an issue area become more powerful over time relative to newcomers and thus occupy a disproportionately influential role within a given network (Lake and Wong 2005). Professional experience confers not only recognition but also the skill-sets and attributes requisite for effective multilateral diplomacy, such as expertise in diplomatic protocols and treaty-making procedures, or what Joachim (2007, 37) calls "procedural expertise." This expertise is an important resource in itself, and also places the organization in a position to garner additional mobilizing resources and political opportunities unavailable to more marginal players. As Merry writes (2006, 54), "attending UN meetings is expensive, but it facilitates fundraising. Since funding comes primarily from the global North, NGOs in consultative status that come to New York or Geneva have the opportunity to meet with funders, find out what the current hot topics are, learn the appropriate language in which to phrase funding proposals, and hear what other groups are doing."

But this position at the center of transnational conferences not only constitutes access to the agenda, but also signifies a given organization's stature and multiplies its social connections with a wider advocacy network, including other NGOs, the media, governments, and other movers and shakers. In turn, this status makes the center-player more attractive as an ally to edge-players. If an issue

contributions from national affiliates, individual members, or other nongovernmental components."

[17] Even among NGOs that earn consultative status there is a hierarchy that affects such matters as the word limit for statements that may be submitted to government delegates at UN conferences. The most privileged status is reserved for the older and larger NGOs. See Merry (2006, 53).

entrepreneur without such skills can attract the support of an NGO that can facilitate such access, it enhances its chances of being heard by the councils of nations. For these reasons, such leading organizations themselves constitute coveted access points for newcomers or issue entrepreneurs with an idea to pitch to transnational civil society.

In short, to a large extent the relevant gatekeeper is constituted by the goals of the norm entrepreneur. If the goal is a multilateral treaty among governments, then governments themselves must be brought on board for any successful action. Hence advocates of debt relief appealed in person to specific decisionmakers in the US Congress who they had identified as the veto players in launching debt relief on to the global agenda (Busby 2007). But if the goal is specific types of programs within multilateral agencies, the civil servants in those agencies themselves play an important role in shaping these more specific "institutional agendas" (Joachim 2007, 17). If the goal is simply to have a concern raised within the UN General Assembly or at multilateral conferences, then UN secretariats are the primary targets of advocacy organizations, because of the role they play in preparations for UN meetings, including drafting supporting documents (Willetts 1996, 49).

Within the children and armed conflict network, UNICEF constitutes a gatekeeper because of both its centrality and moral authority in defining the concept of "child rights." By any measure, UNICEF is the organization outside the UN Secretariat itself most closely associated with the issue area of children and armed conflict. It appears near the top of a Google search for the term, is frequently cited by interviewees when asked which organizations come to their minds, and receives the largest number of incoming hyperlinks from other websites of any organization in the area. UNICEF has long been acknowledged as a leader in the child rights movement – an irony, since the organization took on this role reluctantly after avoiding the seemingly political discourse of rights for the entire period during which the Convention on the Rights of the Child (CRC) was drafted (Oestreich 2007). Its particular agenda-setting power within the UN system is based in part on its budgetary structure. Unlike many UN organizations with formal budgets from governments, which therefore remain hostage to some extent to state agendas, UNICEF raises a large part of its revenue directly from individuals through a variety of innovative campaigns, thereby maintaining a large measure of flexibility in setting the child rights agenda.[18]

This status and role confers a particular authority upon UNICEF to consider and accept or reject claims about child rights by issue entrepreneurs in international society. It is not that UNICEF's rejection of a proposed issue is sufficient to keep it off the international agenda, because other similarly positioned players exist.[19] But because of the contagion effect likely to occur once UNICEF acknowledges an issue as being a "child rights" problem, the acceptance or rejection of such an issue affects its probability of being picked up by other lead players.

Conversely, UNICEF's rejection of the idea that children-born-of-war have specific rights claims against states – with the corresponding implications for the work of advocacy organizations – is a rejection of a specific interpretation of the Convention on the Rights of the Child. This interpretation invokes a positive claim on states to ensure an environment of protection for children against stigma, rather than a negative claim not to formally discriminate against them. The organization, in effect, is exercising *governance* over the social construction of "children's rights" as an idea (Carpenter 2009). Because of its central position within the network, its choice on this matter signals to other (follower) child rights organizations that this is a low-prominence concern and contributes to the barriers political entrepreneurs will face in other forums.

Gatekeeper interests and strategies

What do gatekeepers want? Above all, it is likely that gatekeepers want to remain gatekeepers. They are concerned with their "market share" in transnational civil society. They wish to retain their niche, and may reject issues that they consider too far afield of their mandate

---

[18] Even this, however, varies within the organization. UNICEF's decentralized structure means that new ideas tend to be best received if they come from field offices, rather than other institutional entities. The Innocenti Research Centre in Florence is abuzz with ideas but must typically persuade program officers in the field to approach officials at headquarters. Author's interviews with UNICEF officials, 2005–6.

[19] In the area of "children and armed conflict" another gatekeeper is the Office of the Special Representative to the Secretary-General for Children and Armed Conflict.

for inclusion. For example, Clifford Bob's gatekeeper model stresses the importance of organizational culture and mandate in engendering sympathy for some causes (or some frames) but not others.[20] "A potential supporter will devote scarce time and resources only to a client whose grievances and goals jibe with the NGO's central mandate" (Bob 2005, 28). If an issue *is* highly suited to the work they are doing and not too sensitive, they often prefer to play a significant role in championing it early on so as to maximize the likelihood that it will be framed in such a way as to draw resources and attention to them rather than their competitors.

Gatekeeping organizations, as bureaucracies, are also concerned with organizational survival and success. They wish to maintain their funding sources, which may entail distancing themselves from issues antithetical to the interests of powerful donors. They also wish to maintain credibility with their targets of influence, which often means creating and maintaining an organizational "niche" that results in many valid causes that do not fit being ignored. For example, Amnesty International developed an early niche in the area of political prisoners. As Hopgood (2006) documents, when pressed to expand their mandate to cover other sorts of human rights abuses, many members of the organization initially balked.[21] As Wendy Wong has detailed (2008), as a result of Amnesty's prestige and centrality within the human rights network, its privileging of political detainees constituted and reconstituted the very conception of what "human rights" and "human rights activism" entailed, inadvertently heightening barriers to entry for other activists.

Pursuing one's organizational mandate may mean more than simply avoiding resource expenditures on issues seen as watering down or failing to serve the mandate; organizations may have an interest in actively blocking issue proponents whose ideas are inconsistent with their principled beliefs. For example, NGOs working in the area of health and humanitarian affairs scaled back their rhetoric with respect to family planning when the United States adopted the global gag rule linking

---

[20] Bob refers to this as "substantive matching" versus "organizational matching," which proceeds according to a more cost/benefit-based logic.

[21] Sexual orientation rights, for example, were for some time subordinated to concerns more traditionally understood to be part of Amnesty's mandate for this very reason. See Hopgood (2006, 117).

funding transfers to certain positions on reproductive health issues. At the same time, similar groups that were aligned with a women's reproductive rights frame sought to block pro-life issue proponents in forums such as the UN Conference on Population and during the negotiations for the International Criminal Court. Individuals arguing for the rights of the unborn in transnational civil society are unlikely to find allies among many agencies within the UN system, given a set of principled and causal beliefs currently present in those agencies concerning the relationship between women's reproductive freedom and human security.

At the individual level, persons in gatekeeper roles are concerned not only with their organizational survival and mandate but also with their personal career trajectories. Concerns over professional reputation may make individuals unlikely publicly to support emergent issues that could be considered unpopular by colleagues (Carpenter 2007b). Beyond this, the intellectual history and professional training of specific career civil servants may predispose them to consider or reject particular principles and causal claims by issue entrepreneurs (Jones and Baumgartner 2005, 7). Those with legal training consider issues very differently from those trained in social work and members of both groups would like to be involved in the promotion of issues that validate their particular perspective on the world.[22] Within UNICEF, for example, those I interviewed tended to vary in their approach to the issue of children-born-of-war depending on whether they saw the problem through an international law lens, a criminal justice lens, a programming lens, or an advocacy lens.

Gatekeeping strategies

As Roger Cobb and Marc Howard Ross (1997) outlined in their analysis of domestic issue opponents in US politics, a number of strategies of resistance are open to gatekeepers who wish to reject particular issues from their formal agendas. One is simply to deny the issue's relevance

---

[22] For example, legal training involves a different set of moral and procedural starting points than does social work or political science. I am indebted to J. P. Singh for the idea that the normative understandings agents bring before they come into the game are likely of importance. Individuals take different pathways into careers as global governors, which should be explored in process-tracing the role they later play as gatekeepers.

to a specific issue agenda. This was long the strategy of UN agencies to suggestions that infant male circumcision be considered a violation of bodily integrity rights. Thus, for example, the UN's understanding of "harmful traditional practices" in the 1990s developed with particular reference to circumcision of women and girls in the global South. Cobb and Ross (1997, 28) argue that opponents may also "invoke procedural reasons that a particular issue is inappropriate for consideration: it does not meet certain technical requirements, [or] the problem has been brought to the wrong person or office." UNICEF's claim that the grievances of children-born-of-war do not fit the procedural language of the human rights regime might be understood in this light, as can comments by human rights advocates that conscription is not a human rights violation unless it involves children under the age of eighteen.

A related strategy can be to offer normative arguments for rejecting an issue. Opponents of debt relief, for example, often argued that rather than helping individuals it would merely prop up corrupt regimes (Busby 2007). In the case of children-born-of-war, an argument used by child rights organizations to avoid addressing the issue has been that doing so could actually compromise the rights of the children themselves by drawing greater attention to them (Carpenter 2010). The same strategy was once used to silence victims of rape themselves. Prosecutors at the Tokyo and Nuremberg tribunals were hesitant to allow women to testify about such crimes because of the "delicate" nature of the issue. It took years of campaigning by women's organizations to challenge this mindset (Joachim 2003).[23]

Selectively engaging issue entrepreneurs is a third strategy: Cobb and Ross (1997, 34) refer to this as "symbolic placation." Gatekeepers may allow an issue entrepreneur limited access and an audience as a way to diffuse a new or controversial issue without formally accepting it on their agenda. This has the effect of monopolizing the time and attention of the issue entrepreneur, slowing advocacy efforts in other directions. It also maintains the relational hierarchy between the gatekeeper and issue entrepreneur, as the entrepreneur focuses on engaging

---

[23] Notably, such activists did not merely lobby states, but used amicus briefs to pitch their revisions of international law to those global governors in positions of institutional authority: the judges at the International Criminal Tribunals (see Danner and Voeten, 2007).

the gatekeeper instead of forum shopping. Such strategies are particularly effective against small or underfunded organizations that typically lack the resources to court multiple gatekeepers simultaneously.

Through selective engagement, gatekeepers may also attempt to reframe an issue in a way suitable to them, allowing them to forestall advocacy frames that would undermine their own work and maintaining their privileged position in the issue creation process. Because of their influence, gatekeepers are in a position to coopt the frame proposed by the issue entrepreneurs. This means that while an issue might be selectively incorporated into the formal agenda, it might become a different issue through that process. In recent years, male circumcision has grown in salience on the World Health Organization agenda, but the practice is now framed as a public health issue because of its purported value in preventing the spread of HIV/AIDS. The new public health frame has served to preempt further discussions of the trade-offs with the practice as a human rights issue within the UN system. Rather than being seen as analogous to female genital mutilation, the practice is currently treated as analogous to receiving a vaccination, setting back activists' efforts to frame it as a form of mutilation.[24]

Selective issue adoption can explain the gap in transnational civil society between the issue frames of local or marginal NGOs around an issue and their powerful counterparts in UN agencies or influential NGOs. For example, Rogers and Marres (2000) analyzed advocacy groups involved in the Narmada Dams controversy. Their analysis of advocacy websites found that smaller NGOs were articulating the issue of Narmada through the lens of displacement, in much the way it had been articulated on the ground in India. But the UN agencies and environmental NGOs to which these issue entrepreneurs were hyperlinked in web space (such as Friends of the Earth) included almost no reference to displacement on their websites dealing with Narmada. The dams controversy was acknowledged by major players in the environmental network, but not through the frame of reference identified by the issue entrepreneurs.

---

[24] In response, the anti-cutting network has reframed the issue as one of "genital integrity," attempting to link infant male circumcision more closely with female circumcision, to graft both to the human right to bodily integrity, and to emphasize the involuntary aspect of circumcision performed on children, as opposed to voluntary body modification practices of consenting adults. See www.icgi.org/.

Similarly, while UNICEF has resisted constructing children-born-of-war as a category of concern, the organization has been somewhat more willing to situate some references to such children in its emerging programming on gender-based violence (GBV) in armed conflicts.[25] Subsuming programming for such children of war under women's issues rather than incorporating it as part of a child-protection initiative, and limiting it to children born of rape rather than all children conceived by foreign soldiers in war, is very different from the way in which political entrepreneurs are approaching the issue.

(Such selective framing decisions are highly significant in determining policy responses to problems. In this case, dealing with a child rights problem through a gender-based violence frame has consequences for the way the issue is conceptualized in civil society, as well as for the types of programming available to such children. For example, initiatives aimed at assisting birth mothers alone would not address the range of rights violations experienced by these children, such as the right of older "war children" to information about their identities.[26] In integrating a limited discourse on such children into its GBV programming rather than constructing their concerns as an issue in its own right, UNICEF exercises power over the meanings attached to this discourse and affects the environment in which political entrepreneurs can press future claims on behalf of this population.

Studying issue adoption: some empirical challenges

I have argued so far that all of these actions and inactions constitute central mechanisms of global governance and, as such, decisions about issue adoption bear investigation by IR theorists. How does the combination of gatekeeper influence, interests, and strategies outlined above

---

[25] For example, an outcome document of a meeting at the UNICEF New York office in 2005 expressed a consensus that "children born of sexual violence in armed conflict zones should be addressed within the context and framework of gender-based violence (GBV)" (UNICEF 2006).

[26] Nonetheless, effective responses to survivors of wartime sexual violence could do much to reduce the incidence of attachment difficulties these children may face with their birth mothers, as well as the incidence of stigma from the women's families and socioeconomic deprivation; and such initiatives are of course vital in their own right. The point here, however, is to highlight the gap between the frames of political entrepreneurs and those of gatekeeping organizations in the child rights sector.

shape issue adoption decisions? What can broadly be said about how gatekeepers in global civil society select or reject issues around which to mobilize? Is there an underlying logic that can help us understand transnational politics more clearly? How generalizable, for example, are the patterns that I noted in my UNICEF case data across other gatekeeping organizations in the child rights network when asked to consider the issue of children-born-of-war? How generalizable are these patterns across *other* potential issues pitched to that same set of gatekeepers? Are these patterns generalizable across other sub-networks in the human rights area, and to networks focused on the environment, free trade, social justice, and peace, when faced with new claimants or problems pitched by political entrepreneurs?

Although the sections above distilled several factors that may underlie this process, there is little systematic research that explains which factor or combination of factors best explains empirical variation in the issue adoption decisions of major players in transnational civil society. Several testable assumptions, however, warrant further empirical investigation. Here I outline some hypotheses before turning to methodological issues associated with the study of issue adoption in TANs.

One generalizable factor across cases may be that some attributes of specific problems better lend themselves to international advocacy than others. Keck and Sikkink's (1998) groundbreaking study on TANs developed an implicit theory of issue emergence within networks, emphasizing the importance of *issue attributes* in advocates' selection of specific campaigns. The attributes most helpful in terms of framing issues are "causes [that] can be assigned to the deliberate actions of identifiable individuals"; "issues involving bodily harm to vulnerable individuals, especially when there is a short and clear causal chain assigning responsibility"; and "issues involving legal equality of opportunity" (1998, 27). The idea that the intrinsic nature of an issue can explain its success in efforts to build new international norms is shared by a variety of scholars (Nadelmann 1990; Bob 2002) and echoed by Price (2003).

Can these "attributes" also explain why certain problems are defined and then adopted as issues in the first place? If so, then attributes such as perceived innocence, vulnerability to bodily harm or equal rights violations, and a short causal chain should correspond to issue emergence, and the lack of such attributes should correspond to issue non-emergence. It is also likely that problems for which proposed solutions are readily available may be more likely to succeed than those considered "irredeemably structural" (Keck and Sikkink 1998).

A second explanation for the emergence of certain international standards but not others, which might plausibly be applicable to issue adoption, as well, is the extent to which advocates can link a new set of intersubjective understandings to preexisting moral standards. This perspective, associated in particular with Richard Price's work on weapons taboos, argues that the promotion of new moral standards is most likely to succeed if these can be "grafted" on to preexisting taboos. For example, the chemical weapons taboo was popularized partly because it built upon an earlier prohibition on the use of poisons in warfare (Price and Tannenwald 1996). And advocates of the Ottawa Convention banning anti-personnel landmines sought to move debate over landmines away from arms control discourse and graft it on to the relatively robust norm of civilian immunity by emphasizing landmines' indiscriminate effects (Price 1998).

Although Price's coinage of the term "grafting" is meant to highlight the strategic and conscious aspect of this process, the notion that new issues must "resonate" with existing frames has been articulated in earlier constructivist literature. Florini (2000) discusses the relationship of emerging norms to other norms in the "pool." In the human rights sphere, Bob (2002) argues that the groups most likely to have their oppression championed by international human rights networks are those that suffer from violations *recognized* by the networks: "International human rights organizations have long focused their concern on basic rights rooted in the International Covenant on Civil and Political Rights. Groups suffering abuses that fit into these categories have a better chance of gaining international support than groups suffering other forms of oppression." If the grafting thesis can explain issue nonemergence in the human rights area, we would expect to see nonemergent issues clash with existing human rights standards, while emergent issues would fit more easily; likewise, we would expect issue adoption rates to shift in response to strategic shifts in issue language.[27]

---

[27] For example, it remains to be seen whether the anti-circumcision activists' new strategy will attract greater attention from gatekeepers in the human rights movement.

According to a third line of thinking, international advocacy is best understood as a marketplace for short-term contracts (Cooley and Ron 2002), in which public visibility with respect to a problem generates pressure to appear to be addressing it (Bob 2005); meanwhile, savvy advocates gravitate toward "hot" issues likely to draw donor funding and good media coverage for their organizations. Similarly, the global media itself also sometimes describes momentum around specific issues as a possible source of advocacy (Dale 1996). The contagion effect of targeted media coverage is often cited as a driving force behind disproportionate attention to certain regions (Ramos 2005) or categories of victim (Carpenter 2005a).[28] The logic of this argument is that greater public awareness of a social problem contributes to market incentives for transnational advocates to adopt it as a cause: "Today's dominant issue areas and their thriving niches reflect broad agreement among powerful publics in the developed world about today's most important social problems" (Bob 2005, 29). If the political economy thesis can explain issue emergence, we would expect to see issues with the strongest media visibility or donor interest end up on gatekeepers' agendas, and we would expect those issues absent from the agenda to lack such champions.

Clifford Bob's organizational culture argument should be empirically tested on additional cases as well. Certainly, concerns about suitability to one's mandate are cited in internal gatekeeper documents regarding the evaluation of new causes. The hypothesis also finds some support in the case described here: UNICEF's perception that one can adequately protect children-born-of-war by meeting their mothers' needs may stem from the particular configuration of gender discourse prevalent at UNICEF as an organization, suggesting the importance of institutional factors in driving issue-framing decisions in this case.[29]

However, there are limits to organizational culture as an explanation for variation in issue adoption, since literature has shown the

[28] However, advocacy networks also utilize the media to set their own agenda (Ron *et al.* 2005), so it is not always so clear whether the media drives issue emergence, with advocates responding to it strategically, or more accurately reflects advocacy frames given other necessary conditions.

[29] In Maggie Black's (1996, 183) words, "From the moment of its birth, UNICEF accepted as a matter of course that the well-being of children was inseparable from the well-being of those in whose wombs they were conceived."

malleability of organizational mandates over time, as they evolve to embrace new identity frames and tap into emerging resource pools. For example, Joel Oestreich (2007) has documented the emergence and diffusion of rights-based programming in multiple organizations, such as the World Bank, as a rational response to ideational innovation within global civil society. It should be possible, at any rate, to test empirically the relative importance of organizational mandate in driving consideration of new issues by gatekeepers.

My work on the children and armed conflict network (Carpenter 2007b) suggests another analytical direction for research on issue adoption, one which moves outside the black box of specific organizations to focus on relationships *between* "adjacent" issue networks.[30] Perhaps issue emergence is more likely when two or more networks for which the problem is perceived to be salient agree on an advocacy frame for the issue. According to this hypothesis, *issue concordance* – inter-network agreement over the appropriate frame for an issue – increases the likelihood of successful agenda setting within any specific network when a problem is salient for two or more networks (Carpenter 2005a); such network "spillover" effects, as described by Meyer and Whittier (1994), conversely pose disincentives for selection of issues ill fitted to multiple network agendas. If this hypothesis is borne out, we would expect to see the greatest discordance (and least activity) around issues that engage two or more adjacent networks, but where significant disagreement exists on the appropriate advocacy frame.

How might this subject be studied empirically and the above hypotheses explored and expanded on? To date, empirical work on the emergence of transnational issues has consisted largely of inductive case studies, in essence working backwards from successful campaigns to trace the process by which they emerged. For example, Keck and Sikkink (1998) have traced the emergence of violence against women as an issue within the broader human rights network; Clifford Bob (2009a) describes how India's Dalits went from being members of

---

[30] Network adjacency can be operationalized according to the number of reciprocal links between network organizations; cross-network references in advocacy content; number of focus group participants wearing "hats" in both networks over time; and references within focus groups and interviews to cross-network collaboration.

a marginalized category to successful rights claimants with a corresponding issue campaign around work-and-descent-based discrimination; and Daniel Chong has described Amnesty International's gradual and belated embrace of economic, social, and cultural rights (Chong 2009).

This methodology is limited in at least two ways. First, it can explain only issues that have emerged successfully, but not those that have failed to emerge. By contrast, I argue that exploring *negative* social outcomes – in this case, problems that have not been constructed openly as transnational "issues" – can provide important clues as to the causal factors underlying issue emergence (Lewis and Lewis 1980; Mahoney and Goertz 2004). Understanding what is left off the global agenda and why can add to our understanding of successful issue emergence, as well as the politics and pathologies of transnational advocacy networks more generally (Barnett and Finnemore 2004).

Second, there is reason to think that the hypotheses developed by selecting on the dependent variable may be insufficient to explain variation in transnational issue adoption. This is because the same factors said to correlate with successful issue emergence (as described in the various inductive research available) can also co-occur with *nonemergence*. For example, my earlier research on the humanitarian response to children born of wartime rape found that this issue is of low prominence within the children's rights network (Carpenter *et al.* 2005). Yet as I have recently argued, this cannot be explained easily by any of the implicit hypotheses in the TAN literature (Carpenter 2007a). It is likely that stigma against children born of rape is but one of many existing problems that might be, but have not been, adopted by "gatekeepers" in the human rights network. To build a generalizable theory of issue emergence, we need data on many more such low-prominence issues, better data on prominent issues for comparison, and, perhaps, hypotheses better suited for the questions of issue adoption in global civil society.

To study issue adoption more systematically, three steps are required, each offering separate empirical challenges. The first is to determine as objectively as possible which organizations serve as "gatekeepers" in a particular advocacy domain. The second is to determine which issues are or are not prominent within that policy domain. This involves not only operationalizing and measuring variation in the existing issue pool, but also identifying "nonissues" or "low-prominence" issues – quiet or "softly barking" dogs that might be but have not (yet) been adopted by gatekeepers as issues.[31] Third, one must analyze gatekeepers' own rationale for why certain issues but not others are suitable for adoption. How precisely are such decisions made, and what is at stake for these governors in making such choices? This requires gathering data on gatekeeper decisionmaking on positive, as well as negative, cases.

Although each of these steps involves certain challenges, I propose that a combination of web-sphere analysis and human subjects work with gatekeepers themselves (through either surveys, interviews, or focus groups) can yield data that might be systematically and reliably analyzed to generate better answers.

Operationalizing the "gatekeepers"

For any given issue network, a small number of powerful organizations will dominate issue space, but the most central nodes will vary according to the specific network or sub-network under study. How can one determine in a replicable way who is "doing" a particular issue? How can a researcher approximate the conditions faced by a would-be political entrepreneur in order to identify the organizations with the most influence in a specific issue domain?

One replicable and systematic approach to identifying gatekeepers in a specific network would be looking to cyberspace as a virtual context in which network actors both associate and construct shared meanings. Price (2003, 597) reminds us that the TAN literature has not adequately exploited the internet as a data resource or systematically analyzed it as an organizational medium for advocacy networks.

According to the emerging field of <u>hyperlink network analysis,</u> cyberspace also provides us with data about how organizations within a network interface (Park 2003; Thelwall 2004). Networks themselves are defined in terms of relational links between discrete nodes; hyperlinks in cyberspace connect websites much as social relations connect agents in real space (Wasserman and Faust 1994). But hyperlinking practices between online organizations are not simply an instrumental means by which to navigate from one cyber-locale to another.

---

[31] For articulating the distinction between silence and soft barks, I thank Stephen Rothman.

They also constitute recognition of organizational membership in a community of understanding (Barabasi 2002, 5; Henzinger 2001, 45). Thus, within advocacy communities, linking practices between organizational websites in cyberspace function similarly to academic citations – providing indicators of who is considered a member or a player within a specific community of shared knowledge and practice. "On the web, the measure of visibility is the number incoming links. The more incoming links point to your web page, the more visible it is" (Barabasi 2002, 5). Similarly, Park and Thelwall (2003) discuss hyperlinks as a function of the "credibility" among websites, a reflection of the perception within an issue network of who the key agenda setters are. If advocacy networks are communities of shared meaning, the linking structure and content of web-based advocacy sites around an issue tell us both about specific discourses through which that shared meaning is constructed, and also about which actors' participation is understood to matter in that community of meaning.

Second, hyperlink analysis tells us who the leaders or authorities are within the network, as represented by the relative number of incoming and outgoing links (Park and Thelwall 2003). Of major importance to studying agendas is identifying network "hubs." In social network theory, hubs are nodes with greatly disproportionate numbers of incoming links. Organizations with a larger-than-normal number of outgoing links are "connectors." The key players in a network tend to be both hubs and connectors. For example, in cyberspace one of the key players in the CaAC network is the Office of the Special Representative to the Secretary General for Children and Armed Conflict (OSRSG). This is evident both in the number of links outgoing from the OSRSG's website to other organizations in the network (the OSRSG is a "connector") but also in the number of incoming links: the number of times another organization refers the cyber-citizen to the OSRSG (the OSRSG is also a "hub").

A critique of relying on cyberspace for operationalizing an issue network's gatekeepers is that this method discriminates against less-connected organizations within a network (for example, those in developing countries with lesser access to the internet). However, for our purposes this bias works methodologically in our favor, assisting in identifying organizations with the highest centrality. This is because advocacy networks themselves discriminate in this way, with central nodes (in our case, leading human rights NGOs such as Amnesty

International) exercising a gatekeeping role owing to their disproportionate access, resources, and prestige (Lake and Wong 2005). One
could supplement this method with a survey of "real-space" advocates,
disseminated through a network listserv, asking them to name the five
organizations that come to mind when they think about the issue area.

Operationalizing "issue prominence" in advocacy domains

A helpful and reliable measure of the issue pool for a given set of
gatekeepers (that is, the range of issues on their official agenda) is,
once again, their advocacy websites. Previously I discussed examining hyperlinks between websites as indicators of who is considered
an authority in a given issue area. But an examination of how those
websites define the issue area also provides data on the range of issues
attended to by these powerful gatekeepers. Norm advocates will themselves argue that organizational websites, particularly mission statements, are a vital source of content about the issues that define the
organizations. "In creating an online persona, NGOs engage in framing activities ... by shaping the ways that issues are conceptualized
and understood" (Warkentin 2001, 36–7). As I have argued elsewhere
(2005b) with respect to advocacy around the protection of civilians,
the rhetorical content of websites, the accompanying images, the way
content is categorized, and the way in which different themes and
frames are connected in cyberspace matter enormously in terms of the
construction of advocacy frames in transnational civil society.

A drawback of using website content analysis as a proxy for the
gatekeeper issue agenda could be the lag time in updating web content – organizations vary in the extent to which they keep their sites
updated. For this reason, it is recommended that researchers triangulate web-sphere analysis with data drawn from sources in the real-space
network, such as surveys or focus groups. By recruiting respondents
from the same organizations and asking them to list "the most important issues" in a particular issue area, one can again measure both the
presence and relative prominence of particular issues on a network's
agenda.[32] In studying the network around children and armed conflict,

---

[32] This measure is similar to that used in domestic agenda-setting literature to
measure "issue salience" (Epstein and Segal 2000); while imperfect (Wlezien
2005), it is a useful means of triangulating the frequency analysis of the web
text data.

I found a close correlation between the issue pool as it appeared online and the answers given to this question by focus group participants. It is likely that the internet both constructs and reflects advocates' understanding of the most salient issues in an advocacy sphere at any given time.[33]

A more important reason for supplementing web-sphere analysis with human subjects research is to generate data on negative cases. Web content *can* provide data on failures in issue adoption: an issue such as children born of rape might be conspicuous by its absence from leading advocacy websites, once an investigator has thought to look for its presence. However, it cannot give us clues as to the range of possible problems that might be, but are not, adopted by gatekeeping organizations. Selecting cases on the basis of issues to which a researcher happens to be attuned introduces an unacceptable amount of bias to any study. Instead, survey or interview respondents might be asked which problems they can think of that are not receiving adequate attention from major NGOs, a method similar to that used by Kingdon (1995) in his landmark study of domestic agenda setting.

Capturing the correlates of issue adoption → from P. 229

Scholars of issue adoption also need to generate hypotheses and gather data on the *reasons* why gatekeepers in advocacy organizations select certain issues and not others for advocacy attention. Process-tracing of successful issues is, again, helpful but limited. For one thing, it is hard to know how generalizable it is. Asking advocates of the Ottawa Treaty why they decided to adopt "landmines" as a human security issue and lobby for a global ban will provide context-specific answers, whereas what is needed are general patterns in organizations' issue adoption behavior: generally, what are the constraints faced by an organization in deciding whether to adopt a new issue? How do political entrepreneurs attempt to draw the attention of your organization,

---

[33] Data so collected could also enable researchers to explore gaps between how the issue agenda is articulated by real-space activists as compared with how it is represented in cyberspace. This could provide insights about the significance of the internet in reflecting or indeed constructing the global issue agenda, or whether in fact hyperlink analysis distorts that agenda in favor of the most powerful and technologically savvy agents of global change.

and how many of them are successful? On what basis are such decisions made? Second, it is important to gather data on the decisionmaking process in negative cases, as well as positive ones. Why did landmines and small arms become salient issues, while incendiary weapons have not?

Focus groups with representatives of gatekeeping organizations may be a useful way to gather primary information on advocates' decision-making regarding issue adoption and to explore the value of inductively derived hypotheses. Focus groups, as conversational settings, provide an environment in which to examine what ideas, assumptions, and discourses advocates across issue networks hold in common: they are "particularly suited to the study of attitudes and experiences around specific topics" and the ways in which those topics are articulated in social settings (Barbour and Kitzinger 1999, 5).

Participants should be recruited from gatekeeping organizations themselves – those that have been identified through web analysis or surveys as authorities within a particular issue domain. In the focus groups themselves, such "governors" can be asked to describe the factors their organization considers when adopting new issues; responses can later be coded as corresponding to different themes in the TAN literature. They can also be asked to discuss their own current and emerging issue agendas, and to brainstorm about particular issues that are not receiving advocacy attention, culled from survey and interview responses to the question about low-salient problems. Thus, in addition to substantive information on how advocates explain their issue selection decisions, focus group transcripts can provide data on the way in which particular issues are currently conceptualized, constructed, and discussed among advocates themselves; which issues are conceptually linked to which other issues; how gatekeepers react when asked to justify inattention to specific low-prominence issues; and the extent to which advocates can agree that particular "low-prominence issues" lack some factor required for advocacy.

The text data from these various sources can be compared with the implicit hypotheses on issue emergence drawn from the TAN literature. Exploratory work with focus group data gathered from the children and armed conflict network suggests it is possible to create a coding scheme to capture reliably the type of substantive comments and discursive properties that might be expected to correspond to the factors described above (Carpenter 2007b). Advocates' perceptions of various issue attributes, of organizational constraints in lobbying on a particular problem, of tension between issue networks over a particular problem, or of the ease and difficulty of linking a problem to existing issues are all measurable in text data resulting from directed discussions in focus group settings.

Data need to be collected and coded in such a way as to measure both *what* advocates talk about unprompted and *how* they react when prompted to think about issues that may, or may not, already be on their agenda. Once we have coded the data to reflect not only the issue agenda but also advocates' discursive strategies when asked to discuss a nonissue, we can examine whether the discourse varies in ways that resemble the predictions described above, or whether new or modified hypotheses emerge from an immersion in this text data.

For example, if advocates typically argue that issue attributes matter or are unconvinced that specific low-prominence issues have the appropriate attributes for advocacy, this would lend support to Keck and Sikkink's "issue attributes" hypothesis; to the extent that practitioners invoke the agenda-setting constraints posed by the media and donors, this would lend support to the political economy thesis. Using this method, my exploratory work on the children and armed conflict network found in fact that intra-network concerns were more often mentioned than issue attributes or cost/benefit factors; but the study needs to be duplicated across many more cases in order to determine which results, if any, are generalizable. While this would not constitute a robust test of any of these hypotheses, the annotated text data should provide some insight into which, if any, of these theoretical predictions correspond to advocates' own understanding of why certain issues do or do not lend themselves to transnational advocacy. One might also anticipate that the process of engaging practitioners on these points would produce a better, more refined set of hypotheses amenable to later testing.

Conclusion

I have argued that an important category of global governor is an agent of influence who chooses whether or not to exercise institutional authority by endorsing an emerging issue that has been defined as a significant problem by issue entrepreneurs. The exercise of this choice constitutes "gatekeeping" and is a powerful form of global governance,

How does issue adoption by TANs compare in [currency] to 2 [relational] aspects of domestic/int'l politics in policymaking?

TANs when there are other avenues available for lobbying policymakers?

as issues that do not receive lip service by central players in global civil society rarely receive policy attention by states.) Using the case study of children-born-of-war, I have outlined the political significance of gatekeepers, their relational power vis-à-vis more marginal transnational players, and the strategies they use to shape the global agenda in the service of their own vision or organization interests. As Clifford Bob states, "'Non-policy' constitutes a form of governance every bit as powerful as policy, even if its perpetrators leave no fingerprints and its 'products' are invisible" (2007, 2; see Bob, this volume).

This chapter illustrates several of the dynamics to which the introductory chapter to this volume refers. First, the model and cases presented here constitute (a clear affront to functionalist accounts of global agenda setting.) The existence of pressing global needs does not automatically give rise to governance arrangements to meet them. Rather, such governance is generated when a peculiar confluence of factors is present: when an issue entrepreneur possesses the dedication, resources, diplomatic skill, and tactical savvy to market a problem to an appropriate gatekeeper; when the gatekeeper – because the issue, the issue pool, and the timing fit with organizational, coalitional, and tactical concerns – decides to bite; and, as Bob (2007) explores, when such claims are not dampened or canceled out by counter-claims from other issue advocates.

Use! :

 ①

In such cases, a contagion effect may take place within global civil society that stands a chance of eventually binding governments to policies aimed at solving human problems (Keck and Sikkink 1998). As several of the authors in this volume have shown (Haufler, Gutner, and Cooley), even that policy process does not ensure successful social change. I have argued, however, that such efforts are still-born in cases where a problem is not identified by a critical mass of actors in the first place.

② Second, this analysis casts doubt on the idea that decisions or non-decisions are made for purely instrumental reasons. Gatekeepers may leave certain problems off the agenda in order to prioritize existing issues about which they feel strongly for normative reasons; and they may do so even when their tactical interests could be served by promoting an issue simply because it is not sufficiently clear to them that it is the right thing to do. In short, while IR scholars may have often wrongly presumed that "global governance is a good thing," global governors themselves often "remain to be convinced" that particular problems are soluble through the forms of governance on offer by transnational power centers.)

Third, this case illuminates what Avant, Finnemore, and Sell refer to as "unintended consequences and path dependence in governance processes.. [R]ules and institutions established at one time may be ... resistant to change even when they prove to be dysfunctional from a larger environmental perspective. My analysis suggests that the pre-existing issue pool exerts significant dampening effects on emergent issues under certain circumstances. Just as a gendered frame associating the protection of civilians with "women and children" has prevented concerted advocacy to protect adult male civilians in armed conflict (Carpenter 2005b), the association of women and children as a single group has stymied agenda-setting efforts around populations whose life experiences complicate this frame (Carpenter 2007b). Greater attention needs to be paid in studies of global agenda setting to the relationship between emergent issues and coalitional politics within and between issue networks and sub-networks.

In general, a research agenda on issue construction and gatekeeping in transnational networks would lead theorists of global civil society in some interesting directions. Is "no" ever final? Do the advocates give up and walk away? Do issues fizzle? Die? Do they get rebranded? Under what conditions do people give up? Many of these questions require a larger dataset of issues and nonissues. They require systematic and imaginative research methodologies capable of mapping out transnational space, capturing a range of nascent issues, and comparing them with cases of successful agenda setting. And they require the study not only of gatekeepers but also of issue entrepreneurs. It is the dialectic between these groups that powers global civil society. And as I have shown, this dialectic produces significant outcomes and nonoutcomes in global governance.

→ She's so interested in how TANs adopt issues that she's failed/overlooked showing how much they matter compared to more institutionalized ways of international policymaking. Is this about research focus or is this a failure of establishing significance of scholarship?

9 | Outsourcing authority: how project contracts transform _global governance networks_ →GGN

ALEXANDER COOLEY

Introduction

How do global governors relate to each other and what, if any, are the consequences of these ties? Although scholars of international organization tend to focus on the purpose and structures of contemporary global governance, the actual ties that bind global governors remain undertheorized. As this chapter will suggest, these linkages not only set parameters on the agency of individual global governors, but they also help to establish their authority over a given sector and structure their interactions with one another. At the extreme, certain types of ties may actually undermine the implementation capacity of governors and, instead, encourage improvisation or counterproductive competition by actors on the ground.

If there is a prevailing wisdom on the topic, it is that global governors are implicated in a set of networks that involve various types of international and transnational actors. Anne-Marie Slaughter (2004) has recently advanced one of the most sophisticated versions of this thesis and argues that these networks comprise a variety of governors, including international organizations, nongovernmental organizations (NGOs), and disaggregated parts of states and their bureaucracies. These actors forge horizontal ties to other organizations to coordinate and manage their regulatory tasks, as well as vertical ties that delegate the governance of particular issues and sectors to specific transnational bodies. From this perspective strong network ties facilitate effective and responsive global governance through increased information flows, coordinated agenda setting, and the use of informational technologies to conduct regulatory functions and transnational campaigns. Other scholars complement this structural view of global governance as a transnational network with the observation that members of such governance networks are also bound together by common social

238

values and normative commitments (Price 2003; Keck and Sikkink 1998).

These formulations are subject to debate. Global governance networks are still unevenly distributed across sectors; similarly, Daniel Drezner (2007) has highlighted the centrality of states in the construction of global civil society and regulatory networks. Scholars have also rightly criticized the "transnational social ties" formulation for its artificial separation of normative and strategic behavior and for its failure to note that many NGOs strategically adopt these universal normative commitments in order to attract the attention of Western IOs and NGOs (Sell and Prakash 2004; Bob 2005 and 2002). And as Clifford Bob points out in this volume, conservative NGOs can just as easily use information technologies, network ties, and transnational mobilization strategies to advance internationally causes that are regarded as illiberal, or to check the advance of other activist networks that may infringe on their values.

Adding to these critiques, this chapter critically examines the *project contract* as a distinct mechanism of global governance. It suggests that contracting is not merely a technical vehicle for delivering or delegating governance. Drawing upon organizational theory, I explore how the introduction of contracts into a previously noncontractual realm affects the incentives and relational ties that bind global governors. At the micro-level, I argue that the terms of a contract influence an organization's strategic behavior, while at the macro-level I explore how contracting influences autonomy, competition, accountability, and trust among global governors. In most of these areas, the introduction of project contracts generally diminishes governance outcomes.

I illustrate these claims by examining the growth of contracting as a governance mechanism in two different contemporary transnational sectors: US-led postwar reconstruction in Iraq and the international humanitarian aid regime. The cases are instructive in that they demonstrate important variation in terms of contracting types, but they also suggest that contracts, more generally, may dissipate accountability and erode trust, even across what are usually regarded as dissimilar types of governors and transnational actors. Consequently, over the long term, the introduction of project contracts can erode the authority of governors. Far from being just a delegation vehicle or technical device, contracting has important, and often unintended, transformative consequences for the roles, priorities, and even legitimacy of

governors. As such, it is imperative that both scholars and practitioners consider how to mitigate the most pernicious effects of contracting
and identify alternative modes of delegation that can better mediate
the interactions of global actors.

The political consequences of contracting: an organizational approach

The rise and significance of project contracting

Contracting is a specific type of delegation that establishes a particular type of vertical tie between governors. The increasing use of the
project contract as a governance vehicle has paralleled the recent rise
of international civil society. Over the past fifteen years, across almost
all areas of global governance – including humanitarian aid (Barnett
2005; Cooley and Ron 2002), post-conflict reconstruction, development (Berrios 2000), healthcare and basic social services (Batley 2006;
Loevinsohn 2000; Mills 1998), the environment, and international
educational programs – contracting has become the principal way by
which new transnational initiatives, campaigns, and services are formulated and delivered. Contracting has even extended into traditional
areas of state monopoly, such as the provision of security (Avant 2005;
Singer 2003). At the same time as scholars and practitioners herald the
growth of a truly global civil society, contracting has become ubiquitous in global governance.

Not coincidentally, the rise of project contracting as a governance
mechanism shares many of the underlying causes of the rise of global
civil society, many of which are identified in this volume's introductory chapter. Since the Cold War and the collapse of the Communist
bloc, ideologies of governance have shifted away from promoting state
planning and toward empowering markets, individuals, and nonstate
organizations as centers of social, economic, and political activity.
The privatization of functions that had previously been administered
exclusively by the state has opened a vast new range of issue areas for
specialization for NGOs and for-profit corporations; consequently, the
number of private actors involved in domestic and global affairs has
increased almost exponentially. Political pressures for more accountability, transparency, and efficiency have also pushed states to outsource services to supposedly more competitive nonstate providers;

likewise, project contracting has become a routine part of the project design of international organizations – including the UN Development Programme (UNDP) and the UN High Commissioner for Refugees (UNHCR) – and international financial institutions, such as the World Bank and the Asian Development Bank. All of this has occurred in parallel with the rise of public–private partnerships as vehicles for delivering public goods within states.

Definitions

For the purposes of this study I define a contract as a formal agreement under which a "donor" (the offeror of a contract) pays a "contractor" (the implementing actor) to provide a service or discrete project for a fixed period of time. Contracts are usually, but not always, awarded through a competitive project tender in which multiple parties submit their bids for the donor's project. <u>Donors select the successful</u> bid based on factors such as the contractors' expense schedule, reputation, and past performance on other projects.

Strictly speaking, some legal systems consider verbal agreements, nods, and guarantees to be legal contracts. However, for the purposes of this study, when using the terms "contracting" or "contract," I refer to the formal and binding written agreements between transnational actors that stipulate payment for a specific project. I differentiate formal contracts from more informal cooperative relationships, communications, or understandings that are reached without a formal written legal agreement and bidding process.

Micro-level effects: contractual terms and organizational incentives

Contracts vary in their exact scope and terms. Six specific aspects of contracts – cost structure, completeness, duration, monitoring, performance sanctions, and renewal potential – can all shape the incentives of contracting organizations (Cooley 2004).

First, contracts vary in their <u>cost structure and fee schedule.</u> Most commonly, they take the form of "<u>fixed price</u>" (where payment is agreed upon *ex ante* at a set level, regardless of the subsequent costs incurred to complete a project), "<u>incentive fee</u>" (where remuneration is fixed on a sliding scale according to a set of benchmarks), "<u>cost-plus</u>"

(where payment is calculated as a percentage of the project's final costs), or "time and materials" (where payment is billed according to actual labor hours and expenses). Of these, the most favorable to a contracting party is the "cost-plus" contract, under which profits and bonus payments are guaranteed, regardless of a project's expenses, and the contractor assumes no independent risk. The more expensive the project, the greater the fee that the contractor will collect, thus providing a disincentive to cut costs, waste, and inefficiencies. In fact, Ruben Berrios's (2000) quantitative analysis of the US Agency for International Development's (USAID) projects finds that cost-plus projects are significantly more likely to result in poor project performance than other types of contracts.

Second, contracts vary in their completeness – the degree to which they explicitly outline procedures and rules for dealing with contingencies (Hart 1995; Schmitz 2001). Routinely, contracting parties cannot anticipate every contingency that is likely to arise outside of the contractual framework. As a result, many contracts are left incomplete with the understanding that they will be renegotiated after a certain period to deal with unforeseen circumstances and issues that have arisen over the contract's duration (Koremenos 2001). However, the more incomplete a contract, the more likely it is that an organization will use its residual rights of control over a project and its assets to expand its jurisdiction and, when possible, appropriate any available surplus rent or opportunities not assigned by the original contract (for EU applications, see Farrell and Héritier 2006; Hix 2002). Residual rights of control will also determine the *ex ante* incentives for contracting parties to make transaction-specific investments within a contractual relationship (Hart 1995; Klein 1988).

Third, contracts vary in their duration. Some developmental and technical assistance projects sponsored by international lenders can last for several years, but typically USAID and other government contracts last for one year as they are tied to an annual budget cycle. At the other end of the spectrum, humanitarian contracts can be granted for just a few weeks or even days, especially in the initial stages of a complex emergency or relief effort. In general, the shorter the duration of the contract, the greater the organizational uncertainty faced by a contractor.

Fourth, a contract's monitoring mechanisms can vary significantly across donors. Government contracts are usually subject to periodic review and evaluation by a national legislature and almost all project contracts include some form of project assessment and financial audit that takes place toward the end of the project. But donors may also send monitors during the project to gather information and identify midstream difficulties. In fact, in certain humanitarian and developmental sectors project monitoring itself has become somewhat of a growth industry and may be "outsourced" to a pool of independent auditors and specialized consultants.

Fifth, contracts differ in the performance incentives, bonuses, and sanctions that they detail for superior or inferior performance. Many project contracts, especially in the area of infrastructure development, contain bonus clauses for work completed in a timely fashion. Conversely, sanctions for poor work or performance can range from financial penalties to the actual termination of the contract.

Sixth, and perhaps most importantly, contracts can be fixed-term or renewable. In cases of renewable contracts, as James Ron and I have argued in a study of donor–NGO relations, contractors tend to privilege contract renewal above all other organizational goals, including even effective project implementation (Cooley and Ron 2002).

Macro-level effects: how contracts might affect relations among governors

If the terms and incentives offered by contracts affect a contracting governor's overall organizational strategy and behavior, how might contracting impact the broader relations among governors that are under consideration in this volume? In keeping with Slaughter's map of global governance networks, I explore how the adoption of contracts might impact both the horizontal and vertical ties of contracting governors. I consider the relational issues of competition, autonomy, accountability, and trust.

Contracting and competition (horizontal ties)

Contracting governors, especially those without an alternative private revenue stream, must compete for contracts for their organizational survival. Competition for contracts privileges the importance of the tender process within the organization's planning and strategy. The more reliant an organization becomes on external contracts for its fiscal survival, the greater the chance that its internal staffing and activities

[handwritten margin notes: priorities of those who tax & make profits, no? The money trail as a means of locating authority? → ties my pentagon bjdlo?]

will be geared toward securing and maintaining external contracts. Further, when an exogenous shock generates a complex emergency or an otherwise new potential source of funding, organizations that rely on contracts have little choice but to join the contracting frenzy, regardless of the state of their existing project portfolio (Cooley and Ron 2002). Thus, the greater the reliance of governors upon project contracts for their organizational survival, the greater the competition that will be engendered with other governors over existing and new contracts.

Over the longer term, competition over contracts may also affect the scope of issues and functions that governors choose to undertake. Competition over project tenders encourages contracting governors continuously to amend and expand their capabilities and task specialization in order to bid on new contracts that may not necessarily be directly related to their traditional area of expertise. In organizational terms, the increasing competition for contracts may actually decrease the functional specialization of global governors. For example, both "international humanitarianism" and "post-conflict reconstruction" have dramatically expanded in recent years to include myriad issues and areas that traditionally were not understood to be parts of these sectors (Macrae 2002b). This parallels Tamar Gutner's observation in this volume about lurking mission creep in international organizations.

Contracting and autonomy (vertical ties)

Our expectations of how contracting might affect the autonomy of governors is more mixed. On the one hand, scholars of the domestic and international non-profit sector have made strong claims that some types of financing, especially government contracting, curtail the autonomy and the decisionmaking space of NGOs (Chikoto 2007; Wang 2006; Hulme and Edwards 1997). Donors that dispense contracts are more likely to leverage their financial power to affect the goals and implementation choices of the contractor. From this perspective, organizations that rely on funding from membership dues or investment incomes will retain more autonomy from outside pressures than organizations that are funded primarily through contracts (Wang 2006, 22–4).

However, these general observations about the contrasting effects of different funding sources may not hold in all contracting situations, especially when we consider different types of contracts and monitoring provisions. For one, autonomy is more likely to be constrained in a fixed-price contract than in a cost-plus contract; in the latter, a governor presumably will still have great leeway to make decisions and incur costs without jeopardizing its revenue source. When monitoring and sanctioning mechanisms are weak, contracting governors will not be as constrained or pressured to comply with a donor's directives. This is especially true of transnational environments where legal oversight is absent or, at the very least, considerably weaker than in an institutionalized domestic legal setting. Many of the international settings that are most likely to witness a sudden proliferation of contracting governors – that is, complex emergencies, disaster relief situations, and post-conflict reconstruction – are characterized by political uncertainty, legal vacuums, and a lack of capacity that renders states and international organizations unable adequately to monitor the operations of contracted governors.

At the extreme, principal–agent theory suggests that too much autonomy with inadequate oversight may encourage opportunistic behavior, corruption, and graft by the contracted governor. Thus, the exact type of contract and the strength of its oversight provisions may well determine the extent of a contractor's autonomy.

Contracting and accountability (vertical ties)

Contracting is also likely to affect the accountability of governors. By separating the roles of mandate (donor) and implementation (contractor), contracts actually split the responsibility for a governance initiative and project. This split creates "plausible deniability" for donors, who can take credit for relatively successful projects, but can attribute less successful outcomes to the contractor's poor execution. Moreover, as Avant (2006, 511–12) describes in her examination of private security companies, contracting for services can also bypass traditional mechanisms of legislative oversight in donor countries, thereby empowering the executive and shifting internal balances of power. The legal uncertainty of the transnational environment further dissipates traditional chains of accountability, as contractors may even be granted immunity for their actions from the laws of the country that they are operating in. To be sure, as Ruth Grant and Robert Keohane (2005) remind us, there are several types of accountability involved in global governance, and not all of them are legal or participatory. However, with the exception of the reputational effects, none of the other accountability mechanisms that Grant and Keohane identify (hierarchical, supervisory, legal, market, and peer) actually appears in many transnational settings.

Over the longer term, this dissipation of accountability also raises serious concerns about the sources of political authority for global governors. Already, in both the development and humanitarian worlds, actors on the ground view outside contractors, especially project consultants, with great suspicion and skepticism (War on Want 2004). Thus, contracting governors may continue to operate in various areas of global governance, but their credibility and even authority may be greatly diminished if target groups view them as self-interested contractors as opposed to committed governors who represent the international community.

Contracting and trust (horizontal and vertical ties)

The use of contracting also affects the social ties among networks of global governors. Specifically, contracting tends to erode trust along their horizontal and vertical ties.

International relations scholars have recognized for quite some time that, even in the absence of a central authority, iterated interactions among self-interested actors can yield greater cooperation (Axelrod 1984; Oye 1986). Similarly, Russell Hardin's (2004) influential rationalist-behavioral account views trust between actors as mutually encapsulated self-interest that is premised upon the expectation of steady future interactions; without the expectation of future interaction, trust is unlikely to be sustained between parties. However, whether we view trust through this rationalist perspective or as a "social capital" phenomenon based on norms and social commitments (Putnam 1994), there are important reasons to expect that the introduction of contracting would erode trust in transnational settings.

First, introducing contracting into situations where global governors had previously networked exclusively through their common values or informal ties may change the way governors perceive each other's motives. As Diego Gambetta (1988) reminds us, true cooperation must be interpreted as a reflection of the cooperator's predisposition and not situational or environmental factors. A party that is coerced into cooperation or has no other alternative but to cooperate cannot be deemed "trustworthy" solely on the basis of that interaction. A formal contract between parties creates a binding and legal obligation, backed by prevailing enforcement mechanisms, but it does not increase the iteration necessary to build trust.

In a fascinating and theoretically instructive experimental study, management scholars Deepak Malhotra and J. Keith Murnighan (2002) compared and contrasted the effects of formal (or binding) contracts and nonbinding (or informal) contracts on the development of trust among players in an iterated game. The authors suggest that a tradeoff exists between the mitigation of risk and the development of trust. Informal contracts are riskier endeavors; however, they are more likely to produce the iteration that ultimately generates trust. Conversely, formal contracts may reduce risk through their explicit provisions, but will restrict the development of trust and mutually positive dispositional attributions due to their legally binding enforcement mechanisms. In post-game surveys and interviews, participants in the game with binding contracts attributed the plays of others to their contractual terms and constraints, rather than to their disposition, even if they had been previously deemed trustworthy (Malhotra and Murnighan 2002, 547). By contrast, the authors found that when the experiment was repeated using nonbinding contracts, levels of trust increased significantly, even in an anonymous, computer-mediated environment (p. 552).

Second, the anticipation of contractual renewal is not the analytical equivalent to an iterated interaction among agents. For one, contracts in many sectors of global governance are offered by donors in response to single events or catastrophes that will not recur. Moreover, the immediate goal of contracting governors, especially those that are fiscally insecure and engage in short-term contracts, will be to secure contractual renewal for the current project rather than attain future projects. When certain negative information about a project threatens to curtail the renewal of the contract, contracting governors will hide this information or purposefully paint an upbeat picture in order to secure renewal (Cooley and Ron 2002). Again, only effective monitoring can combat such manipulation of information, but the subsequent disclosure of hidden information or actions would itself erode trust among donors and contractors.

[1] I thank Henry Farrell for his comments on this issue in an earlier draft.

Thus, the introduction of binding contracts into existing networks among global governors may have profound implications, whether we view trust as a rationalist or social capital type of phenomenon. For example, if we accept the constructivist assumption that transnational networks are bound together by actors that share common values about certain global issues, introducing formal contractual relations into these networks may erode these ties by changing the dispositional relationship to a contractually situational one. Similarly, from a rationalist perspective, the prospect of contractual renewal may displace the prospect of iteration upon which trust had been built. Accordingly, contracting has the potential to restructure relational ties among governors through its particular situational logic and constraints.

Hypotheses on contracting and global governance

The above discussion suggests the following general hypotheses about contracting and global governance:

Working assumption: The terms of a contract – its payment structure, completeness, duration, monitoring mechanisms, performance sanctions, and renewal prospects – provide the incentives for the behavior of a contracted governor.

Hypothesis 1: Contracting engenders competition among actual and prospective contracted agents.

Hypothesis 2a: Contracting is more likely to reduce the organizational autonomy of contracted agents when agents: (a) depend on the contract for fiscal survival; (b) are monitored effectively; (c) are sanctioned for noncompliance; and (d) adopt "fixed-price" contracts.

Hypothesis 2b: Contracting is more likely to enhance the organizational autonomy of contracted agents when agents: (a) do not depend on the contract; (b) are inadequately monitored by the donor; (c) are not sanctioned for noncompliance; and (d) adopt "cost-plus" or other non-"fixed-price" contracts.

Hypothesis 3: Contracting, regardless of type, dissipates the accountability of governors.

Hypothesis 4: Contracting erodes trust among global governors, even if previous cooperative ties were built upon longstanding and common normative commitments.

> **Hypothesis 5:** *The above hypotheses should hold regardless of a global governor's for-profit status, the issue area, network ties, or the strength of normative commitments.*

Conversely, <u>these claims about the transformative effects of contracting would be falsified if: the terms of a contract did not affect a governor's incentives and strategic behavior; contracting did not encourage competition among governors; contracts did not predictably affect a governor's autonomy; contracting concentrated accountability; contracting parties maintained or enhanced their trust; or these contracting processes differentially impacted various sectors of global governance.</u>

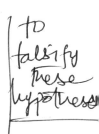

to falsify these hypotheses

Illustrative cases: Iraq's reconstruction and the new humanitarian regime

Logic of the cases

To illustrate some of the mechanisms and hypotheses proposed above, I examine the role of contracting in the US-led reconstruction of Iraq and in the contemporary international humanitarian aid sector. Although these discussions can in no way be considered anything more than anecdotal evidence for some of these claims, I have selected them with <u>two important criteria in mind</u>.

First, the terms of these contracts vary across cases. Many of the initial Iraq contracts were of the "cost-plus" variety, whereas humanitarian contracts are nearly always "fixed price." In terms of duration, Department of Defense (DoD) and USAID contracts in Iraq tended to be for a single year and renewable, while humanitarian contracts can range from just a few weeks to a year. Second, the contractors and donors in these transnational sectors vary in their for-profit status, overall organizational missions, and normative commitments. In the case of Iraq, <u>private corporations executed most of the reconstruction contracts</u> tendered by the US government, while <u>in the humanitarian sector most implementing actors are not-for-profit NGOs</u> that remain committed to their humanitarian ideals. Thus, the cases are meant to show some of these contractual dynamics across a number of quite different governors and agents.

Comparing contracting in Iraq's reconstruction and the new humanitarianism

The US-led reconstruction of Iraq provides a clear case of governance through contracting. While others have comprehensively examined the numerous reasons behind the US failure to enact successful institutional change in the wake of toppling Saddam Hussein's regime (Chandrasekaran 2006; Diamond 2005; Packer 2005), an analytical focus on the actual organization of the reconstruction effort shows that the US government's use of project contracting of the cost-plus variety, coupled with poor oversight, promoted gross inefficiencies, corruption, and waste across almost all sectors (Cooley 2005, 143–56).

The prevailing wisdom about postwar planning and reconstruction in Iraq is that authorities within DoD paid little attention to postwar planning and were thus unprepared for the complexities of nation-building posed by the post-Saddam power vacuum. This view is partially correct, but fails to acknowledge that DoD actually believed that outsourcing major infrastructural and development projects to the private sector was the best way to tackle postwar reconstruction. Unlike the organization of the postwar occupations of Japan and Germany where various US government agencies and departments directly governed the rebuilding effort, US officials in Iraq stated that allowing the private sector to lead the reconstruction would put experienced multinational companies in charge of these difficult projects, prevent the need to deal with corrupt Iraqi enterprises, and demonstrate to Iraqis the capabilities and ingenuity of the US private sector (Miller 2006, 111–31). According to David Nash, head of the coalition's original Project and Contracting Office, the overall contracting model promised to be a "win-win" for American companies and the Iraqi people (p. 115).

From March 2003 through June 2004, during the formal occupation and administration of Iraq by the Coalition Provisional Authority (CPA), US planners awarded individual project contracts to 125 different companies, the vast majority of them from the United States. Each of these contractors assumed a set of distinct functional tasks (see Figure 9.1). Twenty-four contractors were awarded projects worth more than $100 million, with sixteen of them winning contracts in excess of $1 billion each (see Table 9.1). The largest of these was the contract awarded to KBR (formerly Kellogg, Brown & Root), a

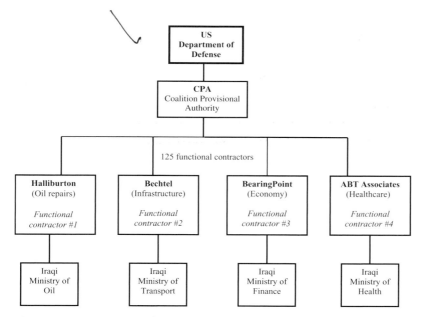

Figure 9.1 Organization of contractors in US-occupied Iraq

subsidiary of Halliburton, to repair Iraq's oil infrastructure and provide oil supplies, a contract valued at more than $10 billion. Other noteworthy contracts were awarded to Parsons Corporation ($5.3 billion for construction services), Bechtel Group ($2.3 billion for rehabilitating Iraqi infrastructure and public works), International American Products ($628.4 million for rebuilding the electrical grid), Creative Associates ($273.5 million for providing educational supplies and training), and BearingPoint ($240.2 million to plan and manage economic recovery) (Cooley 2005, 147). Most of these initial contracts were of the cost-plus variety, as US officials now insist that given the great uncertainty of a post-conflict situation, only this type of contract could guarantee the private sector's engagement.

In the humanitarian sector, we also see the increasing importance of contracting. Contracting has risen in response to perceptions of chronic waste and inefficiency in the sector, as well as the emerging trend of states directly or bilaterally funding NGO activities (more on this later). In 2004, major humanitarian NGOs received about $2 billion from public fundraising, $1.2–2.0 billion from government agency contracts, and $500–800 million in channeled funds, most of

Table 9.1 *Postwar contractors ranked by total contract value in Iraq and Afghanistan, from 2002 through July 1, 2004*

Contractor	Contract total (US$)
Kellogg, Brown & Root (Halliburton)	11,431,000,000
Parsons Corp.	5,286,136,252
Fluor Corp.	3,754,964,295
Washington Group International	3,133,078,193
Shaw Group/Shaw E & I	3,050,749,910
Bechtel Group Inc.	2,829,833,859
Perini Corporation	2,525,000,000
Contrack International Inc.	2,325,000,000
Tetra Tech Inc.	1,541,947,671
USA Environmental Inc.	1,541,947,671
CH2M Hill	1,528,500,000
American International Contractors, Inc.	1,500,000,000
Odebrect-Austin	1,500,000,000
Zapata Engineering	1,478,838,958
Environmental Chemical Corporation	1,475,000,000
Explosive Ordnance Technologies Inc.	1,475,000,000
Stanley Baker Hill LLC	1,200,000,000
International American Products Inc.	628,421,252
Research Triangle Institute	466,070,508
Titan Corporation	402,000,000
Louis Berger Group	327,671,364
BearingPoint Inc.	304,262,668
Creative Associates International Inc.	273,539,368
Readiness Management Support LC	214,757,447
Chemonics International Inc.	167,759,000
Harris Corporation	165,000,000
Science Applications International Corp.	159,304,219
Total contractors in Iraq (2003–4): 125	
16 contractors > $1 billion	
24 contractors > $100 million	
46 contractors > $10 million	

Source: Public Center for Integrity, Windfalls of War Project.

Table 9.2 *(Allocation of humanitarian funding among NGOs, UN agencies, and the Red Cross, 2005)*

Major humanitarian donors	Allocations to UNHCR, WFP, and UNICEF (millions US$)	Allocations to NGOs (millions US$)	Allocations to the ICRC and IHRC (millions US$)
Canada	150.6	30.4	35.4
ECHO	151.7	402.9	54.9
Finland	39.8	3.4	16.6
Ireland	26.1	23.9	9.6
Norway	128.5	130.0	36.5
Portugal	1.8	0.3	1.3
Sweden	132.7	92.5	69.0
UK	101.8	73.0	91.2
Total	733.3	756.4	314.6

Source: Development Initiatives (2006, 2). Totals may not add up owing to rounding. Donors were chosen by OCHA on the basis of their importance and the availability of data.

them contracts, through UN agencies. Of these, seven or eight international NGOs received the bulk of this assistance. In 2005, Walker and Pepper (2007, 5) estimated that about one-third of the $8.4 billion state-donor funding ended up in NGO coffers, either directly or through UN agency projects. A 2006 UN Office for the Coordination of Humanitarian Affairs (OCHA) assessment of eight major donors shows that NGOs received roughly equal amounts of humanitarian aid as three UN agencies and about twice the amount received by the International Committee of the Red Cross (ICRC) and Islamic Human Rights Commission (IHRC) (see Table 9.2). And as Table 9.3 suggests, some NGOs are considerably more reliant on external contracts for funding than others. In fact, a few NGOs – most notably Oxfam and Médecins Sans Frontières (MSF) – make a point of emphasizing that they do not accept grants or contracts from governments, although they do take UN funds.

In terms of contract type, humanitarian contracts tend to be of the fixed-fee variety and can vary considerably in their duration. When provided by a government or an international organization (IO), such as USAID or the European Community Humanitarian Aid Office

Table 9.3 *Major humanitarian NGOs and reliance on contracts for revenues, 2006*

Humanitarian NGO	Total revenues (thousands US$)	Revenues from government and IO contracts	% of revenue from contracts
Care USA	655,481	396,281	60.5
Catholic Relief Services	376,331	227,385	60.4
Mercy Corps	218,900	98,286	44.9
Médecins Sans Frontières[a]	804,800	112,000	14.0
Save the Children	264,874	18,792	7.1
International Rescue Committee	138,579	13,350	9.6
World Vision	335,502	15,641	4.7

Source: Author's calculations based on organizations' individual financial statements for 2006.

[a] MSF totals include all nineteen global chapters and are from 2005.

(ECHO), they can last for as long as a year. However, in cases of complex emergencies they can be much shorter, sometimes even lasting just a few weeks. Monitoring practices also vary considerably across humanitarian donors. For example, the US government and most UN agencies perform evaluations almost exclusively toward the end of the project, while the European Union sends periodic evaluators during a project's midstream to conduct financial audits and complete assessment reports.

The relational effects of contracting reconsidered through the cases

With these rough sketches of the role and structure of project contracts in these two sectors, we can compare some of the broader network effects that these forms of contracting had on relations among governors operating within these sectors.

Contracting and competition

One immediate difference between the cases lies in the level of competition among contractors. Whereas the humanitarian sector does show signs of significant competition between NGOs for government and IO grants, such competition was significantly muted in the Iraq case, owing to pre-standing agreements between major contractors and the US government and the use of no-bid contracts.

Competition for contracts has been a hallmark of the humanitarian sector for the past twenty years. Competition is most intense in the wake of disasters or complex emergencies, when scores of humanitarian NGOs descend upon the area in search of relief work. This tends to cluster both NGOs and donors into just a few global humanitarian hotspots every year. Donors tend to concentrate their efforts in a few high-priority settings, usually with high international visibility or media coverage, while NGOs must follow donors in order to secure funding. For example, in 2004 six countries – Iraq, Sudan, Palestine, Ethiopia, Afghanistan, and the Democratic Republic of Congo (DRC) – received about half of all humanitarian contracts from Development Assistance Committee (DAC) countries (Walker and Pepper 2007, 3).

But even setting up shop in a new crisis zone can be financially risky. Humanitarian agencies incur significant start-up costs when they establish a field operation, as constructing shelters, hiring new staff, and establishing supply lines are heavy expenditures (Stephenson 2005, 344). Thus, securing a contract and its renewal is essential for organizational survival and maintaining individual employment, as such costs will only be reimbursed if the NGO subsequently secures the project contract. Complex emergencies are also the most likely to engender short-term contracts, which places a premium on securing continuous renewals.

A compelling example of this dynamic remains the now infamous inaction of certain international humanitarian NGOs in the Goma (former Zaire) refugee camps following the Rwandan genocide. When Hutu rebels started to divert relief supplies and rearm within the protection of the camps, NGOs did not take collective action or alert UNHCR out of fear that it would revoke their contracts and replace them with any one of the other two hundred NGOs that were working in Goma's "hypercompetitive" relief market (Lischer 2005; Cooley and Ron 2002, 25–31). Although Goma remains a cautionary tale that NGOs have vowed never to repeat, similar types of aid frenzies have characterized nearly every subsequent post-conflict and emergency situation. Similar competitive scrambles for contracts have characterized NGO activities in Kosovo and Afghanistan, where some NGOs reportedly resorted to deliberate underbidding to secure project contracts. And although in the wake of the tsunami in Southeast Asia a wave of private donations reduced the financial importance of contracting, NGOs nevertheless competed intensely for international media attention and bid up salaries for local staff members in order to spend these sizable earmarked funds on suitable projects (Harris 2006; Stirrat 2006). *establish consortiums to reduce competition*

One measure that some NGOs are now adopting to curb such potentially destructive competition is to cartelize the distribution of aid by establishing a consortium or "trust fund" in the field to allow reputable NGOs to pool their resources. For example, major consortia to deliver relief and medical supplies now exist in Somalia, southern Africa (Malawi, Zambia, and Zimbabwe), Sri Lanka, and Iraq.[2] However, the procedures for establishing interorganization cooperation remain ad hoc and informal, while excluded NGOs are often resentful and continue to campaign for projects outside of the cartel.

In Iraq, by contrast, the initial problem during the formal occupation and reconstruction effort of 2003–4 was not too much competition, but the lack thereof. Various US government agencies awarded twenty-five major contracts, comprising about 97 percent of the initial $3.7 billion in funds, none of which met the standard of "full and open competition." Of these, fourteen were new contracts that included five sole-source contracts (including KBR) and nine limited competition contracts, while the other eleven were task orders issued under existing contracts (GAO 2004, 1–4). Later audits observed a significant increase in competitive awards after October 2003, although important exceptions were highlighted and comprehensive data regarding competition practices still remain difficult to attain (GAO 2006).[3]

---

[2] Author interviews with various humanitarian NGO practitioners.
[3] According to the 2006 report, almost all of USAID's awards featured a competitive process, while only 10 percent of State Department contracts were awarded competitively. Post-October 2003, 82 percent of DOD's contracts adhered to federal competitive guidelines.

Competition in the initial stage was further curtailed by the US government's controversial decision to exclude from consideration bids from companies whose host governments did not support the initial US-led military campaign. In fact, the reconstruction effort in Iraq seemed to have inverted the normal market mechanism of a competitive tender among established firms, as many companies were themselves created by ex-pats in Baghdad who reacted to the ample available contracting opportunities.

Contracting and agent autonomy

On the issue of autonomy among contracting governors, the two cases also reveal significant differences. In the Iraq case, the adoption of cost-plus contracts, poor oversight, and a lack of central coordination and management led to nearly unchecked autonomy on the part of larger contractors. By contrast, the increasing use of fixed-price, "bilateral" contracts in the humanitarian sector has constrained the actions and autonomy of NGOs, forcing them to align their own organizational missions and priorities with those of donors in order to secure and maintain external funding.

Contracting and autonomy under cost-plus contracts in Iraq

In Iraq, major reconstruction contractors were initially too autonomous. In organizational terms, contracts were awarded by distinct reconstruction function, but contractors lacked any kind of central coordination mechanism to plan or even exchange basic information about reconstruction priorities. For example, the major reason behind the difficulties in generating power in Baghdad during the formal occupation was that, as separate contractors with distinct functions, Bechtel and Halliburton were each respectively responsible for restoring the electric grid and operating oil refineries. However, in a textbook case of organizational pathologies, the two had no mechanism to account for or coordinate deliveries of intermediary inputs that each needed, so that Bechtel power grids lacked necessary oil and Halliburton's refineries lacked electricity (Cooley 2005, 150).

Beyond these coordination problems, the CPA's lax oversight – combined with the adverse incentives in cost-plus contracts – precipitated almost unprecedented corruption, waste, and opportunism. A scathing July 2004 report on the reconstruction contracts by the CPA's own Inspector General Stuart W. Bowen Jr. launched sixty-nine criminal investigations (of which twenty-seven were still active after the turnover of sovereignty) and found widespread fraud, abuse, and "manipulation of the contracting system" by senior advisors and major contractors.

The most high-profile of these scandals involved the multiple allegations of overspending and overbilling by KBR, the largest of the reconstruction contractors. KBR emerged from the war with a multibillion-dollar, no-bid contract to repair Iraq's oil infrastructure and was also contracted to supply US military camps with meals and amenities. According to investigative reporter Christian Miller (2006), KBR delivered on its overall obligations, but did so at exorbitant cost. Audits by the Defense Contracting Agency, the Pentagon's primary oversight office, concluded that the company had inflated its costs and failed to keep track of expenditures and revenues. Extreme examples abound: in one cycle, KBR billed the government $100 per bag of laundry it serviced and approximately $247 for soda per soldier (Miller 2006, 81–3). KBR employees reported that rather than repair components of existing equipment, such as oil filters in trucks, they were encouraged by management actually to destroy the entire piece of equipment (in what became known as the "burning pit") and simply bill for a replacement. Several executives were accused of taking millions of dollars in kickbacks from subcontractors across various projects, while the company was caught billing $70 million for a contract that had been previously canceled and was accused of charging $200 million for meals that were never actually served to soldiers (pp. 81–2). By August 2004 a DoD auditor found that KBR could not substantiate $1.8 billion in expenses or about 42 percent of the $4.3 billion in bills that were reviewed (O'Harrow 2004).

Similarly, a recent report by the Special Inspector General for Iraq Reconstruction on the performance of Bechtel – the first comprehensive evaluation of a contractor's performance in Iraq (as opposed to a project evaluation) – found that the company met only ten of its twenty-four original project goals, while most projects were canceled, reduced, or never completed as designed (Glanz 2007). Overall, as of August 2007, Pentagon inspectors were still investigating abuse and corruption in about 6 billion dollars worth of military contracts, most of them for supplies (Thompson and Schmitt 2007).

What led KBR, Bechtel, and other US contractors to act in such a blatantly opportunistic manner? Above all, the uncertainty of the post-conflict environment, the lack of oversight, and the cost-plus contracts gave every incentive to these companies to inflate costs and indulge in excesses without fear that US regulators would sanction them. As Marie deYoung, a Halliburton employee in Kuwait, observed of these contractual incentives and lax monitoring, "there was this whole thought process that we could spend whatever we want to because the government won't crack down in the first year of a war. They have no incentive whatsoever to be prudent. It's cost plus" (Miller 2006, 81). Despite numerous critical reports, neither the Pentagon nor the CPA seemed concerned with reining in excesses or punishing offending contractors, while Congressional oversight into the issue was minimal. Although the failure of the CPA's initial reconstruction effort was most likely overdetermined by a number of factors, including the deteriorating security situation in Iraq, the extreme autonomy of contractors was clearly a major contributing factor to its dysfunction.

Contracting and autonomy under fixed-price contracts in the humanitarian sector

By contrast, the rise of contracting in the humanitarian sector has tended to curtail the autonomy of contracting NGOs. The biggest check on the autonomy of humanitarian NGOs has been the spectacular growth in the "bilateralization" of humanitarian aid over the past decade, as states have halted general donations to humanitarian-oriented IOs and replaced them with earmarked funds and project contracts directly targeted for NGOs in the field.

Foreign policy considerations have also played a critical role in this trend, as leading states such as the United States and UK, especially since the Kosovo conflict, have wanted to assert greater control over NGO activities and bypass the mediating authority of UN agencies. In turn, as Michael Barnett (2005) has argued, this new state control has fundamentally challenged the traditional organizational cultures of neutrality and independence associated with many NGOs. The reassertion of state control over NGOs and humanitarian activities has been especially noteworthy in Kosovo, Afghanistan, and Iraq, and has initiated profound debates within NGOs regarding their purpose and autonomy in undertaking humanitarian action. For example, in 2003 USAID administrator Andrew Natsios cautioned NGOs working in Afghanistan that they had an obligation to fly the American flag or they would be replaced (Barnett 2005, 731). Smillie and Minear (2003) suggest that with the rise of the war on terrorism and the interest in the security vacuums left by failed states, dealing with humanitarian emergencies has now become an integral part of the new reconfigured security agendas of states. The authors predict that states will continue to increase their control over humanitarian activities, thereby further clashing with the original organizational missions and cultures of many NGOs.

It is therefore difficult to disentangle the organizational effects of bilateralization on humanitarian NGOs from those of project contracting, as the former has brought much more of the latter. Nevertheless, bilateralization, from the donor's perspective, is effective to a large degree because states now can use funding directly as a mechanism of control. From 1990 to 2000, official humanitarian assistance skyrocketed from $2.1 billion to $5.9 billion, and since the mid-1990s, about half of the revenues to NGOs focusing on humanitarian aid came from government contracts, a figure that suggests that NGOs are increasingly becoming actual instruments of state policy (Barnett 2005, 727).

The broader turn to contracting has also redefined the organizational missions of humanitarian IOs such as UNHCR and ECHO. Previously, these IOs traditionally retained broad discretion over how best to allocate funds and respond to humanitarian crises, but changes in funding practices have turned these organizations now into overseers of multiple outsourced projects. While in 1990 the European Union's humanitarian arm ECHO spent 27 percent of its funds on NGO contracts, by 2000 this had risen to 67 percent; by 1999, only 20 percent of contributions to UNHCR were not earmarked (Macrae 2002a, 16). Overall, then, the rise of contracting and aid bilateralization has transformed the internal organizational structures and priorities of both NGOs and multilateral donors.

Contracting and accountability

The extensive activities of contractors in both settings have also raised concerns over their accountability. Under Order 17 issued in June

---

[4] I thank Jodi Nelson of the IRC for her thoughts on this point.

2004 by the Coalition Provision Authority in Iraq, which was in effect until the implementation of the US–Iraq Status of Forces Agreement in 2009, all contractors were granted immunity from prosecution under Iraqi law. Until 2007, contractors for DoD were also not subject to US military laws and codes of conduct, leaving them to operate in legal limbo, subject to neither the jurisdiction of the sending state nor that of the host country. The immunity clause also meant that the only real disciplinary measure available to authorities against contractors was to expel them from Iraq. However, even in these cases, such exiled personnel could be rehired later to work on other contracts.

The now infamous Abu Ghraib and Blackwater scandals both drew attention to the lingering accountability issues raised by the persistence of contractor immunity. In both cases, neither the Iraqi government, with allegedly sovereign authority, nor the US government held contractors accountable for their abuses. In the case of Abu Ghraib, about one-half of the interrogators involved in the prison abuse scandals were hired as contractors by the firms CACI and Titan, as the former had been given the prison contract as a follow-on to its project to extract data from Iraqi government information systems. None of CACI's civilian contractors were charged or prosecuted for their role in the scandal. Similarly, the Blackwater episode of September 2007, in which a team of security guards contracted to protect US State Department personnel allegedly opened fired on a group of Iraqi civilians, killing sixteen in the process, prompted the Iraqi government to try to terminate Blackwater's contract and revoke the immunity guarantee for foreign contractors. Thus, Blackwater's very status as a contractor in a transnational setting has greatly complicated Iraqi and US efforts to establish effective regulation and mechanisms of accountability.

The fragmentation of accountability is also a major concern in the humanitarian sector. As in the reconstruction case, it remains unclear where actual responsibility for a project lies among the various contracting NGOs and donors. *Ex post* investigations into accusations of wrongdoing and misappropriation once funds have been dispersed are difficult and burdensome for all parties involved. Interviewed officials who work in the humanitarian sector admit that such investigations are very rarely, if ever, undertaken. On the other hand, in some settings some degree of collusion among donors, contractors, and project targets seems to be systematically tolerated. Some have even argued that the parties involved in the contracting system have few incentives to investigate thoroughly allegations of financial irregularities or errors in the field. For example, Nicholas Stockton (2005) has observed that the audit department of a major donor's foreign ministry in Kosovo did not find a single case of financial misappropriation or corruption in any of the 217 contracts (worth $220 million) that were implemented by 44 different agents in what is ranked by Transparency International as the eighth most corrupt country in the world. Stockton attributes such systemic underreporting to donor and contractor fears of poor public relations, as well as the lack of access by local media to the international aid presence. Indeed, citing a recent article by Michael Wrong of the UK's *Financial Times*, Stockton points out that even foreign correspondents are now reluctant to file negative stories about the aid sector as they depend on aid workers and their resources for access and travel to remote field sites (Stockton 2005, 4).

Contracting and trust

Finally, in terms of the effect of contracting on the development of trust among networks of contractors, donors, and recipients, the Iraqi case also conforms to the theoretical expectations that contracting will erode or inhibit the development of trust. By all accounts, neither the CPA nor DoD compelled any sort of loyalty on the part of contractors faithfully to serve the US government and internally curb excesses. Nor has the system of contracting found favor with the Iraqi government itself. In fact, the Iraqi government's recent clampdown on Blackwater testifies to the alarming mistrust that now characterizes relations between the Iraqi government and more than 100,000 foreign contractors that operate in Iraq (Rubin and Kramer 2007).

Indeed, the whole "occupation by contract" model and widespread allegations of unchecked contractor opportunism raise serious questions about whether the contracting system actually encourages contractors to promote their self-interest in the name (and at the expense) of the US government. Anthropologist Janine Wedel (1998 and 2005) has termed this behavior "transactorship politics" and has compared the opportunistic behavior of private US contractors in Iraq to the unchecked self-serving actions of Western economic reformers who administered USAID contracts in Russia in the early 1990s. And although Iraq may be an extreme example of "nation-building by contract," this is not an exclusively American paradigm. For example, the United Nations, the European Union, and various international financial institutions (IFIs) now carry out most of their projects in "post-conflict" environments and peace-building missions through contractors.[5] One observer has even termed this the rise of the international "relief-and-reconstruction complex" (Bello 2006).

The increasing use of contracting has also eroded trust and redefined the relationship between actors in the humanitarian network. Among NGOs, the scramble for relief contracts has led to competitive behavior over project contracts and an unwillingness to exchange even the most basic information about their activities and plans in the field. In their comprehensive review of humanitarian financing, Ian Smillie and Larry Minear (2003, 5–6) find that "mistrust and opacity pervade humanitarian financing and donor behavior." They observe that the "unhealthy degree of reciprocal antipathy" between donors and NGOs "contrasts sharply with the optimism and transparency which the public associates with the humanitarian enterprise." Moreover, they observe that the project evaluations by donors of NGOs that deliver emergency assistance contribute to this prevailing attitude of mutual mistrust and cynicism (pp. 37–8). Project evaluation has become a "mechanism of control," as it threatens project funding and contractual termination, rather than serving as a means for learning (pp. 40–1).

Inevitably, many of these issues are brought up in the context of a discussion about the need to improve "aid coordination," a topic that remains ubiquitous in the industry literature. However, what very few practitioners acknowledge is that the contracting system itself may structurally inhibit effective coordination and may actually erode the very trust necessary to improve it. Max Stephenson's (2005, 345) overview of humanitarian coordination and the development of interorganizational trust observes that, "as for commitment-based trust, if a coordinator must rely on 'the contract' to secure cooperation and coordination, it seems likely that matters between the organizations have descended to a difficult place." But if the theoretical analysis advanced in this chapter is correct, it is the very contract itself that may be eroding trust within the humanitarian network. It is

---

[5] For similar complaints about the role of Western contractors in the reconstruction of Bosnia, see Smillie and Todorovic (2001).

unlikely, therefore, that trust can be generated on top of these formal contractual relationships.)

Conclusion: the challenges of contractual governance

To the champions of global civil society, some of the perspectives offered in this chapter may seem unnecessarily downbeat. After all, even within the framework of a contract, global governors including NGOs, IOs, and corporations execute their projects across a wide range of issue areas and many are effective and important. Here, however, I have suggested that contracting – which is central to the concerns raised in this volume – is inseparable from the actions and strategies of governing agents. Ultimately, contracting may even recast their authority and transform their relations.

(The terms of contracts provide incentives for actions and actually alter the internal priorities of organizations. As the cases of Iraqi reconstruction and the international humanitarian sector suggest, such incentive-based behavior can also affect relations among governors and their implementation capacity. The cases suggest that the type of contract and oversight can differentially impact the autonomy and the competitive behavior of governors. However, in both cases the use of contracting was found to dissipate accountability among governors and erode trust. Of course, these findings may not travel to all instances of global governance, and future studies should try to discern the actual effects of contracts in individual sectors by comparing the behavior of governors operating on contracts with those that are not. For example, in the humanitarian sector we would expect that NGOs with alternative sources of funding, such as MSF which relies on membership dues and individual contributions, would behave differently in the field than NGOs primarily reliant on external contracts. Similarly, we should expect significant differences in the behavior of administrators of earlier reconstruction and occupation efforts who were members of the militaries and governments of the occupying powers, such as in post-World War II Japan or Germany, compared with that of their counterparts in Iraq. In these earlier cases, relations were structured not by contracts, but by long-established official bureaucracies and institutional hierarchies within the American government. All of these may be fruitful areas for future comparisons.

However, if this analysis is at least partially correct, it suggests that as global civil society continues to adopt contractual ties, relational and organizational changes will also follow. Taking contracting seriously does not mean rejecting the value of these projects or these areas of global governance. Rather, it necessitates treating contracting not merely as a technical matter but rather focusing more explicitly on the shifts in authority, accountability, and organizational behavior that contractual relations generate.

One measure of just how deeply institutionalized contracting has become across all aspects of domestic and global governance is to consider the simple, but nearly impossible, counterfactual of what contemporary governance would be like without project contracts. And even as the media and watchdogs call out specific contractors for their actions, inefficiencies, and excesses (for example, criticizing Halliburton's no-bid contract), the necessity of contracting is rarely criticized in and of itself, thereby reifying its centrality and seeming indispensability within global governance.

Practically, this analysis suggests *Remedies* two remedies to some of the problems caused by the introduction of contracts. First, donors may want to consider disbursing more grants to NGOs as opposed to contracts. Grants would specify the same project aims as contracts, but would allow NGOs to retain more flexibility over procedures and instruments, without the legal stipulation that the contracting agent deliver its services in the manner specified *ex ante*. Grants would potentially allow for more honest assessments of project faults and midcourse adjustments without the NGO fearing the loss of a project or resources as a result of its honesty. Such collaborative reviews, as opposed to formal monitoring and periodic audits, could potentially also help to rebuild trust between grantees and donors. Second, contracts, when awarded, should carry longer time frames. One way of mitigating the destructive effects of NGOs constantly securing contractual renewal would be to grant contracts well in excess of one year. Multi-year projects would allow contractors more breathing room and space for experimentation and actual learning without the prospect of incurring financial penalties. Since contracting is here to stay, how it influences and transforms the goals and authority of global governors needs to be much more extensively analyzed by scholars and practitioners alike.

10 | *When "doing good" does not: the IMF and the Millennium Development Goals*

TAMAR GUTNER

Complex Delegation ! [handwritten]

Global governors commonly interact in hopes of cooperating and coordinating in order to tackle global problems, but these attempts can also result in unintended or poor outcomes that risk undermining the entire process. This is especially true in cases in which global governors diffuse common goals, rules, or norms horizontally and/or vertically across a variety of international actors without ensuring that there are clear, workable mechanisms by which they may be translated into specific policies. International organizations (IOs) are increasingly struggling with the effects of these efforts at cooperation, as they find themselves juggling a growing number of issues and programs. In fact, all major IOs are being asked to address, in one form or another, the *same* common (and big) issues, such as poverty reduction, the environment, corruption, terrorism, human rights, and gender. The problem IOs face is the growing gap that exists between global governors' attempts to affect policy and IOs' ability to translate new issue areas into tangible outcomes, particularly where accountability mechanisms are weak and the "fit" between idea and institution is poor. As economist William Easterly (2005) has pointed out, "Collective responsibility for big goals doesn't hold any one agency accountable if the effort fails; they can always point to others as the ones who are to blame." As the editors note in the opening chapter of this volume, this problem is especially acute when a governor is drawn to new competencies outside its delegated areas of comparative advantage. Not only would it struggle to elicit deference from other actors, but people may not defer to it all.

Many thanks to the participants of the "Who are the Global Governors?" workshops and especially to Deborah Avant, Martha Finnemore, and Susan Sell for their helpful comments on earlier drafts. I am also grateful to Jason Rancatore and Courtney Radsch for their research assistance.

This chapter illustrates the negative consequences of noble attempts by global governors to spread poverty reduction goals across IOs and other actors, by focusing on how these global norms impact a major IO that is poorly equipped to address them. This is a tale of two failures. One is relatively well known: the expected failure of the Millennium Development Goals (MDGs). The MDGs are a set of eight ambitious international goals endorsed by heads of state in 2000, aimed at halving poverty and improving the welfare of the world's poor by 2015. They have been touted as "an unprecedented promise by world leaders to address, as a single package, peace, security, development, human rights, and fundamental freedoms" (United Nations 2005). The goals are an affirmation of the ability of the international community to agree on a set of international norms and take steps to address them (Mundy, this volume). Yet, it is also widely recognized that most countries will fail to meet most goals, and no particular actor is responsible for failure.[1] The global financial crisis has hit the poorest countries hardest, making prospects for MDG goal achievement even more elusive. The second tale of failure, and the focus of this chapter, is the impact of the MDGs on the major IO least equipped to implement them: the International Monetary Fund (IMF).

Using this volume's definition of governors as actors that "create issues, set agendas, establish and implement rules or programs, and evaluate and/or adjudicate outcomes," we find in this case study that governors – states, IOs, and other actors – have indeed created issues, set an agenda, and established rules, but these have not been well implemented (Avant *et al.*, this volume). As a result, the chain between the "upstream" area of ideas and the "downstream" area of efficient or effective outcomes is broken. In fact, the failure of the MDGs may go beyond mere ineffectiveness if it ignites a fresh round of aid fatigue among donor countries. This case also provides an example of how

---

[1] Mundy's chapter in this volume presents a rosier picture of the MDGs, although her emphasis is more on acceptance of a global norm rather than evidence that Target 3, which seeks to "ensure that by 2015 children everywhere . . . will be able to complete a full course of primary schooling," is being implemented. The "failure" I refer to is one of implementation, rather than norm acceptance. Recent data show mixed evidence on the implementation side of the MDG for education, with many obstacles remaining, especially in sub-Saharan Africa. See, for example, www.dfid.gov.uk/pubs/files/mdg-factsheets/educationfactsheet.pdf.

muddy the distinction may be between governor and governed. IOs like the IMF are receiving new mandates from their member states, but they also have a voice in shaping the ideas behind these mandates. Meanwhile, IOs are working to implement their goals in poor countries, which, in turn, are also their principals. The result is that complex delegation leads to marginal adaptation of existing policies and procedures rather than bold new initiatives.)

While a great deal has been written on the MDGs and the challenges many countries will face in meeting them (for example, Sahn and Stifel 2003; Black and White 2004; Sharma 2004), there has been little attention to the specific negative consequences that arise when governors seek to diffuse a common set of goals that fit poorly with the practices of some of the major actors involved. I am particularly interested in how the MDGs impact the IMF, a powerful actor whose behavior is important to the success or failure of the MDGs and other poverty reduction initiatives, given its role in helping countries devise macroeconomic stabilization programs that may be tied to concessional lending and debt reduction. In other words, this chapter does not focus on the sources of the MDGs or the role of global governors in creating them; instead it addresses the consequences of the MDGs' diffusion by highlighting what happens when they reach a major IO.)

The IMF is expected to help implement the MDGs, and its managing director has even declared that bridging the poverty gap should rank equally as high as the IMF's traditional goal of helping solve the world's financial imbalances (Freeland and Luce 2007). In fact, the global financial crisis instantly lifted the IMF from a steady decline in lending and legitimacy and put it back into the frontline of actors expected to help poor countries respond to the crisis. At their April 2009 summit, the leaders of the G-20 industrialized and emerging market countries agreed to triple the Fund's lending capacity to $750 billion.

Yet the IMF is perhaps the major IO least capable of embracing any bold new initiatives for poverty reduction in general, and the MDGs in particular. Indeed, its impact on poverty has long been a source of contentious debate within policy, academic, and activist circles. Critics see IMF intervention via austerity programs as *increasing* rather than reducing poverty. Defenders argue that while stabilization measures may increase poverty in the short run, sometimes such bitter medicine is necessary to spark sustained economic growth and poverty reduction in the long run.

This chapter proceeds by unpacking the traditional principal–agent (P–A) model as a useful tool for examining the IMF's mixed behavior in poverty reduction and showing ways in which the model may be modified to explain more precisely the Fund's dysfunctional performance. It then describes the MDGs and their status before returning to the case of the IMF. It concludes by revisiting the issues and questions raised by Avant, Finnemore, and Sell. Not only does the IMF's struggle with the MDGs challenge functionalist assumptions about governance that the editors also critique, but it also shows the complexity of delegated authority in practice. When IOs like the IMF have a dual role as both principal and agent, and when member states are simultaneously governors and governed, the lines of authority are muddied in ways that help explain poor outcomes.

Principal–agent models and delegation pathologies

The fit between the MDGs and the IMF is uncomfortable for two reasons. First, the IMF is already struggling to implement its joint program with the World Bank to address poverty-related issues through the Poverty Reduction Strategy Paper (PRSP) process, which is linked to the Fund's concessionary lending facility (Poverty Reduction and Growth Facility, or PRGF); and second, the goals of the MDGs do not clearly complement the goals of the PRSP process, and there is little consensus about what the relationship between the two should be.

The challenges facing the IMF may be usefully explained by using a P–A model to highlight a set of delegation pathologies rooted in the relationship between member-state principals and the IMF as agent, but also adversely influencing the reverse relationship between the IMF as principal and recipient state as agent. Delegation pathologies occur under conditions in which principals delegate to agents tasks that are unclear, unrealistic, or highly complex. Mixed performance by the IO or recipient countries may involve shirking, as classic P–A models predict, but shirking may also reflect principals delegating tasks that are simply too difficult to implement. This is an ironic conclusion, given that one of the perceived strengths of the MDGs is that they consist of measurable targets and indicators that are supposed to offer donors greater clarity and more opportunities for coordination. The idea is that if all actors are on the same page, trying to achieve identifiable goals, the goals are more likely to be met. Yet this approach ignores the problem that if the goals are not met, it becomes difficult to identify who is to blame. At the very least, some blame should be placed squarely on the shoulders of the global governors who have developed and diffused the goals.

Some of the most compelling research to date seeking to explain dysfunctional IO performance comes out of the constructivist camp, arguing that IO bureaucracies are "social creatures" that use power, authority, and expertise to act autonomously in ways that clearly impact how IOs respond to new mandates (Barnett and Finnemore 1999 and 2004; Barnett 2002). For example, in analyzing the IMF's performance, Barnett and Finnemore (2004) argue that one important indicator of the IMF's ability to address poverty reduction in its work is "the degree to which staff understand it to be logically connected to the realization of more fundamental economic stability goals." The reaction of IMF officials to poverty alleviation goals is mixed. One official interviewed felt that poverty alleviation goals were imposed on the IMF by major donor countries, while another felt that addressing macroeconomic problems without attention to poverty reduction "was probably impossible." While poverty alleviation is related to the traditional work undertaken by the IMF, it is not a clear fit with the IMF's expertise and analytical tools, which tend to focus on correcting macroeconomic imbalances in the domestic economy (Barnett and Finnemore 2004).

This constructivist analysis is useful in illuminating what happens to new mandates when they confront a potent bureaucracy with a comparative advantage in a particular set of tools, skills, and ideologies. It offers a microperspective on sources of disconnect or clash between broad norms and entrenched bureaucracy. Yet the constructivist focus on what happens inside IO bureaucracies downplays the external side of the equation – *what* IOs are being asked to do by member-state shareholders and other global governors, *why* they are being asked to adopt certain policies, and *how* the politics and relationships that extend beyond the bureaucracy to include donors and recipient states impact IOs' ability to carry out their tasks.

Agency theory brings the external side of the equation back into the picture by widening the focus beyond the bureaucracy to include the broader linkages between IO shareholders, the bureaucracy itself, and recipient countries. As a result, agency theory offers a useful tool for analyzing IO performance because by capturing external politics and interests along with internal incentives and responses, it allows analysts to pinpoint better when and how external and internal factors shape IO performance as new policy goals are translated into action.

Agency theory is premised on the simple assumption that performance problems naturally result when one actor (the principal) delegates authority to another actor (the agent) to carry out the principal's designs. Agency theory anticipates the existence of performance problems because, by definition, there is a divergence of interests between principals and their agents, which results in agent behavior that differs from principal expectations. Agency losses are understood to be the biggest side-effects of delegation. Principals can try to reduce opportunistic agent behavior through screening, contracting, and oversight mechanisms.

Agency theory has two major blind spots, however, that may be remedied by widening the angle of its conceptual lens. First, the literature overwhelmingly emphasizes the agent as the source of all poor outcomes; and second, most P–A scholars focus on IOs solely as agents to member states' principals. There has been little attention to problems on the *principal*'s side of the P–A relationship and the fact that, at least in the case of international financial institutions (IFIs), the IO may be *both* principal and agent. A better understanding of these two issues contributes to stronger explanations of IO performance problems. The first point reflects the fact that much of the traditional P–A literature, with its roots in studies of economic contracting and corporate governance, is based on the assumption that the central problem is how to induce the agent to maximize the principal's welfare (Alchian and Demsetz 1972; Jensen and Meckling 1976). In other words, the onus of performance is on agents, who pursue their own interests and behave opportunistically. There is some recognition that the principals can create problems in the sense that the existence of multiple principals reduces the incentives agents face to meet the principals' preferences, and that agency slack is also to be expected when the goals are unclear (Moe 1984; Kiewiet and McCubbins 1991; Tirole 1994). Yet, to date, there is little research that closely examines the troubled institutional behavior that may be caused by multiple principals delegating overly ambitious or complex goals to their institutional agents. Better recognition of whether a performance problem has its roots in agent opportunism or complex delegation not only reveals more precisely the sources of performance difficulties but also informs attempts to correct them. For example, fixing performance problems through techniques such as screening and oversight – traditional tools suggested by agency theory for solving agent shirking – is clearly not the most useful approach if the main problem is that state principals are asking IO agents to do too much or to take on tasks that do not fit the institutions' main strengths.

Recognition of the dual role of IFIs, such as the IMF, as both agents of member states and principals to recipient states also reveals more opportunities for gaps between an IO's policy goals and its on-the-ground behavior. Most of the recent IO literature using P–A models to explain IO performance only addresses the first level of delegation – member states (as principals) delegate to the bureaucracy (as agent) – in order to explain why states delegate, and how delegation may increase IO autonomy (Pollack 2003; Talberg 2002; Nielson and Tierney 2003). Stopping the chain of delegation at the organization's doorstep offers no means of explaining what the IO does or does not do with its delegated authority on the ground and hence does not explain what factors shape IO actions. For example, an IO may have the incentives to properly and carefully adopt a new mandate, but that new mandate may still fail when implemented in a particular country for reasons outside the IO's control.

Analyzing IFIs as principals to recipient-country agents is especially appropriate since the major activity of IFIs is the granting of loans, and the relationship between lenders and borrowers is widely recognized in the field of economics as a typical principal–agent relationship. Banks use screening, monitoring, and other tools as ways of reducing moral hazard and adverse selection problems that are common to P–A relationships. Indeed, development economists have long analyzed the relationship between IFI principals and recipient-country agents as a means of showing how IMF and World Bank conditionality fails to elicit the expected behavior from the recipient (Drazen 2002; Kahn and Sharma 2003; Killick 1997; Martens 2002; Svensson 2000).

Conditionality is a classic P–A issue, because it is the tool used by donor-principals to induce policy change in recipient-country agents in return for aid. The recipient-country agents have incentives to pursue their own interests, and donors work on offering positive and negative incentives to ensure that the aid is properly spent.

A closer examination of problems inherent in delegation and a fuller view of the chain of delegation offer the means for identifying sources of faltering IO performance. They also add to our understanding of the complexity of what global governors do and how they interact. In this case, both member states and the IMF are global governors. States delegate authority to the IMF, although the IMF is involved in shaping its new tasks. The IMF, in turn, has expertise- and institution-based authority, but this does not extend well to issues of poverty reduction, which are outside the IMF's traditional strengths and comparative advantage. In effect, authority delegated to the IMF by member-state governors undermines the IMF's expertise-based authority. Stated differently, the IMF as agent may receive mandates or instructions that conflict with the IMF as a principal. The next section describes the MDGs and their progress, before turning to the case of the IMF to illustrate how delegation tensions impact the IMF both as agent and as principal, resulting in an institution ill equipped to address many of the expectations placed upon it for addressing poverty reduction.

MDGs and their progress

The MDGs offer measurable, tangible goals for mobilizing international aid and support, and a means for measuring progress. They draw from a decade of previous global initiatives, translated into eight goals, eighteen targets, and forty-eight indicators. The first seven goals are directed at reducing poverty in a variety of forms: (1) eradicating extreme poverty and hunger; (2) achieving universal education; (3) promoting gender equality and empowering women; (4) reducing child mortality; (5) improving maternal health; (6) combating HIV/AIDS and malaria; and (7) ensuring environmental sustainability. The eighth goal is to "develop a global partnership for development," which is essentially the means for achieving the first seven goals. Such a partnership would include developing countries implementing rule-based trade, while developed countries increase net development aid. The targets and indicators that accompany each goal are yardsticks by which progress may be measured.

Recent evidence shows that while some countries are making progress in achieving at least some of the MDGs, most countries will fail to meet most of them, with the biggest failures occurring in sub-Saharan Africa. While many analysts were pessimistic before the global financial crisis that the MDGs would be reached, the crisis has obviously made the situation even more dire. A recent report published by the World Bank estimated that 50 million more people would find themselves "trapped in extreme poverty" than expected just a year before, and warned the crisis would imperil the MDGs as it creates "an emergency for development" (World Bank 2009).

The IMF and its poverty reduction efforts

The IMF was created in 1944 to be the guardian of the post-World War II international monetary system by promoting and supervising exchange rate stability, facilitating international trade, and helping countries facing balance of payments problems (IMF 1944). While its mission has clearly evolved over the years, its basic goal has always been "safeguarding financial stability" (de Rato 2004). In turn, it states that it will contribute to the MDGs "through policy advice, technical assistance, financial support, and debt relief" (IMF 2006).

The MDGs were given to an IMF already struggling to address poverty-related concerns through an effort that did not fit well with the MDG goals. The IMF's first direct commitment to poverty reduction was launched in 1999 when the IMF and World Bank announced the Poverty Reduction Strategy Paper (PRSP) process along with the IMF's new PRGF in response to member-state interest in improving World Bank and IMF concessional lending and debt relief actions.

Under the new initiative, qualifying highly indebted poor countries (HIPC) were required to organize and implement a PRSP as a condition for debt relief, so that resources freed up by debt relief could be focused on poverty reduction. As the World Bank noted, the PRSP became "a centerpiece" for relations between the two Bretton Woods institutions and low-income countries (World Bank Operations Evaluations Department 2004, 2). Michel Camdessus (1999), the IMF Managing Director at the time, announced that member states had given the Fund a "clear mandate . . . to integrate the objectives of poverty reduction and growth more fully into its operations." To date, more than fifty countries have prepared their poverty reduction strategies.

The philosophy behind the new process was that countries would be in the development "driver's seat" in creating their own poverty reduction strategies for a three-year period, eventually presenting them through the PRSP. This idea reflects a growing body of research that argues development aid is more effective when backed by domestic commitment and political will (Dollar and Svensson 2000; Burnside and Dollar 2000; Sachs 1994). Governments would take charge of their poverty reduction destinies though a broad participatory process involving civil society actors and donors. The resulting PRSP, then, is actually a document produced by the recipient, with IMF and World Bank support, which lays out the country's poverty reduction objectives and policies, as well as specific targets and measurement indicators for achieving goals. The document should also describe the participatory approach undertaken by the country, including a summary of the format, location, and number of consultations, the issues raised, and the role expected of civil society in monitoring and implementing the plan (World Bank Operations Evaluation Department 2004).

Typically, the reports are organized by sector or theme, with each including a list of itemized actions and their estimated costs. The PRSPs must then be "considered" or "endorsed" by the boards of the IFIs, although in recent years the IFIs have tried to reduce the perception that the boards officially "sign off" on a country's PRSP. PRSPs, and in some cases the interim-PRSP (I-PRSP) and annual progress report, are then linked to specific lending facilities at the IFIs.[2]

At the IMF, the PRSP is linked to its Poverty Reduction and Growth Facility, which offers concessional lending to poor countries with per capita gross national income of $895 in 2003 (IMF 2005b).[3] The PRGF programs are aimed at achieving the joint goals of poverty reduction and economic growth and are supposed to be framed by the PRSP. At the same time, the PRGF programs are also designed to cover only the areas that are the IMF's main responsibilities (as opposed to the World Bank's), namely macroeconomic policies, exchange rates, tax policies, and fiscal management (IMF 2005b).

Problems with PRSPs/PRGFs

The PRSP process is widely accepted to be valid in principle and there is anecdotal evidence of progress in individual countries on issues ranging

---

[2] I-PRSPs outline steps needed to develop a full PRSP – in other words, they are a road map to the road map.

[3] The annual interest rate for PRGF loans is 0.5 percent, with semi-annual payments beginning after a five and a half year grace period, and ending ten years after the disbursement. As of August 2008, seventy-eight countries were eligible for the PRGF loans.

from more sustained participatory processes to shifts in government expenditures toward poverty reduction (World Bank and International Monetary Fund 2005; IMF 2003a). At the same time, there is consensus among IFIs, donors, and NGOs that the performance of the PRSP process to date is mixed to poor. Many of the NGOs argue that the PRSP process is simply an exercise in pouring old structural adjustment wine into new bottles, with "poverty reduction" as a new label (Malaluan and Guttal 2002; Oxfam International 2004; Whaites 2002). The IFIs' own evaluations, in turn, tend to point to the complexity of undertaking PRSPs but are still fairly critical of the outcomes. After all, the process requires low-income countries to take on a challenging set of tasks that include creating and managing a complex policy dialogue, developing a poverty reduction strategy with various goals and monitoring systems, and all in the context of very weak administrative and technical capacities. Adding to the complexity is the fact that many goals are interconnected, and therefore progress in one influences progress in another.[4] As the authors of a joint International Development Association (IDA) and IMF study on the process point out, "These are a set of tasks that few industrial countries could systematically do well" (International Development Association and International Monetary Fund 2002, 4). And the IMF's Independent Evaluation Office (IEO) admits that "actual achievements thus far fall considerably short of potential" (IMF 2004, 3).

An examination of the major tasks that member states delegated to the IMF, and that the IMF delegated to recipient countries, shows how and why the PRS process is fraught with tensions, and why its implementation has been extremely difficult.

What the IMF is being asked to do by its principals

Member-state principals have asked the IMF to develop and implement an approach to addressing poverty that runs into three important sets of problems. First, the entire PRSP process is a significant departure from the IMF's traditional approach to negotiating programs with recipient countries, involving the IMF explicitly in domestic political processes in those countries. Second, the links between promoting

---

[4] One example would be how a child's level of health and nutrition impacts his/her likelihood of enrolling in school. See World Bank and IMF (2005).

economic growth and reducing poverty are still unclear. And third, as discussed in the subsequent section, the PRSP process does not fit well with the MDGs. As a result, even many IMF officials feel the institution's own role in this process is unclear (IMF 2004, 63–5).

The PRS approach puts the IMF squarely in the poverty reduction business, which is quite different from its main mission of promoting economic stability. In fact, the IMF's efforts to promote stability in countries in crisis often contribute to worsening poverty in the short term before alleviating it. For example, traditional IMF conditionality calling for cuts in government spending and other anti-inflation measures obviously directly impact a country's ability to increase spending to meet the MDGs. The IMF's view has always been that the adverse short-term effects of its conditionality will be offset by long-term benefits of economic stability, market efficiency, and growth, although there is also internal recognition that sometimes the IMF's policies are overly austere (IMF 2005a). Former World Bank chief economist Joseph Stiglitz snidely interpreted the IMF's philosophy as "Soaring interest rates might, today, lead to starvation, but market efficiency requires free markets, and eventually, efficiency leads to growth, and growth benefits all. Suffering and pain become part of the process of redemption . . . " (Stiglitz 2003, 36).

But beyond the fundamental clash between the IMF's primary mission and this new task, the entire PRS approach also requires that the IMF work with countries in new ways that require it to engage in activities and processes that it is ill equipped to handle. As the IMF's Independent Evaluation Office's review of PRSP/PRGF notes,

The implications of the PRS approach for the IMF "way of doing business" have not yet been fully acknowledged or acted upon. The approach implies a very different way of organizing IMF inputs based on: a country-driven strategy that sets priorities within a long-term time frame; emphasizing contributions to informing a broader policy debate rather than traditional program negotiations . . . (IMF 2004, 6)

Perhaps the most dramatic illustration of this shift is the fact that the PRS process requires the IMF and the World Bank to be more explicitly involved than ever in the delicate business of encouraging what may be significant *political* change in recipient countries, by nudging countries toward greater accountability and participatory policymaking. In effect, this means that the IFIs are asking governments to change their approach to governing in fundamental ways. Granted, politics are always implicitly involved in IFI negotiations with recipient countries, but it is rare for this role to be made part of the IMF's explicit mandate.[5]

The IMF is especially poorly equipped to encourage countries to engage in more participatory practices for devising macroeconomic policies. Fund and Bank staff have argued that public participation makes sense in the context of a specific lending project, such as when the Bank consults the public before building a power plant or highway. Negotiating macroeconomic policy is a different kettle of fish. As one Fund official noted, "you cannot negotiate macroeconomic policy on the street," because discussion of issues like exchange rates and interest rates can immediately impact stock and bond markets, with potentially highly destructive results.[6] As he pointed out, even the US Federal Open Market Committee does not open its doors to the public when debating changes to US interest rates. As a result, the Fund is not in a position to negotiate in public, but it can encourage a government to inform the public of its decisions and encourage debate on its policies. In other words, while the IMF is not equipped to encourage macroeconomic policy decisions to be decided in public, they can certainly be debated in a public forum. The onus, then, is on the government to specify to the public what are the "rules of the game." To date, it appears that while more stakeholders are increasing their involvement in the process, it is still the case that broad, substantive debates about policy options are rare. As the 2004 IEO report noted, "The PRS process has had limited impact in generating meaningful discussions, outside the narrow official circle, of alternative policy options with respect to the macroeconomic framework and the macro-relevant structural reforms" (IMF 2004, 3).

Another tension between the IMF and the PRS approach stems from the fact that the IMF's business is to help countries to stabilize troubled economies, which is not always the same as promoting economic growth or reducing poverty. And while the IMF has turned its attention

[5] A notable exception is the IMF's involvement since 1996 in the promotion of "good governance in all its aspects, including by ensuring the rule of law, improving the efficiency and accountability of the public sector, and tackling corruption, as essential elements of a framework within which economies can prosper" (IMF 2003b).

[6] Author interview with senior IMF official, August 19, 2005.

to poverty reduction, the linkages between aid, growth, and poverty reduction are still fuzzy.[7] Two of the IMF's own economists have even published a study concluding that there is no robust evidence that aid has any impact on growth, positive or negative (Rajan and Subramanian 2005). As IMF official historian James Boughton (2004, 13) has pointed out, "The challenge here is to provide macroeconomic policy advice to low-income countries that is consistent with the country's requirements for growth and the reduction of poverty, not just the requirements for stability." This recognizes that policy advice geared toward long-term poverty reduction and policy advice geared toward short-term macroeconomic stability may be very different. Traditional IMF advice, after all, calls for countries to tighten their economic belts, cut spending, raise interest rates, and so on. Such measures can work directly against poverty reduction in the short run, either by slowing economic growth, or by making it impossible for governments to increase or focus spending in ways necessary to achieve the MDGs.

In terms of the PRGF, the key challenge facing the IMF has been how to align these programs better with the PRSP process. Ideally, the PRGF-supported programs should be embedded into the PRSP. Not only should the goals be aligned, but this also means that there has to be coordination between organizations on the process of developing both PRSP and PRGF. Also required is a good fit between the PRSP/PRGF program and a government's national budget cycle. The evidence to date shows that the alignment process has not worked very well. The IMF's IEO report (2004, 43) notes, "In most PRGFs, key strategic priorities and policy choices in both macroeconomic and structural areas in program design are still not guided by the PRSP." Problems include a "lack of specificity" in the PRSPs, and the fact that in some cases the numerical targets set by PRSP are out of whack by the time the PRGF is formulated (2004, 45).[8]

The IMF's official response to the PRSP/PRGF challenge has mainly been to assume a "business-as-usual" approach, which is to say that its traditional work in helping countries achieve sustainable growth is the

---

[7] See, for example, the literature that examines how aggregate growth is distributed, particularly whether or not it increases the income of the poor. Examples include White and Anderson (2001).

[8] In the cases examined by the IEO, the average amount of time between presentation of PRSP and PRGF-supported programs was six months.

best way for it to help to reduce poverty. The IMF also touts its other skills in offering policy advice, in monitoring state economies, and in helping strengthen the broader international financial architecture. Finally, it points out that it has taken new steps to write off qualified poor countries' debt.[9] This type of response is clearly insufficient, since it neither addresses IMF staff concerns about what exactly they should be doing to juggle MDGs with their ongoing tasks, nor does it explicitly recognize the very real problems discussed above that cannot be properly addressed with traditional responses. Ultimately, while classic agency theory usually blames agents for performance problems, the IMF's struggles make clear the need for more guidance and leadership from its member-state shareholders. In fact, there is evidence that the IFIs are speaking out critically, calling for donor countries to coordinate their aid better, to fulfill their pledges to improve aid quality, and to target their aid to meet their own goals, which often differ from those of the MDGs. An MDG *Global Monitoring Report*, published by the IMF and World Bank, is concerned that "aid remains poorly coordinated, unpredictable, largely locked into 'special purpose grants,' and often targeted to countries and purposes that are not priorities for the MDGs" (World Bank 2006a).

Problems at the recipient-country level

A number of the PRS performance problems occur when the IMF and World Bank themselves act as principals in delegating tasks that are difficult to implement and measure to recipient countries. Recipients, as a result, face additional incentives for agency slack, usually by seeking the minimal compliance necessary to receive the desired concessionary aid and debt relief.

One of the key challenges at this stage may be called "taxicab delegation," an example of delegation pathology. IFI principals are delegating processes to support "country ownership" in principle, but not clearly

---

[9] This debt relief is a product of the Multilateral Debt Relief Initiative (MDRI) agreed to in June 2005 by the Group of 8 industrial countries, which proposed that the IMF, IDA, and African Development Fund would cancel all of the debt to heavily indebted poor countries that met a set of criteria under the World Bank/IMF Heavily Indebted Poor Countries (HIPC) Initiative, created in 1996 to help eligible countries receive debt relief. MDRI was created specifically to help countries make progress toward achieving the MDGs.

in practice. Countries are told they are in the driver's seat, but the IFIs are perceived as telling them where to go, and of course, paying the fare (Pincus and Winters 2002, 14).[10] The mixed message is "You're in charge as long as you do it our way." Interpretations as to what exactly "country ownership" means in theory and practice also differ. This adds to unrealistic expectations or confusion. For example, what does "country ownership" mean if key domestic policymakers disagree on the goals to be pursued? Is their commitment what matters, or must they also be the source of the policy ideas? Is commitment an adequate reflection of country ownership if implementation is poor? (See, for example, World Bank and International Monetary Fund 2005, 10–11.) A common response among many countries has been to figure out what procedural hoops to jump through to receive debt relief and concessional funding. This has contributed to numerous cases of superficial participation processes with a short-lived impact (IMF 2004, 22). In Guinea and Tajikistan, for example, government consultations with civil society groups ground to a halt after the PRSP was approved by the government (in the case of Tajikistan) and completed (in the case of Guinea) (World Bank Operations Evaluations Department 2004, 10).

Taxicab delegation is created by structuring the PRS as a process by which the country is supposed to be in charge of its policy goals while it must also present a document that passes muster with the IMF and World Bank boards, for the obvious reason that there must be some mechanism to determine whether the PRSP is sufficiently sound as a basis for financial support. Before September 2004, PRSPs and their related annual progress reports were presented to the boards with a four- to five-page "joint staff assessment" (JSA) by IMF and World Bank staffs that stated whether progress in implementation was satisfactory. While World Bank and IMF staff say this procedure was never intended to be an "approval" or "endorsement" of the documents, it was certainly perceived as such and hence undermined the sense of "ownership." JSAs have also been criticized by internal IMF and Bank evaluations as being of mixed quality, in many cases lacking substantive advice on how a country could strengthen its program. As a result of some of these problems, in September 2004 the JSA

---

[10] Pincus and Winters use the taxicab metaphor as an "approach to partnership," but I argue it is a more important pathology that results from delegation challenges facing the IFIs.

evolved into a "joint staff advisory note" designed to provide stronger advice on how PRSPs can be strengthened and how implementation may be improved. However, the JSA no longer includes the concluding paragraph that explicitly recommended the Bank and Fund boards to find the document satisfactory for concessional lending (World Bank Operations Evaluations Department 2004).

A second challenge with IMF delegation of its PRS objectives at the country level is the perennial problem of mixed country capacity. At least one country hired an outside consulting firm to draft its interim PRSP (Brainard *et al.* 2003). Even in cases where countries are able to complete a satisfactory PRSP, integrating the process into existing government decisionmaking processes poses another set of challenges (Hudock 2002; International Development Association and International Monetary Fund 2002). "It is not clear," concludes the IMF's independent evaluation report (2004, 6), "how much countries have to gain by treating the PRSP as an effective strategic road map, rather than as a procedural formality." Poor countries also have difficulty juggling the full range of projects and goals that IOs and donor countries impose upon them. One single country may find itself involved in literally hundreds of aid-related operations.[11]

Ultimately, the PRSP process creates enormous expectations for the IMF and recipient countries to meet. Perhaps no one should be surprised that given the complexity of the strategy, evidence of progress is so mixed.

How do the MDGs fit?

When the objective of the MDGs is placed on top of the PRS, the process and picture become even more complicated. In principle, the PRSPs are supposed to be the mechanism by which governments translate MDGs into practice. PRSPs, therefore, are expected to be aligned with the MDGs. However, the IMF's ability (as well as that of other donors) to encourage this convergence and strengthen the recipient countries' implementation capacity has been elusive for several reasons.

---

[11] Data for Albania in the late 1990s, for example, show it dealing with more than three hundred operations, coming from almost thirty different donors (World Bank and International Monetary Fund 2005, vi).

First, the MDGs and PRSP goals are driven by two different processes that do not overlap well. MDGs are a set of ambitious, global goals, coordinated by the United Nations and devised in international summits and global conferences. Success is thus ultimately measured at the global level, for example, when the *world* cuts poverty. Measuring success also runs into the problem that many developing countries lack the capacity to compile the required statistics. When a country does not produce the required data, the United Nations and other IOs come up with estimates based on "the data of neighboring countries or countries with similar levels of income" (United Nations 2006a, 26). Meanwhile, the PRSPs are the IFIs' own strategy, linked to concessional lending and debt relief. The PRSP is supposed to be tailored to a country's specific circumstances, to fit limited abilities and resources. Individual countries have strengths and weaknesses in various development areas. There is a lot of talk about using the PRSPs as a means to operationalize the MDGs, so the government can organize its priorities and coordinate external aid, but for most countries a realistic PRSP simply may not be enough to reach the MDGs. Equally important, PRSP goals may differ from MDG goals at the country level. For example, Vietnam has prioritized addressing tobacco use as a health priority under its PRSP, but this health issue is not a part of the MDGs (World Bank and International Monetary Fund 2005, 13). As countries try to respond to both MDG and PRSP requirements, many feel they must undertake multiple externally driven processes that do not have much to do with their own economic plans.[12] This situation is further aggravated when donors' efforts to achieve divergent goals are not well coordinated at the domestic government level (World Bank and International Monetary Fund 2005, 13).

That said, there is some evidence that many MDG indicators are included in PRSPs. Researchers at the World Bank have put together data showing that of the forty PRSPs surveyed, all had at least one indicator for poverty headcount, education enrollment, and maternal health (Harrison *et al.* 2005). At the same time, fewer than 30 percent of the PRSPs had indicators for the MDG goals for malnutrition, biological diversity, housing, and air quality. The authors posit that some of the gap may reflect the fact that in some of these areas international indicators are less standardized.

---

[12] Author interview with senior World Bank official, August 2005.

How can these two different sets of processes be better aligned? One idea that the World Bank and IMF staff have suggested is to encourage countries to consider alternative frameworks for achieving the MDGs and to fit these within their poverty reduction strategies (Development Committee 2005). Alternative scenarios can lay out different combinations of resources and policies that would be required to achieve particular results. Making policymakers aware of different policy packages would allow more focus on short- and long-term measures and goals. This seems sensible and may work in countries that better address the more ambitious MDGs, but it also requires imagination in creating more visionary PRSPs. Another proposal calls upon donor countries to work harder at addressing recipient country priorities, instead of serving their own narrow concerns (World Bank and International Monetary Fund 2005, 18). Other proposals look at ways in which recipient countries can strengthen their ability to develop and meet new policies and strategies by, for example, better involving parliaments, creating better monitoring systems, linking annual budgets and other public spending to specific objectives, and so on (World Bank and International Monetary Fund 2005, 25).

A second tension facing the IMF in its attempts to address the MDGs is that the MDGs require increased donor country aid. Indeed, Target 12 of Goal 8 of the MDGs is "more generous official development assistance for countries committed to poverty reduction." For example, the UN Millennium Project (2005) has argued that if industrialized countries increase their aid from 0.44 percent of their GNP in 2006 to 0.54 percent by 2015, the goals may be achieved. This increase is also less than the 0.7 percent that countries agreed to in 2002 at their Monterrey conference on financing development. The IMF is supportive of calls for development aid to be doubled over the next five years, in order to make more progress toward reaching the MDGs, but it has historically been uncomfortable with increases in aid to unstable countries that lack the capacity to absorb increased external flows of resources. In particular, before the current financial crisis, there was much talk about "Dutch disease" – instances where increases in wealth (from aid flows or, as in the Dutch case, the discovery of large natural gas deposits) create unintended outcomes, such as exchange rate appreciation, inflation, and reduced competitiveness (Ebrahim-zadeh 2003). The global financial crisis will push some of these issues to the sidelines, given the desire by G-20 countries and the IMF to inject liquidity into the world economy. But these concerns are likely to resurface.

Conclusion

The MDGs show every indication of heading toward collapse, although no doubt the rhetoric seeking to explain their failure will focus on the few intact pieces found amid the rubble and the bulk of the blame will be placed on the global financial crisis rather than specific actors. Nonetheless, the failure will also underscore how international attempts to create a common set of norms complete with targets and timetables run into trouble when the norms are not diffused evenly or well, and when no one is held accountable for the outcome. As Easterly (2002, 43) put it, "The buck stops nowhere in the world of development assistance."

The IMF's response to the MDGs has been similar to its response to the PRSP/PRGF, and that is one of marginal adaptation rather than a significant deviation from its usual approach. The G-20 leaders have given the IMF a central role in combating the global financial crisis, but the IMF's response is mainly in areas such as making its conditionality more flexible, increasing the amount and speed of its lending, and implementing some quota reforms. It is difficult to imagine the IMF fulfilling director Dominique Strauss-Kahn's commitment to be "the voice for low-income countries" ("G-20 Reaffirms IMF's Central Role in Combatting Crisis" 2009).

This chapter has shown how the MDGs fit poorly – and indeed, sometimes directly conflict – with the IMF's own poverty reduction strategies and policies. Its efforts then to delegate tasks to recipient countries through its conditionality and policy processes run into additional challenges in cases where countries lack the capacity to carry out their end of the deal, or face increased incentives for shirking, or both.

Tracing the path of the MDGs through the IMF to recipient countries reveals a process where what exactly is being delegated, by whom, and to whom, is diffuse and complex. It highlights some of the negative consequences of this diffuse delegation and points to the need for more attention to the global governors' role and responsibility in what and how they delegate. If states or others give IOs goals that are unclear, overly ambitious, unattached to incentives for accountability, or simply too complex to carry out, some responsibility for failure should fall on these principals. The agents may fail, but their inability to undertake their job (which may or may not be due to shirking in pursuit of self-interests) is ultimately traceable to something going wrong at the point of delegation. Put in the language of this volume, governors can undermine IOs by delegating a task that undermines the latter's expertise-based authority.

While this chapter has focused on some of the consequences of complex delegation, there is also a need for research that examines the reasons behind such delegation – that is, why do global governors delegate tasks that are overly ambitious or poorly conceived and, ultimately, so difficult for agents to carry out? And why do they choose to delegate tasks and diffuse global norms without clear accountability mechanisms? We also need to understand better the implications of actors simultaneously constituting both governor and governed, as is the case with IOs such as the IMF. Developing country clients of the IMF, in turn, are impacted by the behavior of the IMF, but are also involved to some degree in the IMF's own governance, as members of its governing bodies.

Complex delegation raises important questions about the efficacy of what is popularly understood as "global governance." The effects of complex delegation vary; sometimes, as in Newman's chapter (this volume), it provides opportunities for entrepreneurial governors to engineer flexible alliance strategies that enhance the governor's influence. At other times it renders general aspirational goals incoherent and exacerbates the gap between goals and norm acceptance (Mundy, this volume). Examining complex delegation highlights the fact that no one governs alone, and that the relationships between and among global governors tell us much about processes and the disjuncture between goals and results. The policy implications of this case are also important, given the ripple effect MDG failure will have on debates about aid effectiveness.

In the end, one hopes the buck has to stop somewhere.

Appendix *Millennium Development Goals, targets, and indicators*

Millennium Development Goals	Indicators	Targets
Goal 1: Eradicate extreme poverty and hunger	Reduce by half the proportion of people living on less than a dollar a day	1. Proportion of population below $1 (PPP) a day 1a. Poverty headcount ratio (percentage of population below national poverty line)
	Reduce by half the proportion of people who suffer from hunger	2. Poverty gap ratio (incidence × depth of poverty) 3. Share of poorest quintile in national consumption 4. Prevalence of underweight in children (>5 yrs) 5. Proportion of population below minimum level of dietary energy consumption
Goal 2: Achieve universal primary education	Ensure that all boys and girls complete a full course of primary schooling	6. Net enrollment ratio in primary education 7a. Proportion of pupils starting grade 1 who reach grade 5 7b. Primary completion rate 8. Literacy rate of 15 to 24 year olds
Goal 3: Promote gender equality and empower women	Eliminate gender disparity in primary and secondary education preferably by 2005, and at all levels by 2015	9. Ratio of girls to boys in primary, secondary, and tertiary education 10. Ratio of literate women to men ages 15 to 24 11. Share of women in wage employment in the nonagricultural sector 12. Proportion of seats held by women in national parliament

(cont.)

Appendix *(cont.)*

Millennium Development Goals	Indicators	Targets
Goal 4: Reduce child mortality	Reduce by two-thirds the mortality rate among children under five	13. Under-five mortality rate 14. Infant mortality rate 15. Proportion of one-year-old children immunized against measles
Goal 5: Improve maternal health	Reduce by three-quarters the maternal mortality ratio	16. Maternal mortality ratio 17. Proportion of births attended by skilled health personnel
	Halt and begin to reverse the spread of HIV/AIDS	18. HIV prevalence among pregnant women ages 15 to 24 19. Condom use rate of the contraceptive prevalence rate 19a. Condom use at last high-risk sex 19b. Percentage of 15 to 24 year olds with comprehensive correct knowledge of HIV/AIDS 19c. Contraceptive prevalence rate 20. Ratio of school attendance of orphans to school attendance of non-orphans ages 10 to 14
Goal 6: Combat HIV/AIDS, malaria, and other diseases	Halt and begin to reverse the incidence of malaria and other major diseases	21. Prevalence and death rates associated with malaria 22. Proportion of population in malaria-risk areas using effective malaria prevention and treatment measures 23. Prevalence and death rates associated with tuberculosis 24. Proportion of tuberculosis cases detected and cured under directly observed treatment short course

Goal	Target	Indicators
Goal 7: Ensure environmental sustainability	Integrate the principles of sustainable development into country policies and programs; reverse loss of environmental resources	25. Proportion of land area covered by forest 26. Ratio of area protected to maintain biological diversity to surface area 27. Energy use (kg of oil equivalent) per $1 GDP (PPP) 28. Carbon dioxide emissions (per capita) and consumption of ozone-depleting chlorofluorocarbons (ODP tons)
	Reduce by half the proportion of people without sustainable access to safe drinking water	29. Proportion of population using solid fuels 30. Proportion of population with sustainable access to an improved water source, urban and rural 31. Proportion of population with access to improved sanitation, urban and rural
	Achieve significant improvement in lives of at least 100 million slum dwellers, by 2020	32. Proportion of households with access to secure tenure
Goal 8: Develop a global partnership for development	Develop further an open trading and financial system that is rule-based, predictable, and nondiscriminatory. Includes a commitment to good governance, development, and poverty reduction – nationally and internationally	Official development assistance 33. Net ODA total and to the least developed countries, as a percentage of OECD/DAC donors' gross national income 34. Proportion of bilateral, sector-allocable ODA of OECD/DAC donors for basic social services (basic education, primary healthcare, nutrition, safe water, sanitation)

(*cont.*)

Appendix (*cont.*)

Millennium Development Goals	Indicators	Targets
	Address the least developed countries' special needs. This includes tariff- and quota-free access for their exports; enhanced debt relief for heavily indebted poor countries; cancellation of official bilateral debt; and more generous official development assistance for countries committed to poverty reduction	35. Proportion of bilateral official development assistance ODA of OECD/DAC donors that is untied 36. ODA received in landlocked countries as proportion of their gross national incomes 37. ODA received in small island developing states as proportion of their gross national incomes Market access 38. Proportion of total developed country imports (by value and excluding arms) from developing countries and from least developed countries, admitted free of duty
	Address the special needs of landlocked and small island developing states	39. Average tariffs imposed by developed countries on agricultural products and textiles and clothing from developing countries
	Deal comprehensively with developing countries' debt problems through national and international measures to make debt sustainable in the long term	40. Agricultural support estimate for OECD countries as a percentage of their gross domestic product

In cooperation with the developing countries, develop decent and productive work for youth	41. Proportion of ODA provided to help build trade capacity
	Debt sustainability
	42. Total number of countries that have reached their HIPC decision points and number that have reached their HIPC completion points (cumulative)
In cooperation with pharmaceutical companies, provide access to affordable essential drugs in developing countries	43. Debt relief committed under HIPC initiative
	44. Debt service as percentage of exports of goods and services
	Other
	45. Unemployment rate of 15 to 24 year olds (male, female, and total)
	46. Proportion of population with access to affordable, essential drugs on a sustainable basis
In cooperation with the private sector, make available the benefits of new technologies – especially information and communications technologies	47. Telephone lines and cellular subscribers per 100 population
	48a. Personal computers in use per 100 population
	48b. Internet users per 100 population
	(Some indicators will be monitored separately for the least developed countries, Africa, landlocked countries, and small island developing states)

Adapted from the following sources: The World Bank Group (2004) *Millennium Development Goals*, retrieved November 9, 2005 from http://ddp-ext.worldbank.org/ext/GMIS/gdmis.do?siteId=2&menuId=LNAV01HOME1; United Nations (2005) *UN Millennium Development Goals*, retrieved November 9, 2005 from www.un.org/millenniumgoals/; United Nations Development Programme, *Millennium Development Goals*, retrieved August 5, 2008 from www.undp.org/mdg/basics.shtml.

11 The power of norms; the norms of power: who governs international electrical and electronic technology?

TIM BÜTHE

Introduction

"Who governs?" Robert Dahl (1961) asked in his classic pluralist study of New Haven politics. This volume takes his question to the international level, asking a series of related questions about the actors in "global governance." I apply Dahl's deceptively simple core question to the governance of terminology, measures, design, and performance characteristics of electrical and electronic phenomena and products. Electrical and electronic technology is governed internationally through the technical standards of the International Electrotechnical Commission (IEC). In this international nongovernmental organization, as elsewhere, governance involves the exercise of power and hence warrants political analysis.

There are many reasons – at least 5,425 of them, as of the end of 2008 – to concern oneself with IEC standards. Three brief examples will illustrate the point. When I take a picture with a digital camera, I can view the image on the camera's LCD screen or send the image to a printer, almost anywhere in the world. While resolution, clarity, and quality of display and printout might differ by manufacturer and

For very helpful comments on previous drafts, I am grateful to Deborah Avant, Daniel Drezner, Martha Finnemore, Jim Goldgeier, Susan Sell, J. P. Singh, and participants of the Global Governors workshops at George Washington University and the 2008 Annual Convention of the International Studies Association. I gratefully acknowledge a research fellowship from the Robert Wood Johnson Foundation Scholars in Health Policy Research Program at the University of California, Berkeley, during which this chapter was completed. For sharing background information, I thank Jack Sheldon, IEC Standardization Strategy Manager, and participants of IEC Technical Committee meetings from various national member bodies of the IEC.

model, the screen and the printer will both recognize and produce essentially the same colored image, *even though the LCD screen uses a mix of red, green, and blue light to produce each color whereas the printer uses cyan, magenta, yellow and black ink or dyes.* How is this possible? Second, when a patient needs x-ray images, s/he usually can trust that the x-ray machine will emit a sufficiently high dose of radiation to ensure that a usable x-ray image is taken without exposing him/her to exceptionally dangerous doses, *even though neither the patient nor the physician has measured the radiation emitted from the x-ray machine* (and in fact, neither may fully understand the technology). Why are we willing to have such trust? Third, as recently as ten to twenty years ago, many vacuum cleaners, hair dryers, and other motorized electrical appliances would interfere with the reception of nearby TVs or radios; some microwaves and cordless phone sets would interfere with each other, etc. Today, a manufacturer of these products can, usually truthfully, give a blanket assurance that such interference will not occur (or can be easily fixed by the consumer), *even though the product has probably not been tested for interference with the consumer's TVs, radios, phones, etc.* How is this possible?

The answer to all three questions is, at least in part, IEC standards. IEC 61966-series "color management" standards define colors so as to allow reliable communication of color data between a broad range of devices with very different ways of reproducing those colors (see IEC 2007a for more details).[1] These IEC standards ensure interoperability. IEC standard 60580, "Medical Electrical Equipment – Dose Area Product Meters" specifies where and how to measure the dosage emitted by radiological devices. Such measurement standards allow the manufacturers of these devices, if they implement IEC 60580, to provide technical data about their products, which can be meaningfully compared across competing products and against regulatory specifications of maximum permissible radiation levels based on the same standard.[2] Finally, IEC 61000-series standards for electromagnetic compatibility

---

[1] Parts of these standards originated in the strictly private "ICC" standards consortium, founded and operated for profit by Adobe, Agfa, Apple, Kodak, Fogra, Microsoft, Sun Microsystems, and Taligent, but 61966 is a series of IEC standards. For a discussion of different ways of setting technical standards, see Büthe and Mattli (2009).

[2] As this example illustrates, nongovernmental IEC technical standards are often used (explicitly or implicitly) by governments and regulatory agencies.

specify thresholds for electromagnetic disturbances that may be emitted by electronic and electrical products and the level of insulation/immunity a product must have from disturbances in its environment, so as to ensure noninterference even when they are operated in close proximity to each other – crucial for pacemakers, electronic components of brakes for cars and trucks, and laptop computers running essential applications.

These IEC norms get producers to design their products or operate their production processes differently than they otherwise would and they get consumers to blindly trust otherwise suspicion-evoking equipment. In other words, they have power (Dahl 1957). Yet, since all of the above sounds rather technical, some observers have concluded that international standardization is purely a science and engineering optimization problem. For Loya and Boli (1999), for instance, international technical standardization is evidence of the triumph of universalistic/global technical rationality over the use of political or economic power to "settle" conflicts of interest. There are, however, many reasons to doubt this harmonious image. Standards are prominent nontariff barriers to trade; where their harmonization opens markets, it benefits firms that are more competitive at the expense of less-competitive ones. Standards also affect the value of patents, which was the root cause of Thomas Edison's ruthless multi-year campaign to keep the United States from adopting alternating rather than direct current as the standard for household electricity (for example, McNichol 2006). And although IEC standards as such are merely prescriptive (that is, they are explicit norms in technical language), the increasing reliance of governments on these standards as the technical basis for regulatory measures means that IEC standards often are effectively mandatory rules for much of the global economy (ISO/IEC 2007, esp. 19ff.).[3]

In addition, whenever prior practice differs, standardization entails switching costs and thus distributional conflicts, as I have shown in previous work about ISO and IEC standardization, based on a survey among firms in five countries and five industries (Büthe and Mattli 2010a; Mattli and Büthe 2003; see also Krasner 1991). Despite these indications that standardization is often as intensely political as

---

[3] There is a close affinity here to the practice, analyzed by Danner and Voeten (this volume), of governments writing into later international treaties the definitions, rules, and procedures originally developed by expert judges.

it is technical, however, social science analyses of international standardization and standards-developing organizations are still few and far between. Most of the existing work focuses on the International Organization for Standardization (ISO) and specifically its 9000- and 14000-series process and management standards (Brunsson and Jacobsson 2000; Casper and Hancké 1999; Guler *et al.* 2002; Kollman and Prakash 2001; Prakash and Potoski 2006b and this volume). I focus here on the IEC, which has received hardly any attention in social science scholarship, even though it is one of the oldest institutions for transnational governance in the international political economy.

In the century since it was founded in 1906, the IEC has grown from nine to seventy-one member bodies (fifty-four electrotechnical bodies with active full membership, seventeen with associate membership; one per country) and affiliates in eighty-two countries (see the section on "Expanding depth, scope, and membership" and Table 11.2 for an overview of the evolution of IEC membership; see also IEC 2008b). The IEC has vastly expanded the scope of its activities from the international "standardization of the nomenclature and ratings of electrical apparatus and machinery" (1904 declaration calling for the establishment of the IEC) to setting international standards for measurement, compatibility, performance, design, engineering development, and safety of industrial and consumer products in "all electrotechnologies including electronics, magnetics and electromagnetics, electroacoustics, multimedia, telecommunication, and energy production and distribution, as well as associated general disciplines" (IEC Mission Statement, 2006). As a result, there are now 5,425 IEC standards, most of them developed anew or updated/revised within the past decade (IEC 2009).[4] Over the course of a century, the IEC has thus developed from informal meetings among representatives of often nascent domestic groups of electrotechnical experts into a firmly established international organization that plays an important and well-institutionalized part in governing the international political economy. For international standard-setting, the IEC is today in most electrotechnologies "the only game in town" – similar to the European Union (EU) for much of European-level regulatory governance (McNamara, this volume). How did this happen? Who defined the vastly expanded

---

[4] Figures are current as of December 31, 2008.

range of issues over which the IEC came to claim governance authority? What is the IEC and who really "governs" electrical, electronic,
and related technologies through IEC standards?

To answer the first two questions, I trace the process of institutional
change that has allowed the IEC to attain its contemporary prominence
and broad scope of authority.[5] I find that the IEC has broadened its
authority by supplementing its initial expertise-based authority with
institutional and delegated authority, as well as by proving competent in those areas of electrotechnical standardization in which it was
already involved (what Avant, Finnemore, and Sell, this volume, call
"capacity-based" authority). Synergies among these authority sources,
in turn, allowed the IEC to broaden the scope of issues for which
it developed international standards. This evolution of IEC governance was driven or at least made possible by the structural changes
emphasized by Avant, Finnemore, and Sell: globalization, technological change, even the end of the Cold War, and deregulation (or, more
precisely, what I call "the privatization of regulation"). However, these
structural factors must be embedded in an analysis of actors, with real
agency and economic as well as political interests, to explain the institutional evolution of the IEC from 1906 to 2008.

In the final section, I analyze who actually exercises power within the
IEC[6] (and beyond) in each stage of the governance sequence: agenda
setting, rulemaking, implementation, monitoring, enforcement, and
adjudication.[7] I argue and show that the cast of actors is diverse and
varies greatly depending on the specific governance activity considered.
Even at face value, Dahl's question of "who governs?" thus does not

---

[5] The IEC's own archive of historical documents is unfortunately very limited,
consisting mostly of the minutes of meetings, though these minutes were often
quite detailed until the 1970s. This scarcity of historical evidence is a common
problem for research about "governors" that operate without a public mandate
for record-keeping.

[6] As I discuss below, the IEC has organizational interests that make it useful at
times to treat the institution as an actor in its own right (see also Büthe 2007;
Hawkins *et al.* 2006). Yet, scholars of institutionalized nonstate actors in world
politics should not replicate at the level of inter/transnational organizations the
analytical sleight of hand for which many of us criticize state-centric theories of
IR, namely the reification of structures as agents, such that the individuals and
groups disappear who exercise power via the institutional structure.

[7] I treat implementation and enforcement as well as monitoring and adjudication
as separate activities, respectively (and do not examine adjudication here; see
Bradley and Kelley 2008; Hawkins *et al.* 2006; Abbott and Snidal 2009).

Table 11.1 *Founding dates of the first national*
electrotechnical societies

1871	Institution of Electrical Engineers (IEE), UK (first founded as Society of Telegraph Engineers)
1883	Société Internationale des Electriciens, France
1883	Elektrotechnischer Verein, Austria-Hungary
1884	American Institute of Electrical Engineers (AIEE)
1884	Société (Royale) Belge des Électriciens (SRBE)
1891	Canadian Electrical Association
1893	Verband Deutscher Elektrotechniker (VDE), Germany
1897	Associazione Elettrotecnica Italiana

have a simple, context-independent answer. Moreover, I demonstrate that formal and informal institutions at the international and domestic levels largely shape who governs and what means they can use to do so. This finding has important implications for the study of global governance more broadly: even in transnational nongovernmental governance, where states as such play only a limited role, cross-national differences in *domestic* public and private institutions matter. Analyses of the ways in which institutions and "institutional complementarity" constrain and empower the diverse actors at the various stages of governance (Büthe and Mattli 2010a) therefore hold great promise for improving our understanding of global governance.

Scope of electrotechnical governance

Founding the IEC: institutionalizing cooperation

The rapid development of electrical engineering in the late nineteenth century led to the establishment of "electrotechnical societies" in most of today's "advanced industrialized" countries (see Table 11.1). Most of them were professional associations of physicists and electrical engineers, who sought to institutionalize their information exchange. The historical documents of the early international meetings of these organizations' representatives, however, also convey a sense that having a national electrotechnical association was considered at the time an increasingly "necessary" part of being a modern, industrializing country (see Finnemore 1992; Meyer 1980).

The push for electrotechnical standardization – at the domestic and the international levels – arose largely out of these societies, often initially motivated by a desire to have common measures in order to be able to replicate and build on each other's research, but increasingly also out of commercial interest, as the development of electrical technology and machinery proceeded at breakneck speed. The planning committee for the sixth International Electrical Congress in St. Louis (1904) thus invited all (then independent) countries to send official delegates for a special meeting to consider international cooperation. These delegates (in what was essentially an assertion of authority) issued a formal declaration, calling on the "technical societies of the world" to come together and create a "representative commission" to "consider questions of the standardization of the nomenclature and ratings of electrical apparatus and machinery." This proclamation led to the founding of the IEC by representatives from Austria, Belgium, Canada, France, Germany, Great Britain, Holland, Hungary, Italy, Japan, Spain, Switzerland, and the United States, meeting from 26 to 28 June 1906 in London (Ruppert 1956). Why did they create a transnational organization for electrical and electrotechnical standardization – and who were "they"?

An important part of the explanation for the creation of the IEC and the initial scope of its authority is functional. There was a widespread belief that, for basic research and technological development to be fruitful and cumulative, common terminology, measures, and symbols were needed not just at the national level but, given the rapidly increasing transnational flow of ideas and products, at the international level, too (Hughes 1983, esp. 47ff., 79ff., 140ff.; see also O'Rourke and Williamson 1999; Rodgers 1998). Market selection *can* create de facto standards (the VHS video format and the Windows operating system for PCs are prominent examples), but the participants of the early international electrical congresses saw that harmonization was not happening "naturally": the exhibits that occupied the "Palace of Electricity" at the 1904 World's Fair in St. Louis, for instance, not only required electricity of numerous different voltages, but differed in whether they needed direct current, or a 1-, 2-, or 3-phase alternating current, with frequency ranging from 25 to 60 cycles.[8] Moreover, the slow, limited success of attempts to achieve harmonization informally in the context

---

[8] See Erdmann (2007) for details; see also AIEE (1904).

of the international electrical congresses, which took place at irregular intervals, suggested that ad hoc cooperation was insufficient: while the delegates of the first International Electrical Congress in Paris in 1881 adopted Ampere, Volt, and Ohm as common "practical units" from among no fewer than ten different units of electric current, twelve different units of electromotive force, and fifteen different units of resistance previously in use, it took another twelve years to agree on common definitions of these units at the fourth international congress in Chicago (Raeburn 2006b, 1). In their exchanges of letters in the early years of the twentieth century and in their ensuing discussions in London in 1906, those who founded the IEC explicitly expressed the hope that institutionalizing this kind of cooperation – giving it a formal institutional structure – would facilitate and speed up standardization on a global level (see e.g., IEC 1906).

As noted in the introduction, however, harmonization of previous divergent standards creates winners and losers. Largely devoid of actors, the functional explanation for the creation of the IEC, sketched above, ignores these distributional considerations. Taking them into account leads me to ask: Who actually founded the IEC? And whose interests was standardization meant to serve?

The official delegates at the 1904 Electrical Congress and the 1906 founding meeting in London were mostly private individuals, often highly respected technical experts in physics or engineering at universities or polytechnic institutes; yet they also played an important role in industrial application and were usually selected by their national electrotechnical societies. It was this group that initially defined the general issue area over which the IEC was to acquire global governance authority. Scientific considerations and the desire to advance the understanding of electricity and related phenomena surely motivated many of them. But commercial rather than purely scientific interests were the driving force behind electrotechnical standardization at the national and international levels. Inventors and commercial developers of electric technology and machinery realized in particular that the lack of standardization of such basics as the type of current (direct vs alternating), or even the way in which voltage was measured, impeded their ability to achieve economies of scale in the production of anything from light bulbs and telephones to electrically powered machinery. As one of the participants noted at the time, a difference of "1/10th of a Volt" in 110 Volts could make a difference of "large sums of money in regard to a contract for incandescent lamps" (Erdmann 2007, 4). Consequently, usefulness for the development of technologies with commercial application was a key criterion for decisions concerning where to focus standardization efforts, and protecting or enhancing the value of one's technology and patents often drove support and opposition to the development of any particular standard. The rapid advances in electrotechnology at the time, however, ensured that standardization usually opened many more new, profitable opportunities than it foreclosed. And IEC standardization – carried out through correspondence and regular plenary sessions every two to three years – was often close behind the cutting edge of technological development. In some cases, international standards were therefore developed before national standards had been firmly established and before a great many had developed a stake in a particular standard or practice. In the realm of electrotechnology, the speed of innovation of new technologies in the *first* decades of the twentieth century, not only created an opening for private transnational governance by technical experts, but helped electrotechnology in its early years to avoid the kind of lock-in that can impede shifting to a new standard even if that new one is clearly superior (David 1985). Drawn-out battles were therefore rare.

Equally important, who was *not* sitting at the table? Some governments saw electrotechnology as holding great promise for economic and industrial development. The Prussian/German government, for instance, set up extensive basic research and standardization facilities for the physical sciences at the Physikalisch-Technische Reichsanstalt, founded in 1887 as an incubator of scientific knowledge to supercharge Germany's electricity-driven late industrialization (Cahan 1989; Hughes 1983, 178; Warburg 1916).[9] Some of the leading figures

---

[9] Countries and empires since ancient times had thrived on trade enabled by the availability of common "weights and measures." Economic historians began to understand and advertise this benefit of standardization in the late ninteenth and early twentieth century in the context of the intellectual ascendancy of models of free trade. Governments therefore supported and encouraged the development of "basic" standards, via institutions such as the US National Bureau of Standards (today NIST), founded in 1901 – secure in the knowledge that protection of industry was still available at all times and could be achieved more profitably (for the government's coffers) by raising tariffs than by fragmenting markets through differing standards. For an excellent historical analysis of the development and economic importance of basic standards, see Spruyt (2001).

in national electrotechnical societies had appointments in public universities or as lead scientists in publicly funded research institutes. Yet, even they hardly acted predominantly as representatives of the state. Rather, the scientists and engineers who were the individual actors in the technical discussions in the early years often acted as representatives of industry or even of their own personal commercial interests, as many of them had a personal financial stake in the commercial applications.[10] Governments as such generally played little or no role in the IEC (see also section on "The power of norms of power" below).

Other forms of exclusion are equally or even more important for the question of who governs. Reflecting the social status afforded to many of the pioneers of the "electrical age," the founding meeting of the IEC in June 1906 was held in London's premier luxury hotel, the Hotel Cecil, assuring in effect (if not necessarily intentionally) the exclusion of stakeholders from poorer parts of the world. The organizational features of the IEC (some of them arguably inevitable, given the technology at the time) also meant that only those able and willing to pay the costs of international travel were able to participate fully in IEC standardization. This, in turn, affected whom a national member body could appoint to be the country's official representative on any given IEC technical committee: participants paid their own way, even though they attended the meetings as representatives of their national electrotechnical societies. The structure, rules, and norms of those domestic-level institutions might have ensured that the national delegates would represent a broad set of interests. Yet, the material costs of participation clearly created a bias in favor of commercially successful stakeholders from rich countries. From the start, economic resources, technical expertise, and institutions at the *domestic* level thus determined what interests would be represented at the international level.

In sum, in the early years the IEC focused on measurement and nomenclature, establishing electrical and magnetic units such as Hertz

---

[10] Many of the key figures, including Ichisuke Fujioka (Japan), Lord Kelvin (UK), Elihu Thomson (USA), and Eugen Wüster (Austria) had both scientific and commercial interests. Even the German Reichsanstalt owed its existence and success at least as much to Werner von Siemens as "first man of German industry" as to Hermann von Helmholtz as "first man of German science" (Cahan 1989). See also Murphy and Yates (2008, 11–17); Yates and Murphy (2008).

and Gauss, as well as developing a unified "International Electrotechnical Vocabulary" (now the thirteen-language *IEC Multilingual Dictionary*, first published in 1938). These were essential building blocks in the industrialization process, the formation of international markets, and the development or "social construction" (Herrigel 1996) of electrical engineering as a universal (global) scientific profession (Ruppert 1956, 4–5). IEC standardization in the early years thus had the characteristics of a public good, with the promise of substantial benefits for most participants, but effectively participation was limited to a small set of countries whose technical and socioeconomic elites shared a common understanding of modern science. Moreover, those who sought electrotechnical standardization had learned from the difficulties of establishing common basic measures of length and volume in the nineteenth century. That experience suggested that the adoption of a standard derived from "universal" scientific principles or from "nature" by a transnational body of experts generates less resistance than the adoption of another country's or ruler's standard (see also Trapp and Wallerus 2006, 28).[11] From the start, the IEC therefore adopted a strong norm that arguments over the specific provisions of a standard – or even the desirability of having an international standard at all – had to have a scientific rationale (that would be open to investigation) and be presented in terms of scientific or engineering optimization.

Expanding depth, scope, and membership: changes in IEC governance, 1906–2008

Over time, the IEC has in several ways broadened the sources of its authority. From the start, the IEC's authority was based on technical expertise. Soon, it also developed an institutional structure that channeled and amplified the expertise of the individuals who came together at the IEC, as a resource for global governance. As early as the 1910s, proposals for standardization work became so numerous and electrotechnologies so differentiated that the member bodies of

---

[11] For example, the meter, defined as 1/40,000,000 of the circumference of the earth at the equator, was far more palatable as a base metric for length than some king's or prince's foot, allowing the meter to persist after the defeat of Napoleon, whose regime had in many places imposed it.

the IEC agreed to assign the detailed technical work to more specialized advisory committees (today's Technical Committees, TCs) rather
than try to discuss every issue in plenary meetings. The number of
such committees grew to more than fifteen by the mid-1920s, which
led to the creation of the Committee on Action (predecessor of today's
Standardization Management Board, discussed below) to coordinate
the activities of the various committees. Early on, the institutional
structure of the IEC thus became one of hierarchy, though with strong
emphasis on bottom-up rather than top-down agenda setting and rulemaking (see sections on "Agenda setting" and "Rulemaking" below).
Delegating the technical work to more specialized committees was
accompanied by the institutionalization of what are today known as
the General Meetings, which bring representatives from all of the member bodies together in one place once a year. The practice of assigning
administrative responsibility for each TC to a "secretariat" hosted
by one of the member bodies was also started in the mid-1920s, not
least to control the costs of operating the IEC Central Office, initially
established in London when the IEC was founded (IEC 1906; Ruppert
1956, 3). In sum, technical work on generating electrical power – a
key technological issue then as now – was in the early years of the
IEC accompanied by institutional changes that generated power for
governance.

   This internal institutional development was accompanied by external institutional development. In the 1920s, the IEC started to develop
informal, as well as formal, links with other public and private organizations engaged in technical standardization, such as the International
Conference on Large Electric Systems of 1921 and the World Power
Conference of 1924 (Ruppert 1956, 5). It speaks to the IEC's savvy
as an organizational actor that it has outlasted almost all of the other
international and transnational organizations with which it cooperated in the interwar period, though very few documents from that
period have survived to assess the extent to which the IEC's persistence was a function of conscious, strategic actions. When the IEC
was revived after World War II, its officers moved swiftly to safeguard
its organizational independence while also establishing a close working relationship with the newly founded International Organization
for Standardization (ISO), which modeled its standard-setting process
on the IEC's (today governed by joint documents). IEC–ISO cooperation has been complemented by the establishment of consultative or

cooperative relationships with international organizations such as the International Telecommunications Union and, in more recent years, the World Health Organization and the World Trade Organization (WTO), with transnational nongovernmental organizations such as Consumers International and the International Amateur Radio Union, and with regional electrotechnical standard setters, in particular the European CENELEC, with which the IEC entered into the formal "Dresden" cooperation agreement in 1996 (Egan 2001). These institutional arrangements have bestowed upon the IEC additional institutional authority and the added legitimacy that comes from the explicit recognition of IEC standard-setting as exemplary.

Some of these arrangements have even given the IEC additional delegated authority, explicitly or implicitly. Most important in this respect has been the Agreement on Technical Barriers to Trade (TBT-Agreement), which came into force on January 1, 1995 as an integral part of the treaty establishing the WTO and is hence binding on all WTO member states. In this treaty, the member states committed themselves and their sub-units to use *international* standards as the technical basis for laws and regulations whenever international standards exist and can achieve the legitimate objectives of such laws and regulations, such as health, safety, or consumer protection (TBT-Agreement, Articles 2.2 and 2.4). Annex 3 of the Agreement contains a "Code of Good Practice for the Preparation, Adoption and Application of Standards," which is based on IEC and ISO principles and obliges standard-setting organizations at any level to notify the joint ISO/IEC Information Center of their acceptance of (or withdrawal from) the Code. "At least every six months," standard-setting organizations at the national/local and regional levels must also notify ISO/IEC of any standards they are currently developing. The Agreement merely defines "international" standards contextually as "issued by international standardizing bodies" (for example Art. 5.4, 12.6), where an "international body" is defined as "open to the relevant bodies of at least all Members" (Annex I.4), but the IEC and ISO are the only standards-developing organizations explicitly recognized in the text of the TBT-Agreement as sources of such standards.[12] WTO member states have thus delegated

---

[12] Documents from the negotiations also show a consensus that ITU standards would be considered international standards. Annex 1 of the Agreement defers to the ISO/IEC definitions of terms for "standardization and related activities."

significant regulatory authority to the IEC (see also Marceau and Trachtman 2002).[13]

Finally, over time, the IEC has acquired what Avant, Finnemore, and Sell (this volume) call "capability-" or "competence-based authority." The IEC standard-setting process (analyzed in section on "IEC standards as instruments of governance" below) is designed to ensure that any IEC standard meets the needs of a large majority of those who have a stake in the matter, including both producers and consumers (manufacturers and users) of the product in question. Although no systematic data exist on the level of use or implementation of IEC standards, it is clear that many IEC standards are widely used in hardware and software design, industrial processes, and product specifications for internal use and purchase orders – from basic terminology and measures to detailed specifications for high-tech products. This implies that IEC standards are considered "useful" by many stakeholders, including increasingly government regulators. As a long-time participant in IEC standardization put it when he explained why he had devoted countless hours of his employer's and his personal time to IEC standardization over the years: "They work." This is not to say that there are no conflicts over international standards – there certainly are, since there are often winners and losers from IEC standardization. Yet, negative votes on draft and final draft standards are very rare (see sections on "Agenda setting" and "Rulemaking" below), and even those who oppose a final draft standard sometimes privately admit that it offers a techn(olog)ical improvement. And internationally, as well as within countries, IEC standardization has for many decades worked *for those interested in international electrotechnological harmonization*. This has made IEC an easy focal point for those seeking further international standardization in old or new areas of electrotechnology.

Indeed, the IEC has successively broadened the scope of its global governance authority over the course of the century since it started with the standardization of basic terminology, symbols, and measurements (which remain important areas of its standardization work). In the

---

[13] Unlike the delegation of standard setting in the WTO's SPS-Agreement (Büthe 2008a), this legal recognition is nonexclusive, but it safeguards the IEC against the controversies encountered by some other (mostly USA-based) standards-developing-organizations (SDOs) that have sought to be considered international standard-setters under the terms of the TBT-Agreement.

1920s, the IEC added developing standards for consumer products to its portfolio, starting with the US-chaired technical committee (TC6) for "lamp sockets and caps" (Raeburn 2006b). Developing standards for consumer products grew into a major area for the IEC after World War II, with the widespread electrification of households throughout advanced industrialized countries and the mass market production of electrical devices for household use (Raeburn 2006a; Ruppert 1956, 6–7f). The IEC's committee structure further expanded as technology changed, with committees being added for computing and information-processing standards in the 1960s, laser equipment in the 1970s, fiber optics, superconductivity, and wind turbines in the 1980s, and fuel cell technology in the 1990s.

The third and final dimension of institutional change is the expansion of IEC membership. From nine official member bodies in 1908 (the year of the IEC's first meeting after it was constituted), the IEC grew to twenty-seven national member bodies (including bodies from four non-European developing countries: India, Egypt, China, and South Africa) by 1939, when it was put on hold for the duration of World War II. Membership grew slowly during the Cold War but has increased rapidly thereafter (see Table 11.2). The current fifty-four full member bodies (one per country) pay annual dues, which depend upon each country's size and level of economic development, measured by its GDP and level of electricity consumption. Associate membership provides for more limited participation (in up to four TCs) in exchange for reduced membership fees. It is intended for small or developing countries with a stake in only a limited number of electrotechnologies.

If associate members are included, members from developing countries now outnumber members from advanced industrialized countries, though the latter still send the overwhelming majority of the technical experts who carry out the technical work (see final columns of Table 11.2). As in the case of international tribunals (Danner and Voeten, this volume), the individuals who collectively govern the IEC come disproportionately from "powerful states." In contrast to the case of ICTY/ICTR, however, participants in IEC standardization from advanced industrialized countries are generally not selected by their governments, and power is here defined by level of economic development and electrotechnical expertise, as well as complementarities of domestic institutions with the IEC, as discussed in greater detail below.

Table 11.2 IEC membership (full and associate members), 1906–2008

Full members	(year joined)	Participant memberships	Observer memberships
Algeria	(1913)	0	0
Argentina	(1913)	4	11
Australia	(1927)	84	71
Austria	(1910)	109	49
Belarus		1	25
Belgium	(1909)	97	70
Brazil	(1952)	25	50
Bulgaria	(1958)	4	142
Canada	(1908)	93	24
China	(1936)	169	1
Croatia		7	58
Czech Republic	(1908)	84	81
Denmark	(1908)	119	48
Egypt	(1930)	35	9
Finland	(1949)	124	45
France	(1907)	154	17
Germany	(1907)	170	1
Greece	(1930)	11	94
Hungary	(1949)	49	90
India	(1929)	67	86
Indonesia	(1954)	17	49
Iran	(1966)	1	33
Ireland	(1974)	22	86
Israel	(1951)	25	56
Italy	(1907)	163	8
Japan	(1910)	169	2

Year columns: 1946–50, 1951–5, 1956–60, 1961–5, 1966–70, 1971–5, 1976–80, 1981–5, 1986–90, 1991, 1992, 1993, 1994, 1995, 1996, 1997, 1998, 1999, 2000, 2001, 2002, 2003, 2004, 2005, 2006, 2007, 2008

(cont.)

Table 11.2 (*cont.*)

Country	Entry year(s)	Participant memberships	Observer memberships
Korea (South)	(1964)	135	33
Libya		0	0
Luxembourg		4	2
Malaysia	(1990)	16	77
Mexico	(1980)	46	57
Netherlands	(1911)	119	35
New Zealand	(1912) (1979)	28	86
Norway	(1959)	81	76
Pakistan	(1912)	0	0
Philippines	(1923) ? (suspended)	0	0
Poland	(1923)	72	96
Portugal	(1929)	71	50
Qatar		0	0
Romania	(1927)	105	55
Russia	(1911)	143	15
Saudi Arabia		12	1
Serbia	(1936)	49	102
Singapore	(1990)	7	88
Slovakia	(1993)	13	84
Slovenia	(1992)	21	68
South Africa	(1939)	67	50
Spain	(1907)	130	39
Sweden	(1907)	144	24
Switzerland	(1911)	119	19

Year columns (across top): 1946–50, 1951–5, 1956–60, 1961–5, 1966–70, 1971–5, 1976–80, 1981–5, 1986–90, 1991, 1992, 1993, 1994, 1995, 1996, 1997, 1998, 1999, 2000, 2001, 2002, 2003, 2004, 2005, 2006, 2007, 2008

Country	First year	Technical committees (col 1)	Technical committees (col 2)
Thailand	(1956)	29	47
Turkey		27	53
Ukraine		27	129
UK	(1906)	166	4
USA	(1907)	153	0
Associate members			
Bosnia		0	0
Colombia		4	0
Cuba	(1969)	4	0
Cyprus		1	0
Estonia		1	0
Iceland		1	0
Kazakhstan	(Affiliate)	2	0
Kenya		4	0
Korea (North)	(1963)	3	0
Latvia		0	0
Lithuania		0	2
Malta		4	0
Nigeria	(Affiliate)	4	0
Sri Lanka		3	1
FYR Macedonia	(Affiliate)	0	0
Tunisia	(1985)	0	0
Vietnam		0	0

Notes: Bosnia stands for Bosnia Herzegovina; Cuba was a full member from 1969 to 1980; membership by the Czech and Slovak member bodies was preceded by Czechoslovakian membership from 1921 to 1939 and from 1956 through 1992; FYR Macedonia stands for Former Yugoslav Republic of Macedonia; Russia/USSR/Russia treated as one continuous membership; Serbia continues the membership of Yugoslavia (2003–6 as Serbia and Montenegro); Thailand was a full member for one year in 1955. Years in parentheses indicate first year of membership where left edge of bar may be ambiguous. Final two columns indicate number of technical committees in which the country's member body holds memberships as of August 15, 2008.

Moreover, in 2001, the IEC turned its policy of encouraging developing countries to join the organization through informal "pre-associated" status into an official "Affiliate Program," in which more than eighty countries now participate. Affiliate membership allows nonvoting participation in exchange for having to pay no membership fees at all (unlike earlier "pre-associated" status), while still being allowed to use two hundred IEC standards as national standards.[14] The program has been vastly successful in increasing the number of countries that have a formal institutional link with the IEC (it grew from thirty-five affiliates in November 2001 to eighty-two affiliates in August 2008).[15] Three current associate members started their relationship with the IEC as affiliates.

In sum, expertise-based authority continues to be essential for the IEC, but IEC authority has deepened over the years as internal and external institutional changes have additionally provided the IEC with institutions-based and delegated authority. And success – in the interest of those seeking international technological harmonization, often for commercial reasons – has allowed the IEC to develop a reputation for competence, further boosting its authority. In addition to broadening the sources of its authority, the IEC has massively broadened the scope of its activities and greatly expanded its membership.

Explaining institutional change in IEC governance

What explains this institutional evolution of the IEC over the past century? Each of the four structural changes identified by Avant,

---

[14] Adopting an IEC standard as a national standard allows national member bodies to raise funds through the sale of those standards.

[15] As of August 15, 2008, there are IEC affiliates in Afghanistan, Albania, Angola, Antigua and Barbuda, Armenia, Bangladesh, Barbados, Belize, Benin, Bhutan, Bolivia, Botswana, Brunei Darussalam, Burkina Faso, Burundi, Cambodia, Cameroon, Central African Republic, Chad, Comoros, Congo, Congo (Democratic Republic of), Costa Rica, Côte d'Ivoire, Dominica, Dominican Republic, Ecuador, El Salvador, Eritrea, Ethiopia, Fiji, Gabon, Gambia, Georgia, Ghana, Grenada, Guatemala, Guinea, Guinea Bissau, Guyana, Haiti, Honduras, Jamaica, Jordan, Kyrgyzstan, Lao, Lebanon, Lesotho, Madagascar, Malawi, Mali, Mauritania, Mauritius, Moldova, Mongolia, Mozambique, Myanmar, Namibia, Nepal, Niger, Panama, Papua New Guinea, Paraguay, Peru, Rwanda, Saint Lucia, Saint Vincent and the Grenadines, Senegal, Seychelles, Sierra Leone, Sudan, Swaziland, Tanzania, Togo, Trinidad and Tobago, Turkmenistan, Uganda, Uruguay, Venezuela, Yemen, Zambia, Zimbabwe. For details, see www.iec.ch/affiliates/acp_about-e.htm.

Finnemore, and Sell in the introduction played a role in this process. Globalization raised the importance of cross-national differences in product standards as nontariff barriers to trade and thus increased the demand for international standards. Since the use of IEC standards was not mandatory as such, the science and engineering experts at the IEC were "nonthreatening" (McNamara, this volume) to governments and their domestic stakeholders, which made delegation of international harmonization of technical standards to the IEC an attractive solution. Delegation of standard-setting to the IEC also merely extended to the international level the domestic practice of government endorsement of standards developed by private sector bodies, consistent with a general trend toward privatization of regulation and the broader shift toward neoliberal economic ideas (Braithwaite and Drahos 2000; Brunsson and Jacobsson 2000, 10ff.). The end of the Cold War increased the number of countries in the world and their international orientation, which contributed to the growth in IEC membership, and the invention of "new technologies" has driven much of the increasing scope of IEC governance.

Together, these structural changes offer a baseline, functional explanation for the broadening of the IEC's sources of authority, changes in the IEC's institutional structure, broadening of the range of issues over which the IEC exercises a global governance role, and the growth in IEC membership. Structural changes, however, were at most a necessary condition. As Avant, Finnemore, and Sell (this volume) note, the demand for governance is rarely universal (some would have preferred the IEC not to develop standards for a given product), and does not automatically lead to the provision of governance. Why did those who sought international or transnational governance win out over those who opposed it?

The institutional structure of the IEC provides a large part of the explanation. Transnational or global technical standardization is in the interest of those who are competitive producers and would benefit from increased market size. These producers are therefore likely to push for the IEC to expand its issue space to include the technical issues that impede their global market access by requesting that their national IEC committee propose the development of standards or the establishment of new technical committees or subcommittees to cover those issues. Under these conditions, those who have the technical expertise to develop a particular standard (that is, make the rules and in that sense supply governance) should be willing to do so as long as the difference between the standard that they expect to be developed with their participation and the standard (or nonstandard) that they expect to be developed without their participation exceeds the costs of supplying governance. The institutional structure of the IEC and international standard-setting thus favors the expansion of the scope of IEC governance by empowering those who (for usually entirely self-interested reasons) seek such an expansion (see also Büthe 2008b). The IEC itself (treated here analytically as an actor in its own right), acting to advance its own self-interest (for example, Fligstein 2009; Michels 1966), should be a ready accomplice to increasing its supply of governance and, more specifically, to the broadening (and deepening) of its authority sketched above, as long as such changes do not risk undermining it (though there is no guarantee against "pathological" expansion; see Barnett and Finnemore 1999). The IEC has also actively sought to broaden its membership in recent years, thus giving a large number of developing countries a stake in the continued centrality of the IEC, making it less likely that competing institutions will challenge the preeminence of the IEC in this realm of global governance.

The power of norms of power: the IEC as a nongovernmental organization

Despite seeking governmental recognition, the IEC was founded as and remains a nongovernmental organization. In order to have no "bureaucratic influence imported into the Commission" (IEC 1906, 10), national technical societies, rather than governments, were to constitute each country's "local [IEC] committee" and appoint representatives to the IEC.[16] These national bodies constitute the IEC's member bodies to this day (see IEC 2007c).[17]

Why did the founders put such emphasis on the IEC being a nongovernmental organization? Institutional mimicry may have played

---

[16] Governments were to be asked to appoint a local committee only in countries "having no Electrotechnical Institution," and if technical societies were subsequently founded in those countries, they could appoint a new local committee (IEC 1906, 18, 20).

[17] Member bodies may be public agencies, hybrid public–private entities, or private bodies with public financial support and regulatory oversight.

some role, as the nongovernmental British Institution of Electrical Engineers served as the explicit inspiration for the IEC. But the commitment to the nongovernmental character of the IEC had broad support from many countries' delegates because it served quite diverse interests. For electrical engineers from Britain and the United States, self-regulation was among the hallmarks of the traditional liberal professions (law and medicine) which they sought to emulate (Abbott 1988; Brint 1994, 5; Gispen 1990). In continental Europe, with its different political traditions and lack of the liberal Anglo-Saxon notion of the "profession" (Jarausch 1990), the explicit recognition of autonomy and self-government in professional and industry associations (even if sometimes more apparent than real) compensated for the lack of democracy in political life (Blackbourn and Evans 1991; Sciulli 2005).[18]

The sometimes adamantly nongovernmental character of the IEC has had three important consequences to this day. First, to underscore the nongovernmental cooperative character of the organization, the founding delegates agreed that "every country joining the Commission [should be placed] on an absolutely equal footing" (IEC 1906, 10, 34), with one vote per country whenever decisions were to be taken by vote. This system ensures that countries do not have influence in the IEC merely because they are large or possess economic or military power resources.

Second, the nongovernmental character of the IEC has restricted the fungibility of power resources. Economically or militarily powerful states have often been able to use seemingly unrelated power resources to influence outcomes in international governmental organizations, such as ITU and WTO – allowing their economic interests sometimes to dominate the preferences of smaller/weaker states (through issue linkage and other means; see, for example, Davis 2004; Krasner 1991; Steinberg 2002). In IEC standardization, attempts at direct governmental interference are considered illegitimate and rarely even tried: in the International Standards Project's survey about international product standards among manufacturing firms in five industries, barely 6 percent of those who most frequently use IEC standards said they

---

[18] See, however, Philip Nord's historical analysis of France for an account of rapid change in political culture (1995); see also Di Palma (1990).

"sometimes" or "often" ask for help from the government (see also Mattli and Büthe 2003, 38–9).[19]

Here, norms really have power: consensus procedures in the standard-setting process stipulate that all arguments for or against specific provisions of a standard or even its desirability have to be considered and, if possible, accommodated. Interviews with participants suggest that this really occurs, except when those who object violate the norms by failing to provide a scientific or engineering rationale that can be investigated (or to present a national consensus position when they make demands for changes to a standard's provisions; see below, and Murphy and Yates 2008, 30). To be sure, technical and scientific reasoning can be used instrumentally, to achieve standardization outcomes that yield commercial advantages or shift adjustment costs to others. The core procedural norm of IEC standardization – that a technical rationale must be presented for all objections – provides no safeguard against such political use of science and engineering. Yet, if the norms are overtly violated, the technical committee may dismiss such objections for lack of a "technical basis."[20] This limits governments' ability to intervene in the process.

Finally, the nongovernmental nature of the IEC has caused the organization to operate "under the radar" of scholars of the international political economy who take a statist analytical approach to questions of global governance (for example, Drezner 2007a). Its important role

---

[19] Includes US respondents who reported requesting help from their members of Congress. Note that it is not possible to distinguish definitively between a direct operation of normative constraints and a strategic allocation of scarce resource, given a perception that government intervention is likely to be ineffective: only 3 percent of the respondents for whom IEC standards are the most important international standards thought that support from the government had "often" helped them in their attempts to influence international standards, though a further 31 percent acknowledged that government is "sometimes" helpful. Consistent with a view that governments are not expected to play a role, only 32 percent blamed the lack of government support in any way for their failures in those instances when they try but fail to influence the content of the standard, and almost all of these respondents were the same ones who credited government support for (a small part of) their success in cases when they succeeded.

[20] None of this is to say that all countries are equal in IEC standardization. Countries with greater scientific and engineering expertise and an ability and willingness to devote more resources to the IEC standardization process clearly are in a better position to influence IEC standards than poor, developing countries, *ceteris paribus*; see, for example, Büthe and Witte (2004).

in global governance has therefore been overlooked. I submit that it is worth taking note of the IEC.

IEC standards as instruments of governance

Standards are explicit norms, often written in highly technical language (Büthe and Mattli 2010a). An IEC standard specifies the characteristics that a phenomenon or device must exhibit in order to be classified as being of a particular type. For instance, IEC 61000, used as an illustration in the introduction to this chapter, specifies electromagnetic (non)interference thresholds that a TV or vacuum cleaner must meet or exceed to be considered "electromagnetically compatible" by IEC standards.

Standards as such are "merely" prescriptive; they are not binding rules. They become instruments of governance only if those whose behavior they target have legal, material, normative, or other incentives to adopt, implement, or comply with the standards. To understand the role of IEC standards in global governance and properly answer the question of who governs, we must consider five stages in what I call the governance sequence (see also Avant, Finnemore, and Sell, this volume; Abbott and Snidal 2009): first, agenda setting, focused on the decision whether an international (IEC) standard for a particular product or process should be developed; second, rulemaking, that is, the process of developing specific IEC standards; third, the adoption or implementation of the IEC standard by manufacturers and other potential users; fourth, the monitoring of compliance with the IEC standard; and fifth, enforcement in cases where compliance is mandatory.[21] For each of these activities, I seek to identify the key groups with a stake in IEC governance, their motivations and resources, and why they do or do not play a role as "governors."

---

[21] I do not here consider adjudication, which takes place, with respect to IEC standards, at three levels. The IEC's Standards Management Board (SMB) (described below) adjudicates between competing claims of authority between different technical committees. Second, the IEC has set up various arrangements with other international organizations with which a conflict of responsibility might arise (ISO, ITU, etc.). Third, national and supranational judicial institutions, such as the WTO Dispute Settlement Mechanism, deal with conflicts of interest over the (ab)use of IEC vs differing domestic standards (e.g. as nontariff barriers to trade).

Agenda setting in the IEC

A proposal to develop a standard for a product or technical issue for which no IEC standard currently exists can only originate from an IEC national member body or from within the organization.[22] Each national IEC member body may make proposals for "new work" to the IEC upon the request of its domestic constituents (scientists, firms, government regulators, consumer advocates, etc.). How any given member body decides whether or not to make the proposal depends on the decisionmaking procedures of each national committee, that is, on domestic standard-setting institutions.

Proposals for new work usually specify the technical committee or subcommittee (SC) that should develop the new standard.[23] Only the "participating" or "P-members" of that committee – that is, the representatives of the national member bodies which regularly participate in the technical work of that committee – vote on the proposal. Acceptance of the new work item requires a positive vote from at least a simple majority of the P-members of the specified TC or SC *and* a commitment from a minimum number of P-members to participate actively in the development of the standard from the preparatory stage through the drafting and revising of the draft standards.[24]

To assess the effect of these requirements and gain a sense of the breadth of support for (and opposition to) new IEC standards among the IEC member bodies, I obtained from the IEC the complete record of votes submitted by P-members from August 1999 through

---

[22] Proposals for new work can be made by any IEC technical committee (TC) or subcommittee (SC), or the secretariat of the TC or SC that is supposed to develop the new standard. The IEC chief executive officer, the IEC Standards Management Board (see below), and its advisory groups also can propose new work. Finally, the IEC recognizes a number of transnational professional and industry associations, many of which are also standard-setters, as well as intergovernmental organizations as "liaison" organizations for certain technical committees (see IEC 2008c) and thereby grants them the right to make proposals for new work in those committees.

[23] Proposal without *ex ante* TC specification are assigned to a TC or SC by the Standards Management Board, which can decide to set up a new committee to deal with the new item.

[24] This minimum number is four for committees with sixteen or fewer P-members and five for committees with seventeen or more P-members; individual TCs/SCs may raise this minimum threshold (IEC 2005 and interviews with Jack Sheldon, Oct. 2007 and Jan. 2008).

Table 11.3 *Votes on proposals to launch development of a new IEC standard*

Vote	# of votes	% of total votes cast
Yes	5,887	78.4
No	410	5.46
Abstain	1,216	16.2
Total	7,513	

Notes: Raw data from IEC. Data management and analysis in Stata 10.1. Data cover all votes submitted by P-members in 453 committee-level ballots covering all proposals for new work items (NP documents) from August 1999 to September 2002.

September 2002.[25] During those thirty-eight months, 453 proposals for new standards came to a vote. Of 8,963 possible votes, 7,513 were cast by P-members of the committees considering the proposals.[26] As Table 11.3 indicates, fewer than 5.5 percent of the total votes cast at that stage were negative. What about the distribution of those negative votes? More than 59 percent of the 453 proposals received no negative votes at all; less than 3 percent received more than four negative votes. Only two proposals (one in 1999 and the other in 2001, constituting just 0.4 percent of all proposals) failed because there were more negative votes than positive ones.

The decision whether to revise an existing standard follows a different procedure. Unlike in the ISO, where all standards come up for review at regular five-year intervals (see Prakash and Potoski, this volume), the "maintenance procedure" in the IEC is specific to each standard. When a TC or SC approves a standard for publication (see below), it also decides when the next review of that standard should occur. The date set at that time must be at least two and no more than

[25] The starting date of the analysis was dictated by the beginning of electronic balloting for new work item proposals; the end (September 2002) was the presumably arbitrary end of an IEC internal study, for which the data were systematically compiled. I am grateful to the IEC for making the data available to me.

[26] Since committee membership varies, the number of member bodies eligible to vote on any one proposal ranged from nine to thirty-six for the proposals for new work analyzed here.

twenty years into the future. As that date approaches, the P-members of the TC or SC with responsibility for the standard examine all proposals for changes submitted since the last revision. They then decide whether to develop a revised standard (subject to the "rulemaking" procedure discussed below), confirm the standard without changes for some period (newly specified at that time), or possibly even withdraw the standard. The IEC thus guarantees that a standard, once adopted, will remain unchanged for at least the time specified in the maintenance procedure, thus assuring users that they will not have to face further switching costs for the specified number of years.

More limited, issue-specific agenda-setting power is exercised by those who hold particular positions within the institutional structure of the technical committees and subcommittees. Each committee has a "secretariat" as well as a chairman; by custom, these positions are held by individuals from different countries.[27] The secretariat provides the administrative support for (and between) the meetings; the chair conducts the meetings. The resources for this work are provided by the national member bodies and do not count toward their contributions to the IEC budget. Together, chair and secretary have significant control over schedule and substantive priorities (within the rules of procedure of the IEC) and, in that sense, possess agenda-setting power.

Finally, an important body for the agenda-setting stage of IEC governance is a special committee of the organization, the Standardization Management Board (SMB). Six of the fifteen seats on the SMB are reserved for the six member bodies that make the largest contributions to the IEC budget and provide the staff support for the largest number of technical committee secretariats. The remaining nine seats are filled

---

[27] Here lies one of the (few) differences between ISO and IEC: in ISO, the national member body as an institution provides the personnel and administrative support for secretariats. In the IEC, TC or SC secretaries are typically themselves standards users, mostly from industry. (The chairmen are in both cases from among the users.) During the early stages of the standardization process (described in more detail in the next section), national member bodies therefore do not to the same extent play the role of intermediary between domestic stakeholders and international-level standard-setters in the IEC as in the ISO. This might explain why in ISO it has traditionally taken seven years to develop a standard initially (Brunsson 2000, 35), though ISO has sought to shorten greatly this time in recent years. In the IEC, developing a new standard has typically taken about three years, according to the IEC's own estimate from recent years.

for three-year terms through elections in the assembly of the member-body presidents, the "Council" (IEC 2005, Art. 10).[28] The SMB wields considerable power, coordinating and overseeing the work of 174 IEC TCs and SCs with their 505 working groups and 1,399 ongoing standards projects (IEC 2009).[29] Most importantly, the SMB reviews regular reports from the TCs about their standardization work and the success of their SCs and working groups in meeting target dates for progress on their work items. If there is a persistent lack of progress on a work item, the SMB is empowered to terminate work on that item. Under these conditions, the SMB has negative agenda-setting power.

In addition, the SMB can reorganize technical work by merging TCs (or creating new ones) if it determines that the structure of the technical work no longer reflects the structure of the marketplace. For instance, the old TCs 12 (radio communications), 60 (recording equipment), and 84 (audio, video, and audiovisual engineering) were in 1995 combined into a new TC100 for "Audio, video and multimedia systems and equipment," because technological developments had rendered the distinctions between the three original TCs less and less meaningful and interoperability between different audio, video, and communications devices was becoming a key issue for consumer electronics. The SMB thus pursues the IEC's organizational self-interest in retaining its relevance to industry (and arguably other stakeholders). It also appoints TC secretariats and chairmanships, adjudicates

---

[28] For the six appointed seats, budget contributions and committee secretariats are each calculated as a percentage of the total and the percentages are added together. In case of a tie, committee secretariats are given greater weight (IEC 2005, Appendix 1). IEC budget contributions are today based on GDP and electrical power consumption, subject to the stipulation that no single country may pay more than 9 percent of the dues portion of the IEC's budget. The member bodies from the United States, Japan, Germany, the United Kingdom, and France therefore jointly account for almost 40 percent of the dues budget (21.5 percent of the total budget); for full member bodies from small countries, a contribution equivalent to 0.9 percent of the IEC dues budget is the minimum (personal communication with Jack Sheldon, January 2008). By contrast, all seventeen associate members (who have full voting rights where they participate) jointly account for 3.6 percent of the IEC dues budget, less than 2 percent of the total budget (IEC 2007d). For the nine elected seats, the Rules of Procedure stipulate that member bodies aim for a "balanced geographical distribution" among qualified candidates. An IEC vice president (an honorary position) and two IEC senior staff members also sit on the SMB *ex officio* (non-voting).

[29] Number of projects underway on December 31, 2008.

jurisdictional conflicts between the TCs, and is responsible for relations with other organizations (IEC 2005).

In sum, at the agenda-setting stage, the key actors are the national member bodies of the IEC (particularly those active in the TCs), with special powers reserved for the six largest contributors to the IEC's work and the nine elected members of the SMB. Within the national IEC member bodies, the primary actors tend to be firms, especially manufacturers of electrical and electronic products and energy/power suppliers, followed by electrical/electronics engineers. But since agenda setting is conducted via the IEC member bodies, the *domestic institutions* – which differ in their legal status, organizational structure, and voting rules (Büthe and Witte 2004; Mattli and Büthe 2003; Tate 2001) – play a key role in this realm of global governance.

Rulemaking: *the development of an IEC standard*

The actual technical work of standard-setting is carried out in the IEC's technical committees (TCs) and subcommittees (SCs) and their "working groups" and "project teams." These committees and groups are staffed by often highly specialized technical experts, mostly from industry, but sometimes also from government regulatory agencies, academia, or research laboratories. The IEC also encourages the participation of labor union representatives and consumer groups, though they constitute only a very small portion of the approximately 10,000 technical experts directly involved in IEC standard-setting worldwide.[30] The participating experts (or their public or private sector employers) volunteer their time, and the resulting technical documents become the common property of the IEC. As far as the rule-making function of global governance is concerned, it is these technical experts who collectively govern.

Individual technical experts, however, cannot claim this power on their own. Participation in a technical committee is limited to those nominated by their respective national IEC member bodies (each of which may nominate several individuals to a given committee, albeit

---

[30] Many member bodies additionally create "shadow" or "mirror committees" at the domestic level to coordinate input from stakeholders in their respective countries. No systematic data exist about the number of participants without commercial interests in IEC standards.

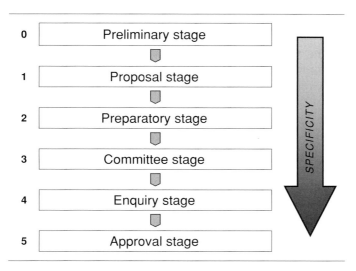

Figure 11.1 Stages of the IEC standardization process

with only one vote collectively). Accordingly, the experts on any TC are to represent the interests of their country's stakeholders as a whole, as established (if so) through the national institutions (Mattli and Büthe 2003). Every full member body has the right to nominate participants with voting rights to every committee (which makes the member body a "P-member" of that committee); associate members can become P-members of up to four technical committees only, though they may send technical experts without committee-level voting rights to any number of additional committees.[31]

Importantly, standard-setting takes place in six stages, as illustrated in Figure 11.1 (see also Büthe and Witte 2004, 37ff.). During the "preliminary" stage, often informal discussions within and among member bodies explore the level of interest in developing a new standard at the international level. If one or more stakeholders consider it desirable

[31] As specified in paragraph 1.7.4 of the ISO/IEC Directives, which specify the rules and procedures for the technical work in both organizations, a P-member can be downgraded to observer (O-member) status if s/he fails to participate for two consecutive meetings of the TC or SC, where participation is defined as a substantive (technical) contribution in person or by correspondence. Having the resources to make such regular contributions is thus effectively a prerequisite for retaining a voice at all stages of the standardization process.

to develop an international standard, then the submission of a formal proposal to develop a standard starts the standardization process in the "proposal" stage (see above for the procedure for launching the process for revisions of existing standards). If that proposal is successful, a first working draft of the new standard is developed during the next, "preparatory" stage. This draft takes into account comments and specific submissions from the national member bodies represented on the TC or SC charged with developing the standard, but it is usually drawn up by the leader of a "project team" within that committee. The work then moves to the committee level, where a full-fledged draft standard is developed with participation from all P-members of the TC or SC during the fourth, "committee" stage (the standard often goes through several drafts during this stage, with increasing specificity). During the "enquiry" stage, a bilingual "Committee Draft for Voting" (CDV) is then circulated among all of the national member bodies (regardless of committee representation) for comment and an initial vote.[32] If the CDV passes this vote, the TC or SC may proceed by revising the standard one last time to take into account technical comments that may have been submitted along with or in lieu of a vote. The resulting revised standard then undergoes a two-month "approval" stage, during which it is circulated among all national member bodies as a Final Draft International Standard (FDIS) for an up or down vote (member bodies have the right to abstain). If approved, the standard is then published by the central office within two months.

Since the specificity of the standard increases as it moves through the six-stage process, early involvement in the process is essential to exercising influence. This makes national member bodies that are involved at the TC level – *and are able to formulate a coherent position on behalf of their domestic constituencies in a timely fashion* – the key actors during the rulemaking process (Büthe and Mattli 2010a; Mattli and Büthe 2003).[33] That said, the enquiry stage procedures and the final approval stage vote ensure that stakeholders from a broader

---

[32] In the otherwise identical ISO process, Committee Drafts for Voting are called "Draft International Standards."

[33] The number of respondents that answered all questions of the survey specifically with regard to IEC standardization is too small to conduct multivariate statistical analyses separately, but given the nearly identical standardization processes of ISO and IEC, the findings from Mattli and Büthe (2003) should be fully applicable to IEC standardization.

spectrum of countries will also have an opportunity to make their voices heard: in both stages that involve formal voting, every member body has one vote, effectively retaining the one-country-one-vote system created in 1906. At both stages, moving forward requires that two-thirds of the submitted, nonabstention votes *from the P-members of the committee that developed the standard* are votes in favor of the draft *and* that no more than 25 percent of all vote-casting member bodies vote against it (ISO/IEC 2004).[34]

It is rare but not unheard-of that a CDV fails to gather the required affirmative support from two-thirds of the voting P-members of the responsible committee. In the 1,578 CDV ballots taken in the IEC from January 1999 to September 2002, the CDV failed to reach that threshold in 34 cases (2.15 percent). Final Draft International Standards fared better: only in 5 of the 1,509 ballots taken (0.33 percent) did an FDIS fail to garner the required support. Since my data only cover the votes submitted by P-members of the committee responsible for a given standard, they do not allow me to assess how commonly CDVs or FDISs fail because more than 25 percent of the submitted, non-abstention votes are negative. Voting records from the P-members suggest that this might be the higher hurdle, though by no means prohibitive.[35]

---

[34] Interviewees with many years' experience in IEC standardization confirmed that these formal institutional rules indeed describe IEC practice.

[35] More than 45 percent of CDVs pass the ballot without a single negative vote, and a further 25 percent with only one negative vote, though 153 of the 1,578 CDV ballots (9.7 percent) saw more than three negative votes; 86 CDV ballots (5.4 percent) saw more than 25 percent of voting P-members oppose the CDV. By all indications, IEC TCs seek even greater consensus between the CDV ballot and the presentation of the FDISs: of the 1,509 FDISs that came up for a ballot between January 1999 and September 2002, more than 65 percent passed without a single negative vote from P-members; almost 93 percent with fewer than 3 negative votes, though 27 cases (just under 1.8 percent) had more than 25 percent of P-members vote against adoption of the technical specification as an IEC standard. The national member bodies that most frequently object at the CDV stage are those from Germany (15.6 percent), the United States (14.5 percent), France (13.7 percent), and the United Kingdom (11.6 percent); all other countries voted "No" on fewer than 10 percent of the CDVs under consideration in committees in which they were P-members between January 1999 and September 2002 (except for Luxembourg, which cast one negative vote in three votes total, and Indonesia, which cast four negative votes in eight total votes cast). At the FDIS voting stage, only Croatia and Germany have cast negative votes in more than 10 percent of the FDIS ballots (11.5 and 10.2 percent, respectively).

Moreover, note that here, again, the norm that pursuing one's self-interest is only legitimate as a technical or engineering improvement has procedural bite in that "negative votes not accompanied by technical reasons" are "excluded when the votes are counted" (ISO/IEC 2004, 2.6.3 and 2.7.3).

At either stage, if the draft or final draft does not gather the required level of support, it is referred back to the TC, which may either drop the standardization project or restart the process from stage 2 or 3. Consensus procedures require (at stages 2 through 4) that all criticisms, objections, or suggestions for improvement of a standard be taken up for substantive discussion and accommodated if possible, though only if underpinned by specific technical arguments. This procedure ensures that any intense conflicts of political-economic interest are blunted, if only in appearance, because they are carried out in terms of scientific/engineering optimization and highly technical language (Mattli and Büthe 2003).

Adoption – implementation – compliance

A standard as such is merely an explicit norm. Setting standards by no means guarantees that the targets of the norm will behave accordingly, especially since the actors who are supposed to "comply" by adopting or implementing the standard may have played no role during the two prior stages except in ideal cases of self-regulation.

Reasons for compliance vary for technical standards, just as for other norms. Electrical engineers use the standard international nomenclature and units of measurement, developed by the IEC in its early decades – Ampere, Volt, Hertz, Ohm, etc. – in part simply because they are practical: the internal logic and the relationship between the basic units used in IEC definitions, along with the reliance on the decimal system, allow simple calculations of various properties of electric phenomena and electronic devices (see Figure 11.2). But even more important are the positive network externalities obtainable from using these standards: since they are familiar and have an agreed-upon definition around the globe, using them facilitates scientific communication and ensures that product specifications, such as information about energy use and interoperability, will be easily understood by suppliers and customers. Compliance with IEC standards thus often stimulates commerce.

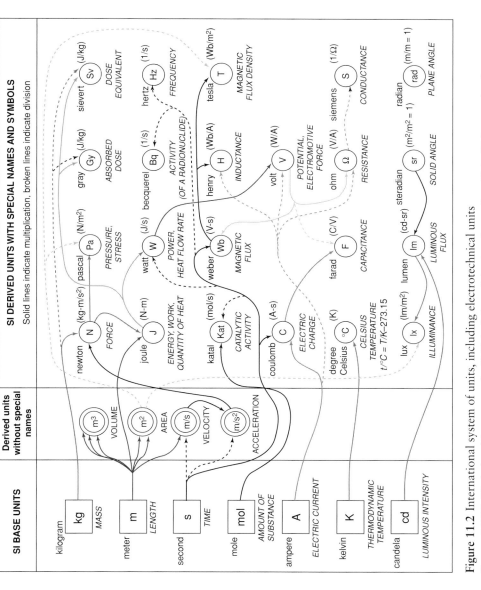

Figure 11.2 International system of units, including electrotechnical units

Source: NIST, "Relationships among the SI Units", http://physics.nist.gov/cuu/Units/SIdiagram.html

The flipside is that standards with strong network effects are hard to dislodge, even by technically superior – more rational or more efficient – ones (David 1985; Katz and Shapiro 1985). For the same reason, if prior standards differ and, therefore, implementation of a single common standard entails substantial switching costs, actual convergence of nomenclatures or technologies may fail – as illustrated by decades of resistance to the introduction of metric units for distance, volume, and weight in the United States.

Similarly, positive network externalities and the technical quality of standardized solutions to a practical problem create incentives for firms to implement IEC standards in their production processes; switching costs create disincentives. But for commercial actors, additional competitive and political considerations come into play (de Vries 2007). Consumers – individual end-users or, more likely, managers or procurement officers buying intermediate industrial goods as inputs – may directly demand implementation from producers. In addition, marketing opportunities, particularly if a standard is widely perceived to constitute a technical advance, may create economic incentives for implementation.[36] These decisions whether to implement a given standard are faced by firms in the pertinent industry *regardless of whether they had any involvement at the agenda-setting or standard-setting stage*.

The key actors at the implementation stage, however, need not be economic actors such as firms, each acting independently. Local or national governments may instead be the key actors at this stage if they decide to incorporate IEC standards directly into laws or regulations, or if they reference IEC standards in such legal documents.[37] In fact,

---

[36] If it is instead the case that deviating from a standard provides an opportunity for product differentiation, producers may consciously decide not to implement the standard. Note that IEC standards generally reflect what is technologically feasible to meet actual or imagined consumer demand in advanced industrialized countries. As a consequence, an electric appliance with metal exterior parts may have double-insulation, auto-shut-off to guard against overheating, and numerous other safety features – which make producing it so expensive as to price it out of the market of many developing countries (see, e.g., Maskus *et al.* 2005). Producing for these markets may then require using divergent, less stringent standards.

[37] The IEC now has a publication and a page on its website to guide government agencies in referencing IEC standards, so as to make such referencing compatible with continuous updating of the standard as technology evolves.

Table 11.4 *Importance of specified reasons for the use of product standards within respondent's firm*

Specified reason	Cumulative percentage "important" or "very important"
Compliance with demand by private sector customers	85
Compliance with demand by public sector customers (government procurement)	65
Compliance with government regulations (not related to sales to the government)	85
Specification of inputs (products you buy)	56
Specification of output (products you sell)	85
Measurement and improvement of internal processes	71

Note: N = 34; firms from Germany, Spain, Sweden, UK, and USA for which IEC standards are the most frequently used international standards.
Source: International Product Standards Survey, principal investigators: Tim Büthe and Walter Mattli.

compliance with government regulation featured prominently among the reasons for the use of standards by firms that ranked IEC standards as the most important nondomestic standards (see Table 11.4). At the same time, it may be firms that ask governments to require everyone to comply, so as to level the playing field (Vogel 1995; cf. Woll 2008).

A final motivation for adoption/implementation by firms is anticipation of the risks of noncompliance in the event of civil litigation, most importantly product liability lawsuits. Since IEC standards often define "best practices," implementing them may provide one of the few available safeguards against being in a weak legal position. Firms may therefore try to make sure that their products comply with applicable IEC standards, even if they do not advertise that fact or seek certification.

Monitoring

As the IEC became increasingly involved in setting standards for industrial and consumer products in the post-World War II period, the question of how to safeguard the value of the IEC trademark became more prominent. As the IEC website puts it: "How can the industrial user and the final consumer be sure that the product they buy conforms to the criteria of an IEC standard?" (IEC 2007b). Conformity assessment has been the IEC's answer. IEC conformity assessment operates largely like a certification scheme (Cashore *et al*. 2004; Meidinger *et al*. 2003; Prakash and Potoski, this volume): producers submit their products to a conformity assessment body, which uses a series of IEC-standard-specific but otherwise general procedures to test it. If the product conforms to the specifications of the particular standard, the conformity assessment body certifies this finding and grants the producer a license to use its name in conjunction with statements about the product's compliance with the applicable IEC standards.

National member bodies of the IEC can conduct conformity assessments themselves, but in many countries the tasks of testing, certifying, etc., are delegated to independent labs and agencies, such as Underwriter Laboratories (UL) in the United States. In either case, the IEC does not accredit the conformity assessors, but instead oversees a system of "peer assessment" among the conformity assessment bodies to verify their competence and veracity within each of three distinct IEC conformity assessment systems or "schemes."[38]

In monitoring adoption, implementation, and compliance, the key actors are thus the conformity assessment bodies (CABs), both individually and collectively (due to the peer review process). In addition, anyone can become a monitoring agent by testing products for

---

[38] The three systems are: IECEE, the conformity assessment scheme for electrotechnical equipment and components; IECQ, the quality assessment system for electronic components; and IECEx, the scheme for certification of compliance with Standards Relating to Equipment for Use in Explosive Atmospheres. Conformity assessment is only available for a limited number of IEC standards, since the IEC considers such an assessment unimportant for many of its standards, given the multitude of incentives for implementation/ compliance of product standards, discussed above. When conformity assessment is available, each national member body decides *for each standard* whether or not to participate in the IEC-sponsored conformity assessment scheme. This decision is completely independent of that body's decision as to whether to participate in the standard-setting work for the standard. A decision to participate in IEC conformity assessment for a given standard, however, entails a commitment to mutual recognition of conformity assessments for this standard in any of the countries that participate in IEC conformity assessment for that standard.

compliance and publicizing the results. That said, unlike the ISO 14000-series standards, where highly motivated NGOs can play an important monitoring role (see Prakash and Potoski, this volume), atomistic third-party monitoring outside the CAB framework appears to play virtually no role in monitoring compliance with IEC standards. Nonetheless, the possibility of such monitoring illustrates the relative openness of the governance process at this stage.

Finally, when governments write IEC standards into laws and regulations (or incorporate them by reference) and thus make compliance mandatory, they may empower public regulatory agencies to monitor (and possibly enforce) compliance. Strictly speaking, such government agencies monitor compliance with public laws or regulations, but whenever IEC standards constitute the technical basis for these measures, governments effectively become actors in the IEC-based governance of electric or electronic technology at the monitoring and enforcement stage – even though they may have played no direct role at the rulemaking or implementation stage.

Enforcement

Firms making capital investments and firms or consumers making purchasing decisions can provide "enforcement" if they demand compliance of a product with certain standards and refrain from purchasing it (or demand a lower price) if the product fails to comply. Such enforcement works in part through the market mechanism, relying on a mix of Hirschmanian exit and voice (Hirschman 1970), and is likely to have its greatest effect because its anticipation motivates firms to comply with the standard.[39] Notice that the key actors here are again actors – mostly firms other than those whose products and actions are directly targeted by the standards – who have played no significant role at prior stages of the governance sequence.

The other key actors for enforcement are governments and state bureaucracies. States that use IEC standards in, for instance, consumer and workplace safety regulations tend to put in place various enforcement mechanisms. Regulatory agencies are often empowered

---

[39] *Ex post* punishment by these actors for noncompliance should be rarely observable, making it difficult to assess the magnitude of the effect.

to levy fines for noncompliance; private actors may be empowered to bring suits against noncompliant firms, thus involving the judiciary in enforcement, too. A comprehensive analysis of the full range of ways to bring public authority to bear to enforce compliance with laws and regulations that (may) make norm-consistent behavior mandatory is beyond the scope of this chapter but not necessary to make the main point for purposes of the current analysis: governmental actors that had little role during previous stages, especially during agenda setting and rulemaking, may play a key role at the enforcement stage. By contrast, the IEC and its national member bodies play hardly any significant role at this late stage.

Conclusion

As a corollary of the rationalization and ever-greater division of labor that are the hallmarks of Weberian modernity, we take for granted the functioning of infrastructures and technologies that most of us do not understand. We want sewer systems to carry our wastewater without emitting unpleasant odors or feeding back into the fresh water supply; we think we should be able to plug electrical devices into an outlet and have them "just work" without having to worry about them being damaged or burning down the house; we are delighted if x-ray machines can wirelessly transmit the image of our bone structure on to the physician's computer screen if that speeds up our visit to the hospital or improves the quality of care. In short, we desire and expect all kinds of technology to be safe and durable; we expect it to deliver reliably a certain level of performance – without any need for us to worry about how this result is achieved. Technical standards allow this to occur.

Since technical standards, by and large, fulfill these objectives, there is a strong temptation to think that technical standards are just about science. But science is not monolithic, and because science is a social process (Weber 1991 [1919]), it is far from certain that a unique technically optimal solution will be reached, even when it exists. Moreover, there are often multiple technically "optimal" solutions, increasing the importance of the nontechnical elements of the standardization process. And because standards are instruments of governance, setting these rules and norms is bound to be a political process, too; and it is far from certain that any technical maximum/optimum constitutes a sociopolitical equilibrium. Consequently, understanding global governance – in electrotechnology as much as elsewhere – requires political analysis of the *actors* in the process: the global *governors*.

This chapter has sought to contribute to our understanding of global governance through an actor-centric analysis of the global governance of electrotechnology. I started with an analysis of the institutional evolution of the International Electrotechnical Commission (IEC), an international nongovernmental organization headquartered in Geneva, with members and affiliates in 153 countries. It develops today the vast majority of international electrotechnical standards for industrial and consumer products alike and, in that sense, is an important governor in the international political economy. The second section of this chapter traced and sought to explain the evolution of the IEC from 1906 through 2008 on four dimensions: (1) growth and diversification of membership; (2) scope of activities; (3) increasing breadth of the sources of the IEC's authority; and (4) IEC insistence on its nongovernmental character. I have sought to show that an analysis of the economic and political interests of the individuals and firms involved in the IEC, as well as the IEC's organizational self-interest, needs to complement the analysis of broader structural changes, such as technological change and the privatization of regulation, in order to explain institutional persistence and change in this realm.

The third section then turned more directly to Dahl's deceptively simple question – "Who governs?" – in an analysis of the actors at each of the five stages of the governance sequence: agenda setting, rulemaking, implementation, monitoring, and enforcement. The cast of actors is diverse and changes across the five stages. Outcomes arise from the interactions between these actors and are therefore unlikely to be simply a manifestation of the preferences of any one actor. So far, these interactions between the different governors of electro-technology have mostly reinforced the central role of the IEC. That said, it is possible that the heightened importance of IEC standards will reduce the efficiency of the standardization process and thus undermine the IEC's authority insofar as it is based on a reputation for competence (Simcoe 2006). It is equally possible that the resulting politicization will undermine the IEC's expertise-based authority, though my findings suggest that this is not generally happening in the IEC so far. Only the close relationship with CENELEC, the regional standards "governor" for Europe, may reduce its legitimacy in other parts of the world, but this is considered necessary to bolster the IEC's centrality and support within Europe.[40]

Finally, taking the actors and domestic institutional structures into account when we try to understand outcomes in the international political economy allows us to understand the evolution of governance of electrical and electronic technology (for example, why the scope of IEC governance has so greatly increased over the past century), as well as the limitations of global standards (why having global standards does not guarantee global uniformity of behavior), given the changing cast of actors and relevant institutional mechanisms during the post-rulemaking stages of the governance process.

[40] Not-for-attribution interviews.

12 | *"Education for all" and the global governors*

KAREN MUNDY

Introduction

International efforts to support a universal right to education have been a ubiquitous part of international society over the past five decades. Today it would be difficult to find any meeting of world leaders in which the universal right to education is not trumpeted as an international goal. Yet despite the engagement of a variety of global governors in "education for all" (EFA) efforts, a wide gulf has historically divided global EFA aspirations and achievements.

This chapter looks at the history of global governors and their "education for all" initiatives, focusing in particular on the changing relational dynamics among EFA governors. Over the past six decades, EFA has become a prime venue for displaying commitments to equity, economic redistribution, and human rights – attracting an expanding cast of governors precisely because it can enhance their legitimacy and authority. Yet ironically, the growth in the number of EFA governors has led to competition and fragmentation in international EFA activities. EFA's global governors have deployed competing technical repertoires, been guided by strikingly different bureaucratic and geopolitical interests, and have drawn on different sources for their authority. The result has been a system-wide form of "organized hypocrisy," in which global governors repeatedly set wide-ranging international targets and goals, for which neither global governors nor developing country states are held responsible (Barnett and Finnemore 2004). Only recently, with the establishment of a new consensus about global development among OECD governments, the emergence of new constraints on the World Bank as EFA's lead governor, and the growth of transnational advocacy groups, has EFA moved from being a widely accepted but unimplemented international norm, to one that is more efficaciously governed. The congruence of reputational and legitimacy concerns among multilateral actors and rich country governments, along with the rising capacity of advocacy networks to invoke global accountability in EFA commitments, seems to have produced a significant expansion of concrete global governance efforts around "education for all."

The EFA case raises several important issues for scholars of global governance. The first concerns expectations about historical efficiency in the evolution and enactment of international norms. The EFA case illustrates how both intra-organizational pathologies and relational dynamics among governors create historically inefficient and meandering normative cycles within the international community. Clearly, this is not a straightforward case of norm advocacy, adoption, cascade, and institutionalization (Finnemore and Sikkink 1998; Keck and Sikkink 1998). Nonetheless, the history of EFA and its global governors suggests that the balance between symbolic and concrete action (and between normative aspirations and their achievement) can shift dramatically, especially when changing relational dynamics invite greater accountability across governors.

The origins of "education for all"

The idea of a universal right to education, and of an international mechanism for its achievement, can be traced to the first half of the twentieth century, when numerous transatlantic organizations advocated for the formation of an intergovernmental educational organization, and the United Nations Educational, Scientific and Cultural Organization was established. Two enduring dynamics among EFA's global governors can be traced to this period. The first is the tension between states' ambivalence about the construction of a global authority in education, and their continued attraction to international educational cooperation. This tension would result in large gaps between rhetoric and funding for EFA. The second is the deep vein of civil society advocacy for the construction of a global authority in education.

In the period between the late nineteenth century and World War I, teachers associations, suffragette groups, and other transatlantic professional organizations lobbied governments for an intergovernmental educational association to ensure equality of access, and pacifist curricula – each working, in the words of the USA based World Federation of Education Associations, to represent "comprehensively the forces working for universal free public education" (World Federation of Education Associations 1923). Later, suffragette organizations, the

British Workers' Educational Association, international peace networks, and international federations of teachers lobbied the founders of the League of Nations to include an educational organ (Fuchs 2007, 398). League officials and state parties dismissed such proposals, however, adopting the view that "national education lies outside and will always lie outside the competence of any official committee of the League" (Davies 1943, 12). Nonetheless many League states later joined the privately established International Bureau of Education (IBE), keen to participate in the setting of international policies and norms for education during its International Conference on Public Education (UNESCO 1997, 58). By 1935, the International Bureau of Education had transformed itself from a private organization into an intergovernmental organization with two dozen state members.

Even before the conclusion of World War II, allied states had begun to discuss the formation of an educational body within the United Nations system. However, during the 1945 San Francisco conference concerns about national sovereignty again caused widespread hesitation about the inclusion of an educational mandate for the UN. These concerns were only overcome by the advocacy efforts of American nongovernmental actors (many drawn from American institutions of higher education) (Jones 1988). Ultimately, a compromise framing of the UN's mandate in education was agreed to, limiting the role of the UN in education to promoting "international cultural and educational cooperation," rather than full-scale international "solutions" (as in the case of health) (United Nations 1945, Chapter IX, Article 55).

The United Nations Educational, Scientific and Cultural Organization was established shortly after the UN conference. Here too, the process was characterized by a significant degree of ambivalence among education's potential global governors. Dominant states and nongovernmental actors held competing views about the scale and purposes of international educational cooperation. The United States, for example, wanted an international agency focused on postwar reconstruction and the expansion of Anglo-American scientific supremacy; the French sought a more elite organization focused on cooperation among leading intellectuals and scientists (Jones 1988). The Soviets and several Latin American states hoped for an organization focused on the expansion of mass schooling, and mass literacy, a focus generally supported by nonstate actors, who saw the universal provision of schooling as a universalizing force that could break down the forms

of nationalism that contributed to the war. The final UNESCO constitution commits state parties to support *"full and equal opportunities
for education for all"* (UNESCO 1945; emphasis added). However, to
realize this broad mandate the organization was given a budget never
larger than that of a medium-sized university, and views among states
about educational priorities for the organization became ever more
highly politicized.

If UNESCO's constitution marked the first formal recognition of the
need for international cooperation in the achievement of education for
all, the need for such cooperation was later reinforced by the inclusion
of a universal right to free elementary education within the Universal Declaration of Human Rights (1948). Here, too, the recruitment
of state signatories to the broader declaration required considerable
nonstate advocacy: state reticence based on concerns about territorial sovereignty later impeded its full adoption. Curiously, however,
Article 26 regarding education caused relatively little debate among
the Declaration's drafters or in the General Assembly. This was especially surprising in light of the contradictory or seemingly arbitrary
way educational rights are defined:

(1) Everyone has the right to education. Education shall be free, at least
    in the elementary and fundamental stages. Elementary education
    shall be compulsory. Technical and professional education shall
    be made generally available and higher education shall be equally
    accessible to all on the basis of merit.
(2) Education shall be directed to the full development of the human
    personality and to the strengthening of respect for human rights
    and fundamental freedoms. It shall promote understanding, toler-
    ance and friendship among all nations, racial or religious groups,
    and shall further the activities of the United Nations for the main-
    tenance of peace.
(3) Parents have a prior right to choose the kind of education that shall
    be given to their children. (United Nations 1948)

As with UNESCO's constitution, Article 26 can be understood as
reflecting an ideational convergence among governments about the
appropriate level and form of public intervention in education. Such
ideational convergence was drawn from the experience of Allied states,
both Western and Soviet, which had rapidly expanded mass systems
of public schooling in the first half of the twentieth century. Global

declarations on EFA in the UNESCO constitution and the Declaration of Human Rights in turn played a chartering role for developing countries, further institutionalizing the notion that free education at the elementary level should be supported by the global community (Cox 1968). Yet despite this normative convergence, tensions over the construction of a global educational authority among states remained deep seated, reflected not only in the inadequate funding and steady politicization of UNESCO itself, but in the decision, described below, to channel the bulk of international educational funding through bilateral development agencies.

Implementing education for all: global governors after WWII

How, then, was the rhetorical embrace of a universal educational entitlement by UN member states during the 1940s translated into a program of international EFA action? As I describe below, the process was neither linear nor straightforward, and it led to a highly diffuse and uneven history of implementation. The global governor with the clearest formal mandate in education, UNESCO, was quickly overtaken by the competing efforts of other emergent global governors (or governor-clusters). These governors included newly created national agencies for international development (such as USAID, CIDA, etc.), the World Bank, and UNICEF.

Between 1945 and the late 1960s, UNESCO scrambled to develop a program of work in education (Jones 1988). The most immediate demands on UNESCO and the UN in the field of education came from the newly independent governments of former colonies, for which UNESCO's budget was far from adequate. Added to UNESCO's fiscal limitations were political challenges derived from its one-nation-one-vote governance structure (Sewell 1975; Preston *et al.* 1989). In the 1950s, '60s, and '70s, UNESCO's education activities increasingly became a focal point for geopolitical contests, both between the Soviets and the United States,[1] and later on, between Western powers

---

[1] The United States and the Soviet Union repeatedly conflicted over UNESCO's work in the field of basic education, most severely around efforts in the field of adult literacy, where the United States blocked a Soviet proposal for a world literacy campaign modeled on the Soviet experience, and instead guided UNESCO to sponsor an "experimental" project in functional literacy (Jones 1988).

and nonaligned countries seeking a "new international economic (and information) order" (Mundy 1999). While UNESCO's education program concentrated on universal standard setting and convening large regional conferences on educational development, the politicization of its activities created mounting frustration among member states, leading them to channel funding for education to other governors (Jones 1988; Imber 1989; Sack 1986).

UNESCO's activities were thus quickly overshadowed by the emergence of a new set of EFA governors, ready to channel rich country resources directly to meet developing countries' growing educational demands. By the mid-1960s, virtually every industrialized country supported educational development through a rapidly expanding bilateral development assistance program (OECD/DAC 1974). In the early 1970s, 8–10 percent of total Official Development Assistance (ODA) was being earmarked for educational purposes. More than three-fourths of all official international loans and grants for education in the developing world have continued to flow through these bilateral channels. Surprisingly little of this bilateral aid, however, was to focus on the costs of basic levels of schooling. More than half went for provision of "technical assistance" from donor countries, while much of what remained was allocated to higher-level education infrastructure projects like the construction of colleges and technical institutions. Bilateral donors eagerly sought to tie their educational aid to their own institutions, goods, and services; and they overtly used educational aid to enhance geopolitical allegiances. Recipient countries found themselves with dozens of uncoordinated, short-term bilateral education projects, few of which contributed directly to the expansion of universal, free, and publicly provided primary education, where costs stemmed mainly from teachers' salaries.

In addition to new bilateral flows of aid for education, the late 1960s and early 1970s saw multilateral organizations with no formal mandate in education develop substantial education sector portfolios. The World Bank entered the EFA arena in the early 1960s, just after the creation of its concessional loan facility, the International Development Association (IDA). Joining together with the economists at the Organization for Economic Cooperation and Development (OECD), the Bank's staff initially organized its educational lending around support for manpower planning and training. But by the 1970s both organizations had developed the empirical tools (drawn from the field of economics) that would allow them to frame their work in education as an economic investment in "human capital" (Resnick 2006). The Bank flirted briefly with a basic-needs approach to education in the 1970s, at least partly responding to legitimacy concerns generated by heightened Third World radicalism (Mundy 1998; Jones 1992). But this brief surge of interest in basic education was quickly displaced by structural adjustment policies in the late 1970s. Because structural adjustment lending targeted the reduction of public sector costs, public education systems emerged as a natural target for World Bank reform efforts in the public sector, feeding the expansion of the Bank's technical capacity and authority in this sector (Carnoy 1995). By the mid-1980s, the Bank had become the single largest global governor in the field of education, with a technical staff and budget far larger than that of UNESCO and a unique technical competency drawn almost entirely from the discipline of economics.

Despite its emergence as the most powerful global governor in the field of education, the Bank remained far from endorsing universal free education as a principle for international action. From the mid-1980s, research from within the Bank on investment in education at the elementary level set off what might appear, in the context of the Bank's broader structural adjustment and liberalization policies, a surprising shift of Bank lending toward elementary-level education projects (Mundy 2002; Heyneman 2003). However, the Bank looked at primary education primarily through an investment lens, arguing for incremental growth in enrollments; the reform of educational systems; the development of strategies such as cost-recovery (school fees); the recruitment of paraprofessional teachers; and private service delivery (Colclough 1996; Alexander 2002; Jones and Coleman 2005; Samoff 1996; Nelson 1999; World Bank 1995). The Bank's emerging EFA agenda had considerable impact on OECD donor organizations, many of which began to shift their limited aid for basic education away from a unique focus on public, state-delivered educational services.

UNICEF also emerged as a significant global governor in education in the 1970s and 1980s, developing a reputation for being both entrepreneurial and innovative. In the late 1960s and early 1970s, for example, facing Third World calls for a new international economic order, UNICEF made a bid for increased funding from OECD governments by focusing a part of its work on basic educational needs, grassroots community development, and non-formal education (Phillips 1987). In the late 1970s and 1980s, it attracted large amounts of funding from OECD governments for its work on the education of girls and the provision of alternative forms of schooling (Black 1996). For most of the period, UNICEF's EFA efforts mirrored its broader strategy of promulgating targeted technologies, such as oral rehydration and immunization, to produce rapid improvements in child survival and life chances. Much like the EU experience described by McNamara in this volume, UNICEF's efforts proved to be highly generative, influencing a much wider reframing of global EFA efforts around "quick" fixes and the targeted needs of specific populations.

Only much later, after 1989 and a protracted advocacy campaign by nongovernmental actors, did UNICEF adopt a rights-based focus for its educational work, speaking out directly against the impact of Bank- and IMF-led structural adjustment reforms of basic social programs for children. As we shall explore below, UNICEF then became the institutional home of a burgeoning transnational children's rights movement, and a strong advocate for the right to education (Fuchs 2007). However, UNICEF's entrepreneurial organizational culture and its reliance on voluntary funding from OECD countries and individual donors has continued to limit its willingness to pool its resources with other UN and bilateral partners.

Throughout the period between 1970 and 2000, interorganizational competition and fragmentation characterized the activities of EFA's global governors. Multiple global and regional summits on education (see Table 12.1), backstopped by an expanding expert community on education, failed to produce a focused and coordinated EFA effort: their result was rather a permissive menu of models and theories about educational development (King 1991; Chabbott 2003; Birdsall and Vaishnave 2005; Clemens 2004). This situation held true even in the late 1980s and early 1990s, when UNICEF, UNESCO, and the World Bank came together for the first time in an effort to stimulate renewed funding for basic education from Western donor countries. At their jointly organized World Conference on Education for All, held in Jomtien, Thailand, in 1990, the Bank and UN bodies called upon both Western governments and the NGO community to renew their commitment to funding basic education. Much of the conference

Table 12.1 *International EFA declarations and commitments,*
1934–2005

Goal year	Date	Forum
–	1934	International Conference on Public Education, Geneva
–	1946	Formation of the United Nations Educational, Scientific and Cultural Organization (UNESCO)
–	1948	UN Universal Declaration on Human Rights, New York
–	1951	International Conference on Public Education, Geneva
–	1952–4	UNESCO Regional Conferences on Free and Compulsory Education; Bombay, Cairo, and Lima
EFA by 1980	1960	UNESCO Meeting of Representatives of Asian Member States on Primary and Compulsory Education, Karachi ("Karachi Plan")
EFA by 1980	1961	UNESCO Conference of African States on the Development of Education in Africa, Addis Ababa ("Addis Ababa Plan")
EFA by 1980	1962	UNESCO Conference of Ministers of Education and Ministers Responsible for Economic Planning, Santiago ("Santiago Plan")
EFA by 1980	1966	UNESCO Conference of Ministers of Education and Ministers Responsible for Economic Planning in the Arab States, Tripoli
EFA by 1980	1970	International Development Strategy for the Second UN Development Decade, New York
EFA by 2000	1979	UNESCO Conference of Ministers of Education and Ministers Responsible for Economic Planning of Member States in Latin America and the Caribbean, Mexico City
EFA by 2000	1980	International Development Strategy for the Third UN Development Decade, New York
–	1989	Covenant on the Rights of the Child (including the right to education)
EFA by 2000	1990	World Conference on Education for All, Jomtien ("Jomtien Declaration")

(cont.)

Table 12.1 (*cont.*)

Goal year	Date	Forum
EFA by 2000	1993	Education for All Summit of Nine High-Population Countries, Delhi ("Delhi Declaration")
–	1995	World Summit for Social Development ("universal and equitable access to education" is one of ten commitments)
EFA by 2015	1996	Shaping the 21st Century, OECD Development Assistance Committee (makes universal primary education top priority)
–	1999	IMF/World Bank Poverty Reduction Initiative launched (establishes expected norms for the proportion of educational expenditure in national budgets)
EFA by 2015	2000	World Education Forum, Dakar ("Dakar Declaration on EFA")
–	2000 and 2002	G-8 Ministerial Meetings (promise to fund all viable national EFA plans through the World Bank's Fast Track Initiative)
EFA by 2015	2000	Millennium Summit, New York ("Millennium Declaration")
EFA by 2015	2001	Road Map towards the Implementation of the United Nations Millennium Declaration
Funding to end fees	2005	G-8 Ministerial Meetings: commits adequate funding for universal abolition of primary school fees

Source: Adapted from Clemens (2004) and Mundy (2006).

was spent debating the cause of the reversals or stagnation in rates of access to schooling in the poorest developing countries, with particularly acrimonious criticisms targeting Bank-supported structural adjustment programs.

In the decade that followed the Jomtien conference, bilateral aid – the largest source of EFA finance – actually fell, and competition among multilateral EFA governors increased. Tensions between the market-led liberalization programs advocated by the Bank and the "human development" models promoted by the UN continued to underscore the competing principles upon which each governor staked its authority in the field of education (Jolly 1991; Therien and Lloyd 2000; Therien 2002). Leading states in the EFA arena were faced with their own domestic adjustments to economic globalization and found little incentive or opportunity for the expansion of a common approach to global poverty and the related question of "education for all." OECD nations simply sat out this round of EFA initiatives, ignoring the entrepreneurial efforts of the multilaterals.

Because no concrete plan for a coordinated, global-level intervention followed the World Conference on Education for All, many have regarded it as the peak of organized hypocrisy in the global governance of education – a moment in the history of EFA that crystallized the disjuncture between collective promises of global coordination and the failure to realize concrete mechanisms for coordinated and well-funded EFA initiatives (Torres 2000; Chabbott 2003).

This section has highlighted relational dynamics among EFA's global governors as a key source of this dysfunctionality. Fragmentation grew from the decision by OECD governments to channel the bulk of their educational development funding through bilateral channels, which have been historically biased towards higher education projects and initiatives that satisfy domestic geopolitical and economic interests. Competition emerged around the different ideological frames and technical competencies of the three big IO governors, and from their resource dependency on member governments. One final trend during this period is important to note. As expertise and bureaucratic forms of authority grew among international organizations, the voice of nongovernmental actors – the traditional advocates of a coordinated international authority for EFA – were increasingly marginalized in the community of EFA governors (Mundy and Murphy 2001).

Education for all on the rebound

Ten years after the Jomtien meeting in 1990, international declarations on education for all emerged in a wide range of intergovernmental and international venues (see Table 12.1). Such commitments culminated in the adoption of universal primary education as one of the Millennium Development Goals (MDGs) and the development of the Dakar Framework for Action on Education for All at the World Education

Forum in 2000 (World Education Forum 2000). Viewed on their own, these commitments might seem like little more than an extension of the EFA promise-making that has characterized international society for the past half-century. As I argue below, however, this time promises came with concrete plans for coordinated action, new financial commitments, renewed participation by nonstate actors, and new mechanisms of accountability. Both in terms of resource commitments and in the development of structures for coordinating and delivering educational aid, a very different environment emerged for EFA. Explanations for this shift can be found in the mounting legitimacy pressures on IOs and Western governments over the 1990s, the successful bridging of the ideological divide between UN and Bretton Woods institutions, and in the resurgence of nonstate global governors focused on accountability and results.

Education re-embedded in a new development compact

After more than a decade of declining aid and the promulgation of neoliberal policy reforms, the late 1990s saw OECD governments and their multilateral institutions begin to develop a consensus about international poverty and inequality that has been described by several authors as a global "Third Way," bridging the divide between the neoliberal and social welfare orientations of the UN and the Bretton Woods organizations (Therien 2002 and 2005; Ruggie 2003; Noel 2005). Ruggie describes this new global compact as encompassing

> the centrality of governance, the rule of law, education, and health to economic success; the positive role of investment, including skills and technologies embodied in foreign direct investment; the need for further debt relief and other forms of development assistance for poor countries; the urgency of lowering trade barriers imposed on developing country exports by agricultural subsidies and other non-tariff barriers in the rich countries; the protectionist potential posed by pursuing social and environmental objectives through linkages to trade agreements; and the need for governments and international institutions alike to forge partnerships with the private sector and a wide range of civil society actors. (Ruggie 2003, 305)

The emergence of this consensus can be traced back to the OECD Development Assistance Committee's endorsement of *Shaping the*

21st Century (OECD/DAC 1996), in which OECD governments promised to increase bilateral aid, harmonize their activities, and focus on a handful of top development priorities, including universal education. In 2000, the IMF, OECD, World Bank, and UN also promised closer coordination, more attention to country ownership of development, and tighter focus on specific development priorities (again including education) in a document entitled *A Better World for All* (IMF *et al.* 2000). Both agreements fed into the Millennium Development Summit and Millennium Development Declaration, which aligned the United Nations and its agencies, the Bretton Woods institutions, and OECD governments behind a unifying framework (United Nations General Assembly 2000; OECD/DAC 2003 and 2005).

Several authors have characterized this new "consensus" as part of a broader rapprochement between the neoliberal approaches to globalization and development, which were endorsed by the IMF and the World Bank in the 1980s and 1990s, and the more equity- and redistribution-focused, globalization-skeptical approaches adopted by the United Nations and the more expansive social welfare states of the OECD. One of the drivers of this rapprochement has clearly been a need, both within Bretton Woods organizations and among G-8 governments, to respond to rising international protests against globalization and the aftermath of the East Asian economic crisis of the late 1990s (Stiglitz 2003). Many also credit the rising importance of the European Union, with its more expansive approach to welfare state capitalism, as playing an important part in the emergence of this consensus (Noel 2005; Held 2005).

Education, and particularly primary education, has played a central part in this new international consensus. Its centrality is reflected not only in the priority given to achieving a basic right to education within the Millennium Development Goals, but also in the nearly revolutionary attention that the World Bank and the IMF now pay to the achievement of what they have come openly to describe as a fundamental obligation to ensuring primary education as a right or entitlement (Aoki *et al.* 2002; Bruns *et al.* 2003).

Clearly, the attention given to primary education in the most recent period derives from the bridging role it plays between liberal and more social-democratic political ideologies. In the policies of the Bretton Woods organizations, of Anglo-American states within the OECD, and increasingly of UN organizations, education is explicitly described as straddling both equity- and productivity-conceptualizations of development, as in the following quote from the World Bank (2002, v):

The expansion of educational opportunity, which can simultaneously promote income equality and growth, is a win-win strategy that in most societies is far easier to implement than the redistribution of other assets, such as land or capital. In short, education is one of the most powerful instruments known for reducing poverty and inequality and for laying the basis for sustained economic growth, sound governance and effective institutions.

Simon Maxwell sums up the important bridging role played by education in the new consensus somewhat more critically: "A crude characterization of the current approach is to encourage internal and external trade liberalization, and simultaneously invest in health, education and good governance, so that people are able to take advantage of new economic opportunities" (Maxwell 2005, 3). In summary, because the idea of education for all marks a comfortable middle ground between liberals' faith in equality of opportunity, and the more redistributive emphases apparent in theories of social democracy, it became a natural focal point for the enactment of this new development compact.

New resource flows and commitments

In the period since 2000, both the volume of official development assistance and the proportion of ODA targeted for primary education have increased substantially. The emergence of a common set of development priorities, as embodied in the MDGs, set the stage for the first increases in official development aid from OECD countries in more than a decade, beginning with announcements to that effect by the European Union and the United States at the March 2002 Financing for Development conference in Monterrey, Mexico. The OECD Development Assistance Committee projects upward of a 50 percent increase in total ODA over the period between 2000 and 2008, with roughly three-fourths of this increase coming from the accelerated promises of members of the European Union to meet the 0.7 percent ODA/GDP international target for aid levels. Furthermore, the concentration of

ODA on least-developed countries has continued to rise (Gupta *et al.* 2006).[2]

These substantial increases have been matched by several interesting proposals for raising immediately available funding for development, such as the UK's proposal for an International Financing Facility and France's proposal for a new international tax (Atkinson 2005).[3] A large number of OECD governments (including the six largest ODA donors) have also made clear pledges to increase funding for universal primary education. Among the most noteworthy has been the 2006 announcement by British Chancellor of the Exchequer Gordon Brown that the United Kingdom will provide $15 billion for basic education over ten years – double the current volume of British aid to basic education. The Netherlands has acted on its pledge to devote more than 20 percent of its ODA to education and recently made a $201 million pledge to UNICEF in support of basic education programs for children in conflict and disaster areas, the largest single donation ever received by the organization. Meanwhile, the European Union has emerged as the second largest multilateral provider of aid for basic education (after the World Bank). Aid to all levels of education has now reached the levels it enjoyed in the 1980s and early 1990s, increasing 85 percent in constant-dollar terms between 2000 and 2004 (UNESCO 2006b, 87). Flows to basic education have also grown very rapidly and now account for more than 30 percent of all bilateral aid to education – up from less than 5 percent in the early 1990s (UNESCO 2006b, 88). Overall, the largest movers on the EFA front are EU countries that endorse a more expansive and redistributive approach to both domestic and global public policy.

Nonetheless, UNESCO estimates that even with existing commitments we are less than 50 percent of the way toward closing the financing gap for EFA. There are still wide variations in the commitments made by individual bilateral donors. Three-quarters of aid to

---

[2] However, it is important to note that at least some of the official increase in ODA is the result of debt forgiveness rather than direct increases in bilateral aid budgets; in addition, a substantial share of recent ODA has gone to Afghanistan and Iraq (Gupta *et al.* 2006; UNESCO 2006a, 108).

[3] The IFF would take donor commitments and a down payment and use these to back international bonds that could generate an immediate expansion of funds for development.

basic education comes from six countries (France, Germany, Japan, the Netherlands, the United Kingdom, and the United States).

Restructuring the education for development regime

Since 2000, it has become increasingly common to hear OECD government leaders, business organizations, advocacy groups, and prominent political or intellectual figures call for a new, global-level "Education for All Compact" (Sperling 2001a and 2001b; Birdsall and Vaishnave 2005; Pritchett 2004; Clinton 2007; World Economic Forum 2005). For example, the UN Millennium Project (2005) urges governments to develop a new global compact for EFA, in which donors "commit new funds [$7 billion per year] in a new way through a strong coordinated global effort that rewards and reinforces countries' measurable progress." At Dakar, each of the four main global governors in education – the World Bank, UNICEF, UNESCO, and the bilateral donors (coordinated through the OECD's Development Assistance Committee) – has endorsed the creation of a long-term, steady, and reliable source of funding for the recurrent costs of schooling in the poorest countries of the world. Each has also committed itself to major improvements in terms of donor coordination, concentration of aid on the poorest countries, the untying of aid to education, and direct funding for recurrent costs of education.

Today, both bilateral and multilateral development organizations increasingly work in a coordinated fashion with recipient governments to produce carefully crafted education sector plans that focus on the achievement of universal access to education. Implementation of these plans is typically monitored through a joint external review process – a far cry from the isolated, project-by-project evaluations of a decade ago. In addition, many bilateral organizations and advocacy groups now support the World Bank-led "Fast Track Initiative," a pooled fund that helps support governments in the development of national EFA plans and management of pooled or coordinated forms of assistance (World Bank 2004a, 2004b, and 2004c; UNESCO 2005 and 2006a). They also fund an annual Global EFA Monitoring Report, an enterprise hosted by UNESCO in which bilateral and multilateral activities are carefully scrutinized and compared (UNESCO 2004, 2005, 2006a, and 2006b). These new coordinating mechanisms imply an increasing willingness on the part of OECD nations to forgo the traditional sovereignty-based bilateral model of foreign aid in favor of global-level collective action. They also mark a sharp change in the behavior of multilateral organizations, in the direction of greater coordination and harmonization of their activities.

Experimentation with pooled funding, direct budgetary support, and funding of recurrent costs of primary-level education also suggests that universal primary education is being recognized by many OECD governments as a global public good in need of collective rather than unilateral action. What is sometimes not recognized is how frequently education has emerged as the key sector in which donors experiment with historically novel efforts at donor coordination, harmonization, and pooling of resources (OECD/DAC 2003 and 2005; Riddell 2000; Samoff 2001 and 2004; Dyer 2005; UNESCO 2005 and 2006a). Where national education plans are endorsed, much (though far from all) aid is now given directly to the education ministry or as general budget support.[4] Donor organizations using budget or sectoral support as their main modalities explicitly recognize that much of the additional funding for the achievement of basic education will require the international community to assume some of the recurrent costs of the primary education systems of least developed nations for an extended period of time. In some countries (for example, Zambia and Tanzania), significant portions of the national recurrent costs of education are now funded by international donors – an impossibility a mere decade ago.

However, commitment to these new forms of coordination is not complete: Japan and the United States, for example, refuse to pool funds and still prefer project-by-project grants; UNICEF and the World Bank remain reluctant to pool their funds in joint programs of educational support. Many critics also question the "tough political reforms" advocated in calls for a new global compact on education. For example, the Millennium Project and the Fast Track Initiative advocate reductions in the unit costs of primary education, greater involvement of private sector service deliverers, introduction of standardized testing regimes, and the decentralizing of educational systems (UN Millennium Project 2004 and 2005; World Bank 2004a, 2004b, and 2004c;

---

[4] Gupta *et al.* (2006, 15) report that donor countries have increased their commitments of budget support from about 10 percent to new highs of 20 percent of total aid commitments since 2000.

Rose 2003). The Bank-led Fast Track Initiative, which certifies national EFA plans as fit for funding, sets a minimum level of 10 percent private sector delivery of basic education services.

Most of these more debated aspects of the new EFA agenda originate from the World Bank and reflect the organization's continued support for the domestic reorganization of public education to accommodate an expanded role for the private sector and market-like mechanisms of governance. Officially, a significant group of governors opposes this reinterpretation of EFA (including the UN organizations, the European Union, and many nongovernmental actors). Yet these same governors have agreed to allow the Bank to lead the Fast Track Initiative, which sets the standards and benchmarks that guide international EFA efforts, including those directing the rising and increasingly coordinated EFA funding from bilateral donors (Mundy 2006). Even the EU governments, which have the strongest commitment to education as a public good, now channel large portions of their new funding for EFA through the Bank-led Fast Track Initiative and give generously to newly created trust funds managed by the Bank.

The continued role of the Bank as the most powerful governor in the EFA arena underscores the extent to which a combination of expertise and perceived efficacy can reinforce the authority of a global governor, even where its principals continue to voice significant disagreement with the details of its policies. Even NGO actors now treat the Bank as the "only train leaving the station" and work to maintain continuous high-level dialogue with its staff in the education sector (Murphy 2005). At the same time, it is important to recognize that EFA also acts as an important source of legitimacy for the World Bank, at a time when its activities and raison d'être have been hotly criticized by both right and left. In the past, the Bank was very hesitant about committing itself to goals for which funding had not already been secured. But this is exactly what President Wolfensohn did in 2000, when he promised that the Bank would ensure that no country with a credible plan for achieving EFA would fail for want of adequate resources. Even today, some Bank staff view the Bank's Fast Track Initiative as misguided for its emphasis on the rapid expansion of enrollments.[5] Yet the odd mix of demand for action from its principals and the

---

[5] Author's private communication with Bank staff, March 2007.

internal legitimacy concerns that underpin the Bank's preeminence on EFA has yielded both a greater inclination to monitor and scrutinize Bank activities among the wider community of EFA governors and incentives for the Bank to work in cooperation and partnership with them. Changing relational dynamics among EFA's global governors have forced the Bank to work towards a commonly defined EFA goal.

New actors and a new global politics of accountability

Another striking aspect of the recent episode of EFA internationalism is the unprecedented inclusion of nongovernmental actors in both international and national education-for-development policy arenas. It is not just that new partnerships with civil society and private sector organizations have come to be seen as essential by official political actors on the international stage (Ruggie 2003 and 2004; Scholte 2005). There has also been a remarkable growth of effective transnational networks representing coalitions of civil society and private sector actors. These organizations often link local-level coalitions to transnational campaigns in ways that have proven effective in shaping educational policies at both the national and the global levels.

In recent years, transnational advocacy networks on such issues as human rights, debt relief, ODA reform, and globalization have frequently taken up the issue of the universal right to education as one part of their broader advocacy efforts (Mundy and Murphy 2001; Oxfam International 1999). In addition, a strong transnational advocacy network on education for all emerged in 2000, initiated by Oxfam International, ActionAid, and Education International (the international association of teachers unions). The Global Campaign for Education (GCE) now counts among its members a large number of national civil society EFA coalitions around the world, as well as some of the largest international nongovernmental organizations involved in education (Oxfam, CARE, Save the Children, ActionAid, and Global March on Child Labour). It has been instrumental in pushing bilateral donors, international organizations, and G-8 members to make concrete commitments of resources for EFA, and offers salient criticism wherever IO policies veer toward privatization of educational services (Rose 2003; Mundy and Murphy 2002).

The GCE and other transnational coalitions committed to EFA have also been quite effective in bringing critical issues raised by civil society organizations in recipient countries to the attention of the international community (Global Campaign for Education 2004; Miller-Grandvaux *et al.* 2002; Dyer and Pain 2004). In one oft-cited example, civil society actors succeeded in persuading the Tanzanian government to abolish primary school fees. In that case, research by Tanzanian groups on the impact of fees on health and education was used by US NGOs to press the US Congress to enact legislation prohibiting funding to the World Bank if any of its lending programs imposed any form of user fees as part of its loan conditionality (50 Years is Enough 2000). The World Bank subsequently removed all user fees conditionalities, and the government of Tanzania declared free primary education. The Tanzania experience, in turn, goaded a number of other African governments to remove school fees in education and declare universal free primary education (Sumra 2005; TEN/MET 2006; Mundy *et al.* 2007). Here a new form of global accountability spurred significant advance in the achievement of "education for all."

In addition to these nongovernmental organizations and civil society coalitions, several private sector organizations have recently become active supporters of a global education for all initiative. These include the World Economic Forum (2005), a consortium of business organizations that has spearheaded a Global Governance Initiative to monitor achievements of the MDGs (including education) and is actively pursuing discussions about private/public EFA partnerships; the Commonwealth Education Fund (which brings private sector and public sector funding in the United Kingdom); the International Business Leaders Forum (IBLF 2005); and a new $60 million program of EFA funding from the Hewlett and Gates foundations. Compared with civil society coalitions, these private sector coalitions have different rationales for supporting a global EFA effort: they are more closely interested in trained labor and more sympathetic to private sector service provision. Nonetheless, they appear to support the general idea that access to basic education is a public good that should be universally available, and they increasingly work through public–private partnerships with major multilaterals like the World Bank and UNESCO on education for all efforts, providing yet another example of mutually reinforcing forms of authority on the issue.

Conclusions: EFA and its global governors

In this chapter, I have sought to present a rough history of international action around the notion of "education for all." I think it is clear that EFA has had an extremely uneven history, one characterized by bouts of reticence and attraction on the part of nation-states; entrepreneurial periods of issue (re)definition by multilateral organizations; an interrupted history of transnational advocacy; and great gaps in intergovernmental coordination and collective action. The most recent period stands out precisely because it has seen both a widely shared acceptance among established global governors of the universal right to education, *and* the first convincing efforts to construct a globally coordinated mechanism for action.

Why has EFA moved from being a widely accepted but unimplemented international norm to one that is more consistently acted upon today? As I have argued, the EFA case is, in part, an ideational story about a widely accepted but diffuse norm that has attracted a widening range of governors: bilateral aid organizations, multilateral organizations, international financial institutions, and, more recently, transnational advocacy networks and new transnational private sector associations. Historically, each member of this shifting cast of global governors has sought to redefine the EFA project in ways that enhance its particular status and legitimacy within the world polity. Despite the formal EFA mandates created at the end of World War II, not all (and, in some periods, even most) global governors have framed their EFA activities as part of a collective effort to achieve a global entitlement or create a global public good. They have continued to differ substantially in their views about the scale at which the governance of EFA should be carried out (that is, by states, bilaterally, or multilaterally).

Only in the most recent political period has the potential for collective action and cross-governor accountability begun to materialize. Four factors have contributed to this change. First, attention to EFA has clearly been fed by a new consensus among OECD governments about the importance of education as a domestic response to the challenges of economic globalization and competitiveness. Furthermore, both OECD governments and the Bretton Woods institutions see the right to education as an issue that can bolster their legitimacy as governors of economic globalization, bridging neoliberal and more socialdemocratic ideologies. Substantial commitments to EFA have also been

spurred by rising pressures for greater attention to global inequality –
both from transnational advocacy movements that have made education a fundamental part of their agenda for global social justice,
and from EU states that share more expansive views about social
democracy. Finally, the legitimacy deficits that plagued UN and Bretton
Woods organizations in the 1990s have propelled them to act more
cooperatively than ever before. All of these factors have created a positive context for the emergence of new forms of global coordination
around EFA, yielding new aid commitments and new opportunities
for cross-accountability and collective authority among EFA's global
governors.

Yet the EFA norm has still not become "historically efficient" in
the sense of permanently shifting actor commitments toward a multilaterally endorsed and guaranteed educational entitlement. Ironically,
though today's global governors in the EFA arena appear to agree
more consistently than ever before that EFA needs globally coordinated action, they still disagree about something the initial framers of
EFA took for granted: that education should be viewed as a public
good, and therefore should be publicly provided. The most powerful
governor in today's EFA arena, the World Bank, favors the delivery
of public services through a mix of public and private means. Other
institutional governors, significantly weaker in terms of expertise and
financial power, have tended to band with the Bank in new attempts at
EFA fundraising and coordination, while reserving the right to criticize
new benchmarks for public education at the recipient country level.
As noted above, the Bank's leadership suggests that expertise and perceived efficacy can reinforce the authority of a global governor, even
when its principals continue to voice significant disagreement with the
details of its policies. However, the wild card in this arena remains
the transnational issue networks which have taken up the EFA norm.
Their bid to link international civil society to domestic citizen groups
inside both donor and recipient countries could amount to a sophisticated new form of transnational accountability that revitalizes the
idea that education should be free, publicly available, and equal, on a
world scale.

Universal access to free, publicly provided basic education has now
achieved status and legitimacy as a global public good on a scale not
realized during the twentieth century. But its story is far from over.
A surprising finding from the EFA case is that enhanced authority

on an issue among individual governors (in terms of either capacity, expertise, moral authority, material resources, or formal delegation) can produce interorganizational competition. Competition based on expertise can act as a disincentive to concrete and coordinated action, and sometimes contributes to what we might think of as "interorganizational" hypocrisy: many actors, shared goals and norms, little effective change. Contexts in which governors are subject to greater scrutiny and contest from others, are faced with greater constraints on their authority, and are forced to work productively toward what Inis Claude (1966) once described as "collective legitimation," may be a more important trigger than single actor authority in the realization of highly aspirational global commitments such as "education for all."

13 | *Conclusion: authority, legitimacy, and accountability in global politics*

DEBORAH D. AVANT, MARTHA FINNEMORE, AND SUSAN K. SELL

Asking questions about who actually does the governing we see in contemporary politics has led us through some rocky terrain, analytically. It required us to define what global governors are (*"authorities who exercise power across borders for the purpose of affecting policy"*). This, in turn, raised questions about the sources of these authorities and how they change over time. It has also forced us to rethink many of our initial assumptions. When we began this project, we expected to focus on different *forms* of governors – NGOs, IOs, corporations, even states. These standard categories produced far fewer regularities than we expected. Over the course of our research we became convinced that the key to understanding these governors lay not in their form but in their relationships. Governors' relationships with constituencies and with one another shape how and whether governors become authorities in the first place and how they affect governing outcomes.

Our hope is that these chapters are only the beginning of research on global governors. The framework we developed suggests a research agenda for global politics that has analytical implications for our understanding of multiple authorities in global politics. It has implications for our assessment of the normative value of different arrangements and it has implications for international relations theory. We outline these, in turn, below.

Analytical implications: multiple authorities in global politics

The connection between governance and the state is very deep in our collective subconscious. To the extent that analysts have focused on the growing importance of nonstate or supra-state actors it has been in terms of their competition with states as ultimate authorities. Debates about whether to join a new IO, like the World Trade Organization or the International Criminal Court, are often framed as surrenders of sovereignty, at least by opponents. Critiques of expanding NGO power and influence are often taken as testaments to state weakness, particularly in the developing world.

Our analysis and the chapters presented here suggest that this assumption requires serious reconsideration. Authority in contemporary global life has many sources. The state is certainly one – a big one – but it is far from the only source. Professions, corporations, advocacy groups, and others who "exercise power across borders for purposes of affecting policy" (our definition of governing) draw their authority from expertise, morality, competence, and other sources that are independent of the state. These varied sources create authority of different types, and different types of authority may work through unlike mechanisms, some global but some very local. This diversity opens the way for fruitful conversations between comparative politics and international relations scholars about the internal politics of various authorities. Our argument thus challenges many entrenched divides in international relations and comparative politics, suggesting much more need for research on the microfoundations of global politics.

Multiple authorities with political effects

The web of global governors investigated here includes states and diverse other actors. The fact that nonstate governors have power does not necessarily – or even normally – shrink the power of states. Indeed, it may enhance state power. The capacity of the USA to stall control of small arms was enhanced by the mobilization of WFSA (Bob, this volume). Nor do other governors necessarily aspire to be states (or anything like them) and, based on the issues examined in this volume, we see little evidence of states as a group lining up against other governors. The authority of states may have some distinctive qualities, but we see little evidence that the authority states wield is "ultimate" or that it is in zero-sum opposition to other types. Instead different states join with various governors depending on the respective goals and constituencies of each.

Thinking about sources of authority outside the state is not new. Others have noted the potential for "varied" rather than "like" units in the international system – both historically (Ruggie 1993; Spruyt 1994) and in contemporary times (Cerny 1998). Neomedievalists of various stripes have predicted contrasting worlds. Some see vicious cycles in which overlapping authorities provide avenues for evading rules and accountability, degrading the efficiency of what gets done, serving fewer interests, and inciting conflict (Cerny 1998). Others have posited the prospects for more virtuous cycles in which multiple functional and territorial jurisdictions offer opportunities for new rules and accountability structures that enhance governance efficiency, serve more interests, and engender cooperation (Ruggie 1998).

We find examples of both dynamics. This suggests that the interesting next step is not a prediction of order or disorder resulting from diverse authority structures, central concerns of earlier scholarship on the topic. Rather, our next step is to investigate the conditions under which governors consolidate their authority (or not) and the varied outcomes produced by their efforts.

Beyond global pluralism: microfoundations of global political space

Thinking of multiple governors with various authorities suggests a different world than the imagined Westphalian one of like, territorially bounded units that underpins so much international relations (IR) theory. Once we remove the assumption that global political space is built on states, the microfoundations of this space loom large. One might be tempted simply to toss the varied authorities into an arena and think of the process as something like global liberalism (Gilpin 1975; Krasner 1978) or "global pluralism" in which the various governors jockey for advantage and compete to cement their preferred outcomes. However, the cases presented in this volume suggest that the solution cannot be so simple.

Global governance as we are characterizing it analytically, and as the empirics in these chapters suggest, is distinct from a simple translation of pluralism to the global level. As the nod to Dahl in this volume's title suggests, global politics does bear some similarities to domestic politics largely writ, but there are also some key differences. For example, the advocacy groups researched by Carpenter and Bob (this volume) work hard to set agendas, lobby, and obtain favorable outcomes on their issues, much as domestic interest groups do. Interest group politics as comparative or American politics scholars understand it, however, makes little sense without a constitution, an executive, or a legislature, all of which are missing in a global context. Whom should an advocacy group target? For what action should they lobby? The targets of their work are not at all clear. In fact, as these chapters show, there are multiple targets and the governing "game" has many more than the two levels envisioned by Robert Putnam (1988).

Much of the structure of governing globally is informal, as these cases show, yet how we should think about this analytically is unclear. Carpenter's "gatekeepers" are such only informally, begging questions about how one becomes a gatekeeper. Do gatekeepers arise only under certain conditions? Not only are many arrangements informal, but membership in these arrangements is often overlapping and fluid. Peter Drahos has written of "nodal governance" in which overlapping membership in different authority structures reinforces positions of privilege. For example, Microsoft participates in a number of governance venues and interacts with counterparts from PhRMA and MPAA, etc. to create mutually reinforcing systems of lobbying, advocacy, campaign financing, etc. Perhaps those with this kind of overlapping membership can more easily shift forums to gain bargaining advantage. We can imagine other structures buttressing this kind of power as well. More organized structures such as professions and professional organizations may both provide the road maps that link individuals to authority structures and also provide the mental software that shapes how they think about problems (Danner and Voeten, this volume). We see great need for research aimed at making sense of informal global structures and their various microfoundations.

Normative implications: legitimacy, democracy, accountability, and the global public good

Thinking about the agents of global governance has the useful consequence of casting these politics in a new light and inviting different kinds of questions. "Why are you in charge?" for example, is asked much less frequently than one might suppose at the global level. It is all too easy for us, as analysts, to take the status quo as given and ask standard questions about its efficacy. Putting the spotlight on agents – on governors – and making the dynamics of their authority (who defers and why) central to analysis also highlights important normative and ethical issues that deserve more consideration from scholars. In some cases, our framework provides assistance in grappling with these. Other issues will require more thought.

Legitimacy

Our definition of global governors implies that they have some measure of legitimacy. "Legitimacy is a generalized perception or assumption that the actions of an entity are desirable, proper, or appropriate within some socially constructed system of norms, values, beliefs and definitions" (Suchman 1995: 574). The governed should be much more inclined to defer to and recognize the authority of a governor they perceive to be legitimate. Legitimacy can thus play a crucial role in the construction and exercise of authority. Governors understand this well and often go out of their way to emphasize the normative desirability and appropriateness of their actions, thus bolstering legitimacy. Perceptions that a governor is legitimate can enhance her capacity to act and the prospects of success for her policies.

The types and degrees of legitimacy can vary significantly. Some governors have legitimacy within a narrow audience tied to a very specific source of authority. Others are considered legitimate among a much broader population and draw on many sources of authority. Furthermore, legitimacy can be tied to a governor's abidance by particular procedures and/or a governor's ability to deliver substantive ends consistent with a particular value system.

The link between legitimacy and authority is not simple or automatic, though. We cannot assume that compliance and deference means that the governed accept an authority or her actions as legitimate. As students of authoritarian regimes understand well, there are many reasons why the governed may defer or comply with dictates of an authority. They may have few other options. They may be fearful of noncompliance. They may simply lack the time, knowledge, attention, or energy to object or resist. Just as there can be "reluctant governors" (Haufler, this volume), so too can there be "reluctant governed."

Reluctance among the governed is a tension that governors must manage. It creates instability in the governor's authority and opportunities for change. Someone among the governed might organize the reluctant constituency against her and/or challenge her rules. Under-standing the characteristics of the governed and their reactions to governors' policies is crucial for a governor's success, but it is also important for us as scholars. Understanding what governors do is only half the intellectual task. The other side of this relationship deserves equal attention and this framework helps us focus on it.

The nature of global governors (as often multifaceted and chameleon-like) both gives them tools to manage their legitimacy and exposes them to risks and challenges to their legitimacy. Governors that draw on more than one source of authority may have a deeper pool of resources to draw upon to establish and maintain their legiti-macy, but they are also more likely to find situations in which what is proper by one source of authority is problematic by another. Or the legitimacy of a governor at one level of aggregation – an international organization, for instance – may be undercut by lack of legitimacy at another level – say member states that are viewed as illegitimate by their populations. The UN's ability to claim it is a legitimate represen-tative of the world's people has been challenged on this very count. Finally, as governors widen the scope of their appeals for legitimacy, they may find it difficult to manage various value systems that do not mesh easily. The decidedly liberal bias of many international organi-zations, for instance, is challenged on the basis that it conflicts with various elements of Islam.

One tool that can help governors manage these contradictions is trust. Trust is "a set of expectations held by one party that another party or parties will behave in an appropriate manner with regard to a specific issue" (Farrell and Knight 2003, 541) Thus, by building trust a governor can make it more likely that her legitimacy will not suffer – at least in the short term – in response to unexpected contra-dictions. Trust may be built between individuals and groups through "other regarding" behavior. Institutions can also bolster trust by gen-erating expectations about the likelihood of compliance with rules and by establishing expectations about how others should act in particu-lar situations (Farrell and Knight 2003, 542). The EU governors Kate McNamara documents as working so hard to build a new kind of insti-tutional authority can expect enhanced trust to be one of its products. As Alex Cooley's chapter demonstrates, though, by focusing actors on situational rather than dispositional factors, some kinds of contracting relationships undermine trust.

Democracy

Abiding by democratic principles has been another mechanism linked to trust building but translating the principles to the global level has proved challenging. Benedict Kingsbury and others have argued that the principles embodied in public law can generate expectations about proper behavior – what we might term "publicness" – that can be used to judge the democratic basis of anyone claiming to govern – be it an organization, a state, or a transnational governor (Kingsbury *et al.* 2005). A key feature of "publicness" in global administrative bodies is the promotion of accountability of global bodies to ensure that they meet adequate standards of transparency, consultation, participation, rationality, legality, and provide effective review of rules and decisions that bodies make (Kingsbury *et al.* 2005). It aims at instilling processes associated with deliberative democracy even in situations that do not have the electoral trappings of democracy.

One interesting feature of the global governors in this volume is that many of them actively see these "public" features – including transparency, consultation, and accountability – as a means of increasing their authority and legitimacy. In several instances governors have responded to critics who challenge their legitimacy by becoming more transparent and opening up a dialogue with critics. The IMF and the World Bank fit this model, and so do the movements toward corporate social responsibility in the global private business sector. Thus, while some governors may try to escape scrutiny, many others seek it out as a means of gaining more influence. Whether these choices actually enhance accountability in ways that make for earned legitimacy or whether they are merely fig-leaves that allow the governors to continue operating is a pressing question for future research.

Accountability

Our focus on the relationships between governors and governed illuminates the need for a more sophisticated approach to the question of accountability. Often the problems critics complain of when they call global governors like the World Bank "unaccountable" are not really problems with the degree of accountability, per se, but problems with who is holding the accounts. As the scandal surrounding Paul Wolfowitz's tenure at the Bank made clear, in many ways the institution was quite accountable to the interests of its major sponsors, like the US government. What really worried the critics was the fact that it was not accountable to the people on whose behalf it was lending money. Cries for greater accountability in this instance would be more accurately described as cries for different account holders or attention to the variety of constituencies to whom a governor *should* be accountable.

Our volume demonstrates at least two ways in which global governance does pose problems for the degree of accountability – or the ability to hold a governor to account by anyone. The first can be illustrated by a continuation of the example above. If one were simply to switch the Bank's account holders from major shareholders to major borrowers one might be able to devise an effective system of accountability. If one tries to design a system of accountability that satisfies both, however, one may end up with results that satisfy neither. As Tamar Gutner's chapter illustrates, the system set up to hold the IMF accountable to both donors and constituent countries has reduced rather than enhanced the ability of anyone to hold the IMF to account.

The second serious accountability problem arises when many different governors participate in the governance process in ways that make it hard to allocate responsibility or blame to any one of them. This is particularly problematic when governors are acting in a way that is (arguably) legitimate on procedural grounds to a rather narrow audience. In the 1990s this kind of issue led rich Western countries and the UN essentially to turn their backs on the genocide in Rwanda with little capacity to hold anyone to account for inaction.

In many more situations, however, the issue is not so much lack of accountability but how to manage competing demands for accountability to different constituencies, for different ends, and by different mechanisms. Thus we suggest any analysis of accountability begin with careful attention to the following questions:

(a) Accountable to whom? Most governors are the object of accountability claims by more than one constituency. The World Bank is accountable to its member states but has found itself increasingly under pressure to be accountable to both NGOs who work with it and monitor its actions as well as to the populations affected by its projects. These constituencies may not all want the same things from the Bank, creating dilemmas that Bank staff must manage.

(b) Accountable for what? Many governors have multifaceted missions which may include very abstract or diffuse goals that are hard to measure. Worse, many demand contradictory actions. The UN is supposed to safeguard the sovereignty and independence of its members, but it also has a "responsibility to protect" people who may be endangered by the actions of a member government. How, then, does one hold such a governor to account? What, exactly, would constitute "good performance" for this governor? Different constituencies may have very different views on this, vastly complicating the life of the governor, and managing these conflicting demands can be a challenge.

(c) Accountable by what mechanism? As constituencies have demanded more accountability from governors, an impressive array of mechanisms has appeared to accomplish this end. *Transparency* is one particularly common tool for monitoring what governors do. The explosion in information governors of all kinds release about themselves and their activities is largely driven by these accountability demands. *Participation* by concerned constituencies in governor decisionmaking is another. The international financial institutions now pride themselves on including representatives of borrower states and affected populations in decisionmaking about their work, albeit with controversial results. Offering or withholding funding based on performance is another obvious way to hold governors to account. Donors to NGOs often use this tool and the USA withheld dues to the UN to induce performance changes.[1]

Careful analysis of accountability demands and governor responses can be revealing. It helps us understand more about who has power and who is likely to benefit from governance arrangements, but it also says something about how governors, themselves, understand their responsibilities and their missions. Crafting policies that successfully address accountability demands can be tricky when actors have such different views about what, exactly, governors should be accountable

---

[1] Grant and Keohane (2005) describe seven different accountability mechanisms. On accountability in NGOs, see Slim (2002).

for and to whom. This is hardly a unique problem, however. Similar accountability issues pervade all levels of politics and a broader conversation with scholars in other parts of political science may be beneficial.

The global public good

Global governance itself is widely assumed to be "a good thing." We equate it with activities that are hard to dislike – cooperation, problem-solving, and the provision of public goods. A hard look at some of the actual governing that goes on in the world, however, suggests that this positive aura surrounding the term may not always be warranted. Ethical implications of much governing activity are often mixed and complex. Whether governance activities are "a good thing" depends a great deal on answers to the questions "good for whom?" and "good for what purpose?"

One reason analysts have neglected to ask these questions may be the language they use to talk about governance. The rhetoric commonly utilized carries a normative bias about which scholars have not always been self-conscious or reflective. Two terms, in particular, are loaded: "cooperation" and "public goods." In a world where conflict and violence are all too common, cooperation is often portrayed (sometimes implicitly) as the cure for these ills. If only states could cooperate, we would have fewer wars, solve more problems, and live in a more harmonious world, or so the rhetoric goes. As analysts, though, we know that cooperation itself is neither good nor bad; it is the ends to which we cooperate that can be normatively judged. Hitler and Stalin cooperated to invade Poland and cooperation is required to undertake genocide and exploitation. The fact that cooperation is occurring to produce governance does not, by itself, say anything about the ethics or the merits of that activity.

Another rhetorical source of analytic confusion lies in the treatment of the term "public good." Governors may have a variety of motivations. Some may be self-interested, some principled, some may be acting for profit, others may be altruists, but many (probably most) are some combination of these. Whatever their motive, a common tactic among global governors is to appeal to the greater collective – or public – good to legitimate their action. Such appeals, after all, provide the basis for claiming that others should defer and grant them

authority to govern. One result of such appeals in the academic literature has been some conflation of global governance "for the public
good" with provision "of public goods" in an economic sense. The definition of a public good in economics is a good that is both nonrival and
nonexcludable. Clean air, clean water, and national defense are classic
examples. The term "public good" is thus a technical description of a
product; it is not a statement of its normative value. Americans "benefit" from the government's provision of national defense in a technical sense even when they disagree with it or think it undermines their
security. Analyses are not always clear about this distinction, however,
and sometimes conflate products ("goods") with what is desirable (or
"good"). This tendency has deep roots in academic thinking. Much
of the work on hegemonic stability as a form of global governance in
the 1980s was driven by worries over US decline and the effects this
might have on global stability and the "public goods" US hegemony
provided. Whether the loss of US hegemony was good or bad was
not much debated in this work, nor was the normative value of the
US-sponsored order and public good (or goods) it created.[2]

Cui bono? Who benefits from the actions of global governors and,
conversely, who is hurt? While most governors make broad claims
about widespread public benefits of their action, not all do. Some governors work openly for the benefit of one specific group – an industrial
sector or an oppressed population, for example. They may argue that
benefiting this group somehow has diverse benefits for all, but the par-
ticularism of their actions is openly proclaimed. Other governors may
claim to be working in the public interest and for everyone's benefit,
but find that their vision of who is "the public" and what the public wants is not shared by all. Economists working in both IOs and
governments may find that what they assume to be pareto-improving
free trade arrangements are not seen that way by participants. Some
people's resistance to these "goods" may be driven not by economic
concerns, per se, but because they value other things such as local
cultures, traditions, and community that may be crushed by global
markets. Even when governors work for some reasonably consensual
goal, like controlling disease, governors may find that intended bene-
ficiaries are not the actual ones if corrupt distribution systems siphon

---

[2] For more contemporary work that does engage some of these issues, see Kaul
et al. (1999).

valuable medicines away from the needy and enrich local middlemen. Clashes among governors (and with the governed) over who should benefit, who does benefit, and what is actually a benefit permeate many efforts by governors.

Implications for IR theory

We began this inquiry by making three theoretical moves. First we put agency and governors, rather than structures, at the center of the framework we offer here. In addition, we consider a wide range of agents, not just states. Finally, we investigate diverse outcomes, many of which raise serious questions about common functionalist assumptions. If we abandon statism and problematize structuralism and functionalism, where does that leave us theoretically?

It leads us away from structural or "systemic" theory for a start. IR theory has long privileged theories pitched at the level of what it calls the "international system" and has understood that system to be a system of states. This style of theorizing became fashionable in the 1980s and is a legacy of the forceful arguments that Kenneth Waltz (1979) made about the dangers of "reductionism" and nonsystemic theory. Without denying the value of Waltz's contribution, we respectfully submit that this kind of theorizing has limitations. Waltz, himself, was modest in his claims. He claimed to explain "a small number of big and important things" with his systemic and structural theory (1986, 329). That leaves a large number of important things unexplained. We situate ourselves in that large space. Other kinds of theories have value in explaining outcomes in the contemporary world. Among them are theories centered on agency rather than structure. Even among structural theories, there is no obvious reason why the only structure of interest should be one created by a distribution of power among states.[3]

The focus on agency also gets us away from equilibrium and stasis. Instead, our emphasis has been on dynamics and transformation. Governors are generative. They create issues, set agendas, construct new power and authority. Dynamics and change are normal in our

---

[3] Of course, other types of international systems may also exist and occasionally IR scholars have noted these. Immanuel Wallerstein's conception of a capitalist "modern world system" has, perhaps, received the most attention, but even it has a strong statist component (Wallerstein 1974, 1980, and 1989).

view. We freely admit that we do not fully understand these dynamic processes. Our hope here was to offer some initial ideas that will open up these questions to more sustained investigation. Central among these notions is that tensions and synergies among sources of authority profoundly shape both the influence of governors and their evolution. Much more could be done to investigate the effects of various synergies (or tensions) under different conditions or to investigate the mechanisms by which authority is constructed in the first place. We would welcome such work.

Dynamics that result from tensions and synergies will always be context dependent. Generalizations about them must therefore be contingent and we should expect surprises as we investigate these processes on the ground. Surprises, thus, are integral to the dynamic processes we see. Unintended and unexpected outcomes are not flukes, to be folded into an error term. They are normal parts of the processes we explore. They are natural results of the tensions (or synergies) inherent in the varied constellations of governing authority.

The framework we sketch does not fit neatly into some single "level of analysis" expected by standard IR theory. The processes we investigate in this volume cross levels. They weave back and forth among levels. They may involve the creation of new levels (one possible reading of McNamara's chapter). Rather, the framework we offer is better understood as a problem-solving tool. By focusing on authority and deference, governors and the governed, it draws our attention to the sources of and instabilities in power or leadership in the political arena. By focusing our attention on relations among governors, similarly, the framework exposes cooperation or conflict, not just among states, but among a variety of differently empowered governors.

The result is a much more problem-driven style of theorizing and research than IR often produces. The knowledge that results from application of our approach is less likely to be law-like generalizations about outcomes than deeper understandings of mechanisms and processes. All of this leaves us in much closer partnership with theories commonly used in comparative politics than with paradigmatic IR theories. Substantively, the kinds of cross-level interactions entailed in governing will lead researchers into areas of inquiry where comparative politics has more or better understanding than IR. Conversely, attention to such interactions can free analysts from the territorially bounded assumptions that often drive research in comparative politics. This is already evident from some of the chapters here. Cooley, for example, zeros in on the erosion of trust as a key reason why project contracting produces problematic results regardless of whether the contracting agent is the USA or the UN and whether the contractor is a for-profit firm or a not-for-profit NGO. His investigation suggests fresh ways to address this problem by examining alternative mechanisms that would build rather than erode trust among governors occupying different "levels of analysis" and territorial spaces. Conceptually, the understandings that emerge from such a partnership will likely be more problem- or issue-driven, akin to comparative theories, than grand paradigmatic statements. As a consequence, we expect these findings, while contingent and context dependent, will have the great advantage of being relevant to practical political problems and policies.

Beyond their relevance to practical political problems, these findings suggest opportunities for normative theorizing. If what passes for global governance often eludes both the public and the good, it is hard to conclude that we are living in the best of all possible worlds. We have seen that many problems are not solved; many needs are not met. Carpenter's chapter reminds us that many pressing issues, such as children-born-of-war, are not taken up by activists. Items on actors' agendas are not there owing to their intrinsic virtue, but rather as the result of an intensely political process that silences some worthy contenders and promotes others. Nonadoption of an issue is also a form of governance. As Amartya Sen has argued, "it is possible to attach importance to opportunities that are *not* taken up. This is a natural direction to go if the *process* through which outcomes are generated has a significance of its own" (2000, 76). Processes such as contracting, advocacy, and complex delegation present opportunities and choices to some actors while denying them to others. Freedom to choose, in itself, may have value, as Sen points out. Mechanisms and processes, themselves, thus have normative content which we can judge. The framework here helps uncover these processes and assists our evaluations of them.

Analysis that crosses levels of analysis also helps us go beyond grand schemes to form a deeper apprehension of governance on the ground. Many of our authors look at specific processes and outcomes that may have been badly conceived, inadequately executed, poorly implemented, or harmfully exclusionary. This may not have been intended by governors, but both processes and outcomes should be judged nonetheless. Political theorist Brian Barry argues that social justice refers to the distribution of rights, opportunities, and resources (2005, 33). Who is harmed by and who benefits from particular distributions is context specific, however. Assessments of success, failure, benefit, loss, or dysfunction depend upon the context as well as what the actors *themselves* were hoping or trying to accomplish.

By focusing on governors and foregrounding agency, our analytic approach reveals what functionalist and structural accounts obscure. It places politics at the center of analysis. Authority and legitimacy often are contested; often there are no neutral interpretations of either. Instead of asking about the public good, it allows us to ask "good for whom?" Governing must be understood politically: who governs, what they govern, how they govern, and whom they govern are contentious issues reflecting power, access, mobilization, and agency.

References

50 Years is Enough. 2000. "Congress Requires US Opposition to Health and School User Fees." *Economic and Social Justice News* 3(4); www.50years.org/cms/ejn/story/136 (accessed October 29, 2009)

Abbott, Andrew. 1988. *The System of Professions*. Chicago: University of Chicago Press

Abbott, Kenneth, and Duncan Snidal. 2001."International 'Standards' and International Governance." *Journal of European Public Policy* 8(3): 345–70

    2009. "The Governance Triangle: Regulatory Standards Institutions and the Shadow of the State." In *Politics of Global Regulation*, edited by Walter Mattli and Ngaire Woods. Princeton: Princeton University Press

Ahrens, Joachim, Herman W. Hoen, and Renate Ohr. 2005. "Deepening Integration in an Enlarged EU: A Club Theoretical Perspective." *Journal of European Integration* 27(4): 417–39

AIEE (American Institute of Electrical Engineers). 1904. *The Niagara Falls Electrical Handbook*. Local Reception Committee, Boston, MA, http://ia331337.us.archive.org/2/items/niagarafallselec00ameriala/niagarafallselec00ameriala.pdf (accessed October 30, 2007)

Alchian, Armen A., and Harold Demsetz. 1972. "Production, Information Costs, and Economic Organization." *The American Economic Review* 62(5): 777–95

Alexander, N. 2002. *Paying for Education: How the World Bank & IMF Influence Education in Developing Countries. Research Report, 1998*, updated 2002. Washington, DC: Citizens' Network on Essential Services, www.campaignforeducation.org/resources/May2002/CNES%20Paying%20For%20Education.htm (accessed October 4, 2004)

Alter, Karen. 1998. "Explaining National Court Acceptance of European Court Jurisprudence: A Critical Evaluation of Theories of Legal Integration." In *The European Court and National Courts*, edited by A.-M. Slaughter, A. Stone Sweet, and J. Weiler. Oxford: Hart

    2006. "Delegation to International Courts and the Limits of Re-contracting Political Power." In *Delegation and Agency in International*

Organizations, edited by Darren G. Hawkins, David A. Lake, Daniel L. Neilson, and Michael J. Tierney. Cambridge: Cambridge University Press

2008. "Agents or Trustees? International Courts in their Political Context." *European Journal of International Relations* 14(1): 33–63

Anderson, Benedict. 1983. *Imagined Communities*. New York: Verso

Aoki, A., B. Bruns, M. Drabble, M. Marope, M. Mingat, A. Moock, and P. Murphy. 2002. "Education." In *World Bank. Poverty Reduction Strategy Paper Source Book*. Washington, DC: World Bank

Atkinson, A. B. 2005. "The Way Forward." In *New Sources of Development Finance*, edited by A. B. Atkinson. New York: Oxford University Press

Auty, Richard. 1994. "Industrial Policy Reform in Six Large Newly Industrializing Countries: The Resource Curse Thesis." *World Development* 22(1): 11–27

Avant, Deborah. 2005. *The Market for Force: The Consequences of Privatizing Security*. Cambridge: Cambridge University Press

2006. "The Implications of Marketized Security for IR Theory: The Democratic Peace, Late State Building, and the Nature and Frequency of Conflict." *Perspectives on Politics* 4(3): 507–28

Axelrod, Robert. 1984. *The Evolution of Cooperation*. New York: Basic Books

Ba, Alice D., and Matthew Hoffmann. 2005. *Contending Perspectives on Global Governance: Coherence, Contestation and World Order*. New York: Routledge

Bache, Ian, and Matthew Flinders. 2004. *Multi-level Governance*. New York: Oxford University Press

Bachrach, Peter, and Morton Baratz. 1962. "Two Faces of Power." *American Political Science Review* 56(4): 947–52

1963. "Decisions and Non-decisions: An Analytical Framework." *American Political Science Review* 57(3): 632–42

Bailey, Ian. 2003. *New Environmental Policy Instruments in the European Union*. Burlington, VT: Ashgate

Ballentine, Karen, and Heiko Nitzschke, eds. 2005. *Profiting from Peace: Managing the Resource Dimensions of Civil War*. Boulder, CO: Lynne Rienner

Ballentine, Karen, and Jake Sherman, eds. 2003. *The Political Economy of Armed Conflict: Beyond Greed and Grievance*. Boulder, CO and London: Lynne Rienner

Banfield, Jessica, Damian Lilly, and Virginia Haufler. 2002. *Transnational Corporations in Conflict-Prone Zones: Public Policy Responses and a Framework for Action*. London: International Alert

Barabasi, Albert-Lazslo. 2002. *Linked: The New Science of Networks*. New York: Basic Books

Barber, Benjamin R. 2003. *Fear's Empire: War, Terrorism, and Democracy*. New York: W. W. Norton

Barbour, R. S., and J. Kitzinger, eds. 1999. *Developing Focus Group Research: Politics, Theory and Practice*. London: Sage

Barnett, Michael. 2002. *Eyewitness to Genocide: The United Nations and Rwanda*. Ithaca, NY: Cornell University Press

  2005. "Humanitarianism Transformed." *Perspectives on Politics* 3(4): 723–40

Barnett, Michael, and Raymond Duvall. 2005. "Power in International Politics." *International Organization* 59: 1–32

Barnett, Michael N., and Martha Finnemore. 1999. "The Politics, Power and Pathologies of International Organizations." *International Organization* 53(4): 699–732

  2004. *Rules for the World: International Organizations in Global Politics*. Ithaca, NY: Cornell University Press

Barry, Brian. 2005. *Why Social Justice Matters*. Cambridge: Polity Press

Bartley, T. 2009. "Standards for Sweatshops: The Power and Limits of Club Theory for Explaining Voluntary Labor Standards Programs." In *Voluntary Programs: A Club Theory Perspective*, edited by Matthew Potoski and Aseem Prakash. Cambridge, MA: MIT Press

Bartolini, Stefano. 2005. *Restructuring Europe: Centre Formation, System Building and Political Structuring between the Nation State and the EU*. Oxford: Oxford University Press

Bass, Gary. 2000. *Stay the Hand of Vengeance*. Princeton: Princeton University Press

Batley, Richard. 2006. "Engaged or Divorced? Cross-Service Findings on Government Relations with Non-State Service-Providers." *Public Administration and Development* 26(3): 241–51

Baumgartner, Frank R., and Bryan D. Jones. 1993. *Agendas and Instability in American Politics*. Chicago: The University of Chicago Press

Beetham, David. 1991. *The Legitimation of Power*. Atlantic Highlands, NJ: Humanities Press International

Bello, Walden. 2006. "The Rise of the Relief-and-Reconstruction Complex." *International Affairs* 59(2): 281–96

Bendell, Jem. 2004. *Barricades and Boardrooms: A Contemporary History of the Corporate Accountability Movement*. Geneva: UN Research Institute for Social Development

Benner, Thorsten, Wolfgang Reinicke, and Jan Martin Witte. 2003. "Global Public Policy Networks." *Brookings Review* 21(2): 18–21

Bennett, Colin. 1992. *Regulating Privacy: Data Protection and Public Policy in Europe and the United States*. Ithaca, NY: Cornell University Press

Berdal, Mats, and David M. Malone, eds. 2000. *Greed and Grievance: Economic Agendas in Civil Wars*. Boulder, CO: Lynne Rienner

Berle, A. A., and G. C. Means. 1932. *The Modern Corporation and Private Property*. New York: Harcourt, Brace & World

Berman, Jonathan. 2000. "Boardrooms and Bombs: Strategies of Multinational Companies in Conflict Areas." *Harvard International Review* 22(3): 28–33

Berrios, Ruben. 2000. *Contracting for Development: The Role of For-Profit Contractors in US Foreign Development Assistance*. Boulder, CO: Praeger

Bessen, S. M., and G. Saloner. 1988. *Compatibility Standards and the Market for Telecommunication Services*. Santa Monica, CA: Rand

Best, Joel, ed. 2001. *How Claims Spread: Cross-National Diffusion of Social Problems*. New York: Aldine de Gruyter

Bignami, Francesca. 2005. "Transgovernmental Networks vs Democracy: The Case of the European Information Privacy Network." *Michigan Journal of International Law* 26: 806–68

Billig, Michael. 1995. *Banal Nationalism*. London: Sage

Birdsall, N., and M. Vaishnave. 2005. "Education and the MDGs: Realizing the Millennium Compact." *Columbia Journal of International Affairs* 58(2): 257–64

Black, M. 1996. *Children First: The Story of UNICEF Past and Present*. New York: Oxford University Press

Black, Richard, and Howard White. 2004. *Targeting Development: Critical Perspectives on the Millennium Development Goals*. Routledge Studies in Development Economics 36. London: Routledge

Blackbourn, David, and Richard J. Evans, eds. 1991. *The German Bourgeoisie*. London and New York: Routledge

Bob, Clifford. 2002. "Merchants of Morality." *Foreign Policy* 129: 36–45

    2005. *The Marketing of Rebellion: Insurgents, Media, and International Activism*. Cambridge: Cambridge University Press

    2009a. "Dalit Rights are Human Rights: Caste Discrimination, International Activism, and the Construction of a New Human Rights Issue." In *Rights on the Rise*, edited by Clifford Bob. Philadelphia: University of Pennsylvania Press

    2009b. "Introduction: Fighting for New Rights." In *The International Struggle for New Human Rights*, edited by Clifford Bob. Philadelphia: University of Pennsylvania Press

    2009c. *Rights on the Rise: The Struggle for New Human Rights*. Philadelphia: University of Pennsylvania Press

forthcoming. *Globalizing the Right-Wing: Conservative Activism and World Politics*, Cambridge: Cambridge University Press

Boughton, James M. 2004. "IMF at 60: Reflections on Reform at the IMF and the Demands of a Changing World Economy." *Journal of Finance and Development* 41(3): 9–13

Bourdieu, Pierre. 1991. *Language and Symbolic Power*. Cambridge, MA: Harvard University Press

Boutwell, Jeffrey and Michael T. Klare, eds. 1999. *Light Weapons and Civil Conflict: Controlling the Tools of Violence*. New York: Carnegie Commission on Preventing Deadly Conflict

Boutwell, Jeffrey, Michael T. Klare, and Laura W. Reed, eds. 1995. *Lethal Commerce: The Global Trade in Small Arms and Light Weapons*. Cambridge, MA: Committee on International Security Studies, American Academy of Arts and Sciences

Bradley, Curtis A., and Judith Kelley, eds. 2008. "The Law and Politics of International Delegation." Special issue of *Law and Contemporary Problems* 71(1)

Brainard, Lael, Carol Graham, Nigel Purvis, Steven Radelet, and Gayle Smith. 2003. *The Other War: Global Poverty and the Millennium Challenge Account*. Washington, DC: Brookings Institution Press

Braithwaite, John, and Peter Drahos. 2000. *Global Business Regulation*. New York: Cambridge University Press

Brint, Steven. 1994. *In the Age of Experts: The Changing Role of Professionals in Politics and Public Life*. Princeton: Princeton University Press

Broad, Robin, and John Cavanagh. 1998. *The Corporate Accountability Movement: Lessons and Opportunities*. Washington, DC: World Resources Institute

Bruinsma, Fred J. 2006. "Judicial Identities in the European Court of Human Rights." In *Multilevel Governance in Enforcement and Adjudication*, edited by Aukje van Hoek, A. M. Hol, O. Jansen, P. Rijpkema, and R. Widdershoven. Antwerp: Intersentia

Bruns, B., A. Mingat, and R. Rakotomalala. 2003. *A Chance for Every Child: Achieving Universal Primary Education by 2015*. Washington, DC: World Bank

Brunsson, Nils. 1989. *The Organization of Hypocrisy: Talk, Decisions, and Actions in Organizations*. New York: Wiley

2000. "Organization, Markets, and Standardization." In *A World of Standards*, edited by Nils Brunsson and Bengt Jacobsson. New York: Oxford University Press

Brunsson, Nils, and Bengt Jacobsson, eds. 2000. *A World of Standards*. New York: Oxford University Press

Buchanan, J. M. 1965. "An Economic Theory of Clubs." *Economica* 32: 1–14

Bulmer, Simon. 1994. "The Governance of the European Union: A New Institutionalist Approach." *Journal of Public Policy* 13(4): 351–80

Burgerman, Susan. 2001. *Moral Victories: How Activists Provoke Multilateral Action*. Ithaca, NY: Cornell University Press

Burnside, Craig, and David Dollar. 2000. "Aid, Policies, and Growth." *American Economic Review* 90(4): 847–68

Busby, Joshua. 2007. "Bono Made Jesse Helms Cry: Jubilee 2000, Debt Relief, and Moral Action in International Politics." *International Studies Quarterly* 51(2): 247–75

Büthe, Tim. 2004. "Governance through Private Authority: Nonstate Actors in World Politics." *Journal of International Affairs* 58(1): 281–90

  2007. "Review of Hawkins *et al.*, Delegation and Agency in International Organizations." *Perspectives on Politics* 5(4): 861–2

  2008a. "The Globalization of Health and Safety Standards: Delegation of Regulatory Authority in the SPS-Agreement of the 1994 Agreement Establishing the World Trade Organization." *Law and Contemporary Problems* 71(1): 219–55

  2008b. "Institutional Change in the European Union: Two Narratives of European Commission Merger Control Authority, 1955–2004." Unpublished manuscript, Duke University

Büthe, Tim, and Walter Mattli. 2009. "International Standards and Standard-Setting Bodies." In *Oxford Handbook of Business and Government*, edited by David Coen, Graham Wilson, and Wyn Grant. Oxford and New York: Oxford University Press

  2010a. *Global Private Governance: The Politics of Rule-Making for Product and Financial Markets*. Princeton: Princeton University Press

  2010b. "Standards for Global Markets: Domestic and International Institutions for Setting International Product Standards." In *Handbook on Multi-Level Governance*, edited by Henrik Enderlein, Sonja Wälti, and Michael Zürn. Cheltenham, UK: Edward Elgar

Büthe, Tim, and Gabriel Swank. 2006. "The Politics of Anti-Trust and Merger Review in the EU: Institutional Change and Decisions from Messina to 2004." CES Working Paper 142, Cambridge, MA, Minda de Gunzburg Center for European Studies, Dec. 2006

Büthe, Tim, and Jan Martin Witte. 2004. *Product Standards in Transatlantic Trade and Investment*. Washington, DC: American Institute for Contemporary German Studies

Cahan, David. 1989. *An Institute for an Empire: The Physikalisch-Technische Reichsanstalt, 1871–1918*. Cambridge: Cambridge University Press

Camdessus, Michel. 1999. "Concluding Remarks at the Closing Joint Session of the Annual Meetings, International Monetary Fund." Available from www.imf.org/external/np/speeches/1999/093099.htm

Caporaso, James. 1996. "The European Union and Forms of State: Westphalian, Regulatory or Post-Modern?" *Journal of Common Market Studies* 34(1): 29–52

Carnoy, M. 1995. "Structural Adjustment and the Changing Face of Education." *International Labour Review* 134: 653–73

Carpenter, Charli. 2005a. "International Agenda-Setting in World Politics: Issue Emergence and Non-Emergence around Children and Armed Conflict." In *Human Rights and Human Welfare* Working Paper No. 30. Pittsburgh

2005b. "Women, Children and Other Vulnerable Groups: Gender, Strategic Frames and the Protection of Civilians as a Transnational Issue." *International Studies Quarterly* 49(2): 295–334

2007a. "Setting the Advocacy Agenda: Theorizing Issue Emergence and Non-emergence in Transnational Advocacy Networks." *International Studies Quarterly* 51(1): 99–120

2007b. "Studying Issue (Non)-Adoption in Transnational Advocacy Networks." *International Organization* 61(3): 643–67

2009. "Orphaned Again? Children Born of Rape as a Non-Issue for the Human Rights Movement." In *The International Struggle for New Human Rights*, edited by Clifford Bob. Philadelphia: University of Pennsylvania Press

2010. *Forgetting Children Born of War: Setting the Human Rights Agenda in Bosnia and Beyond*. New York: Columbia University Press

Carpenter, Charli, Kai Grieg, Donna Sharkey, Robyn Wheeler, and Betcy Jose-Thota. 2005. "Protecting Children Born of Rape and Exploitation in Conflict Zones: Findings from Consultations with Humanitarian Practitioners." Pittsburgh: University of Pittsburgh, GSPIA/Ford Institute of Human Security

Carpenter, Charli, Betcy Jose-Thota, and Ben Rubin. 2008. "Assessing Virtual Issue Networks: Transnational Advocacy in Real- and Cyberspace." Presented at the International Studies Association Annual Conference, March 26–30, in San Francisco, CA

Carpenter, Daniel. 2001. *Forging of Bureaucratic Autonomy: Reputations, Networks, and Policy Innovation in Executive Agencies*. Princeton: Princeton University Press

Cashore, Benjamin, Graeme Auld, and Deanna Newsom. 2004. *Governing through Markets: Forest Certification and the Emergence of Non-state Authority*. New Haven: Yale University Press

Casper, Steven, and Bob Hancké. 1999. "Global Quality Norms within National Production Regimes: ISO 9000 Standards in the French and German Car Industries." *Organization Studies* 20(6): 961–85

Casson, Mark. 1994. *The Economics of Business Culture: Game Theory, Transaction Costs, and Economic Performance*. Oxford: Oxford University Press

Cerny, Philip. 1998. "Neomedievalism, Civil War and the New Security Dilemma: Globalization as Durable Disorder." *Civil Wars* 1(1): 36–64

Chabbott, C. 2003. *Constructing Education for Development: International Organizations and Education for All*. New York: Routledge/Falmer

Chandrasekaran, Rajiv. 2006. *Imperial Life in the Emerald City: Inside Iraq's Green Zone*. New York: Knopf

Checkel, Jeff, and Peter Katzenstein. 2009. *European Identity*. New York: Cambridge University Press

Chikoto, Grace. 2007. "Government Funding and INGOs' Autonomy: A Tool Choice Approach." Working Paper 07–06, Andrew Young School of Policy Studies, Georgia State University

Chong, Daniel. 2009. "Economic Rights and Extreme Poverty." In *The International Struggle for New Human Rights*, edited by Clifford Bob. Philadelphia: University of Pennsylvania Press

Clapp, J. 1998. "The Privatization of Global Environmental Governance." *Global Governance* 4: 295–316

Claude, I. L. Jr. 1966. "Collective Legitimization as a Political Function of the United Nations." *International Organization* 20(3): 367–79

Clemens, M. 2004. "The Long Walk to School: International Educational Goals in Historical Perspective." Center for Global Development Working Paper 37, March

Clinton, H. R. 2007. "Security and Opportunity for the Twenty-First Century." *Foreign Affairs* 86(6): 2–18

Club of Rome. n.d. "Initiative for a Global Response System," www.clubofrome.at/grs/ (last accessed 23 April 2009)

Coase, R. H. 1960. "The Problem of Social Cost." *Journal of Law and Economics* 3: 1–44

Cobb, Roger, and Marc Howard Ross. 1997. *Cultural Strategies of Agenda Denial*. Lawrence: University of Kansas Press

Coglianese, C., and J. Nash. 2009. "Applying Club Theory to Government-Sponsored Voluntary Programs." In *Voluntary Programs: A Club Theory Perspective*, edited by Matthew Potoski and Aseem Prakash. Boston: MIT Press

Colclough, C. 1996. "Education and the Market: Which Parts of the Neo-liberal Solution are Correct?" *World Development* 24(4): 589–610

Collier, Paul. 2000. *Economic Causes of Civil Conflict and their Implications for Policy*. Washington, DC: World Bank

    2003a. *Breaking the Conflict Trap: Civil War and Development Policy*. Washington, DC: World Bank

    2003b. *Natural Resources, Development, and Conflict: Channels of Causation and Policy Interventions*. Washington, DC: World Bank, www.gdnet.org/pdf2/online_journals/cerdi/2004_3/Collier.pdf

Collier, Paul, and Anke Hoeffler. 2000. *Greed and Grievance in Civil War*. World Bank Working Paper. Washington, DC: World Bank

Commission on Global Governance. 1995. *Our Global Neighborhood*. New York: Oxford University Press

Cooley, Alexander. 2004. "The Marketplace of Humanitarian Action: A Political Economy Perspective." Paper prepared for the Social Research Council's "The Transformations of Humanitarian Action" Seminar Series, November 9, New York

    2005. *Logics of Hierarchy: The Organization of Empires, States and Military Occupations*. Ithaca, NY: Cornell University Press

Cooley, Alexander, and James Ron. 2002. "The NGO Scramble: Organizational Insecurity and the Political Economy of Transnational Action." *International Security* 27: 5–39

Cooper, Robert. 2003. *The Breaking of Nations: Order and Chaos in the Twenty-first Century*. New York: Atlantic Books

Cornes, R., and T. Sandler. [1986] 1996. *The Theory of Externalities, Public Goods, and Club Goods*. 2nd edn. Cambridge: Cambridge University Press

Cortell, Andrew P., and James W. Davis, Jr. 2000. "Understanding the Domestic Impact of International Norms: A Research Agenda." *International Studies Review* 2(1): 65–87

Cox, R. 1968. "Education for Development." In *The Global Partnership: International Agencies and Economic Development*, edited by R. Gardner and M. F. Millikan. New York: Praeger

Cox, Robert W. 1983. "Gramsci, Hegemony, and International Relations: An Essay in Method." *Millennium: A Journal of International Studies* 12(2): 162–75

Cram, Laura. 2001. "Imagining the Union: A Case of Banal Europeanism?" In *Interlocking Dimensions of Integration*, edited by Helen Wallace. New York: Palgrave Macmillan

    2006. "Inventing the People." In *Civil Society and Legitimate European Governance*, edited by S. Smismans. Aldershot: Edward Elgar

Crenson, Matthew. 1971. *The un-Politics of Air Pollution: A Study of non-Decisionmaking in the Cities*. Baltimore: The Johns Hopkins University Press

Cutler, A. Claire, Virginia Haufler, and Tony Porter, eds. 1999. *Private Authority and International Affairs*. Albany, NY: SUNY Press

Dahl, Robert A. 1957. "The Concept of Power." *Behavioral Science* 2(3): 201–15

  1961. *Who Governs?* New Haven: Yale University Press

  1968. "Power." *International Encyclopedia of the Social Sciences*, vol. XII. New York: Free Press

Dale, Stephen. 1996. *McLuhan's Children: The Greenpeace Message and the Media*. Toronto: Between the Lines

Dallaire, Romeo. 2003. *Shake Hands with the Devil: The Failure of Humanity in Rwanda*. Toronto: Random House

Danner, Allison. 2003. "Navigating Law and Politics: The Prosecutor of the International Criminal Court and the US Independent Counsel." *Stanford Law Review* 55: 1633–65

  2006. "When Courts Make Law: How the International Criminal Tribunals Recast the Laws of War." *Vanderbilt Law Review* 59: 1–68

Dasgupta, S., H. Hettige, and D. Wheeler. 2000. "What Improves Environmental Compliance? Evidence from Mexican Industry." *Journal of Environmental Economics and Management* 39(1): 39–66

David, Paul A. 1985. "Clio and the Economics of QWERTY." *American Economic Review* 75(2): 332–7

Davies, G. 1943. *Intellectual Cooperation between the Two Wars*. London: Council for Education and World Citizenship

Davis, Christina L. 2004. "International Institutions and Issue Linkage: Building Support for Agricultural Trade Liberalization." *American Political Science Review* 98(1): 153–69

Delaet, Debra. 2007. "Framing Male Circumcision as a Human Rights Issue? Contributions to the Debate over the Universality of Human Rights." Paper presented at the International Studies Association Annual Conference, February 28–March 3, Chicago

de Rato, Rodrigo. 2004. "The IMF at 60 – Evolving Challenges, Evolving Role." Paper read at "Dollars, Debt and Deficits – 60 Years After Bretton Woods," Madrid

deSoysa, Indra. 2000. "The Resource Curse: Are Civil Wars Driven by Rapacity or Paucity?" In *Greed or Grievance: Economic Agendas in Civil Wars*, edited by D. M. Malone and M. Berdal. Boulder, CO: Lynne Rienner

Development Committee. 2005. "2005 Review of the Poverty Reduction Strategy Approach: Balancing Accountabilities and Scaling Up Results." Joint Ministerial Committee of the Boards of Governors of the Bank and the Fund on the Transfer of Real Resources to Development Countries, September 12

Development Initiatives. 2006. "Summary Paper on the Financing and Partnerships between UN and non-UN Humanitarian Organizations." Prepared for the conference "Enhancing the Effectiveness of Humanitarian Action: A Dialogue between UN and non-UN Humanitarian Organizations," July 12–13, Geneva

de Vries, Henk J. 2007. "Standards for Business: How Companies Benefit from Participation in International Standards Setting." In *International Standardization as a Strategic Tool*, edited by IEC. Geneva: International Electrotechnical Commission

Diamond, Larry. 2005. *Squandered Victory: The American Occupation and the Bungled Effort to Bring Democracy to Iraq*. New York: Owl Books

Diez Medrano, Juan. 2003. *Framing Europe: Attitudes to European Integration in Germany, Spain, and the United Kingdom*. Princeton: Princeton University Press

Di Palma, Giuseppe. 1990. *To Craft Democracies: An Essay on Democratic Transitions*. Berkeley: University of California Press

Dobbins, James, John G. McGinn, Keith Crane, Seth G. Jones, Rollie Lal, Andrew Rathmell, Rachel M. Swanger, and Anga R. Timilsina. 2003. *America's Role in Nation-Building: From Germany to Iraq*. Santa Monica, CA: RAND

Dogan, Rhys. 1997. "Comitology: Little Procedures with Big Implications." *West European Politics* 20(3): 31–60

Dollar, David, and Jakob Svensson. 2000. "What Explains the Success or Failure of Structural Adjustment Programmes?" *The Economic Journal* 110(466): 894–917

Drazen, Alan. 2002. "Conditionality and Ownership in IMF Lending: A Political Economy Approach." *IMF Staff Papers* 49: 36–67

Drezner, Daniel. 2007a. *All Politics is Global: Explaining International Regulatory Regimes*. Princeton: Princeton University Press

2007b. "When Celebrities Attack." *The National Interest* November/December

Duffield, Mark. 2001. *Global Governance and the New Wars: The Merging of Development and Security*. London and New York: Zed Books.

Dunning, John. 1993. *The Globalization of Business*. New York: Routledge

Dworkin, Ronald. 2006. *Is Democracy Possible Here? Principles for a New Political Debate*. Princeton: Princeton University Press

Dyer, Kate. 2005. "The Cost of Poverty: Transaction Costs and the Struggle to Make Aid Work in the Education Sector in Tanzania." Human Development Report Office Occasional Paper. New York: UNDP

Dyer, K., and C. Pain. 2004. "Civil Society Budget Monitoring for National Accountability." Workshop Report, February 17–19, 2004. Lilongwe, Malawi (mimeo)

Easterly, William. 2002. "The Cartel of Good Intentions." *Foreign Policy* 131: 40–9

2005. "Tone Deaf on Africa." *New York Times*, July 3: C10

Eberlein, Burkard, and Abraham Newman. 2008. "Escaping the International Governance Dilemma? Incorporated Transgovernmental Networks in the European Union." *Governance* 21(1): 25–52

Ebrahim-zadeh, Christine. 2003. "Dutch Disease: Too Much Wealth Managed Unwisely." *Finance and Development*, March: 50–1

EFA/FTI Secretariat. 2005. "Guidelines for Assessment and Endorsement of the Primary Education Component of an Education Sector Plan," www1.worldbank.org/education/efaafti/documents/ assessementguidelines.pdf (accessed January 30, 2005)

Egan, Michelle. 2001. *Constructing a European Market: Standards, Regulation, and Governance*. New York: Oxford University Press

Egeberg, Morten. 1999. "Transcending Intergovernmentalism? Identity and Role Perceptions of National Officials in EU Decision-Making." *Journal of European Public Policy* 6: 456–74

Elazar, D. J. 1987. *Exploring Federalism*. Tuscaloosa, AL: University of Alabama Press

Epstein, Lee, and Jeffrey A. Segal. 2000. "Measuring Issue Salience." *American Journal of Political Science* 44(1): 66–83

Erdmann, Jeanne. 2007. "The Appointment of a Representative Commission." Geneva: IEC, www.iec.ch/about/history/articles/appointment_ commission.htm (accessed October 30, 2007)

European Commission. 2003. "European Commission/US Customs Talks on PNR Transmission Joint Statement." Brussels, February 17/18. Available at http://ec.europa.eu/justice_home/fsj/privacy/docs/ adequacy/declaration_en.pdf

Falk, Richard. 1995. *On Humane Governance: Toward a New Global Politics: The World Order Models Project Report of the Global Civilization Initiative*. University Park, PA: Pennsylvania State University Press

Farrell, Henry. 2003. "Constructing the International Foundations of E-commerce: The EU–US Safe Harbor Arrangement." *International Organization* 57(2): 277–306

Farrell, Henry, and Adrienne Héritier. 2006. "Codecision and Institutional Change." EUI Working Paper, RSCAS No. 2006/41. Florence: European University Institute

Farrell, Henry, and Jack Knight. 2003. "Trust, Institutions and Institutional Change: Industrial Districts and the Social Capital Hypothesis." *Politics and Society* 31(4): 537–66

Farrell, Joseph, and Garth Saloner. 1985. "Standardization, Compatibility, and Innovation." *Rand Journal of Economics* 16: 70–83

Farrell, Mary. 2007. "From EU Model to External Policy? Promoting Regional Integration in the Rest of the World." In *Making History: European Integration and Institutional Change at Fifty*, edited by Sophie Meunier and Kathleen McNamara. New York: Oxford University Press

Favell, Adrian. 2003. "Eurostars and Eurocities: Free Moving Professionals and the Promise of European Integration." Council for European Studies, accessed under "Publications" at www.europanet.org/pub/Favell_jan04.html

Fearon, James. 2005. "Primary Commodity Exports and Civil War." *Journal of Conflict Resolution* 49(4): 483–507

Feigenbaum, Harvey, Jeffrey Henig, and Chris Hamnett. 1998. *Shrinking the State: The Political Underpinnings of Privatization*. Cambridge: Cambridge University Press

Financial Times. 1997. "Bank Role Urged in Chad Oil Plan." *Financial Times* October 27: 4

Finnemore, Martha. 1992. *Science, the State, and International Society*. Stanford: Stanford University Press

   1996. *National Interests in International Society*. Ithaca, NY: Cornell University Press

   2003. *The Purpose of Intervention*. Ithaca, NY: Cornell University Press

Finnemore, Martha, and Kathryn Sikkink. 1998. "International Norm Dynamics and Political Change." *International Organization* 52(4): 887–918

Flaherty, David. 1989. *Protecting Privacy in Surveillance Societies*. Chapel Hill: University of North Carolina Press

Flathman, Richard E. 1980. *The Practice of Political Authority*. Chicago: University of Chicago Press

Flauss, J.-F. 1998. "Radioscopie de l'élection de la nouvelle Cour européenne des droits de l'homme." *Revue trimestrielle des droits de l'homme* 9: 435–64

Fligstein, Neil. 2008. *Euro-clash: The EU, European Identity and the Future of Europe*. New York: Oxford University Press

   2009. "Organizations: Theoretical Debates and the Scope of Organization Theory." UC Berkeley Center for Culture, Organizations, and Politics working paper.

Fligstein, Neil, and Iona Mara-Drita. 1996. "How to Make a Market: The Case of the Single European Market." *American Journal of Sociology* 102(1): 1–34

Florini, Ann M., ed. 2000. *The Third Force: The Rise of Transnational Civil Society*. Tokyo: Japan Center for International Exchange; Washington, DC: Carnegie Endowment for International Peace

Fort, Timothy L., and Cindy A. Schipani. 2004. *The Role of Business in Fostering Peaceful Societies*. Cambridge: Cambridge University Press

Foucault, Michel. 1988. "The Political Technology of Individuals." In *Technologies of the Self*, edited by L. H. Martin, H. Gutman, and P. H. Hutton. Amherst: University of Massachusetts Press

Franchino, Fabio. 2000. "Control of the Commission's Executive Functions." *European Union Politics* 1(1): 63–92

Fratianni, Michele, and John Pattison. 2002. "International Organisations in a World of Regional Trade Agreements: Lessons from Club Theory." *The World Economy* 24: 333–58

Freeland, Chrystia, and Edward Luce. 2007. "Bridging Poverty Gap Should Be IMF Priority, Says Strauss-Kahn." *Financial Times* July 28: 1

Freeman, Bennett. 2000. "Globalization, Human Rights and the Extractive Industries, As Prepared for Delivery: Speech by US Deputy Assistant Secretary of State." Paper read at Third Warwick Corporate Citizenship Conference, July 10, 2000, University of Warwick

Friedman, Milton. 1970. "The Social Responsibility of Business is to Increase its Profits." *The New York Times Magazine*, September 13

Fuchs, E. 2007. "Children's Rights and Global Civil Society." *Comparative Education* 43(3): 393–412

"G-20 Reaffirms IMF's Central Role in Combatting Crisis." 2009. IMF Survey Online

Gambetta, Diego. 1988. "Can We Trust Trust?" In *Trust: Making and Breaking Cooperative Relationships*, edited by Diego Gambetta. Cambridge, MA: Blackwell

Gaventa, John. 1982. *Power and Powerlessness: Quiescence and Rebellion in an Appalachian Valley*. Champaign, IL: University of Illinois Press

General Accounting Office (GAO). 2004. *Contract Management: Contracting for Iraq Reconstruction and for Global Logistics Support*. Prepared Statement of David Walker for the House of Representatives Committee on Government Reform, June 15. Washington, DC

   2006. *Rebuilding Iraq: Status of Competition for Iraq Reconstruction Contracts*. Report to Congressional Committees, October 2006. Washington, DC

Gereffi, Gary, and Miguel Korzeniewicz. 1994. *Commodity Chains and Global Capitalism*. Westport, CT: Greenwood

Gereffi, G., R. Garcia-Johnson, and E. Sasser. 2001. "NGO-Industrial Complex." *Foreign Policy* 125: 56–65

Gilardi, Fabrizio. 2005. "The Institutional Foundations of Regulatory Capitalism: The Diffusion of Independent Regulatory Agencies in Western Europe." *Annals of the American Academy of Political and Social Science* 598(1): 84–101

Gilpin, Robert. 1975. *US Power and the Multinational Corporation: The Political Economy of Foreign Direct Investment.* New York: Basic Books

Ginsberg, Roy. 2001. *The European Union in International Politics: Baptism by Fire.* Lanham: Rowman and Littlefield

    2007. *Demystifying the European Union: Enduring Logic of Regional Integration.* Lanham: Rowman and Littlefield

Ginsberg, Roy H., and Michael E. Smith. 2007. "Understanding the European Union as a Global Political Actor: Theory, Practice and Impact." In *Making History: European Integration and Institutional Change at Fifty*, edited by Sophie Meunier and Kathleen R. McNamara. Oxford: Oxford University Press

Gispen, Kees. 1990. "Engineers in Wilhelmian Germany." In *German Professions, 1800–1950*, edited by Geoffrey Cocks and Konrad H. Jarausch. New York: Oxford University Press

Glaeser, Edward, and Andrei Shleifer. 2002. "Legal Origins." *Quarterly Journal of Economics* 17(4): 1193–229

Glanz, James. 2007. "Bechtel Meets Goals on Fewer than Half of its Iraq Rebuilding Projects, US Study Finds." *New York Times* July 26

Global Campaign for Education. 2004. "Undervaluing Teachers: IMF Policies Squeeze Zambia's Education System," www.campaignforeducation.org/resources/resources_listall.php (accessed January 10, 2005)

Global Witness. 1998. *Rough Trade: The Role of Companies and Governments in the Angolan Conflict.* London: Global Witness

    1999. *A Crude Awakening: The Role of the Oil and Banking Industries in Angola's Civil War and the Plunder of State Assets.* London: Global Witness

Goldring, Natalie J. 1999. "Domestic Laws and International Controls." In *Light Weapons and Civil Conflict: Controlling the Tools of Violence*, edited by Jeffery Boutwell and Michael T. Klare. New York: Carnegie Commission on Preventing Deadly Conflict

Goldsmith, Jack, and Eric Posner. 2005. *The Limits of International Law.* Oxford: Oxford University Press

Goldstein, Judith, Miles Kahler, Robert O. Keohane, and Anne-Marie Slaughter, eds. 2001. *Legalization and World Politics.* Cambridge, MA: MIT Press

Goodman, John. 1991. "The Politics of Central Bank Independence." *Comparative Politics* 23(3): 329–49

Goodman, Ryan, and Derek Jinks. 2004. "How to Influence States." *Duke Law Journal* 54: 621–703

Gorski, Philip S. 2003. *The Disciplinary Revolution.* Chicago: University of Chicago Press

Gower, J. 2001. "Developing a Green Agenda: The Emergence of Environmental Policy within the European Union." In *The Greening of the European Union?*, edited by J. Gower. London: Sheffield Academic Press

Grant, Andrew, and Ian Taylor. 2004. "Global Governance and Conflict Diamonds: The Kimberley Process and the Quest for Clean Gems." *The Round Table* 93(375): 385–401

Grant, Ruth, and Robert Keohane. 2005. "Accountability and Abuses of Power in World Politics." *American Political Science Review* 99(1): 29–43

Grieg, Kai. 2001. "The War Children of the World." War and Children Identity Project, www.warandchildren.org. Bergen, Norway

Gugerty, Mary Kay, and Aseem Prakash, eds. 2010. *NGO Accountability Clubs: Self-Regulation in the Nongovernmental and Nonprofit Sectors*. Cambridge: Cambridge University Press

Guler, Isin, Mauro F. Guillén, and John Muir MacPherson. 2002. "Global Competition, Institutions and the Diffusion of Organization Practices: The International Spread of ISO 9000 Quality Certificates." *Administrative Science Quarterly* 47(2): 207–32

Gupta, S., C. Pattillo, and S. Wagh. 2006. "Are Donor Countries Giving More or Less Aid?" IMF Working Paper WP/06/01. Washington, DC: International Monetary Fund

Gurr, Ted Robert, and Monty Marshall. 2006. *Peace and Conflict 2005*. College Park: Center for International Development and Conflict Management

Gutner, Tamar. 2007. "When 'Doing Good' Does Not: The IMF and the Millennium Development Goals." Paper prepared for the Global Governor's Working Group, George Washington University, November 2007, in Washington, DC

Haas, Peter M. 1990. *Saving the Mediterranean: The Politics of International Environmental Cooperation*. New York: Columbia University Press

Habermas, Jürgen. 2001. *The Postnational Constellation: Political Essays*. Cambridge, MA: MIT Press

Hall, Rodney Bruce, and Thomas Biersteker. 2002. *Emergence of Private Authority in Global Governance*. New York: Cambridge University Press

Hardin, Garrett. 1968. "The Tragedy of the Commons." *Science* 162: 1243–8

Hardin, Russell. 2004. *Trust and Trustworthiness*. New York: Russell Sage Foundation

Harris, Simon. 2006. "Disasters and Dilemmas: Aid Agency Recruitment and HRD in Post-tsunami Sri Lanka." *Human Resource Development International* 9(2): 291–8

Harrison, Makiko, Jeni Klugman, and Eric Swanson. 2005. *Are Poverty Reduction Strategies Undercutting the Millennium Development Goals? An Empirical Review.* Washington, DC: World Bank

Hart, Jeffery A. 2004. *Technology, Television, and Competition: The Politics of Digital TV.* Cambridge: Cambridge University Press

Hart, Oliver. 1995. *Firms, Contracts and Financial Structure.* Oxford: Clarendon Press

Harvey, David. 1990. *The Condition of Postmodernity.* Cambridge: Blackwell

Hathaway, Oona. 2005. "Between Power and Principle: A Political Theory of International Law." *University of Chicago Law Review* 71: 469–536

Haufler, Virginia. 2001. *A Public Role for the Private Sector: Industry Self-Regulation in the Global Economy.* Washington, DC: Carnegie Endowment for International Peace

2003. "Globalization and Industry Self-Regulation." In *Governance in a Global Economy*, edited by M. Kahler and D. Lake. Princeton: Princeton University Press

2004. "International Diplomacy and the Privatization of Conflict Prevention." *International Studies Perspectives* 5: 158–63

2007. "Governing Corporations in Zones of Conflict: Issues, Actors and Institutions." Paper presented to the Global Governors Working Group, George Washington University, November 2007, in Washington, DC

Hawkins, Darren G., David A. Lake, Daniel L. Nielson, and Michael J. Tierney. 2006. *Delegation and Agency in International Organizations.* Cambridge: Cambridge University Press

Hayward, Clarissa Rile. 2000. *Defacing Power.* New York: Cambridge University Press

Held, David. 2005. "At the Global Crossroads: The End of the Washington Consensus and the Rise of Global Social Democracy?" *Globalizations* 2(1): 95–113

Held, David, and Anthony McGrew. 2000. "The Great Globalization Debate". In *The Global Transformations Reader*, edited by David Held and Anthony McGrew, Cambridge, UK: Polity Press

Helfer, Laurence R. 2006. "Why States Create International Tribunals: A Theory of Constrained Independence." In *International Conflict Resolution*, edited by Stefan Voigt, Max Albert, and Dieter Schmidtchen. Tubingen: Mohr Siebeck

Helfer, Laurence R., and Anne-Marie Slaughter. 2005. "Why States Create International Tribunals: A Response to Professors Posner and Yoo." *California Law Review* 93: 901–56

Henderson, Sarah. 2002. "Selling Civil Society: Western Aid and the Nongovernmental Sector in Russia." *Comparative Political Studies* 35(2): 139–67

Henzinger, Monika. 2001. "Hyperlink Analysis for the Web." *IEEE Internet Computing* 5(1): 45–50

Herrigel, Gary. 1996. *Industrial Constructions.* New York: Cambridge University Press

Heyneman, S. P. 2003. "The History and Problems in the Making of Education Policy at the World Bank, 1960–2000." *International Journal of Educational Development* 23: 315–37

Hirschman, Albert O. 1970. *Exit, Voice, and Loyalty: Responses to Decline in Firms, Organizations, and States.* Cambridge, MA: Harvard University Press

Hix, Simon. 1999. *The Political System of the European Union.* Basingstoke: Macmillan/Palgrave

    2002. "Constitutional Agenda-Setting through Rule Interpretation: Why the European Parliament Won in Amsterdam." *British Journal of Political Science* 32(2): 259–80

    2005. *The Political System of the European Union.* 2nd edn. New York: Palgrave

Hobsbawm, Eric, and Terence Ranger, eds. 1983. *The Invention of Tradition.* Cambridge: Canto/Cambridge University Press

Hocking, Brian. 2004. "Privatizing Diplomacy?" *International Studies Perspectives* 5(2): 147–52

Holzscheiter, Anna. 2005. "Discourse as Capacity: Non-State Actors' Capital in Global Governance." *Millennium* 33(3): 723–46

Hondius, Fritz. 1975. *Emerging Data Protection in Europe.* New York: Elsevier

Hooghe, Liesbet. 2005. "Several Roads Lead to International Norms, but Few via International Socialization: A Case Study of the European Commission." *International Organization* 59(4): 861–98

Hooghe, Liesbet, and Gary Marks. 2001. *Multilevel Governance and European Integration.* Lanham, MD: Rowman and Littlefield

Hopgood, Stephen. 2006. *Keepers of the Flame: Understanding Amnesty International.* Ithaca, NY: Cornell University Press

Hudock, Ann. 2002. *Laying the Foundation for Sustainable Development: Good Governance and the Poverty Reduction Strategy Paper.* Washington, DC: World Learning

Hughes, Thomas P. 1983. *Networks of Power: Electrification in Western Society, 1880–1930.* Baltimore: The Johns Hopkins University Press

Hulme, David, and Michael Edwards, eds. 1997. *NGOs, States and Donors: Too Close for Comfort?* New York: St. Martin's Press

Human Rights Watch. 2001. "UN: 'Program of Inaction' on Small Arms." Press release, July 19, http://hrw.org/english/docs/2001/07/19/global308.htm (accessed August 12, 2008)

Human Security Center. 2005. *Human Security Report 2005: War and Peace in the 21st Century*, revised edn. Oxford: Oxford University Press (available online at www.humansecurityreport.info/content/view/28/63/)

2006. *Human Security Brief 2006*, edited by A. Mack. Vancouver: University of British Columbia

Humphreys, Macartan. 2005. "Natural Resources, Conflict, and Conflict Resolution." *Journal of Conflict Resolution* 49(4): 508–37

IANSA. 2003. "United Nations Biennial Meeting of States on Small Arms and the Programme of Action: 7–11 July," www.iansa.org/media/bms.htm (accessed August 12, 2008)

2006. "UN Arms Talks Meltdown: Conference Allows Global Gun Crisis to Continue." Press release, July 7, www.iansa.org/un/review2006/documents/IANSA%20press%20release%20_7%20July%202006_.pdf (accessed August 12, 2008)

IEC. 1906. Report of Preliminary Meeting. London: International Electrotechnical Commission

2005. *IEC Statutes and Rules of Procedure* (2001 edn, as amended on 2004-01-02, 2005-01-07 and 2005-09-02, endorsed by the National Committees). Geneva: IEC.

2006a. *Development and Growth of IEC Technical Committees, 1950–2006*, www.iec.ch/online_news/etech/arch_2006/etech_0206/focus.htm (accessed January 17, 2007)

2006b. *IEC Technical Committee Creation: The First Half-Century. 1906–2006: The Electric Century.* Geneva: IEC, www.iec.ch/online_news/etech/arch_2006/ etech_0106/focus.htm (accessed May 6, 2006)

2007a. *Colour Management*, www.iec.ch/zone/colourgmt/cm_entry.htm (and linked pages; accessed October 29, 2007)

2007b. *Conformity Assessment*. Geneva: IEC, www.iec.ch/conformity/ (accessed October 30, 2007)

2007c. *IEC Membership*, www.iec.ch/about/members-e.htm (accessed October 30, 2007)

2007d. *IEC Performance 2006*. Geneva: IEC

2008a. *International and Regional Partners*, www.iec.ch/about/partners/ (accessed August 10, 2008)

2008b. "Members" and "IEC Affiliate Country Programme Participants," www.iec.ch/cgi-bin/procgi.pl/www/iecwww.p?wwwlang=e&wwwprog=membrs3.p and www.iec.ch/cgi-bin/procgi.pl/www/iecwww.p?wwwlang=E&wwwprog=membrs32.p (accessed March 10, 2008)

2008c. *Organizations and TC/SC Liaisons*, www.iec.ch/about/organ-e.htm (accessed March 18, 2008)

2009. *The IEC in Figures* [as of 2008-12-31]. Geneva: IEC, www.iec.ch/news_centre/iec_figures/ (accessed April 10, 2009)

Imber, M. F. 1989. *The USA, ILO, Unesco and IAEA: Politicization and Withdrawal in the Specialized Agencies*. London: Macmillan

IMF. 1944. *Articles of Agreement of the International Monetary Fund*. Washington, DC: International Monetary Fund

2003a. *Aligning the Poverty Reduction and Growth Facility (PRGF) and the Poverty Reduction Strategy Paper (PRSP) Approach: Issues and Options*, edited by P. D. a. R. Department. Washington, DC: International Monetary Fund

2003b. *The IMF and Good Governance*. Washington, DC: IMF

2004. *Evaluation of the IMF's Role in Poverty Reduction Strategy Papers and the Poverty Reduction Growth Facility*. Washington, DC: International Monetary Fund

2005a. *The Macroeconomics of Managing Increased Aid Inflows: Experiences of Low-Income Countries and Policy Implications*. Washington, DC: International Monetary Fund

2005b. *Review of the PRGF Program Design-Overview*. Washington, DC: International Monetary Fund

2006. *The IMF and the Millennium Development Goals*, wwwlimf. org/external/np/exr/facts/mdg.htm (accessed August 10, 2006)

IMF, OECD, World Bank and UN. 2000. *A Better World for All*. Washington, DC: Communications Development

International Business Leaders Forum. 2005. *Business and the Millennium Development Goals: A Framework for Action*. London: Prince of Wales International Business Leaders Forum and the UNDP

International Development Association and International Monetary Fund. 2002. *Review of the Poverty Reduction Strategy Paper (PRSP) Approach: Main Findings*. Washington, DC: World Bank and International Monetary Fund

ISO. 2004a. *The Founding of ISO*, www.iso.org/iso/en/aboutiso/ introduction/fifty/pdf/foundingen.pdf (accessed July 19, 2004)

2004b. *Frequently Asked Questions on ISO 14001*, www.iso.org/iso/en/aboutiso/introduction/ index.html (accessed July 19, 2004)

2007a. *What "International Standardization" Means*, www.iso.org/iso/en/aboutiso/introduction/index.html (accessed January 19, 2007)

2007b. *Who is ISO?*, www.iso.org/iso/en/aboutiso/introduction/index.html (accessed 19, 2007)

ISO/IEC. 2004. *ISO/IEC Directives, Part 1: Procedures for the Technical Work*. 5th edn. Geneva: International Organization for Standardization and International Electrotechnical Commission

2007. *Using and Referencing ISO and IEC Standards for Technical Regulations*. Geneva: International Organization for Standardization and International Electrotechnical Commission

Jachtenfuchs, Markus. 2001. "The Governance Approach to European Integration." *Journal of Common Market Studies* 39(2): 245–64

Jacoby, Wade. 2004. *The Enlargement of the European Union and NATO: Ordering from the Menu in Central Europe*. Cambridge: Cambridge University Press

Jarausch, Konrad H. 1990. *The Unfree Professions: German Lawyers, Teachers, and Engineers, 1900–1950*. New York: Oxford University Press

Jensen, Michael C., and William H. Meckling. 1976. "Theory of the Firm: Managerial Behavior, Agency Costs and Ownership Structure." *Journal of Financial Economics* 3(4): 305–60

Joachim, Jutta. 2003. "Framing Issues and Seizing Opportunities: The UN, NGOs and Women's Human Rights." *International Studies Quarterly* 47(2): 247–74

2007. *Agenda Setting, the UN, and NGOs: Gender Violence and Reproductive Rights*. Washington, DC: Georgetown University Press

Joerges, Christian, and Juergen Neyer. 1997. "Transforming Strategic Interaction into Deliberative Problem-Solving: European Comitology in the Foodstuffs Sector." *Journal of European Public Policy* 4: 609–25

Johnson, Ailish. 2007. "EU Social Policy, or How High Up Do You Like Your Safety Net?" In *Making History: European Integration and Institutional Change at Fifty*, edited by Sophie Meunier and Kathleen R. McNamara. New York: Oxford University Press

Jolly, R. 1991. "Adjustment with a Human Face: A Unicef Record and Perspective on the 1980s." *World Development* 19(12): 1807–21

Jones, Adam. 2007. *Case Study: Military Impressment and Conscription*, www.gendercide.org/case_conscription.html

Jones, Bryan, and Frank Baumgartner. 2005. *The Politics of Attention: How Government Prioritizes Problems*. Chicago: University of Chicago Press

Jones, P. 1988. *International Policies for Third World Education: Unesco, Literacy and Development*. London and New York: Routledge

1992. *World Bank Financing of Education: Lending, Learning and Development*. London: Routledge

Jones, P. W., and D. Coleman. 2005. *The United Nations and Education: Multilateralism, and Globalisation*. New York: RoutledgeFalmer

Kahl, Inge, Isabelle Grunberg, and Marc Stern. 1999. *Global Public Goods: International Cooperation in the 21st Century*. New York: Oxford University Press

Kahn, Mohsin S., and Suni Sharma. 2003. "IMF Conditionality and Country Ownership of Adjustment Programs." *World Bank Research Observer* 18(2): 227–48

Kaldor, Mary. 1999. *New and Old Wars: Organized Violence in a Global Era*. Oxford: Polity Press

Kaplan, Robert. 1994. "The Coming Anarchy." *The Atlantic Monthly* 273(2): 44–76

Karl, Terry Lynn. 1997. *The Paradox of Plenty: Oil Booms and Petro-States*. Los Angeles and San Francisco: University of California Press

Katz, Michael L., and Carl Shapiro. 1985. "Network Externalities, Competition, and Compatibility." *American Economic Review* 75(3): 424–40

Kaul, Inge, and Katell le Goulven, eds. 1999. *Global Public Goods: International Cooperation in the 21st Century*. New York, Oxford University Press

Keck, Margaret, and Katherine Sikkink. 1998. *Activists beyond Borders*. Ithaca, NY: Cornell University Press

Keen, David. 1998. *The Economic Functions of Violence in Civil Wars*. Adelphi Papers 320. Oxford: Oxford University Press for the International Institute of Strategic Studies

Kennelly, Arthur E. 1933. "Conference of the Symbols, Units and Nomenclature (SUN) Commission of the International Union of Pure and Applied Physics (IPU) in Paris in July, 1932 and its Results." *Proceedings of the National Academy of Sciences of the United States of America* 19(1): 144–9

Keohane, Robert O. 1984. *After Hegemony*. Princeton: Princeton University Press

———. 2003. "Global Governance and Democratic Accountability." In *Taming Globalization: Frontiers of Governance*, edited by David Held and Mathias Koenig-Archibugi. London: Polity Press

Keohane, Robert, and Joseph Nye. 1974. "Transgovernmental Relations and International Organizations." *World Politics* 27(October): 39–62

———. 2001. "Between Centralization and Fragmentation: The Club Model of Multilateral Cooperation and Problems of Democratic Legitimacy." KSG Working Paper No. 01–004 (February), http://papers.ssrn.com/sol3/papers.cfm?abstract_id=262175 (accessed October 21, 2008)

Keohane, Robert O., Andrew Moravcsik, and Anne-Marie Slaughter. 2000. "Legalized Dispute Resolution: Interstate and Transnational." *International Organization* 54(3): 457–88

Khagram, Sanjeev, James Riker, and Kathryn Sikkink, eds. 2002. *Restructuring World Politics: Transnational Social Movements, Networks and Norms*. Minneapolis: University of Minnesota Press

Kiewiet, D. Roderick, and Mathew D. McCubbins. 1991. *The Logic of Delegation: Congressional Parties and the Appropriations Process*. Chicago: University of Chicago Press

Killick, Tony. 1997. "Principals, Agents and the Failings of Conditionality." *Journal of International Development* 9(4): 483–95

Kindleberger, Charles P. 1983. "Standards as Public, Collective and Private Goods." *Kyklos* 36(3): 377–96

King, K. 1991. *Aid and Education in the Developing World: The Role of Donor Agencies in Educational Analysis*. Chelmsford: Longman

King, Kimi, James Meernik, and Geoff Dancy. 2005. "Judicial Decision Making and International Tribunals: Assessing the Impact of Individual, National and International Factors." *Social Science Quarterly* 86: 683–703

Kingdon, John W. 1995. *Agendas, Alternatives, and Public Policies*. 2nd edn. New York: HarperCollins

Kingsbury, Benedict, Nico Krisch, Richard B. Stewart, and Jonathan B. Wiener. 2005. "Forward: Global Governance as Administration – National and Transnational Approaches to Global Administrative Law." *Law and Contemporary Problems* 68: 1–14

Klein, Bradley. 1988. "Vertical Integration as Organizational Ownership: The Fisher Body–General Motors Relationship Revisited." *Journal of Law, Economics and Organization* 4(1): 199–213

Kolk, A. 2000. *The Economics of Environmental Management*. London: Prentice Hall/Financial Times

Kollman, K., and A. Prakash. 2001. "Green by Choice? Cross-National Variations in Firms' Responses to EMS-based Environmental Regimes." *World Politics* 53: 399–430

Koremenos, Barbara. 2001. "Loosening the Ties that Bind: A Learning Model of Flexibility." *International Organization* 55(2): 289–325

Kotchen, M., and Klaas van 't Veld. 2009. "An Economics Perspective on Treating Voluntary Programs as Clubs." In *Voluntary Programs: A Club Theory Perspective*, edited by Matthew Potoski and Aseem Prakash. Cambridge, MA: MIT Press

Krasner, Stephen. 1978. *Defending the National Interest: Raw Materials Investments and US Foreign Policy*. Princeton: Princeton University Press

1983. *International Regimes*. Ithaca, NY: Cornell University Press

1991. "Global Communications and National Power: Life on the Pareto Frontier." *World Politics* 43(3): 336–66

1999. *Sovereignty: Organized Hypocrisy*. Princeton: Princeton University Press

Lake, David. 2006. "Relational Authority in the Modern World: Toward a Positive Theory of Legitimacy." Paper prepared for the workshop on Legitimacy in the Modern World, University of California, San Diego, December 8–9, 2006

2007. "Escape from the State of Nature: Anarchy and Hierarchy in World Politics." *International Security* 32(1): 47–79

Lake, David, and Wendy Wong. 2005. "The Politics of Networks: Interests, Power and Human Rights Norms." Working paper, University of California San Diego

Langer, Maximo. 2005. "The Rise of Managerial Judging in International Criminal Law." *American Journal of Comparative Law* 53: 835–909

LaPierre, Wayne. 2006a. *The Global War on Your Guns: Inside the UN Plan to Destroy the Bill of Rights*. Nashville, TN: NelsonCurrent

2006b. "The Peters Principle." *America's 1st Freedom* (February): 32–7

La Porta, Rafael Florencio Lopez-de-Silanes, Andrei Shleifer, and R. Vishny. 1999. "The Quality of Government." *Journal of Law, Economics and Organization* 15(March): 222–79

Lebovic, James, and Erik Voeten. 2006. "The Politics of Shame: The Condemnation of Country Human Rights Practices in the UNCHR." *International Studies Quarterly* 50(4): 861–88

Lewis, George, and Jonathan Lewis. 1980. "The Dog in the Night-Time: Negative Evidence in Social Research." *British Journal of Sociology* 31: 544–58

Lipschutz, Ronnie. 2005. "Global Civil Society and Global Governmentality." In *Power in Global Governance*, edited by Michael Barnett and Raymond Duvall. Cambridge: Cambridge University Press

Lipson, Michael. 2007. "Peacekeeping: Organized Hypocrisy?" *European Journal of International Relations* 13(1): 5–34

Lischer, Sarah Kenyon. 2005. *Dangerous Sanctuaries: Refugee Camps, Civil Wars and the Dilemmas of Humanitarian Aid*. Ithaca, NY: Cornell University Press

Litvin, Daniel. 2003. *Empires of Profit: Commerce, Conquest, and Corporate Responsibility*. New York and London: Texere

Loevinsohn, Benjamin. 2000. *Contracting for the Delivery of Primary Healthcare in Cambodia*. Washington, DC: World Bank

Loveman, Mara. 2005. "The Modern State and the Primitive Accumulation of Symbolic Power." *American Journal of Sociology* 110(6): 1651–83

Lowi, Theodore J. 1964. "American Business, Public Policy, Case-Studies, and Political Theory." *World Politics* 16(4): 677–93

Loya, Thomas, and John Boli. 1999. "Standardization in the World Polity: Technical Rationality over Power." In *Constructing World Culture*, edited by John Boli and George Thomas. Stanford, CA: Stanford University Press

Lustick, Ian S. 2006. *Trapped in the War on Terror*. Philadelphia: University of Pennsylvania Press

Lutz, Ellen, and Kathryn Sikkink. 2001. "The Justice Cascade: The Evolution and Impact of Foreign Human Rights Trials in Latin America." *Chicago Journal of International Law* 2(1): 1–34

Maas, Willem. 2007. "The Evolution of EU Citizenship." In *Making History: European Integration and Institutional Change at Fifty*, edited by Sophie Meunier and Kathleen R. McNamara. New York: Oxford University Press

McAdam, Doug. 1999. *Political Process and the Development of Black Insurgency, 1930–1970*, 2nd edn. Chicago: University of Chicago Press

McAdam, Doug, Sidney Tarrow, and Charles Tilly, eds. 2001. *Dynamics of Contention*. Cambridge: Cambridge University Press

McCubbins, M., and T. Schwartz. 1984. "Congressional Oversight Overlooked: Police Patrols versus Fire Alarms." *American Journal of Political Science* 28(1): 165–79

    1987. "Congressional Oversight Overlooked: Police Patrols and Fire Alarms." In *Congress: Structure and Policy*, edited by M. McCubbins and T. Sullivan. New York: Cambridge University Press

McNamara, Kathleen R. 1998. *The Currency of Ideas: Monetary Politics in the European Union*. Ithaca, NY: Cornell University Press

McNamara, Kathleen R., and Sophie Meunier. 2002. "Between National Sovereignty and International Power: The External Voice of the Euro." *International Affairs* 78(4): 849–68

McNichol, Tom. 2006. *AC/DC: The Savage Tale of the First Standards War*. San Francisco: Jossey-Bass

Macrae, Joanna. 2002a. "The 'Bilateralisation' of Humanitarian Response: Trends in the Financial, Contractual and Managerial Environment of Official Humanitarian Aid." Background paper for UNHCR. London: Humanitarian Policy Group, Overseas Development Institute

    2002b. *The New Humanitarianisms: A Review of Actions and Trends in Global Humanitarian Action*. HPG Report No. 11. London: Humanitarian Policy Group, Overseas Development Institute

Mahoney, James, and Gary Goertz. 2004. "The Possibility Principle." *American Political Science Review* 98: 653–69

Majone, Giandomenico. 2001. "Two Logics of Delegation: Agency and Fiduciary Relations in EU Governance." *European Union Politics* 2: 103–22

Malaluan, Jenina Joy Chavez, and Shalmali Guttal. 2002. *Structural Adjustment in the Name of the Poor: The PRSP Experience in Lao PDR, Cambodia and Vietnam: Focus on the Global South*

Malhotra, Deepak, and J. Keith Murnighan. 2002. "The Effects of Contracts on Interpersonal Trust." *Administrative Science Quarterly* 47(3): 534–59

Manners, Ian. 2002. "Normative Power Europe: A Contradiction in Terms?"*Journal of Common Market Studies* 40(2): 234–58

Marceau, Gabrielle, and Joel P. Trachtman. 2002. "TBT, SPS, and GATT: A Map of the WTO Law of Domestic Regulation." *Journal of World Trade* 36(5): 811–81

March, James G., and Johan P. Olsen. 1989. *Rediscovering Institutions*. New York: The Free Press

1998. "The Institutional Dynamics of International Political Orders." *International Organization* 52(4): 943–69

Marks, Gary. 1993. "Structural Policy and Multilevel Governance in the EC." In *The State of the European Community, Vol. II: The Maastrict Debates and Beyond*, edited by Alan W. Cafruny and Glenda G. Rosenthal. Boulder, CO: Lynne Rienner

Martens, Bertin. 2002. "Introduction." In *The Institutional Economics of Foreign Aid*, edited by B. Martens, U. Mummert, P. Murrell, and P. Seabright. New York: Cambridge University Press

Maskus, Keith E., Tsunehiro Otsuki, and John S. Wilson. 2005. *The Cost of Compliance with Product Standards for Firms in Developing Countries: An Econometric Study*. World Bank Policy Research Paper 3590 (May)

Mathews, Jessica Tuchman. 1989. "Redefining Security." *Foreign Affairs* 68(2): 162–77

1997. "Power Shift." *Foreign Affairs* 76(1): 50–66

Mattli, Walter, and Tim Büthe. 2003. "Setting International Standards: Technological Rationality or Primacy of Power?" *World Politics* 56: 1–42

Maxwell, S. 2005. *The Washington Consensus is Dead: Long Live the Meta-Narrative*. Working paper 243. London: Overseas Development Institute

May, Christopher, ed. 2006. "Global Corporate Power." In *International Political Economy Yearbook*, edited by C. May and N. Phillips. Boulder, CO: Lynne Rienner

Meidinger, Errol, Chris Elliott, and Gerhard Oesten, eds. 2003. *Social and Political Dimensions of Forest Certification*. Remagen-Oberwinter: Forstbuch Verlag

Merry, Sally Engle. 2006. *Human Rights and Gender Violence: Translating International Law into Local Justice*. Chicago: University of Chicago Press

Meunier, Sophie. 2005. *Trading Voices: The European Union in International Commercial Negotiations*. Princeton: Princeton University Press

Meunier, Sophie, and Kathleen R. McNamara, eds. 2007. *Making History: European Integration and Institutional Change at Fifty*. New York: Oxford University Press

Meunier, Sophie, and Kalypso Nicolaïdis. 2006. "The European Union as a Conflicted Trade Power." *Journal of European Public Policy* 13(6): 906–25

Meyer, David S., and Suzanne Staggenborg. 1996. "Movements, Countermovements, and the Structure of Political Opportunity." *American Journal of Sociology* 101: 1628–60

Meyer, David S., and N. Whittier. 1994. "Social Movement Spillover." *Social Problems* 41: 277–98

Meyer, J., B. Boli, G. Thomas, and F. Ramirez. 1997. "World Society and the Nation-State". *American Journal of Sociology* 103(1): 144–81

Meyer, John W. 1980. "The World Polity and the Authority of the Nation-State." In *Studies of the Modern World-System*, edited by Albert Bergesen. New York: Academic Press

Michels, Robert. 1966. *Political Parties*. New York: Free Press

Miller, Christian T. 2006. *Blood Money: Wasted Billions, Lost Lives and Corporate Greed in Iraq*. New York: Little, Brown

Miller-Grandvaux, Y., M. Welmond, and J. Wolfe. 2002. *Evolving Partnerships: The Role of NGOs in Basic Education in Africa*. Washington, DC: USAID

Mills, Anne. 1998. "To Contract or Not to Contract? Issues for Low and Middle Income Countries." *Health Policy and Planning* 13(1): 32–40

Milner, Helen V. 1988. *Resisting Protectionism*. Princeton: Princeton University Press

—— 1998. "Rationalizing Politics: The Emerging Synthesis of International, American, and Comparative Politics." *International Organization* 52(4): 759–86

Moe, Terry. 1984. "The New Economics of Organization." *American Journal of Political Science* 28(4): 739–77

Moravcsik, Andrew. 2002. "Reassessing Legitimacy in the European Union." *Journal of Common Market Studies* 40(4): 603–24

Mouffe, Chantal. 2005. *On the Political*. New York: Routledge

Mueller, John. 2006. *Overblown: How Politicians and the Terrorism Industry Inflate National Security Threats, and Why We Believe Them.* New York: The Free Press

Mundy, Karen. 1998. "Educational Multilateralism and World (dis)Order." *Comparative Education Review* 42(4): 448–78

    1999. "UNESCO and the Limits of the Possible." *International Journal of Educational Development* 19(1): 27–52

    2002. "Education in a Reformed World Bank." *International Journal of Educational Development* 22(5): 483–508

    2006. "Education for All and the New Development Compact." *International Review of Education* 52(1): 23–48

Mundy, K., and L. Murphy. 2001. "Transnational Advocacy, Global Civil Society: Emerging Evidence from the Field of Education." *Comparative Education Review* 45(1): 85–126

    2002. "New Roles of INGOs in the Education for All Movement." Background Paper for the 2002 EFA Monitoring Report. Paris: UNESCO

Mundy, K., M. Haggerty, S. Cherry, R. Maclure, and M. Sivasubramaniam. 2007. "Basic Education, Civil Society Participation and the New Aid Architecture: Lessons from Burkina Faso, Kenya, Mali and Tanzania." Working Paper 07.3, HakiElimu Working Papers, Dar es Salaam, Tanzania

Murphy, Craig N., and JoAnne Yates. 2008. *The International Organization for Standardization (ISO): Global Governance through Voluntary Consensus.* London: Routledge

Murphy, J. 2005. "The World Bank, INGOs and Civil Society: Converging Agendas? The Case of Universal Basic Education in Uganda." *Voluntas: International Journal of Voluntary and Non-Profit Organizations* 16(4): 353–74

N. N. 1905. *Transactions of the International Electrical Congress, St. Louis, 1904.* Albany, NY: J. B. Lyon

Nadelmann, Ethan. 1990. "Global Prohibition Regimes: The Evolution of Norms in International Society." *International Organization* 44(4): 479–526

Najam, Adil, Mihaela Papa, and Nadaa Taiyab. 2006. *Global Environmental Governance: A Reform Agenda.* Winnipeg: International Institute for Sustainable Development

Nelson, J. 1999. "Reforming Health and Education: The World Bank, the IDB and Complex Institutional Change." Political Essay No. 26. Washington, DC: The Overseas Development Council

Nelson, Jane. 2000. *The Business of Peace: The Private Sector as a Partner in Conflict Prevention and Resolution.* London: Prince of Wales Business Leaders Forum

Newman, Abraham. 2008a. "Building Transnational Civil Liberties: Trans-governmental Entrepreneurs and the European Data Privacy Directive." *International Organization* 62(1): 103–30

2008b. *Protectors of Privacy: Regulating Personal Data in the Global Economy.* Ithaca, NY: Cornell University Press

Newman, Edward. 2004. "The 'New Wars' Debate: A Historical Perspective is Needed." *Security Dialogue* 35(2): 173–89

Nexon, Daniel, and Iver B. Neumann. 2006. "Introduction: Harry Potter and the Study of World Politics." In *Harry Potter and International Relations*, edited by Daniel Nexon and Iver B. Neumann. Lanham, MD: Rowman and Littlefield

Nielson, Daniel L., and Michael J. Tierney. 2003. "Delegation to International Organizations: Agency Theory and World Bank Environmental Reform." *International Organization* 57(2): 241–76

Noel, Alain. 2005. "The New Politics of Global Poverty," www.queensu.ca/sps/the_policy_forum/speakers_series/NPGPDec05.pdf (accessed April 25, 2006)

Nord, Philip. 1995. *The Republican Moment.* Cambridge, MA: Harvard University Press

NRA (National Rifle Association). 2007. "Freedom in Peril: Guarding the 2nd Amendment in the 21st Century," www.boingboing.net/images/NR-F8_PERILFINAL.pdf (accessed August 12, 2008)

NRA-ILA. 1997. "World Forum on the Future of Sportshooting Activities Established." *Fax Alert* 4: 28

Nunberg, Geoffrey. 2007. *Talking Right: How Conservatives Turned Liberalism into a Tax-Raising, Latte-Drinking, Sushi-Eating, Volvo-Driving, New York Times-Reading, Body-Piercing, Hollywood-Loving, Left-Wing Freak Show.* New York: PublicAffairs

OECD/DAC. 1974. *Annual Development Co-operation Report.* Paris: OECD

1996. *Shaping the 21st Century: The Contribution of Development Cooperation.* Paris: OECD

2003. *Rome Declaration on Harmonization,* www.aidharmonization.org/ah-overview/secondary-pages/why-RomeDeclaration (accessed April 25, 2006)

2005. *Paris Declaration on Aid Effectiveness,* www.aidharmonization.org/ah-overview/secondary-pages/editable?key=205 (accessed April 25, 2006)

Oestreich, Joel. 2007. *Power and Principle: Human Rights Programming in International Organizations.* Washington, DC: Georgetown University Press

O'Harrow, Robert, Jr. 2004. "Auditor Criticizes Iraq Contract Oversight: Halliburton Unit Failed to Justify Expenses, Memo Says." *Washington Post*, August 24: E1

Olson, M. 1965. *A Logic of Collective Action.* Cambridge, MA: Harvard University Press

O'Rourke, Kevin H., and Jeffrey G. Williamson. 1999. *Globalization and History.* Cambridge, MA: MIT Press

Ostrom, E. 1990. *Governing the Commons.* New York: Cambridge University Press

Ostrom, V., R. Warren, and C. Tiebout. 1961. "The Organization of Government in Metropolitan Areas: A Theoretical Inquiry." *American Political Science Review* 55: 831–42

Overseas Development Institute, and United Nations Development Programme. 2006. "Meeting the Challenge of the 'Resource Curse.'" London: Overseas Development Institute for the Business and Development Performance Program/UNDP

Oxfam International. 1999. *Education Now.* Oxford: Oxfam International
   2004. "From 'Donorship' to 'Ownership'? Moving Towards PRSP Round Two." In Oxfam Briefing Paper 51. Oxford: Oxford International

Oye, Kenneth, ed. 1986. *Cooperation under Anarchy.* Princeton: Princeton University Press

Packer, George. 2005. *The Assassins' Gate: America and Iraq.* New York: Farrar, Straus and Giroux

Paris, Roland. 2001. "Human Security: A Paradigm Shift or Hot Air?" *International Security* 26(2): 87–102

Park, Han Woo. 2003. "Hyperlink Network Analysis: A New Method for the Study of Social Structure on the Web." *Connections* 25(1): 49–61

Park, Han Woo, and Mike Thelwall. 2003. "Hyperlink Analyses of the World Wide Web: A Review." *Journal of Computer-Mediated Communications* 8(4); available online at www.ascusc.org/jcmc/vol8/issue4/park.html

Pauly, Lou, and Edgar Grande. 2007. *Complex Sovereignty: Reconstituting Political Authority in the Twenty First Century.* Toronto: University of Toronto Press

Peterson, John, and Michael Shackleton. 2006. *The Institutions of the European Union.* New York: Oxford University Press

Petroleum Economist. 1998. "Tapping into a New Frontier Oil Province." *Petroleum Economist* 65(10): 5–10

Phillips, H. M. 1987. *Unicef and Education: A Historical Perspective*. New York: Unicef

Pierson, Paul. 2004. *Politics in Time: History, Institutions, and Social Analysis*. Princeton: Princeton University Press

Pigou, A. C. 1960. *The Economics of Welfare*. 4th edn. London: Macmillan

Pincus, Jonathan, and Jeffrey A. Winters. 2002. *Reinventing the World Bank*. Ithaca, NY: Cornell University Press

Pollack, Mark A. 1997. "The Commission as Agent." In *At the Heart of the Union*, edited by N. Nugent. New York: St. Martin's Press

2002. "Control Mechanism or Deliberative Democracy? Two Images of Comitology." *Comparative Political Studies* 36(1): 125–55

2003. *The Engines of European Integration: Delegation, Agency, and Agenda Setting in the EU*. New York: Oxford University Press

Porch, Douglas. 2003. "Occupational Hazards: Myths of 1945 and US Iraq Policy." *The National Interest* 72: 35–45

Posner, Eric A., and Miguel de Figueiredo. 2005. "Is the International Court of Justice Biased?" *Journal of Legal Affairs* 34: 599–608

Posner, Eric A., and John C. Yoo. 2005. "Judicial Independence in International Tribunals." *California Law Review* 93: 37–74

Potoski, M., and A. Prakash. 2005a. "Covenants with Weak Swords: ISO 14001 and Firms' Environmental Performance." *Journal of Policy Analysis and Management* 24(4): 745–69

2005b. "Green Clubs and Voluntary Governance: ISO 14001 and Firms' Regulatory Compliance." *American Journal of Political Science*, 49(2): 235–48

Potter, Jonathan. 1996. *Representing Reality: Discourse, Rhetoric and Social Construction*. London: Sage

Prakash, Aseem, and Matthew Potoski. 2006a. "Racing to the Bottom? Globalization, Environmental Governance, and ISO 14001." *American Journal of Political Science* 50(2): 347–61

2006b. *The Voluntary Environmentalists: Green Clubs, ISO 14001, and Voluntary Environmental Regulation*. Cambridge: Cambridge University Press

2007. "Investing Up: FDI and the Cross-National Diffusion of ISO 14001." *International Studies Quarterly* 51(3): 723–44

Pratt, John W., and Richard J. Zeckhauser. 1987. *Principals and Agents: The Structure of Business*. Cambridge, MA: Harvard Business School Press

Preston, W., E. Herman, and H. Schiller. 1989. *Hope and Folly: The United States and Unesco, 1945–1985*. Minneapolis: University of Minnesota Press

Price, Richard. 1998. "Reversing the Gun Sights: Transnational Civil Society Targets Land Mines." *International Organization* 52(3): 613–44

   2003. "Transnational Civil Society and Advocacy in World Politics." *World Politics* 55: 579–606

Price, Richard, and Nina Tannenwald. 1996. "Norms and Deterrence: The Nuclear and Chemical Weapons Taboos." In *The Culture of National Security: Norms and Identity in World Politics*, edited by Peter J. Katzenstein. New York: Columbia University Press

Pritchett, Lant. 2004. "Towards a New Consensus for Addressing the Global Challenge of the Lack of Education." *Copenhagen Consensus Challenge Paper*. Copenhagen: Copenhagen Consensus

Putnam, Robert. 1988, "Diplomacy and Domestic Politics: The Logic of Two-level Games." *International Organization* 42: 427–60

   1994. *Making Democracy Work: Civic Traditions in Modern Italy*. Princeton: Princeton University Press

Raeburn, Anthony. 2006a. *Development and Growth of IEC Technical Committees: 1950 to 2006*, www.iec.ch/about/history/overview/overview_1950–2006.htm (accessed August 10, 2008)

   2006b. *IEC Technical Committee Creation: The First Half-Century (1906–1949)*, www.iec.ch/about/history/overview/overview_1906-1949.htm (accessed August 10, 2008)

Rajan, Raghuram G., and Arvind Subramanian. 2005. "Aid and Growth: What Does the Cross-Country Evidence Really Show?" IMF Working Paper WP/05/127, Washington, DC

Ramasastry, Anita. 2002. "Corporate Complicity: From Nuremberg to Rangoon: An Examination of Forced Labor Cases and their Impact on the Liability of Multinational Corporations." *Berkeley Journal of International Law* 20(1): 91–159

Ramirez, F. O., and J. Boli. 1987. "Global Patterns of Educational Institutionalization." In *Institutional Structure: Constituting the State, Society and the Individual*, edited by G. M. Thomas, J. W. Meyer, F. O. Ramirez, and J. Boli. Beverly Hills, CA: Sage

Ramos, Howard. 2005. "Setting the Human Security Agenda: News Media Coverage of International Human Rights." Working paper, Canadian Consortium on Human Security, British Columbia

Raustiala, Kal. 1997. "States, NGOs and International Environmental Institutions." *International Organization* 41: 719–40

   2002. "The Architecture of International Cooperation: Transgovernmental Networks and the Future of International Law." *Virginia Journal of International Law* 43(Fall): 1–92

Raz, Joseph, ed. 1990. *Authority*. New York: New York University Press

Reinicke, Wolfgang, Thorsten Benner, and Jan Martin Witte. 2003. "Innovating Global Governance through Global Public Policy Networks: Lessons Learned and Challenges Ahead." *Brookings Review* 1

Resnik, J. 2006. "International Organizations, the 'Education/Economic Growth' Black Box, and the Development of World Education Culture." *Comparative Education Review* 50: 173–95

Reus-Smit, Christian, ed. 2005. *The Politics of International Law*. Cambridge: Cambridge University Press

Riddell, A. 2000. "Implications for Agencies of Pursuing Sector Wide Approaches in Education." Unpublished paper

Rieff, David. 1996. *Slaughterhouse: Bosnia and the Failure of the West*. New York: Touchstone

Risse, Thomas. 1994. "Ideas do not Float Freely: Transnational Coalitions, Domestic Structure, and the End of the Cold War." *International Organization* 48(2): 185–214

2000. "'Let's Argue!' Communicative Action in World Politics." *International Organization* 54(1): 1–39

2003. "The Euro between National and European Identity." *Journal of European Public Policy* 10(4): 487–503

Risse, Thomas, Maria Green Cowles, and James Caporaso, eds. 2001. *Transforming Europe*. Ithaca, NY: Cornell University Press

Risse-Kappan, Thomas. 1995. *Bringing Transnational Actors Back In*. Cambridge: Cambridge University Press

Rochefort, David, and Roger Cobb, eds. 1994. *The Politics of Problem Definition: Shaping the Policy Agenda*. Lawrence: University of Kansas Press

Rodgers, Daniel T. 1998. *Atlantic Crossings*. Cambridge, MA: Belknap Press of Harvard University Press

Rogers, Richard, and N. Marres. 2000. "Landscaping Climate Change: A Mapping Technique for Understanding Science and Technology Debates on the World Wide Web." *Public Understanding of Science*, 9: 141–63

Ron, James, Howard Ramos, and Kathleen Rodgers. 2005. "Transnational Information Politics: NGO Human Rights Reporting, 1986–2000." *International Studies Quarterly* 49: 557–87

Rose, P. 2003. *The Education Fast Track Initiative*. Report prepared for ActionAid on behalf of the Global Campaign for Education. London: ActionAid

Rosenau, James N., and Ernst-Otto Czempiel. 1992. *Governance without Government: Order and Change in World Politics*. Cambridge: Cambridge University Press

Ross, Michael. 2003. "Oil, Drugs and Diamonds: How do Natural Resources Vary in their Impact on Civil War?" In *Beyond Greed and Grievance: The Political Economy of Armed Conflict*, edited by Karen Ballentine and Jake Sherman Boulder, CO: Lynne Rienner

2004. "What Do We Know about Natural Resources and Civil War?" *Journal of Peace Research* 41(3): 337–56

Ross, Michael L. 1999. "The Political Economy of the Resource Curse." *World Politics* 51(2): 297–323

Rubin, Alissa, and Andrew Kramer. 2007. "Iraqi Premier Says Blackwater Shootings Challenge his Nation's Sovereignty." *New York Times* September 24

Rudolph, Christopher. 2003. "Constructing an Atrocities Regime: The Politics of War Crimes Tribunals." *International Organization* 55(3): 655–91

Ruggie, John. 1993. "Territoriality and Beyond: Problematizing Modernity in International Relations." *International Organization* 47(1): 139–74

1998. *Constructing the World Polity* London: Routledge

2003. "The United Nations and Globalization: Patterns and Limits of Institutional Adaptation." *Global Governance* 9: 301–21

2004. "Reconstituting the Global Public Domain: Issues, Actors and Practices." *European Journal of International Relations* 10(4): 499–531

Ruppert, Louis. 1956. *Brief History of the International Electrotechnical Commission*. Geneva: Bureau Central de la Commission Electrotechnique Internationale

Russo, Michael V. 2001. "Institutional Change and Theories of Organizational Strategy: ISO 14001 and Toxic Emissions in the Electronic Industry," http://lcb1.uoregon.edu/mrusso/ISOstudy.htm (accessed July 11, 2004)

Rysman, Marc, and Timothy S. Simcoe. 2007. "Patents and the Performance of Voluntary Standard Setting Organizations." Manuscript, Boston University and University of Toronto, June

Sabel, Charles, and Jonathan Zeitlin. 2007. "Learning from Difference: The New Architecture of Experimentalist Governance in the European Union." EUROGOV Papers

Sachs, Jeffrey. 1994. "Life in the Economic Emergency Room." In *The Political Economy of Policy Reform*, edited by J. Williamson. Washington, DC: Institute for International Economics

Sack, R. 1986. "Unesco: From Inherent Contradictions to Open Crisis." *Comparative Education Review* 30(1): 112–19

Sahn, David E., and David C. Stifel. 2003. "Progress Toward the Millennium Development Goals in Africa." *World Development* 31(1): 23–52

Samoff, J. 1996. "Which Priorities and Strategies for Education?" *International Journal of Educational Development* 16(3): 249–71

    2001. "The Evolution of Education Aid to Africa: Changing Terminology, Persisting Practice." Paper presented at the Annual Meeting of Comparative and International Education Society (CIES), Washington, DC

    2004. "From Funding Projects to Supporting Sector?" *International Journal of Educational Development* 24(4): 397–427

Samuelson, P. A. 1954. "A Pure Theory of Public Expenditure." *Review of Economics and Statistics* 36: 387–9

Sandler, Todd, and Keith Hartley. 1999. *The Political Economy of NATO.* Cambridge: Cambridge University Press

Sayre, D. 1996. *Inside ISO 14000.* Delray Beach, FL: St. Lucie Press

Schabas, William. 2001. *Introduction to the International Criminal Court.* Cambridge: Cambridge University Press

Schattschneider, E. E. 1960. *The Semisovereign People: A Realist's View of Democracy in America.* Hinsdale, IL: Dryden Press

Schmitt, Carl. 1996. *The Concept of the Political.* Chicago: University of Chicago Press

Schmitz, Hans. 2004. "Impaired Vision: Constructing Protections against Genocide." Paper presented at the Annual Meeting of the International Sudies Association, Montreal, Canada, March 18.

Schmitz, Patrick W. 2001. "The Hold-Up Problem and Incomplete Contracts: A Survey of Recent Topics in Contract Theory." *Bulletin of Economic Research* 53(1): 1–17

Scholte, J. A. 2005. "Civil Society and Democratically Accountable Global Governance." In *Global Governance and Public Accountability*, edited by D. Held and M. Koenig-Archibugi. Malden, MA: Blackwell

Schwartz, John. 2003. "German and US Telecommunications Privacy Law: Legal Regulation of Domestic Law Enforcement Surveillance." *Hastings Law Journal* 54(April): 751

Sciulli, David. 2005. "Continental Sociology of Professions Today: Conceptual Contributions." *Current Sociology* 53(6): 915–42

Scott, James. 1998. *Seeing Like a State: How Certain Schemes to Improve the Human Condition have Failed.* New Haven: Yale University Press

Searle, John. 1995. *The Construction of Social Reality.* New York: The Free Press

Sell, Susan, and Aseem Prakash. 2004. "Using Ideas Strategically: The Contest between Business and NGO Networks in Intellectual Property." *International Studies Quarterly* 48: 143–75

Sen, Amartya. 2000. *Development as Freedom.* New York: Anchor Books

Sewell, J. P. 1975. *Unesco and World Politics*. Princeton: Princeton University Press

Shapiro, Martin, and Alec Stone. 1994. "The New Constitutional Politics of Europe." Special issue of *Comparative Political Studies* 26(4): 397–420

Sharma, Shalendra D. 2004. "The Promise of Monterrey: Meeting the Millennium Development Goals." *World Policy Journal* 21(3): 51–67

Shipan, Charles. 2004. "Regulatory Regimes, Agency Actions, and the Conditional Nature of Congressional Influence." *American Political Science Review* 98(3): 467–80

Shore, Cris. 2000. *Building Europe: The Cultural Politics of European Integration*. London: Routledge

Simcoe, Timothy S. 2006. "Standard Setting Committees." Manuscript, University of Toronto

Simmons, Beth, Frank Dobbin, and Geoffrey Garret. 2006. "Introduction: The International Diffusion of Liberalism." *International Organization* 60(4): 781–810

Simmons, P. J. 1998. "Learning to Live with NGOs." *Foreign Policy* 112: 82–96

Simon, Herbert A. 1947. *Administrative Behavior*. New York: Macmillan

Singer, J. David. 1987. "Reconstructing the Correlates of War Dataset on Material Capabilities of States, 1816–1985." *International Interactions* 14: 115–32

Singer, J. David, Stuart Bremer, and John Stuckey. 1972. "Capability Distribution, Uncertainty, and Major Power War, 1820–1965." In *Peace, War, and Numbers*, edited by Bruce Russett. Beverly Hills: Sage, 19–48

Singer, Peter. 2003. *Corporate Warriors: The Rise of the Privatized Military Industry*. Ithaca, NY: Cornell University Press

Skowronek, Stephen. 1982. *Building a New American State: The Expansion of National Administrative Capacities, 1877–1920*. Cambridge: Cambridge University Press

Slaughter, Anne-Marie. 2000. "Governing the Global Economy through Government Networks." In *The Role of Law in International Politics: Essays in International Relations and International Law*, edited by M. Byers. Oxford: Oxford University Press

    2001. "Agencies on the Loose? Holding Government Networks Accountable." In *Transatlantic Regulatory Cooperation*, edited by G. Bermann, M. Herdegen, and P. Lindseth. Oxford: Oxford University Press

    2004. *A New World Order*. Princeton: Princeton University Press

Slim, Hugo. 2002. "By What Authority? The Legitimacy and Authority of Non-governmental Organizations." *Journal of Humanitarian Assistance*, available at www.jha.ac/articles/a082.htm

Smillie, Ian, and Larry Minear. 2003. "The Quality of Money: Donor Behavior in Humanitarian Financing." Paper prepared for Humanitarianism and War Project, Tufts University

Smillie, Ian, and Goran Todorovic. 2001. "Reconstructing Bosnia, Constructing Civil Society." In *Patronage or Partnership: Local Capacity Building in Humanitarian Crises*, edited by Ian Smillie. Bloomfield, CT: Kumarian

Smillie, Ian, Lansana Gberie, and Ralph Hazleton. 2000. *The Heart of the Matter: Sierra Leone, Diamonds, and Human Security*. Ottawa: Partnership Africa Canada

Smith, Blaine. 2007. "John Howard, What Did You Give Australians for their $500,000,000? Zilch." *America's 1st Freedom* 8(2): 34

Smith, Michael E. 2003. *Europe's Foreign and Security Policy: The Institutionalization of Cooperation*. Cambridge: Cambridge University Press

Snow, David A., and Robert D. Benford. 1992. "Master Frames and Cycles of Protest." In *Frontiers in Social Movement Theory*, edited by Aldon D. Morris and Carol McClurg Mueller. New Haven: Yale University Press

Snyder, Anna. 2003. *Setting the Agenda for Global Peace: Conflict and Consensus Building*. Burlington, VT: Ashgate

Snyder, Jack, and Leslie Vinjamuri. 2003. "Trials and Errors: Principle and Pragmatism in Strategies of International Justice." *International Security* 28(3): 5–44

Soroka, Stuart. 1999. "Policy Agenda-Setting Theory Revisited: A Critique of Howlett on Downs, Baumgartner and Jones, and Kingdon." *Canadian Journal of Political Science / Revue canadienne de science politique* 32(4): 763–72

Sowell, Thomas. 2007. *A Conflict of Visions: Ideological Origins of Political Struggles*. New York: Basic Books

Spar, Debora. 1998. "The Spotlight and the Bottom Line." *Foreign Affairs* 77(2): 7–12

Sperling, G. 2001a. "The Developing World's Quiet Crisis." *The Financial Times* July 17: 15

   2001b. "Toward Universal Education: Making a Promise and Keeping It." *Foreign Affairs* 80(5): 7–13

Spiegel Online. 2005. "'For God's Sake, Please Stop the Aid!'" interview with James Shikwati, director of Kenya's Inter Region Economic Network, July 4, www.spiegel.de/international/spiegel/0,1518,363663,00.html

Spruyt, Hendrik. 1994. *The Sovereign State and its Competitors*. Princeton: Princeton University Press

2001. "The Supply and Demand of Governance in Standard-Setting: Insights from the Past." *Journal of European Public Policy* 8(3): 371–91

Statewatch. 2003. "Massive Majority in European Parliament against Deal with US on Access to Passenger Data." March 12. Available at www.statewatch.org/news/2003/mar/12epvote.htm

Steinberg, Richard H. 2002. "In the Shadow of Law or Power? Consensus-Based Bargaining and Outcomes in the GATT/WTO." *International Organization* 56(2): 339–74

2004. "Judicial Lawmaking at the WTO: Discursive, Constitutional, and Political Constraints." *The American Journal of International Law* 98(2): 247–75

Stephan, Paul B. 2002. "Exploring the Need for International Harmonization: Courts, Tribunals, and Legal Unification – The Agency Problem." *Chicago Journal of International Law* 3: 333–52

Stephenson, Max. 2005. "Making Humanitarian Relief Networks More Effective: Operational Coordination Trust and Sense Making." *Disasters* 29(4): 337–50

Stiglitz, J. 2003. *Globalization and its Discontents.* New York: W. W. Norton

Stirrat, Jock. 2006. "Competitive Humanitarianism: Relief and the Tsunami in Sri Lanka." *Anthropology Today* 22(5): 11–16

Stockton, Nicholas. 2005. "Preventing Corruption in Humanitarian Relief Operations." Paper presented to the ADB/OECD Anti-Corruption Initiative for Asia and the Pacific, September 28–30, Beijing

Stopford, John M., Susan Strange, and John S. Henley. 1991. *Rival States, Rival Firms: Competition for World Market Shares.* New York: Cambridge University Press

Suchman, Mark C. 1995. "Managing Legitimacy: Strategic and Institutional Approaches." *Academy of Management Review* 20: 571–610

Sugden, Robert. 1989. "Spontaneous Order." *Journal of Economic Perspective* 3(4): 85–97

Sumra, S. 2005. *CEF Global Midterm Review: Tanzania Programme Report* (electronic version). Commonwealth Education Fund

Svensson, Jakob. 2000. "When is Foreign Aid Policy Credible? Aid Dependence and Conditionality." *Journal of Development Economics* 61(1): 61–84

Talberg, Jonas. 2002. "Delegation to Supranational Institutions: Why, How and with What Consequences?" *West European Politics* 25(1): 23–46

Tarrow, Sidney. 2002. "The New Transnational Contention: Organizations, Coalitions, Mechanisms." Paper presented at the annual meeting of the American Political Science Association, Boston, MA, August 28

2005. "The New Transnational Activism." In *Cambridge Studies in Contentious Politics*, edited by J. A. Goldstone, D. McAdam, S. Tarrow, C. Tilly, and E. J. Wood. Cambridge: Cambridge University Press

Tate, Jay. 2001. "National Varieties of Standardization." In *Varieties of Capitalism: The Institutional Foundations of Comparative Advantage*, edited by Peter A. Hall and David Soskice. New York: Oxford University Press

Taubes, Gary. 2007. *Good Calories, Bad Calories: Challenging the Conventional Wisdom on Diet, Weight Control, and Disease.* New York: Knopf

TEN/MET. 2006. *Strengthening Education in Tanzania: CSO Contributions to the Education Sector Review 2006.* Dar es Salaam: TEN/MET

Terris, Daniel, Cesare Romano, and Leigh Swigart. 2007. *The International Judge: An Introduction to the Men and Women who Decide the World's Cases.* Waltham, MA: Brandeis University Press

Thelen, Kathleen. 1999. "Historical Institutionalism in Comparative Politics." *Annual Review of Political Science* 2(1): 369–404

Thelwall, Mike. 2004. "Interpreting Social Science Link Analysis Research: A Theoretical Framework." *Journal of the American Society for Information Science and Technology*, www.scit.wlv.ac.uk/~cm1993/papers/Interpreting_SSLAR.pdf

Therien, J. P. 2002. "Multilateral Institutions and the Poverty Debate." *International Journal* 57(2): 233–52

2005. "The Politics of International Development: Towards a New Grand Compromise?" *Economic Policy and Law: Journal of Trade and Environmental Studies Special Issue*, www.ecolomics-international.org (accessed March 15, 2005)

Therien, J. P., and C. Lloyd. 2000. "Development Assistance on the Brink." *Third World Quarterly* 21(1): 21–38

Thompson, Ginger, and Eric Schmitt. 2007. "Graft in Military Contracts Spread from Base." *New York Times* September 24

Thompson, Karen Brown. 2002. "Women's Rights are Human Rights." In *Restructuring World Politics*, edited by Sanjeev Khagram, James Riker, and Kathryn Sikkink. Minneapolis: University of Minnesota Press

Thurner, Paul, Michael Stoiber, and Cornelia Weinmann. 2005. "Informelle transgouvernementale Koordinationsnetzwerke der Ministerialburokratie der EU-Mitgliedstaaten bei einer Regierungskonferenz." *Politische Vierteljahresschrift* 46(4): 552–74

Tiebout, C. 1956. "A Pure Theory of Local Expenditure." *Journal of Political Economy*, 64 (October): 416–24

Tirole, Jean. 1994. "The Internal Organisation of Government." *Oxford Economic Papers* 46(1): 1–29

Torpey, John. 2000. *The Invention of the Passport: Surveillance, Citizenship, and the State.* Cambridge: Cambridge University Press

Torres, R. M. 2000. *One Decade of Education for All: The Challenge Ahead.* Buenos Aires: International Institute for Educational Planning (IIEP)

Trachtman, Joel P. 1999. "The Domain of WTO Dispute Resolution." *Harvard International Law Journal* 40: 333–77

Trapp, Wolfgang, and Heinz Wallerus. 2006. *Handbuch der Maße, Zahlen, Gewichte und der Zeitrechnung.* 5. durchgesehene und erweiterte Auflage. Stuttgart: Philipp Reclam junior

Trondal, Jarle, and Frode Veggeland. 2003. "Access, Voice and Loyalty: The Representation of Domestic Civil Servants in EU Committees." *Journal of European Public Policy* 10(1): 59–77

Turner, Jenia. 2007. "Transnational Networks and International Criminal Justice." *Michigan Law Review* 105: 986–1032

UNESCO. 1945. *UNESCO Constitution*, adopted November 16, 1945, www.icomos.org/unesco/unesco_constitution.html (accessed March 14, 2008)

   1997. *50 Years for Education.* Paris: UNESCO

   2004. *EFA Global Monitoring Report 2003/4: Gender and Education for All: The Leap to Equality.* Paris: UNESCO

   2005. *EFA Global Monitoring Report 2005: The Quality Imperative.* Paris: UNESCO

   2006a. *EFA Global Monitoring Report 2006.* Paris: UNESCO

   2006b. *EFA Global Monitoring Report 2007: Strong Foundations, Early Childhood Care and Education.* Paris: UNESCO

UNICEF. 2006. "Children Born of Sexual Violence in Conflict Zones: Considerations for UNICEF Response." Outcome document of a meeting held November 23, 2005. On file with author

United Nations (UN). 1945. *Charter of the United Nations*, www.un.org/aboutun/charter (accessed June 5, 2008)

   1948. *Universal Declaration of Human Rights*, at http://www.un.org/Overview/rights.html (accessed March 14, 2008)

   2001. *Programme of Action to Prevent, Combat and Eradicate the Illicit Trade in Small Arms and Light Weapons in All its Aspects.* UN Doc. A/CONF.192, http://disarmament.un.org/cab/poa.html (accessed August 12, 2008)

   2005. *The Millennium Development Goals Report 2005.* New York: United Nations

   2006a. *The Millennium Development Goals Report 2006.* New York: United Nations

2006b. "Setting the Record Straight: The UN and Small Arms." Press release, www.un.org/events/smallarms2006/pdf/SettingRecord-Straight.pdf (accessed August 12, 2008)

United Nations Foundation. n.d. *Understanding Public–Private Partner-ships.* Washington, DC: United Nations Foundation

United Nations General Assembly. 2000. *United Nations Millennium Dec-laration.* UN Resolution A/RES/55/3. New York: United Nations

United Nations Global Compact. 2002. "Dialogue on Business in Zones of Conflict: Rapporteur's Report." New York: United Nations

United Nations Millennium Project. 2004. "Interim Report on Achieving the Millennium Development Goal of Universal Primary Education." Report of the Millennium Development Project, www.unmillenni-umproject.org (accessed September 10, 2004)

2005. "Toward Universal Primary Education: Investments, Incentives and Institutions." Report from the Task Force on Education and Gen-der Equality. London: Earthscan and the UN Millennium Project, www.unmillenniumproject.org/ (accessed January 10, 2005)

Uvin, Peter. 1998. *Aiding Violence: The Development Enterprise in Rwanda.* West Hartford, CT: Kumarian

Vachudova, Milada. 2005. *Europe Undivided: Democracy, Leverage and Integration after Communism.* Oxford: Oxford University Press

Voeten, Erik. 2007. "The Politics of International Judicial Appointments: Evidence from the European Court of Human Rights." *International Organization* 61(4): 669–70

2008. "The Impartiality of International Judges: Evidence from the Euro-pean Court of Human Rights." *American Political Science Review* 102(4): 417–33

Vogel, David. 1995. *Trading Up: Consumer and Environmental Regulation in a Global Economy.* Cambridge, MA: Harvard University Press

2006. *The Market for Virtue.* Washington, DC: Brookings Institution Press

Walker, Peter, and Kevin Pepper. 2007. "Follow the Money: A Review and Analysis of the State of Humanitarian Funding." Background paper prepared for the meeting of the Good Humanitarian Donorship and Interagency Standing Committee, Geneva, July 20.

Wallace, Helen, William Wallace, and Mark Pollack, eds. 2004. *Policy-Making in the European Union,* 5th edn. Oxford: Oxford University Press

Wallerstein, Immanuel. 1974. *The Modern World-System, vol. I: Capitalist Agriculture and the Origins of the European World-Economy in the Sixteenth Century.* New York and London: Academic Press

1980. *The Modern World-System, vol. II: Mercantilism and the Consolidation of the European World-Economy, 1600–1750.* New York: Academic Press

1989. *The Modern World-System, vol. III: The Second Great Expansion of the Capitalist World-Economy, 1730–1840s.* San Diego: Academic Press

Waltz, Kenneth. 1979. *Theory of International Politics.* Reading, MA: Addison-Wesley

1986. "Reflections on *Theory of International Politics*: A Response to my Critics." In *Neorealism and its Critics*, edited by Robert O. Keohane. New York: Columbia University Press

Walzer, Michael. 1967. "On the Role of Symbolism in Political Thought." *Political Science Quarterly* 82(2): 191–204

Wang, Shaoguang. 2006. "Money Autonomy: Patterns of Civil Society Finance and their Implications." *Studies in Comparative International Development* 40(4): 3–29

Wapner, Paul. 1996. *Environmental Activism and World Civic Politics.* Albany: State University of New York Press

War on Want. 2004. *Profiting from Poverty: Privatisation Consultants, DFID and Public Services.* London: War on Want, www.waronwant.org/profiting

Warburg, E. 1916. "Werner Siemens und die Physikalisch-Technische Reichsanstalt." *Naturwissenschaften* 4(50): 793–7

Warkentin, Craig. 2001. *NGOs, The Internet and Global Civil Society.* New York: Rowman and Littlefield

2002. *Reshaping World Politics: NGOs, the Internet, and Global Civil Society.* Lanham: Rowman and Littlefield

Wasserman, Stanley, and Kathryn Faust. 1994. *Social Network Analysis: Methods and Applications.* Cambridge: Cambridge University Press

Weaver, Catherine. 2008. *Hypocrisy Trap: The Rhetoric, Reality, and Reform of the World Bank.* Princeton: Princeton University Press

Weber, Eugen. 1976. *Peasants into Frenchmen.* Stanford: Stanford University Press

Weber, Max. 1946. *From Max Weber: Essays in Sociology.* New York: Oxford University Press

1991 [1919]. *Wissenschaft als Beruf. In Schriften zur Wissenschaftslehre.* Stuttgart: Philipp Reclam junior

Wedel, Janine. 1998. *Collision and Collusion: The Strange Case of Western Aid to Eastern Europe.* New York: St. Martin's Press

2005. "US Foreign Aid and Foreign Policy: Building Strong Relationships by Doing it Right!" *International Studies Perspectives* 6(1): 35–50

Weiler, Joseph. 1982. "The Community System: The Dual Character of Supranationalism." In *Yearbook of European Law*, edited by F. G. Jacobs. Oxford: Clarendon Press

1991. "The Transformation of Europe." *Yale Law Journal* 100(8): 2405–83

Weiss, Linda. 1998. *The Myth of the Powerless State*. Ithaca, NY: Cornell University Press

Wendt, Alexander. 2000. *Social Theory of World Politics*. Cambridge: Cambridge University Press

Wessels, Wolfgang. 1998. "Comitology: Fusion in Action." *Journal of European Public Policy* 5(2): 209–34

Whaites, Alan, ed. 2002. *Masters of their Own Development? PRSPs and the Prospects for the Poor*. Monrovia, CA: World Vision

White, Howard, and Edward Anderson. 2001. "Growth versus Distribution: Does the Pattern of Growth Matter?" *Development Policy Review* 19(3): 267–89

Wiener, Antje. 1997. "Assessing the Constructive Potential of Union Citizenship – A Socio-Historical Perspective." European Integration online papers (EIoP) 1(17), http://eiop.or.at/eiop/texte/1997-017a.htm

1998. *"European" Citizenship Practice: Building Institutions of a Non-State*. Boulder, CO: Westview

Wilcke, Richard. 2004. "An Appropriate Ethical Model for Business and a Critique of Milton Friedman's Thesis." *The Independent Review* 9(2): 187–209

Willetts, Peter. 1982. *Pressure Groups in the Global System: The Transnational Relations of Issue-orientated Non-Governmental Organizations*. New York: St. Martin's Press

1996. *The Conscience of the World: The Influence of NGOs in the UN System*. Washington, DC: Brookings Institution Press

Williams, Paul R., and Michael P. Scharpf. 2002. *Peace With Justice? War Crimes and Accountability in the Former Yugoslavia*. Lanham, MD: Rowman and Littlefield

Williamson, O. E. 1985. *Economic Institutions of Capitalism*. New York: The Free Press

Wiseman, J. 1957. "The Theory of Public Utility – An Empty Box." *Oxford Economic Papers* 9: 56–74

Wlezien, Christopher. 2005. "On Issue Salience: The Problem with the 'Most Important Problem.'" *Electoral Studies* 24(4): 555–79

Wolf, Klaus Dieter, and Stefan Engert. 2005. "Corporate Security Responsibility: Towards a Conceptual Framework for Comparative Research." Paper preseted at Corporate Security Responsibility Workshop, Peace Research Institute Frankfurt (PRIF), September 29–October 1

Wolf, Klaus Dieter, Nicole Deitelhoff, and Stefan Engert. 2007. "Corporate Security Responsibility: Towards a Conceptual Framework for Comparative Research." *Cooperation and Conflict* 42(3): 294–320

Wolfsfeld, Gadi. 1997. *Media and Political Conflict: News from the Middle East*. Cambridge: Cambridge University Press

Woll, Cornelia. 2008. *Firm Interests: How Governments Shape Business Lobbying on Global Trade*. Ithaca, NY: Cornell University Press

Wong, Wendy. 2008. "Centralizing Principles: How Amnesty International Shaped Human Rights Politics through its Transnational Network." Doctoral dissertation, UCSD

Wood, B. Dan. 1988. "Principals, Bureaucrats, and Responsiveness in Clean Air Enforcement." *American Political Science Review* 82 (March): 213–34

Wood, B. Dan, and Jeffrey S. Peake. 1998. "The Dynamics of Foreign Policy Agenda Setting." *American Political Science Review* 92(1): 173–84

Woodrow Wilson International Center for Scholars, and International Peace Academy. 2001. *The Economics of War: The Intersection of Need, Creed and Greed*. Washington, DC: Woodrow Wilson International Center for Scholars and the International Peace Academy

World Bank. 1995. *Priorities and Strategies for Education*. Washington, DC: World Bank

    2002. *Achieving Education for All by 2015: Simulation Results for 47 Low Income Countries*. Washington, DC: World Bank

    2004a. "Aid Effectiveness and Financing Modalities," http://image-bank.worldbank.org/servlet/WDSContentServer/IW3P/IB/2004/10/04/000012009_20041004095816/Rendered/PDF/300691put0as0vol.02.pdf (accessed October 4, 2004)

    2004b. "Education for All Fast Track Initiative. Progress Report (March 26)." Washington, DC: World Bank

    2004c. *Fast Track Initiative News August, September, October 2004*. Washington, DC: World Bank

    2006a. *Global Monitoring Report*. Washington, DC: World Bank

    2006b. "Guidelines for World Bank and IMF Staffs for Joint Staff Advisory Notes (JSAN) for Poverty Reduction Strategy Papers," http://siteresources.worldbank.org/INTPRS1/Resources/PDFs/jsan_prsp_guidelines.pdf (accessed September 10, 2006)

    2009. *Global Monitoring Report*. Washington, DC: World Bank

World Bank and International Monetary Fund. 2005. *Review of the PRS Approach: Balancing Accountabilities and Scaling Up Results*. Washington, DC: The World Bank and the International Monetary Fund

World Bank Operations Evaluations Department. 2004. *The Poverty Reduction Strategy Initiative: An Independent Evaluation of the World Bank's Support*. Washington, DC: World Bank

World Education Forum. 2000. *The Dakar Framework for Action, Education for All: Meeting our Collective Commitments*. Dakar, Senegal: World Education Forum

    2005. *Global Governance Initiative Annual Report 2005*, www.weforum.org/site/homepublic.nsf/Content/Global+Governance+Initiative (accessed March 15, 2005)

World Federation of Education Associations. 1923. "Conference Proceedings of the World Federation of Education Associations Meeting," held under the auspices of the National Education Association of the United States, June 28–July 6, 1923, San Francisco

Yates, JoAnne, and Craig N. Murphy. 2008. "Charles Le Maistre: Entrepreneur in International Standardization." *Entreprises et Histoire* 51(June): 10–27

Index

Cambridge Studies in International Relations